# HISTORY OF THE THIRD ORDER REGULAR RULE

# HISTORY OF THE THIRD ORDER REGULAR RULE
## A SOURCE BOOK

edited by

Margaret Carney, O.S.F., S.T.D.
Jean François Godet-Calogeras, Ph.D.
Suzanne M. Kush, C.S.S.F., M.A.

Franciscan Institute Publications
The Franciscan Institute
Saint Bonaventure University
Saint Bonaventure, NY 14778
2008

Cover design: Mark Sullivan
Cover illustration: Volterra, Bibl. Guarnacci, codex 225, f. 148r
Cover texture: photo of the habit of Clare of Assisi,
courtesy of Stefan Diller
Book design: Phillips Robinette, O.F.M.

ISBN: 978-1-57659-149-9

Library of Congress Card Catalogue Number: 2008927723

Printed in the United States of America

Bookmasters, Inc.
Ashland, Ohio

To the honor of Assisi's most beloved Penitents,
Francis and Clare,

To the brothers and sisters of the current age
whose dedication and discipline created this text,

To all of our companions of the BFI, CFI
and International Work Group —
those still living and
those who await us in the New Jerusalem,

We dedicate this work with the prayer
that future generations will, by their study of it, know
our happiness as the men and women who persevered
in doing this work (cf. 2LtF 88).

*Our deepest gratitude goes to the*
*Province of the Most Sacred Heart of Jesus,*
*The Third Order Regular of Saint Francis,*
*and Provincial Minister Christian Oravec, T.O.R.*
*for the generous gift that made*
*this whole project possible*

# CONTENTS

ACKNOWLEDGEMENTS

This source book on the history of the Rule
of the Third Order Regular of Saint Francis
was the work of a *fraternitas*.
It was made possible with the generous assistance
of a community of friends and co-workers:

Kimberly Carney,
Nancy Celaschi, O.S.F.,
Anne Foerst, Ph.D.,
Athena Godet-Calogeras,
Marianne Jungbluth, F.H.F.,
Robert J. Karris, O.F.M.
Beate Kless, O.S.F.,
Veronica Marie Lucerno, C.S.S.F.,
Roberta A. McKelvie, O.S.F.,
Daria Mitchell, O.S.F.,
Elise Mora, O.S.F.,
Alison More, Ph.D.,
Dennis O'Brien,
Margaret Marie Padilla, C.S.S.F.,
Luigi Pellegrini, O.F.M. Cap.,
Noel Riggs,
Phillips Robinette, O.F.M.,
Bert Roest, Ph.D.,
Mark Sullivan,
Mary Joanne Suranni, C.S.S.F.,
Chad Taylor,
Elizabeth Thompson,
Michael Vaile,
and the many others,
who gave us advice and support.

To all we are grateful.

## Abbreviations

| | |
|---|---|
| AAS | *Acta Apostolicae Sedis* (Acts of the Apostolic See) |
| BFI | International Franciscan Bureau (oversight of the Rule Project) |
| CA:ED | *Clare of Assisi: Early Documents*, R.J. Armstrong, ed. and trans. (New York: New City Press, 2006). |
| CFI | International Franciscan Commission (organizational assistant to the BFI) |
| CRIS | The Congregation for Institutes of Consecrated Life and for Societies of Apostolic Life |
| FA:ED | *Francis of Assisi: Early Documents*, R.J. Armstrong, J.A.W. Hellmann, W.J. Short, eds., 3 volumes (New York: New City Press, 1999-2001). |
| Editor's Note: | Readers may notice that in the translation process choices have been made to adjust certain words or phrases according to editorial preferences; therefore, exact agreement with cited sources may vary. |

# INTRODUCTION

The grace of the work that produced the pontifically approved text for The Rule and Life of the Brothers and Sisters of the Third Order Regular of St. Francis in 1982 has several sources. Multiple streams fed the font of energy and enlightenment that gave rise to this first international collaboration in TOR history. Let us enumerate the most important of these.

## PART ONE: THE INTERNATIONAL QUEST FOR A NEW FRANCISCAN RULE

### THE SECOND VATICAN COUNCIL

On the morning of October 11, 1961, a seemingly endless line of bishops processed into the immense nave of St. Peter's Basilica over the rain-washed stones of its grand piazza. The procession, which took most of the morning to complete, was the first ritual of a convocation whose four sessions would leave the Church dramatically altered. From these meetings it emerged as an institution shaking off centuries of placid self-sufficiency in favor of a new engagement with the world. The recognition that certain groups within the Church would serve as important catalysts of the agenda the Council fathers advanced was crystallized in a number of actions they took. After the Council's close (and the death of John XXIII) the implementation phase was deftly led by Paul VI. One of his early actions was the publication of a short *motu proprio* instructing members of religious congregations to update their norms and adjust their customs to the demands of modern society in service of a more effective evangelizing program. Known by its title, *Ecclesiae Sanctae*,[1] this seldom quoted papal directive set in motion a veritable hurricane of

---

[1] This document can be studied in its original form by reference to AAS 58 (1966): 757-87 or retrieved through <http://www.vatican.va/archive/hist_councils/ii_vatican_council/index.htm.>. Part II details the norms for renewal of religious institutes, 775-82.

activity that would later cause serious backlash not only within Vatican circles, but in national episcopacies as well. Nonetheless, during the Council's period of *aggiornamento* the promotion of experimental and democratic processes to do the work of analysis and acceptance of the Council's teaching was decisive. The foundations were being laid for a new moment of opportunity in the Franciscan family which was also moving from a hierarchical model of governance (not unlike most institutions in the church) to a more fraternal and cooperative *modus operandi*.

## FRANCISCAN EDUCATION FOR RENEWAL

Franciscans pondered the exhortation to "return" to the "charism of their founders" found within the exhortations of Paul VI as he invited religious women and men to take up this task at a crucial time. The response to the mandate was, for the most part, enthusiastic. However, the route of return was by no means certain. In spite of decades of scientific research by scholars in Europe, many rank and file Franciscans lacked knowledge of primary sources. The difficulty of creating a modern hermeneutic for the deeds and documents of long ago was substantial. Franciscan friar theologians and other experts, often trained in the leading schools of the continent, were well aware of contemporary scholarship that was launching exciting new approaches to Franciscan source materials. The scholars of Grottaferrata, the faculties of the Antonianum, Laurentianum or Seraphicum, and those editing critical editions in a variety of settings including the Franciscan Institute of St. Bonaventure University, formed a small army of experts making primary resource material available more widely than at any previous time in Franciscan history.

As the necessity of providing Franciscans with the academic programs to augment and support more popular and accessible formation workshops and institutes, a multi-layered response took shape. Programs sponsored by universities at undergraduate and graduate levels provided invaluable educational opportunities to many. At present the English-speaking world enjoys "an embarrassment of riches" in this regard. The Franciscan School of Theology at the Graduate Theological Union of Berkeley, California; the Franciscan Center of the Washington Theological Union; The Franciscan Institute/School of Franciscan Studies of St. Bonaventure University; The Franciscan International Study Centre at Canterbury, England. In addition, the Association of Franciscan Colleges and Universities includes a number of liberal arts colleges with a Franciscan educational institute or a designated academic leader charged with sharing solid Franciscan intellectual preparation with faculty and students alike.

When the Franciscan Institute re-opened its teaching program in 1971 under the direction of Conrad Harkins, O.F.M., its goal was to bridge the gap between the scholarly community and the vast number of Franciscan sisters and friars whose need and desire to master this material was increasingly apparent. By the time the first cohort of M.A. students graduated from the Franciscan Institute, a faint note of frustration was emerging within the student body. Students who were members of the Third Order Regular increasingly sought answers to questions about *their* historical origins, about what differentiated them from the "First Order," or the Order of Friars Minor. Neither faculty nor library had much to offer by way of response. The timing of this emergent and constructive discontent—the late 1970s—was providential. The realization that the Third Order Regular lived and worked in the shadow of its better-known elder brother, the First Order, was taking shape at the very time that the invitations to international assemblies of Third Order Regular congregations were beaming around the globe. It is to these early assemblies that we now turn.

### CONVENING THE THIRD ORDER REGULAR MEMBERS

Prior to the advent of computerized information systems, a large and somewhat awkward item known as a Rolodex stood on the desk of every secretary worth his/her salt. The Rolodex was a miniaturized card catalog that allowed you to record an address and other pertinent data in a small rotating set of cards that could be quickly retrieved by spinning the file with a side handle. It was a marvelous tool and allowed one to add and delete numerous entries with efficiency and speed. As one official of the Vatican Congregation for Religious Life (as it was then known) reminded me, our branch of the Franciscan Order had "no Rolodex" well into the twentieth century. In other words, there was no central office or coordinating body that permitted efficient and regular communications among the nearly four hundred different groups of sisters, brothers, nuns and mixed masculine congregations that comprised the Order. For that reason, while the three branches of friars (Capuchin, Conventual, Observant) began to meet in post-counciliar general and provincial chapters before the end of the 1960s, the Third Order Regular taken as a whole remained de-centralized with disconnected communications. The "Order" was and remains an amalgamation of some four hundred autonomous institutes or congregations.[2] One of the most ancient is the congregation of priests and lay friars, which bears the an-

---

[2]The Third Order Regular is constituted in such a way that new foundations are constantly being incorporated into it. For that reason providing exact statistics on current numbers of congregations is not easy. The International Franciscan Conference of the Brothers and Sisters of the Third Order Regular (IFC-TOR) has its office in Rome and

cient title of Third Order Regular. Its generalate is in Rome, its current corporate lineage dates to the fifteenth century and its general minister in modern times is seated alongside the generals of the three branches of the First Order according to pontifical protocols.

When the "Rule Project" was in its earliest stages, lists of congregations and institutes were laboriously developed. However, certain historical confusion and mis-information prevented many groups from being included in early communications. To give some grasp of the variety this includes we consider that its taxonomy is shared by the friars of the Third Order Regular as described above; multiple monasteries of contemplative nuns; active congregations of sisters and brothers numbering from those of a dozen members to those in the thousands. Some of these are resident in a single diocese. Others are trans-continental in scope. There is no single canonical governing structure and each approved institute has its own superior and recognized status in the Church. If ever an entity was guilty of causing bouts of "seraphic confusion," the Third Order Regular is at the top of the list.

In the more developed nations of that period (e.g., Western Europe, the United States, Brazil) national federations or cooperative organizations were created. The prerogatives were limited; membership was voluntary. However, such national organizations did speed the work of formative education to bridge the gap between the grass roots membership and Franciscan experts. Little by little some of these national groups acknowledged the need for international collaboration. However, in the absence of any central governing body, initial efforts were limited and, at times, communications did not meet their target. Nonetheless, congregations with members in multiple nations were the first to experience and then facilitate the importance of finding unifying threads and congresses to test for international consensus on questions of identity within the Church and mission in the modern world. It is also a credit to the branches of the First Order that many friars whose ministry placed them in frequent contact with Franciscan sisters/brothers, advocated for more national and international exchange during this period of ferment and new educational options. The generals of the three branches were generous in granting financial support to host certain early meetings and releasing some of their best experts to serve as animators of these efforts.

---

its Secretary General will provide current statistics upon request. <ifctorsg@tin.it> or <http://www.infracon.org>.

RENEWAL ASSEMBLIES OF THE THIRD ORDER REGULAR[3]

*Madrid, 1974*

In 1974, the masculine congregations of the Third Order Regular held a congress in Madrid, Spain.[4] The primary directing energy emanated from the TOR generalate in Rome and sought the cooperation of other masculine institutes of the Order. Sponsorship was vested in a structure known as the Inter-obediential Congress. This Congress was a vehicle of communication between and among the masculine entities of the Third Order Regular that dated from the mid-twentieth century. The Madrid Assembly was its first reunion following the close of the Council in 1964. The TOR friars and brothers included a number of guests from conferences of TOR sisters, thus demonstrating an important recognition that the rule and history of the Third Order is not the monopoly of any one canonical institution. The study document issued by this congress found immediate acceptance among Third Order congregations in the U.S. where the new national Federation became the vehicle for its dissemination. It served as a guide for recovery of an authentic and historically rooted appreciation of Third Order identity.

*Assisi, 1976*

In 1976, a group of Western European sisterhoods hosted an assembly in Assisi. They had the blessing and financial backing of Minister General, Constantine Koser and the cooperative approval of Capuchins and Conventuals. At its conclusion, the participants agreed to the utility of additional efforts to work together on documents for formation for future generations of post-conciliar members. Part of the impetus for this meeting was the growing recognition that many national groups were formulating identity statements to be used as the basis for renewal and, in particular, as the basis for renewing formation studies and methods. (Remember that in 1968, the Congregation for Religious had issued its directives on renewing the novitiate programs, *Renovationis causam*, with allowances for dramatic departures from conventional and cloistered programs.)[5] Those in a position to observe the good effects of such efforts (ministers general with international experience, Vatican officials receiving periodic reports and visits) saw an opportunity for synergistic collaboration and offered their services in promoting that.

---

[3]The IFC-TOR (see note above) maintains the archives of the activities that culminated in the papally approved Rule of 1982. Records of the assemblies, communications with congregations, consultation results, and most important materials can be located there.

[4]Full documentation found in *Analecta Tertii Ordinis Regularis Sancti Francisci*, vol. 13: 123, (1974).

[5]*Renovationis causam* in AAS 61 (1969): 103-20.

This assembly traced its beginnings to a Francophone project sponsored by twenty-five congregations headquartered in France and Belgium. Over several years this collaboration produced a text of twelve chapters, following closely the structure and language of the Rule of St. Clare, and disseminated for study in 1972. Before long, this proposed text was known widely as "the French Rule."

Representatives of the masculine branch of the Order registered two concerns: 1) the text was prepared for and directed only to sisters' congregations and 2) the penitential foundations of the Order were not acknowledged in the construction or content of the text. While rediscovery of this font of identity had only recently been publicized, the French project had developed along lines that were questioned by those striving to locate the origins of the tertiary congregations more precisely.

## Structural Support Systems

At this point the superiors who had already experienced international assemblies had established an ad hoc structure to carry the project forward, now normally called "the Rule Project." There were three bodies assigned to this work. The International Franciscan Bureau (BFI) was a governing board made up of superiors from a variety of institutes, and charged by their peers with oversight of this important pioneering effort. The International Franciscan Council (CFI) assisted them. This latter body had several executive directors or secretaries of national federations as members and several other members with specific expertise in organization of international meetings and communication. Their task was the management of documentation, translation, and communication to the growing new "rolodex" of TOR institutes worldwide. Finally, a task force to be known as the International Work Group was appointed. The CFI and BFI invited into this group representatives from North and South America, India, and Western Europe who had sufficient knowledge of sources and texts and sufficient personal expertise to serve as editors and authors of the text that would emerge from such a vast consultation. This Work Group was to function in a tertiary role, serving mostly in the background to provide the BFI members with a well-crafted document for consultation with their peers. This consultation was to be completed in time for the anniversary of Francis's birth in 1982. What follows below is a more detailed exposition of these events.

### Assisi, 1979

When a second general meeting took place in 1979, approval of the adoption of a renewed rule text was the primary goal. The French Rule was voted as the official working text. The assembly did, however, experience the dramatic power of unresolved issues of historical identity, the concerns arising from affiliations with various branches of the Friars Minor, the major differences in the nature of this wide array of institutes with different national and international cultures and apostolic origins, and the lack of precedent for doing an international collaboration of such importance with this group of institutions. The success of the assembly must be acknowledged and its importance cannot be underestimated. The result of honest grappling with these issues led to important resolutions on the part of the leaders of the movement. The following decisions were to have critical importance:

1. The International Franciscan Bureau (BFI) was created consisting of six general superiors of TOR congregations. These six men and women had the responsibility—delegated by their peers—to supervise the entire project and submit its results to the Holy See at the appropriate time.

2. The International Franciscan Commission composed of nine members would organize procedures and criteria for drafting a final rule text.

3. The masculine congregations would be fully included in future deliberations and consultations.

4. Consultors from the four men's branches of the First Order would work with both the BFI and CFI, but would not have voting rights.

The plan articulated by this assembly projected submitting the final text to the Holy See in the name of the whole Order to replace the Rule approved by Pius XI in 1927. In spite of the careful work that multiple European congregations had done to advance this proposal, the lack of widespread consultation beyond Europe gave rise to significant consternation on the part of groups who were newly invited to express their concerns. Those opposing adoption of "the French Rule" also were uneasy with utilization of Clare's Rule adapted for congregations with a history of apostolic works. While for many the outcomes of this assembly were cause for celebration, the unseen discontent soon manifested itself in communications within the order and questions posed to the Congregation for Religious, which at that time was headed by Eduardo Cardinal Pironio. However, the gathering consensus that the project could succeed drove a concerted effort forward.

*Grottaferrata, 1980*
Wise heads prevailed at this perilous intersection and the BFI, CFI and consultors met in Grottaferrata from March 8-10, 1980. At this meeting a plan to insure the project's success and directives of the 1979 assembly were elaborated. The elements were:

1. Recognition that, while the French Rule had received majority support in the Assisi Assembly, it was far from being a document that could unite all constituents. Thus, it was agreed to propose that the Madrid Statement and the Dutch Rule (which contained much contemporary insight into renewal processes) should be harmonized with the French text.

2. An additional committee, the International Work Group, was added to the machinery of the CFI. The members were to read, evaluate and accept, edit or discard all suggestions from all respondents. The methodology and working criteria to be used by the CFI and work groups were carefully outlined at the Grottaferrata meeting, as was a time-table leading to an international Assembly in March 1981 in Rome.

3. All TOR congregations would be notified of the status of the project and provided with necessary documentation to assist in the consultation. It was assumed that the consultation would be at the generalate level, but inclusion of all members of the institute was the prerogative of the superiors responsible for answering on behalf of their congregations.

4. Most important, the Grottaferrata leadership saw that the work that had been done in multiple renewal initiatives could be united around four fundamental values that were clearly present in all versions: Conversion/*Metanoia*, Minority, Contemplation and Poverty. These four values were to be the touchstones of an authentic rule document.

Raphael Pazzelli would later note in his commentary edition of the Rule that by the close of the Grottaferrata meeting a "bilateral agreement" was emerging that would strengthen the prospect of success. The two sides of this agreement were implicit in the four decisions listed above. One position involved the institutes that were convinced that a return to ancient penitential sources and promotion of a renewed penitential identity were critical components for a text to be fully adequate. The other position involved institutes whose origins were more directly dependent upon minorite spirituality and modern apostolic categories. These institutes had legitimate concerns about adopting language and mental categories that appeared—at first blush—somewhat foreign to their historical evolution. Given the intensity of debate about authentic and viable forms of *aggiornamento* for religious life raging at the time, these concerns were at the heart of the responsibility accepted by the women and men who, at that precise moment, bore the responsibility for the Order's future.

*Pittsburgh, 1980*

Following the 1979 Assisi meeting, European sentiment about content and method was almost unanimous. However, significant disagreements were voiced by the masculine congregations of the Order and by the membership of the Franciscan Federation of the USA. The shared concern was exemplified in an emergency meeting of the national federation (at that point still comprised only of women's congregations) and the leaders of masculine TOR entities resident in the United States. The meeting took place at Millvale, Pennsylvania, in the motherhouse where Mother Viola Lenninger had worked to bring the federation into existence. (The Sisters of St. Francis of Millvale merged with the Sisters of St. Francis of New York in 2007.) Roland Faley, T.O.R., who at that point was the American-born Vicar General of the TORs in Rome, was present as well.[6]

There may well have been other such gatherings to examine the "French Rule" Project that was being proposed as the sole draft for international consideration. Let it suffice to say that at this meeting's close, the leaders of these USA congregations decided to act in cooperation with their European counterparts but on condition that additional time be dedicated to exploring other models for revision of the Rule of 1927 which was, at that point, the canonical Rule of all approved TOR institutes. These women acted with a sincere and educated sense of urgency to preserve the authentic historic patrimony of the Order as they had come to understand it through some fifteen years of dedicated renewal studies. The meeting concluded with the public nomination of Sr. Margaret Carney, OSF (Sisters of St. Francis of the Providence of God) and Fr. Thaddeus Horgan (Franciscan Friars of the Atonement) to the International Work Group. Much was at stake. Much needed to be done and to be dared in order to insure an outcome that would truly unify this vast and disorganized branch of Franciscans.

It should be noted that many national and regional gatherings fanned the flame of interest and desire during these years. The instances are far too numerous to recount here. However, it would be the rare congregation whose members have no memory of participation in wonderful and inspiring assemblies or celebrations of Franciscan identity during this era.

---

[6]E. Saggau, O.S.F., *A Short History of the Franciscan Federation of the Third Order Regular of Brothers and Sisters of the United States* (Washington, D.C.: The Franciscan Federation, 1995), 8-12.

## CFI MEETING

Another meeting of the CFI in June of 1980 developed precise regulations for the first gathering of the International Work Group. The first meeting involved ten representatives from various countries accompanied by four consulters and the CFI members who would link the two units. By this time, Sr. Louise Dendooven, F.M.M., was named the General Secretary of the project. She was a Belgian-born missionary with valuable experience in formation and international cooperation. She was also blessed with an iron will and enormous capacity for intricate, inter-cultural work and dialogue. No one who worked with her over the years of her mandate can doubt that her determination was a major factor in the success of a venture which appeared doomed to fail more than once in the course of the program.

### INTERNATIONAL WORK GROUP, REUTE, GERMANY 1980

#### WORK GROUP MEMBERS:

| | |
|---|---|
| Fr. Thaddeus Horgan, S.A. | TOR Masculine Congregations |
| Sr. Margaret Carney, O.S.F. | United States of America |
| Sr. Marie-Benoît Lucbernet | Francophone Congregations |
| Sr. Ignatia Gomez | India/Asia |
| Sr. Maria Honoria Montalvo | Colombia |
| Sr. Maria Luiza Piva | Brazil |
| Sr. Marianne Jungbluth | Germany/Belgium |
| Sr. Elena Maria Echevarren | Spain |
| Sr. Isabella Cieri | Italy |

#### CONSULTORS:

Jean-Francois Godet, O.F.M.[7] (also served as animator/facilitator)
Jaime Zudaire, O.F.M. Cap.
Francesco Saverio Pancheri, O.F.M. Conv.
Tomeu Pastor Oliver, T.O.R.

*Reute, 1980*

The Reute Meeting was the first encounter of the work group with the CFI and the consultants. It was an intense experience and revealed the powerful tensions at work in the pluralistic TOR world. In spite of the efforts of the BFI and CFI to prepare means to insure good working relationships and results, the outcomes were inconsistent and at times contradictory. However, there was sufficient harmony between and among

---

[7]Several years after the project, Jean-François Godet accepted a dispensation to return to the secular path of Franciscan life. He subsequently married (adopting the name Godet-Calogeras) and continues his service as a Franciscan teacher and author in the United States.

various propositions that a unified schema was developed after the close of the meeting. This was accomplished by a sub-committee charged with resolving some inherent difficulties that emerged in the intense atmosphere of that ten-day session in a remote corner of Bavaria.

The Work Group followed the instructions to harmonize the three prevailing project drafts. They exhaustively evaluated the proposals that arrived in huge dossiers from some two hundred congregations. They revised and re-drafted until they were numb. A singular problem arose due to unintended consequences of choosing to separate into two language groups. One group of members and experts worked in German-English-French. The second worked in Italian-Portuguese-Spanish. Unfortunately the experts assigned to the different sectors were operating on very different planes of interpretation of primary sources in relationship to this new text. Serious disagreements punctuated the working sessions. When the ten days were over, the group reported to its CFI superiors that it produced two drafts of propositions for articles. There were strong correspondences and identical draft articles for a substantial portion of the proposed rule. However, there were also draft articles emanating from both language circles that could not be successfully merged into a single text accepted by the group as a whole. (This process of voting on each article, chapter, and complete text was wisely demanded by the CFI as a way of confirming the text in a verifiable way.) It came as a shock to all participants that the first Work Group session failed to achieve this fundamental goal. Needless to say, the CFI and its Secretary were unhappy but they were also determined to eliminate the factors that were preventing the Work Group from successful completion of its task.

When the Reute session concluded, the embarrassed and exhausted Work Group members were informed that there would have to be a reconsideration of the methods to be used in the next phase of work. "Go home and wait for word from us." This was the unvarnished and melancholy directive that echoed as we took to the highways and airports following our German encounter. In spite of the difficulties of these days, factors of lived Franciscan *fraternitas* prevailed in the midst of tension. The work of communication in social situations called for extra sensitivity and time. The work of common prayer rotated among the languages and allowed all to savor the songs, symbols and artistry of different cultures with each day's Divine Office or Eucharist. The dedication of religious who cooked, cleaned rooms, typed until their fingers were blue—all of this created a sense of shared purpose in and through painful moments.

Few can appreciate the difficulty of the work load of the ten day meeting. This session was conducted in French without simultaneous translation.

The text had to be redacted in Latin. The work group members represented five language groups: German, Italian, French, Spanish/Portuguese and English. All drafts had to be "tested" in translation into these languages. This work was being done with typewriters and duplication of materials with a single copier. As time went on, the length of the working day extended so that by the close of the session, many were functioning with little sleep with predictable results. However, the members of the CFI who attended the session and shared the work also conveyed a genuine sense of optimism that we "the little ones" of the grand enterprise, could play our part and play it well.

In the weeks that followed, a new sub-committee took the work of the two language groups and managed to create a new draft document. The French Rule gave way to the Reute Draft. This was then circulated world-wide with instructions to provide feedback due by April 15, 1981. A dramatic decision was made to reduce the number of work group members and expert advisors and the consultation progressed with the goal of a second meeting in Belgium.

Additional sessions of BFI and CFI members took place: November 8-9, 1980 in Rome; December 1-2, 1980 at Savona, Italy; February 26-27, 1981 in Montpellier, France. These sessions set the ground rules and re-cruited personnel for the Rome General Assembly scheduled for March, 1982. In addition to meticulous preparation of norms and agendas, the BFI created a solidarity fund so that no congregation would be denied access to the assembly because of economic need. With amazing speed, given the newness of the work, the elaborate machinery of an historic congress was assembled and the new and tentative relationships of this vast and complex "Order" were being forged in act and intention.

*Work Group, Brussels, 1981*
Springtime in Brussels found the members of the Work Group and CFI arriving at the house of studies attached to the provincial headquarters of the Belgian friars. Fearing a repeat of the difficulties that plagued the Reute meeting, the CFI had reorganized the membership of both Work Group and consultors, reducing the number in both. At the Reute meetings, a retreat house staff provided multiple domestic support. In Belgium the facility did not have a large staff. Thus, Work Group members shared daily household tasks such as cleaning of dishes and assistance with other household duties. This simple necessity created an environment that was conducive to developing elementary human relationships in a new key. Sr. Louise Dendooven, accompanied by Sr. Bernadette Nor-

din and the faithful translators of the Work Group,[8] made clear that a simplified process for the work was being inaugurated and that this action signified a confidence that the group's resources were equal to the daunting task. Gone was the negatively charged air of the last days in Reute. A new fraternal ambience emerged and work, still hard and relentless, went forward quickly.

Two hundred and five congregations submitted revisions to the Reute draft. Each revision had to be evaluated. New schemata were developed for each article and chapter. A draft translation into the five[9] languages was a constant. Finally, after ten days of intense exchange, reflection and attention to the consultation documents, a single text emerged that the Work Group members unanimously approved by formal votation. During this same ten day period, an assassin tried to kill John Paul II and the turning pages of history confronted the project leaders, reminding them of the contingencies of our lives and plans and linking them back to the early Franciscans for whom papal approval of their Rule was the high point of the movement's youthful expansion.

The members of the BFI attended the final session of the Brussels meeting on May 21-22. They reviewed the work on the new draft and concluded that they could confidently place this draft in the hands of the TOR superiors. While certain choices made by the Work Group in redacting the text caused discussion and concern, the Work Group's method and exegesis finally received enthusiastic approval from the members of the Bureau. So enthusiastic was the reception that the BFI decided to increase the role for the Work Group members in the Rome assembly. The original Assembly program placed the Work Group function behind the scenes to do further editing. The BFI members now realized that the presentation of the draft could best be done by these authors. It was a stunning change in plans. To that point, all parties assumed that the primary presentations of the Rome assembly would be done by internationally recognized Franciscan scholars or elected leaders. Now, the Work Group would be placed on center stage, charged with explaining the text, but also expected to communicate the extraordinary experience that resulted in the unity of the Brussels experience.

In the last hours of the session a hasty decision was made to convene the Work Group members for a third session. This time the task would be to prepare the presentations needed for the Assembly. There would

---

[8]Translation was done by a team of volunteers, mostly sisters, who worked one-on-one with Work Group members and others in the CFI or BFI who might need their assistance. Translation equipment was used only in the general assemblies.

[9]While six languages were in use in the group, the assembly program operated in five languages with Portuguese being dependent on the Spanish translation for most of the work.

be four papers on the four fundamental values and exegetical presentations on each chapter. The members would also be present at all plenary sessions to respond to questions and to hear proposals for further amendment. With little time left to prepare and calendars already full of commitments, the members decided to dedicate their Christmas holidays to this task. This was also a commitment to share a beloved feast together—a sign of the new and vibrant solidarity that was born in the days of work on the text.

*Work Group, Oyster Bay, NY, 1981/82*
The BFI/CFI accepted a request to schedule this final Work Group session in the United States. Subsequently the Franciscan Brothers of Brooklyn offered to host the session at their retreat house in Oyster Bay, Long Island. Quiet and memorable hours were shared around a Christmas tree and then the work was taken up again. This time, the nervous anxiety of the group was pronounced. Accustomed to working behind the scenes while BFI and CFI members led the public proceedings, the members faced a daunting challenge as they absorbed the responsibility placed upon them. Several were inexperienced to public speaking, and even those who had experience felt trepidation at the thought of addressing so historic a gathering. Two members had recently suffered significant health crises and the long days of preparatory work took further tolls. Some of the Work Group's requests to alter the proposed schedule of presentations in the assembly schedule caused further anxious exchanges. As the week closed, a New Year's celebration attended by dozens of Franciscans from the New York area brought a break in the work and lightened the tension with a dose of New Year's revelry that included exquisite French champagne presented as a gift from the BFI. The hospitality of the American Franciscans, particularly that of the Brothers of Brooklyn, put to rest any doubts that earlier difficulties about the Rule Project might prevent enthusiastic collaboration on both sides of the Atlantic. As the text became refined and the matrix of its first commentary was written, the fundamental relationships that would support a new international identity for the Order were also being forged.

*General Assembly, Rome, March 1-10, 1982*
The program for the General Assembly exhibited the BFI's concern for legitimate processes that would lead to ratification by carefully elaborated stages and constant monitoring of the voting process. All was developed to provide maximum participation by the superiors in attendance. A series of plenary assemblies and small language group exchanges made up the daily regimen. Three types of votes gradually brought about the hoped-for consensus:

1. A straw vote followed the presentation of each chapter. Proposals for change would then be handed over to the Work Group for redaction;

2. Orientation votes on the basic text with its proposed amendments required a two third majority for text or amendments to go forward;

3. A final deliberative vote on each article and each chapter were required for the parts of the text that did not receive the two-thirds approval in the orientation voting.

The Assembly concluded the votation on the text on March 8th and only two votes prevented the final ballot from being a unanimous approbation of the proposed Rule and Life. The Assembly had, over the course of the week, come to incorporate only seven changes to the basic text. These changes reflected careful study and vigorous exchange among the participants. Several key areas of tension or misunderstanding that had previously dominated the debate on the project were resolved by the painstaking work presented by BFI, CFI and Work Group members. A private audience with John Paul II occurred mid-program. Just as dramatic was the arrival in the Assembly, two days after its start, of two sisters from Poland. The crackdown on Solidarity by military intervention was in full swing. These courageous women managed, in spite of the fragile situation in their homeland, to make the journey. As they entered the aula, a respectful hush fell over the membership. Ashen-faced and solemn, these sisters took their place close to the Work Group. Their determination was a dramatic witness to the life-changing importance of what was transpiring at the *Domus Pacis* in those days. The text is usually referred to simply as "the Rule." But here, again, participants were reminded that it is a Rule and Life—and that it is the life that is the ultimate bull of approbation in a life governed by the workings of the Spirit of the Lord.

*Approbation of the Text*
On December 17, 1982, Cardinal Pironio, Prefect for the Congregation of Religious and Secular Institutes, presented the text *Regula et Vita Fratrum et Sororum Tertii Ordinis Sancti Francisi* to Pope John Paul II. By the time the text reached the pontiff's desk, an important modification had been made. A chapter on chastity composed of articles written by German scholar-friar, Lothar Hardick, O.F.M. had been added. The Cardinal requested the Pontiff's approval and the assignment of the date of December 8th, feast of the Immaculate Conception, to the letter of approbation.

On April 21 of the following year, Cardinal Edward Martines Somalo, Substitute of the Secretary of State, sent a letter containing the papal brief, *Franciscanum Vitae Propositum*, the confirmation of the Rule. On April 30th, Cardinal Pironio sent copies of both the brief of John Paul II and the accompanying letter of Cardinal Somalo to the BFI. Notification had already been provided, according to Roman protocol, to the Minister General of the friars of the Third Order Regular.

The news gradually made its way to the generalates of the Order and a new era for this branch of the Franciscan family began.

The 1982 centenary of the birth of St. Francis of Assisi was filled with opportunities for members of the family to cross the lines of institutional separation and enjoy a wonderful year long celebration of united vision and hope. Indeed, the birthday celebrations of that year marked the culmination of several major projects and works that contributed enormously to a new shared identity. In addition to the approbation of the Third Order Rule, the publication in English of the Paulist Press volume *Francis and Clare: The Complete Works*, initially edited by Ignatius Brady, O.F.M. and completed by Regis Armstrong, O.F.M. Cap., was a singular event that typifies the ground being broken at the time. This volume provided, for the first time, an authoritative translation of the principal sources for both saints in a form that made it the standard text for the next twenty years.

## PART TWO: THE PATH OF PENANCE AND THE MAKING OF PEACE

### AREAS OF CONFLICT AND CONFUSION

In the foregoing description of the Rule Project, indications of serious tensions and misunderstanding abound. In order to better understand the text and the significance of much of its content, it is important to know the content of these tensions and to have some idea of how they were resolved. The following material has that purpose.

### *Lack of Formal TOR Structure*

Here, the hindsight of a twenty-five year experience is helpful. If one looks back to descriptions of the growing friction between advocates of different methods for renewing the TOR rule at that time, several partial explanations for serious difficulties can be identified. One is the lack of structural unity within a vast Order whose member congregations ranged from small "experimental" communities of less than a dozen members to large, well organized multi-national congregations with decades of strong leadership. These latter were often well connected to the authorities of the Friars Minor and close to the Vatican by geography and history.

*Affiliations with First Order[10]*

The ties to the First Order were themselves sometimes part of the friction. Generals of the different branches could act (or refuse to act) in ways that had direct bearing on the deliberations of TOR generals meeting in assemblies and task forces. Since many congregations of women depended literally on First Order authorities to represent their interests to the Vatican or to protect their works in fragile situations of mission, there was sincere desire to avoid any action that might be seen as ungrateful for this patronage or willingness to exchange it for a new identity that stressed autonomy for the TOR too loudly.

Given the affiliations between many TOR women's groups and the Friars Minor the existence of congregations of Third Order Regular friars and brothers was news to some. For example, in France where so much work had been done on a new text, the existence of TOR friars was unknown. There was only one very small house of this branch of friars in Paris. The TOR men were thus "invisible" to the Francophone sisters. Others, while a distinct minority, enjoyed close association, even formal aggregation, with the Third Order Regular friars. Thus, there was a clear note of ambivalence and anxiety about the proceedings of the Assembly and some of the debates about the text's content. Looking back, it is easy to understand that many congregations of women were understandably reluctant to over-identify with the Third Order Regular lest that be interpreted as mitigating their historic ties to the First Order. On the other hand, those whose relationships to the TOR friars were strong were mystified at times by the attitudes of others.

It is fortunate that part of the era of post-counciliar renewal included inter-jurisdictional commissions or meetings that brought the generals of all four groups of friars together regularly. Their mutual respect and experience of cooperation allowed them to define ways of relating to the Rule Project that resulted in steady forward movement and final resolution of these problems.[11]

*Nationalism*

Nationalism and cross-cultural problems could and did play out even in Franciscan working meetings. Bias that was rooted in one's national

---

[10]R. Pazzelli, T.O.R., *The Franciscan Sisters: Outlines of History and Spirituality*, trans. Aiden Mullaney, T.O.R. (Steubenville, OH: University Press, 1993), 197-99. This book also contains a helpful summary of the Rule Project assemblies and key meetings, 183-99.

[11]P. McMullen, T.O.R., *The Development of the New Third Order Regular Rule* (Loretto, PA: St. Francis College, 1986). In this M.A. thesis, Paul McMullen details the entire project from the perspective of the TOR friars. Paul served in the General Curia of the TORs in Rome during this period and served as staff to the Madrid meeting of 1974.

history could easily enter into one's perceptions of others coming to the table of international deliberation and debate. These emerging lines of disagreement about method and content were, for the most part, carried on between leaders of Europe and the U.S.A. whose general superiors were the most numerous participants in the international assemblies. It was generally assumed that these superiors represented sufficient international expertise as they normally came from congregations with missions on almost every continent. However, at a period in which the Church was being confronted by the demand to see life from the vantage point of the world's *comunidade de base*, or base communities, as they were called, the small number of native leaders from Latin America, Asia and Africa was increasingly apparent. It may be safely said that consciousness of the problem was more acute than constructions of solutions. However, events subsequent to the passage of the Rule text would begin to bring solutions forward in helpful ways.

*Scholarly Biases*

Finally, even one's positions in regard to contemporary scholarship and interpretation might result in serious disagreement. Those most familiar with newly published theories about Francis's real intentions, the nature of his writings, the historic accuracy of his biographies, were defensive when asked to look from other frames of reference at their assumptions and convictions. Along with the ubiquitous "Franciscan Question" pondered by every serious student of Franciscan history stood the question of whether or not Francis intended to found what is presently subsumed under the banner of the Third Order Regular. While in scholarly circles this was a minor but contentious motif of classroom and "rec" room debate, Third Order Franciscans were finding a voice and asserting a right to be classified as equal in vocation and dignity with the members of the First and Second Orders. Acknowledgment of the rightness of the claim was not always swift in coming and arguments forged by prominent historians could and did lose sight of the existential fact: Third Order Franciscans were living a complete and authentic Franciscan life in the present and were not about to assume a second class status within the family that they loved and served by their daily lives.

The TOR Rule, whose papally-affirmed status spanned the centuries from 1289 to 1927, was a centuries old cord of connection that rooted the members in a solid lineage even if its historical documentation left much to be desired. Since consistent attention to the sources for the history and spiritual legacy of the TOR tended to be unevenly incorporated into the curricula of major Franciscan study centers, it is also fair to say that members of this branch themselves are often ignorant of the "long and winding road" by which their contemporary inheritance could be validated. Since the vast majority of institutes are modern foundations, lacking a "blood line" back to the earliest Franciscan penitential communities, a commitment to study and preserve this historic consciousness has been in short supply. Happily, the years since the Rule's approval have seen a steady advance in our knowledge, much of it developed by lay scholars. However, there is room for a great deal of research and teaching on this topic. It will be particularly important for this work to be exported to developing nations were the Order sees wonderful growth and a promising future.

### POSTSCRIPT: PEACE AND GOOD

The Franciscan greeting of peace is often accompanied by the wish for "good." It is a quaint way of speaking but conveys a profound belief of Francis and Clare that the nature of God's action in the world is best characterized in one word: good. This is the word that summarizes the activity of each day of creation in Genesis. This is the word used by Bonaventure to describe the inner life of the Trinity. One might be tempted to write the story of this Rule in terms of the trials and tribulations of its authors, the leaders of BFI and CFI and (were we to have access to their diaries!) the leaders of the First Order and certain curial officials as well. There is precedent for this as Franciscan history loves a lurid tale and is punctuated by sad chronicles of brothers rising up against brothers and the quest to live the Franciscan rule. Alas, the followers of the Poverello have their dark chronicles of murder and mayhem, much as they hate to admit it. (Thank God the Rule Project had no murders to recount, but more than one hour of mayhem is remembered by those who were at its center of gravity!)

It is thus very important to write this story as a chronicle of grace. The Order bears the ancient name, The Order of Penance. Much has been done to "excavate" the rich biblical, liturgical and social meaning of this term so central to the self-understanding of today's Third Order members. The call of *penance* is a call to continual conversion. This central understanding was not simply a theoretical template for discussion through the years of work on the 1982 Rule. The lived experience of constant readiness to stand under the correction of the Spirit was the prevailing spiritual experience of all who took part in this chapter in Franciscan history. The justice and judgment of the Spirit expressed itself in manifold ways. At times it took the form of discovery of an historical fact. At times it appeared in the painful dialogue that resulted in new consensus. At times it appeared when cross-cultural bias gave way to new mutual respect. Many times it took the form of long days and nights of difficult work in Spartan conditions, work done by unsung secretaries, translators, office helpers whose names are already lost with the turning of the pages of the story.

Breaking bread together became the nourishment of a new penitential consciousness. In the first place, the members of the various bodies committed themselves to lengthy meetings often held in remote locations. This required travel from one's home base, spending prolonged time together and sharing the rhythm of days of work, meals, recreational diversions, and prayer. Even when tensions were rife, meals and evening periods of relaxation became oases for normal human exchanges. Away from the formal process of translators and mediated committee meetings, the task of sharing table conversation, a joke by the fireside in the evening, a song, a walk to explore nearby sights—all required multiple levels of communication. This put the polyglots to the test and often resulted in hilarious moments. Each sister and brother came bearing the hopes not of a single congregation but, at times, of whole nations. Each came also with personal history and personal *legenda* of living the rule and life handed down for eight centuries. The normal tapestries of family sorrows and joys, health problems and ministerial stresses were part of the exchange as profound friendships germinated out of the soil of such demanding work.

Breaking bread in the form of prayer and worship mirrored the nights and days of dining room encounters. No matter how grievous the discord, no matter how wounded the psyche, no matter how uncertain the opinion of the day's results, the call to join in the liturgy of the hours or the Eucharist provided deep encounter in the Giver of all good gifts. Perhaps none was more poignant than the Christmas Mass celebrated in the small chapel of Oyster Bay. There, without benefit of great choirs and orchestral support, this band of pilgrim authors agreed at one point to simply sing "Silent Night" in all their native languages simultaneously. The result was magical. One harmony out of many tongues rose in the incense-sweetened air that night. It heralded possibilities of a new international penitential brotherhood and sisterhood whose penance was nothing less than a total commitment to be turned to God and turned to neighbor in a life-long covenant of Franciscan evangelical striving.

Is it possible that what was vouchsafed to this group of pioneering sisters and brothers was a taste of the earliest generation's struggles and searching? Their text emerged from a *sacrum commercium*—a sacred exchange of desires, commitments, and prophetic convictions. Aided by technology and the speed and ease of modern travel, a world-wide federation of Franciscan men and women were doing the work that once was done in the hermitages and marketplace ministries of the first Franciscans. And what was that? It was simply the search for a way to simply and in a few words distill the burden and beatitude of being called to walk in the footprints of Jesus the Christ. Out of the short span of years in which all of these were engaged in the rule project's demands arose a new chapter in Franciscan history and new cross-cultural set of structures and options that would build upon this foundation. For these men and women, the blessing invoked in the Early Rule of Francis himself became a text of immediate experience, of beatitude.

### IN THE NAME OF THE LORD!

I ask all my brothers [and sisters] to learn and frequently call to mind
the tenor and sense of what has been written in this life
for the salvation of our souls. I beg God, Who is All-powerful,
Three and One, to bless all who teach, learn, retain, remember,
and put into practice these things, each time they repeat and do
what has been written here for the salvation of our souls, and,
kissing their feet, I implore everyone to keep,
and treasure them greatly.[12]

---

[12]ER XXIV:1-3; FA:ED I, 86.

## "Who's Who" in the Rule Project

### BFI: International Franciscan Bureau

Function:       Acts as Board of Directors representing major superiors

Members:        Sr. Elizabeth Delor, O.S.F. — President
                Sr. Giovanna Achille, F.A.
                Sr. Alma Dufault, F.M.M.
                Sr. Eliska Pretschnerova, O.S.F.
                Sr. Christianne Wittmers, O.S.F.
                Br. Luis Cuesta Y Nozal, T.O.R. Cap.

Coordinator     Sr. Louise Dendooven, F.M.M.
Facilitator     Fr. Frédéric Deblock, O.F.M.

### CFI: International Franciscan Commission

Function:       Acts as "manager" of the Rule Project; directs meeting
                plans, rules for procedure, etc.

Members:        Sr. Carmen Ciria, F.S.S.S.
                Sr. Roberta Cusack, O.S.F.
                Sr. Marie Andrea Frech, S.S.F.
                Sr. Ethelburga Hacker, D.F.S.
                Sr. Bernadette Nourdin, S.S.F.A. — Secretary
                Sr. Romualda Trinchera, F.M.I.H.
                Sr. Augusta Vinsentin, F.M.S.H.
                Br. Columban Keller, C.M.S.F.

Coordinator:    Sr. Louise Dendooven, F.M.M.
Facilitator:    Fr. Frédéric Deblock, O.F.M.

### Consultors: Representative of Superiors of OFM, OFM Cap., OFM Conv., TOR

Function:       Communications liaison with First Order, experts in
                Franciscanism

Members:        Fr. Bernardin Beck, O.F.M.
                Fr. Fidèle Lenaerts, O.F.M. Cap.
                Fr. Candido Lorenzoni, O.F.M. Conv.
                Fr. Raffaele Pazzelli, T.O.R.

## Work Group: Authors, Editors of Rule Text

Function:        Compose text based on results of consultation; amend
                 during the General Assembly of Rome

Members:         Sr. Margaret Carney, O.S.F.
                 Fr. Thaddeus Horgan, S.A.
                 Sr. Ignatia Gomez, M.S.A.
                 Sr. Marianne Jungbluth, O.S.F.
                 Sr. Marie-Benoit Lucbernet, S.S.F.A.
                 Sr. Maria Luiza Piva, C.F.
                 Sr. Maria Honoria Montalvo, F.M.I.

Facilitator      Br. Jean François Godet, O.F.M.

# HISTORICAL SOURCES

# 1

The canonical foundation of the Third Franciscan Order did not happen until 1289 with the Rule of Nicholas IV in the bull *Supra montem*. But, historically, it is clearly documented that the existence of what would later be called the Third Order goes back to the times of Francis himself.

This first chapter presents the historic sources that accompany the development of the Third Order Regular from Francis to modern times: Francis's *Letter to the Faithful* and the Volterra Document, the *Memoriale propositi* of 1221, the Rule of Nicholas IV establishing the Third Order in 1289, the Rule of Leo X establishing the Third Order Regular in 1521, and the Rule of Pius XI renewing the Rule in conformity with the new code of Canon Law in 1927.

The earliest documents are Francis's *Letter to the Faithful* and the text found in the codex 225 of the Guarnacci Library in Volterra. Those documents have been published in Kajetan Esser's 1976 critical edition of the writings of Francis.[1] Since its discovery by Paul Sabatier, the text of the Volterra manuscript has been traditionally considered as a first version of the Letter to the Faithful.[2] There is no doubt that the two documents are closely connected: suffice it to take a quick look at the two texts to see that they share the same author. The Volterra manuscript, written in the middle of the thirteenth century, contains the only known copy of

---

[1] K. Esser, *Die Opuscula des hl. Franziskus von Assisi. Neue textkritische Edition* (Grottaferrata: Collegio S. Bonaventura, 1976). A second edition, prepared by E. Grau, was published in 1989. The Letter to the Faithful is on pages 207-13; the Volterra Document, on pages 178-80.

[2] P. Sabatier, *Fratris Francisci Bartholi de Assisio Tractatus de indulgentia S. Mariae de Portiuncula* (Paris: Fischbacher, 1900), 132-36. K. Esser, "Un precursore della *Epistola ad fideles* di san Francesco d'Assisi," *Analecta TOR* 14:129 (1978): 11-47. R. Pazzelli, "Il titolo della 'Prima recensione della lettera ai fedeli': Precisazioni sul Codice 225 di Volterra," *Analecta TOR* 19:142 (1987): 233-40. L. Temperini, *Frate Francesco a tutti i suoi fedeli* (Rome: Editrice Franciscanum, 1987).

our document, which is part of a collection of four writings of Francis, along with the *Admonitions*, the *Letter to the Custodians*, and the *Letter to the Order*. Although the Volterra Document is composed of passages of Francis's *Letter to the Faithful*, it is not a letter, but rather an admonition to those who do penance and those who do not. A closer look at the texts of the *Letter to the Faithful* and the Volterra Document, which a synoptic presentation makes easier, demonstrates that the story of the dying unrepentant man of the *Letter to the Faithful* (72-81) is omitted in the Volterra Document, although there is mention of a bitter death. The *Letter to the Faithful*, in verse 82, has a correct *eius* when the Volterra Document has an incorrect *eius* (2:15). Copying the conclusion of the story from the *Letter to the Faithful* (83-85), the Volterra Document (2:16-18) hesitates between singular and plural. While the *Letter to the Faithful* was truly a letter Francis addressed to all who live in the whole world, the Volterra Document uses excerpts from its text to draft a simple but strong statement to those who do and those who do not do penance.[3]

At the same time Francis was writing his *Letter to the Faithful*, Cardinal Hugolino was trying to organize the fraternities of penitents in Italy and composed the *Memoriale propositi*, commonly dated as 1221.[4]

The text of the Rule of Nicholas IV is found in the bull *Supra montem*[5]; the Rule of Leo X, in the bull *Inter cetera*[6]; and the Rule of Pius XI, in the bull *Rerum condicio*.[7]

---

[3]Debate on the dating and intention of these texts will undoubtedly continue. Recent examples of such scholarly research include the work of Michael F. Cusato, O.F.M. "An Unexplored Influence on the *Epistola ad fideles* of Francis of Assisi: The *Epistola universis Christi fidelibus* of Joachim of Fiore," in *Franciscan Studies* 61 (2003): 253-78, and Margaret Carney, O.S.F., "The 'Letter' of Fourteen Names: Reading 'The Exhortation,'" in *Francis of Assisi History, Hagiography and Hermeneutics in the Early Documents*, ed. Jay M. Hammond (NY: New City Press, 2004), 90-104.

[4]G.G. Meersseman, *Dossier de l'Ordre de la Pénitence au XIIIe siècle* (Fribourg: Editions universitaires, 2nd ed., 1982), 91-112. L. Temperini, *Testi e Documenti sul Terzo Ordine Francescano* (Roma: Editrice Franciscanum, 1991), 90–108. English translation by T. Zaremba in *Franciscan Social Reform: A Study of the Third Order Secular of St. Francis as an Agency of Social Reform according to Certain Papal Documents*, Ph.D. dissertation (Washington: The Catholic University of America, 1947), 114-21.

[5]Temperini, *Testi e Documenti*, 248-76. English translation in Zaremba, *Franciscan Social Reform*, 123-31.

[6]*Seraphicae legislationis textus originales* (Quaracchi: Collegium S. Bonaventurae, 1897), 287-97.

[7]*Acta Apostolicae Sedis* 19 (1927): 361-67.

spe mercedis nõ cupit maifestare ho
minibus qz ipe altissimus maifestabit
opa eius qbuscuqz ei placuit. Beatus sit
qui secreta dõ obseruabit i corde suo. Ho
hec st uba uite z salutis q si qs legerit
z fecerit i beniet; uita z auiiet saluter
a dño de illis qui fecerit primum.

In noie domini. Bñs qui dñm di
ligunt ex toto corde, ex tota aia
z mente ex tota uirtute z diligunt
proximos suos sicut se ipos z odio hñt cor
porn cor cui. Viciis z pctis z reqz priut
corpus z sanguier dñi nri ybu xpi sa
cunt fructus dignos pñie. Quod qz beñ aie
neccí sci illi uisse dñi talia fecerit; qz
tali ter pseuerazt q regesceir si eos so
dñi z faciet aps eos baptacularz z mansi
onem qst filij pacis celestis cui opa fa
cuuit qst sposi si kiis amatores dñi nri
ybu xc. Sponsi sumus qui spu sco con
iugir fidel aia dño nro ybu xpo. fres
et sumus qui facimus uolutater patris

Et finalzs cui eligir bona fecerit coñidabir illi
dño dicens. Brñe tibi comendo k bonu. u reddes illd
iñ die iudicii. Ego ei su fur z latro. z si mecu
retulerz kunuer k z. sz placeat tibi ur obliuiscar
z z tu teneas

## EPISTOLA AD FIDELES

## EXHORTATIO AD FRATRES ET SORORES DE PENITENTIA

### I. DE ILLIS QUI FACIUNT PŒNITENTIAM

[1]In nomine Domini Patris et Filii et Spiritus Sancti. Amen. Universis christianis, religiosis, clericis et laicis, masculis et feminis, omnibus qui habitant in universo mundo, frater Franciscus, eorum servus et subditus, obsequium cum reverentia, pacem veram de cælo et sinceram in Domino caritatem.

[1]In nomine Domini! Omnes qui Dominum diligunt ex toto corde, ex tota anima et mente, ex tota virtute (Mk 22:39), et diligunt proximos suos sicut se ipsos (Mt 22:39), [2]et odio habent corpora eorum cum vitiis et peccatis, [3]et recipiunt corpus et sanguinem Domini nostri Iesu Christi, [4]et faciunt fructus dignos pœnitentiæ (Lk 3:8):

[2]Cum sim servus omnium, omnibus servire teneor et administrare odorifera verba Domini mei. [3]Unde in mente considerans, quod cum personaliter propter infirmitatem et debilitatem mei corporis non possim singulos visitare, proposui litteris præsentibus et nuntiis verba Domini nostri Iesu Christi, qui est Verbum Patris, vobis referre et verba Spiritus Sancti, quæ spiritus et vita sunt (Jn 6:64).

[4]Istud Verbum Patris tam dignum, tam sanctum et gloriosum nuntiavit altissimus Pater de cælo per sanctum Gabrielem angelum suum in uterum sanctæ ac gloriosæ virginis Mariæ, ex cuius utero veram recepit carnem humanitatis et fragilitatis nostræ. [5]Qui, cum dives esset (2 Cor 8:9) super omnia, voluit ipse in mundo cum beatissima Virgine, matre sua, eligere paupertatem. [6]Et prope passionem celebravit pascha cum discipulis suis et accipiens panem gratias egit et benedixit et fregit dicens: Accipite et comedite, hoc

## LETTER TO THE FAITHFUL

¹In the name of the Lord, Father and Son and Holy Spirit. Amen.

To all Christians, religious, clerics, and layfolk, to men and women, to all who live in the whole world: Brother Francis, their servant and subject, sends deference and respect, true peace from heaven and sincere charity in the Lord.

²Since I am the servant of all, I am held to serve and offer to all the fragrant words of my Lord. ³I thought a while how because of my sickness and weakness I cannot visit each one of you. This made me decide to send you by the present letter and message the words of our Lord Jesus Christ, who is the word of the Father, and the words of the Holy Spirit, which are spirit and life (Jn 6:64).

⁴That Word of the Father, so worthy, so holy, and so glorious, the most high Father, from heaven through his holy angel Gabriel, announced his arrival in the womb of the holy and glorious Virgin Mary. From Mary's womb he took the real flesh of our human fragility. ⁵Though rich (2 Cor 8:9) above all things, together with the most Blessed Virgin his mother, he voluntarily chose poverty in this world. ⁶And near his passion he celebrated the Passover with his disciples. And taking bread he gave thanks, he blessed and broke

## EXHORTATION TO THE BROTHERS AND SISTERS OF PENANCE

### I. ON THOSE WHO DO PENANCE

¹In the name of the Lord! All who cherish the Lord with their whole heart, with their whole soul and mind, with all their virtue (Mk 12:30) and love their neighbors as themselves (Mt 22:39), ²and hate their bodies with vices and sins, ³and receive the Body and Blood of our Lord Jesus Christ, ⁴and do worthy fruits of penance (Lk 3:8):

est corpus meum (Mt 26:26). [7]Et accipiens calicem dixit: Hic est sanguis meus novi testamenti, qui pro vobis et pro multis effundetur in remissionem peccatorum (Mt 26:27). [8]Deinde oravit Patrem dicens: Pater, si fieri potest, transeat a me calix iste. [9]Et factus est sudor eius sicut guttæ sanguinis decurrentis in terram (Lk 22:44). [10]Posuit tamen voluntatem suam in voluntate Patris dicens: Pater, fiat voluntas tua (Mt 26:42); non sicut ego volo, sed sicut tu (Mt 26:39). [11]Cuius Patris talis fuit voluntas, ut filius eius benedictus et gloriosus, quem dedit nobis et natus fuit pro nobis, se ipsum per proprium sanguinem suum sacrificium et hostiam in ara crucis offerret; [12]non propter se, per quem facta sunt omnia (Jn 1:3), sed pro peccatis nostris, [13]relinquens nobis exemplum, ut sequamur vestigia eius (1 P 2:21).

[14]Et vult ut omnes salvemur per eum et recipiamus ipsum puro corde et casto corpore nostro. [15]Sed pauci sunt, qui velint eum recipere et salvi esse per eum, licet eius iugum suave et onus ipsius leve (Mt 11:30). [16]Qui nolunt gustare, quam suavit sit Dominus (Ps 33:9) et diligunt tenebras magis quam lucem (Jn 3:19) nolentes adimplere mandata Dei, maledicti sunt; [17]de quibus dicitur per prophetam: Maledicti qui declinant a mandatis tuis (Ps 118:21).

it, saying: Take and eat together, this is my Body (Mt 26:26). [7]And taking the cup he said: This is my Blood, of the New Testament. For you and for many it will be shed for the forgiveness of sins (Mt 26:27). [8]Then he prayed to his Father, saying: Father, if it is possible, let this cup pass from me. [9]And his sweat was as drops of blood falling on the ground (Lk 22:44). [10]Still, he laid his will in the will of the Father, saying: Father, your will be done (Mt 26:42). Not as I wish, but as you do (Mt 26:39). [11]It was his Father's will that his blessed and glorious Son, whom he gave to us and who was born for us, offer himself with his own blood as a sacrifice and a victim on the altar of the cross. [12]He did not do it for himself, through whom all things are made (Jn 1:3), but for our sins, [13]leaving us an example that we might follow in his footsteps (1 P 2:21).

[14]And he wants us all to be saved by him and to receive him with our pure heart and chaste body. [15]Few however are those who would want to receive him and be saved by him, though his yoke is sweet and his burden light (Mt 11:30). [16]Those who do not want to taste how sweet is the Lord (Ps 33:9), who cherish the darkness more than the light (Jn 3:19), refusing to carry out God's commands, are doomed. [17]About such men does the prophet speak: Doomed are they who stray from your commands (Ps 118:21).

[18]Sed, o quam beati et benedicti sunt illi qui Deum diligunt et faciunt sicut dicit ipse Dominus in evangelio: Diliges Dominum Deum tuum ex toto corde et ex tota mente et proximum tuum sicut te ipsum (Mt 22:37.39). [19]Diligamus igitur Deum et adoremus eum puro corde et pura mente, quia ipse super omnia quærens dixit: Veri adoratores adorabunt patrem in spiritu et veritate (Jn 4:23). [20]Omnes enim, qui adorant eum, in spiritu veritatis oportet eum adorare (Jn 4:24). [21]Et dicamus ei laudes et orationes die ac nocte dicendo: Pater noster, qui es in cælis (Mt 6:9), quia oportet nos semper orare et non deficere (Lk 18:1).

[22]Debemus siquidem confiteri sacerdoti omnia peccata nostra; et recipiamus corpus et sanguinem Domini Iesu Christi ab eo. [23]Qui non manducat carnem suam et non bibit sanguinem suum (Jn 6:55.57), non potest introire in regnum Dei (Jn 3:5). [24]Digne tamen manducet et bibat, quia qui indigne recipit iudicium sibi manducat et bibit, non diiudicans corpus Domini (1 Cor 11:29), id est non discernit.

[25]Faciamus insuper fructus dignos pœnitentiæ (Lk 3:8).

[26]Et diligamus proximos sicut nos ipsos (Mt 22:39). [27]Et si quis non vult eos amare sicut se ipsum, saltim non inferat eis mala, sed faciat bona.

[28]Qui autem potestatem iudicandi alios receperunt iudicium

[18]But oh! how happy and blessed are they who cherish God and do as the Lord himself says in the gospel: You shall cherish the Lord your God with whole heart and whole mind, and your neighbor as yourself (Mt 22:37.39). [19]Let us therefore cherish God and adore him with a pure heart and a pure mind because he himself wants nothing more, as he said: True adorers will adore the Father in spirit and in truth (Jn 4:23). [20]For all who adore him should adore him in the spirit of truth (Jn 4:24). [21]And let us speak our praise and prayers to him day and night, saying: Our Father, who are in heaven (Mt 6:9), because we should always pray and never cease (Lk 18:1).

[22]And so we must confess all our sins to a priest, and let us receive from him the body and blood of our Lord Jesus Christ. [23]Who does not eat his flesh and drink his blood (Jn 6:55.57) cannot enter the reign of God (Jn 3:5). [24]However, one should eat and drink worthily, for the one who receives unworthily eats and drinks unto one's judgment, without distinguishing the body of the Lord (1 Cor 11:29), that is, without seeing what one does.

[25]Furthermore, let us do worthy fruits of penance (Lk 3:8).

[26]And let us cherish our neighbors as ourselves (Mt 22:39). [27]And if one does not want to love them as oneself, at least do them no harm, but do them good.

[28]Those who have received the power to judge others shall exert

cum misericordia exerceant, sicut ipsi volunt a Domino misericordiam obtinere. [29]Iudicium enim sine misericordia erit illis qui non fecerint misericordiam (Jas 2:13).

[30]Habeamus itaque caritatem et humilitatem; et faciamus eleemosynas, quia ipsa lavat animas a sordibus peccatorum (Tb 4:11; 12:9). [31]Homines enim omnia perdunt, quæ in hoc sæculo relinquunt; secum tamen portant caritatis mercedem et eleemosynas, quas fecerunt, de quibus habebunt a Domino præmium et dignam remunerationem.

[32]Debemus etiam ieiunare et abstinere a vitiis et peccatis (Sir 3:32) et a superfluitate ciborum et potus et esse catholici.

[33]Debemus etiam ecclesias visitare frequenter et venerari clericos et revereri, non tantum propter eos, si sint peccatores, sed propter officium et administrationem sanctissimi corporis et sanguinis Christi, quod sacrificant in altari et recipiunt et aliis administrant. [34]Et firmiter sciamus omnes quia nemo salvari potest, nisi per sancta verba et sanguinem Domini nostri Iesu Christi, quæ clerici dicunt, annuntiant et ministrant. [35]Et ipsi soli ministrate debent et non alii. [36]Specialiter autem religiosi, qui renuntiaverunt sæculo, tenentur plura et maiora facere, sed ista non dimittere (Lk 11:42).

[37]Debemus odio habere corpora nostra cum vitiis et peccatis quia Dominus dicit in evangelio:

judgment with mercy, just as they themselves want to get mercy from God. [29]For judgment without mercy shall be theirs who have shown no mercy (Jas 2:13).

[30]Let us have charity then and humility. And let us give alms because they wash the stains of sins from souls (Tb 4:11; 12:9). [31]For people lose all things which they leave in this world, but they carry with them the wages of charity and the alms which they gave, for which from the Lord they will have a reward and an appropriate remuneration.

[32]Furthermore we must fast and abstain from vices and sins (Sir 3:32) and excessive food and drink, and be Catholic.

[33]We must also visit churches frequently and venerate and revere the clergy, not so much for themselves, should they be sinners, but because of their office and administration of the most holy body and blood of Christ, which they offer in sacrifice on the altar and receive and administer to others. [34]And let all of us know for sure that no one can be saved except through the holy words and the blood of our Lord Jesus Christ, which the clergy say, proclaim, and minister. [35]And they alone must minister and not others. [36]But religious especially, who have renounced the world, are held to do more and greater things, but not to disregard these (Lk 11:42).

[37]We must hate our bodies with its vices and sins, for the Lord says in the Gospel: All evils, vices

Omnia mala, vitia et peccata a corde exeunt (Mt 15:18-19; Mk 7:23).

[38]Debemus diligere inimicos nostros et benefacere his, qui nos odio habent (Mt 5:24; Lk 6:27).

[39]Debemus observare præcepta et consilia Domini nostri Iesu Christi.

[40]Debemus etiam nosmetipsos abnegare (Mt 16:24) et ponere corpora nostra sub iugo servitutis et sanctæ obedientiæ, sicut unusquisque promisit Domino. [41]Et nullus homo teneatur ex obedientia obedire alicui in eo, ubi committitur delictum vel peccatum. [42]Cui autem obedientia commissa est et qui habetur maior, sit sicut minor (Lk 22:26) et aliorum fratrum servus. [43]Et in singulos fratres suos misericordiam faciat et habeat, quam vellet sibi fieri, si in consimili casu esset. [44]Nec ex delicto fratris irascatur in fratrem, sed cum omni patientia et humilitate ipsum benigne moneat et sustineat.

[45]Non debemus secundum carnem esse sapientes et prudentes, sed magis debemus esse simplices, humiles et puri. [46]Et habeamus corpora nostra in opprobrium et despectum, quia omnes per culpam nostram sumus miseri et putridi, fœtidi et vermes, sicut dicit Dominus per prophetam: Ego sum vermis et non homo, opprobrium hominum et abiectio plebis (Ps 21:7).

and sins come from the heart (Mt 15:18-19; Mk 7:23).

[38]We must cherish our enemies and do good to those who hate us (Mt 5:24; Lk 6:27).

[39]We must observe the precepts and counsels of our Lord Jesus Christ.

[40]We must also deny ourselves (Mt 16:24) and put our bodies under the yoke of service and holy obedience, as everyone has promised the Lord. [41]And let no one be held in obedience to submit to someone where a crime or a sin would be committed. [42]Instead, the one to whom obedience has been committed and who is taken for greater shall be as the lesser one (Lk 22:26) and the servant of the other brothers. [43]And he shall have and do mercy to each of his brothers, such as he would want for himself, if he were in a similar situation. [44]Nor shall he get angry against a brother because of the brother's fault, but with all patience and humility he shall admonish him kindly and support him.

[45]We must not be wise and prudent according to the flesh but we must rather be simple, humble, and pure. [46]And we shall hold our bodies in scorn and contempt, for all of us, through our fault, are miserable and putrid, rotten and worms, just as the Lord says through the prophet: I am a worm and not a man, a scorn of men and the outcast of the people (Ps 21:7).

[47]Numquam debemus desiderare esse super alios, sed magis debemus esse servi et subditi omni humanæ creaturæ propter Deum (1 P 2:13).

[48]Et omnes illi et illæ, dum talia fecerint et perseveraverint usque in finem, requiescet super eos Spiritus Domini (Is 11:2) et faciet in eis habitaculum et mansionem (Jn 14:23). [49]Et erunt filii Patris cælestis (Mt 5:45), cuius opera faciunt. [50]Et sunt sponsi, fratres et matres Domini nostri Iesu Christi (Mt 12:50). [51]Sponsi sumus quando Spiritu Sancto coniungitur fidelis anima Iesu Christo. [52]Fratres enim sumus quando facimus voluntatem patris eius, qui est in cælo (Mt 12:50); [53]matres quando portamus eum in corde et corpore nostro (1 Cor 6:20) per amorem et puram et sinceram conscientiam; parturimus eum per sanctam operationem, quæ lucere debet aliis in exemplum (Mt 5:16).

[5]O quam beati et benedicti sunt illi et illæ, dum talia faciunt et in talibus perseverant, [6]quia requiescet super eos spiritus Domini (Is 11:2) et faciet apud eos habitaculum et mansionem (Jn 14:23). [7]Et sunt filii patris cælestis (Mt 5:45), cuius opera faciunt, et sunt sponsi, fratres et matres Domini nostri Iesu Christi (Mt 12:50). [8]Sponsi sumus quando Spiritu Sancto coniungitur fidelis anima Domino nostro Iesu Christo. [9]Fratres ei sumus quando facimus voluntatem patris qui in cælis est (Mt 12:50); [10]matres quando portamus eum in corde et corpore nostro (1 Cor 6:20) per divinum amorem et puram et sinceram conscientiam; parturimus eum per sanctam operationem, quæ lucere debet aliis in exemplum (Mt 5:16).

[54]O quam gloriosum et sanctum et magnum habere in cælis Patrem! [55]O quam sanctum, paraclitum, pulchrum et admirabilem habere sponsum! [56]O quam sanctum et quam dilectum, beneplacitum, humilem, pacificum, dulcem et amabilem et super omnia desiderabilem habere talem fratrem et filium, qui posuit animam suam pro ovibus suis (Jn 10:15) et oravit patrem pro nobis dicens: Pater sancte, serva eos in nomine tuo, quos dedisti mihi (Jn 17:11).

[11]O quam gloriosum est, sanctum et magnum in cælis habere Patrem! [12]O quam sanctum, paraclitum, pulchrum et admirabilem talem habere sponsum! [13]O quam sanctum et quam dilectum, beneplacitum, humilem, pacificum, dulcem, amabilem et super omnia desiderabilem habere talem fratrem et talem filium, Dominum nostrum Iesum Christum, [14]qui posuit animam pro ovibus suis (Jn 10:15) et oravit patri dicens: Pater sancte, serva eos in nomine

[47]We must never desire to be above others, but rather we must be servant and subject to every human creature for God (1 P 2:13).

[48]And all the men and women who have done such things and persevered to the end: on them shall rest the spirit of the Lord (Is 11:2) and make in them his home and dwelling (Jn 14:23). [49]And they will be children of the heavenly Father (Mt 5:45) whose works they do. [50]And they are the spouses, brothers, and mothers of our Lord Jesus Christ (Mt 12:50). [51]We are spouses when by the Holy Spirit the faithful soul is joined to Jesus Christ. [52]We are brothers when we do the will of his Father who is in heaven (Mt 12:50); [53]mothers, when we bear him in our heart and body (1 Cor 6:20) through love and a pure and sincere conscience; we give birth to him through a holy activity, which must shine in example to others (Mt 5:16).

[54]O how glorious and holy and great it is to have a Father in heaven! [55]O how holy, consoling, beautiful and admirable to have a spouse! [56]O how holy and how loving, gratifying, humbling, peace-giving, sweet and lovable, and above all things desirable to have such a brother and such a son, who laid down his soul for his sheep (Jn 10:15) and prayed to the Father for us saying: Holy Father, keep in your name those whom you have given me (Jn 17:11). [57]Father, all whom you have

[5]Oh! how happy and blessed are those men and women, while they do such things and persevere in such things, [6]for on them shall rest the spirit of the Lord (Is 11:2), and make among them his home and dwelling (Jn 14:23). [7]And they are children of the heavenly Father (Mt 5:45), whose works they do, and they are the spouses, brothers and mothers of our Lord Jesus Christ (Mt 12:50). [8]We are spouses when by the Holy Spirit the faithful soul is joined to our Lord Jesus Christ. [9]We are brothers to him when we do the will of the Father who is in heaven (Mt 12:50); [10]mothers, when we bear him in our heart and body (1 Cor 6:20) through divine love and a pure and sincere conscience; we give birth to him through a holy activity, which must shine in example to others (Mt 5:16).

[11]O how glorious, holy and great it is to have a Father in heaven! [12]O how holy, consoling, beautiful and admirable to have such a spouse! [13]O how holy and how loving, gratifying, humbling, peace-giving, sweet, lovable and above all things desirable to have such a brother and such a son, our Lord Jesus Christ, who laid down his soul for his sheep (Jn 10:15) and prayed to the Father saying: [14]Holy Father, guard them in your name (Jn 17:11), whom you have given

[57]Pater, omnes, quos dedisti mihi in mundo, tui erant et mihi eos dedisti (Jn 17:6). [58]Et verba, quæ dedisti mihi, dedi eis; et ipsi acceperunt et cognoverunt vere quia a te exivi et crediderunt quia tu me misisti (Jn 17:8); rogo pro eis et non pro mundo (Jn 17:9; benedic et sanctifica eos (Jn 17:17). [59]Et pro eis sanctifico me ipsum, ut sint sanctificati in unum sicut et nos (Jn 17:11) sumus. [60]Et volo, pater ut ubi ego sum et illi sint mecum, ut videant claritatem meam (Jn 17:24) in regno tuo (Mt 20:21).

[61]Ei autem qui tanta sustinuit pro nobis, tot bona contulit et conferet in futurum, omnis creatura, quæ est in cælis, in terra, in mari et in abyssis reddat laudem Deo, gloriam, honorem et benedictionem (Rv 5:13), [62]quia ipse est virtus et fortitudo nostra, qui est solus bonus, solus altissimus, solus omnipotens, admirabilis, gloriosus et solus sanctus, laudabilis et benedictus per infinita sæcula sæculorum. Amen.

[63]Omnes autem illi, qui non sunt in pœnitentia et non recipiunt corpus et sanguinem Domini nostri Iesu Christi, [64]et operantur vitia et peccata, et qui ambulant post malam concupiscentiam et mala desideria, et non observant quæ promiserunt, [65]et serviunt corporaliter mundo carnalibus desideriis, curis et sollicitudinibus huius sæculi et curis huius vitæ, [66]decepti a diabolo, cuius filii sunt et eius

tuo (Jn 17:11), quos dedisti mihi in mundo, tui erant et mihi dedisti eos (Jn 17:6). [15]Et verba quæ mihi dedisti, dedi eis; et ipsi acceperunt et crediderunt vere quia a te exivi et cognoverunt quia tu me misisti (Jn 17:8). [16]Rogo pro eis et non pro mundo (Jn 17:9). [17]Benedic et sanctifica (Jn 17:17) et pro eis sanctifico me ipsum (Jn 17:19). [18]Non pro eis rogo tantum, sed pro eis qui credituri sunt per verbum illorum in me (Jn 17:20), ut sint sanctificati in unum (Jn 17:23) sicut et nos (Jn 17:11). [19]Et volo, pater, ut ubi ergo sum et illi sint mecum, ut videant claritatem meam (Jn 17:24) in regno tuo (Mt 20:21). Amen.

## II. De illis qui non agunt pœnitentiam

[1]Omnes autem illi et illæ, qui non sunt in pœnitentia, [2]et non recipiunt corpus et sanguinem Domini nostri Iesu Christi, [3]et operantur vitia et peccata, et qui ambulant post malam concupiscentiam et mala desideria carnis suæ, [4]et non observant quæ promiserunt Domino, [5]et serviunt corporaliter mundo carnalibus desiderii et sollicitudinibus sæculi et curis huius vitæ: [6]detenti a diabolo, cuius sunt

given me in the world, yours they were and you have given them to me (Jn 17:6). [58]And the words you have given me, I have given them; and they have accepted them and know truly that I have come from you and they have believed that you have sent me (Jn 17:8). l pray for them and not for the world (Jn 17:9); bless them and make them holy (Jn 17:17). [59]And I make myself holy for them so that they may be made holy (Jn 17:17) in being one as we, too, are (Jn 17:11). [60]And I want, Father, that where I am, they also may be with me, that they see my brightness (Jn 17:24) in your reign (Mt 20:21).

[61]To him who has borne so much for us, who has given us so many good things and will do so in the future: let every creature in heaven, on earth, in the sea and in the depths, return praise, glory, honor and blessing (Rv 5:13), [62]for He is our strength and courage who alone is good, alone most high, alone all-powerful, admirable, glorious, and alone holy, praiseworthy and blessed for endless ages. Amen.

[63]However, all those who are not in penance, and do not receive the body and blood of our Lord Jesus Christ, and put their activity in vices and sins, [64]and who wander after evil concupiscence and evil desires, and do not observe what they have promised, [65]and serve the world bodily by the carnal desires, the cares and concerns of this world, and by the cares of this life, [66]deceived by the devil whose

me in the world, yours they were and you have given them to me (Jn 17:6). [15]And the words you have given me, I have given them; and they have accepted them and have believed truly that I have come from you, and they know that you have sent me (Jn 17:8). [16]I pray for them and not for the world (Jn 17:9). [17]Bless them and make them holy (Jn 17:17) and for them I make myself holy (Jn 17:19). [18]Not only for them do I pray, but also for those who are going to believe in me through their word, so that all be made holy in one (Jn 17:23) as we, too, are. [19]And I want, Father, that where I am, they also may be with me, that they see my brightness (Jn 17:24) in your reign (Mt 20:21). Amen.

## II. On those who do not do penance

[1]However, all those men and women who are not in penance, [2]and do not receive the body and blood of our Lord Jesus Christ, [3]and put their activity in vices and sins, and who wander after evil concupiscence and the evil desires of their flesh, [4]and do not observe what they have promised the Lord, [5]and serve the world bodily by the carnal desires and the concerns for the world, and by the cares of

opera faciunt (Jn 8:41), cæci sunt, quia verum lumen non vident Dominum nostrum Iesum Christum. [67]Sapientiam non habent spiritualem, quia non habent Filium Dei in se, qui est vera sapientia Patris; de quibus dicitur: Sapientia eorum devorata est (Ps 106:27). [68]Vident, agnoscunt, sciunt et faciunt mala; et scienter perdunt animas.

filii et eius opera faciunt (Jn 8:41), [7]cæci sunt, quia verum lumen non vident Dominum nostrum Iesum Christum. [8]Sapientiam non habent spiritualem, quia non habent Filium Dei qui est vera sapientia Patris; [9]de quibus dicitur: Sapientia eorum deglutita est (Ps 106:27); et Maledicti qui declinant a mandatis tuis (Ps 118:21). [10]Vident et agnoscunt, sciunt et faciunt mala et ipsi scienter perdunt animas.

[69]Videte, cæci, decepti ab inimicis nostris scilicet a carne, a mundo et a diabolo, quia corpori dulce est facere peccatum et amarum servire Deo, quia omnia mala, vitia et peccata de corde hominum exeunt et procedunt (Mk 7:21), sicut dicit Dominus in evangelio. [70]Et nihil habetis in hoc sæculo neque in futuro. [71]Putatis diu possidere vanitates huius sæculi, sed decepti estis, quia veniet dies et hora, de quibus non cogitatis et nescitis et ignoratis. [72]Infirmatur corpus, mors appropinquat, veniunt propinqui et amici dicentes: Dispone tua. [73]Ecce uxor eius et filii eius et propinqui et amici fingunt flere. [74]Et respiciens videt eos flentes, movetur malo motu; cogitando intra se dicit: Ecce animam et corpus meum et omnia mea pono in manibus vestris. [75]Vere, iste homo est maledictus, qui confidit et exponit animam suam et corpus et omnia sua in talibus manibus;

[11]Videte, cæci, decepti ab inimicis vestris: a carne, mundo et diabolo; quia corpori dulce est facere peccatum et amarum est facere servire Deo; [12]quia omnia vitia et peccata de corde hominum exeunt et procedunt, sicut dicit Dominus in evangelio (Mk 7:21). [13]Et nihil habetis in hoc sæculo neque in futuro. [14]Et putatis diu possidere vanitates huius sæculi, sed decepti estis, quia veniet dies et hora, de quibus non cogitatis, nescitis et ignoratis; infirmatur corpus, mors appropinquat

children they are and whose works they do (Jn 8:41), they are blind, for they do not see the true light, our Lord Jesus Christ. [67]They do not have spiritual wisdom, for they do not have the Son of God in them, who is the true wisdom of the Father. About them it is said: Their wisdom has been swallowed up (Ps 106:27). [68]They see, they recognize, they know and they do what is wrong and knowingly lose their souls.

[69]See, blind people, you are being deceived by our enemies, that is, by the flesh, by the world, and by the devil, for it is sweet to the body to commit sin and bitter to serve God, because all evils, vices and sins come and proceed from the heart of men (Mk 7:21), just as the Lord says in the Gospel. [70]And you have nothing in this world and nothing in the future. [71]You think you possess the vanities of this world for a good while, but you are deceived, for the day and hour will come of which you do not think and do not know and ignore. [72]The body becomes weak, death approaches, relatives and friends come saying: Make a disposition of your things. [73]Look now, his wife and his children, his relatives and friends pretend to weep! [74]Glancing back he sees them crying and is moved the wrong way. Thinking to himself he says: Look, I put in your hands my soul and body and all I have. [75]Truly, this man is doomed who

this life: [6]held captive by the devil whose children they are and whose works they do (Jn 8:41), they are blind, [7]for they do not see the true light, our Lord Jesus Christ. [8]They do not have spiritual wisdom, for they do not have the Son of God who is the true wisdom of the Father. [9]About them it is said: Their wisdom has been swallowed down Ps 106:27); and, doomed are they who stray from your commands (Ps 118:21). [10]They see and recognize, they know and they do what is wrong, and they themselves knowingly lose their souls.

[11]See, blind people, you are being deceived by your enemies: by the flesh, the world, and the devil, for it is sweet to the body to commit sin and bitter to work to serve God; [12]because all vices and sins come and proceed from the heart of men (Mk 7:21), just as the Lord says in the Gospel. [13]And you have nothing in this world and nothing in the future. [14]And you think you will possess the vanities of this world for a long time, but you are deceived, for the day and the hour will come of which you do not think, do not know and ignore; the body becomes weak, death approaches,

[76]unde Dominus per prophetam: Maledictus homo qui confidit in homine (Jer 17:5).

[77]Et statim faciunt venire sacerdotem; dicit ei sacerdos: "Vis recipere pœnitentiam de omnibus peccatis tuis?" [78]Respondet: "Volo". "Vis satisfacere de commissis et his quæ fraudasti et decepisti homines sicut potes de tua substantia?" [79]Respondet: "Non". Et sacerdos dicit: "Quare non?". [80]"Quia omnia disposui in manibus propinquorum et amicorum." [81]Et incipit perdere loquelam et sic moritur ille miser.

et sic moritur amara morte.

[82]Sed sciant omnes, quod ubicumque et qualitercumque homo moriatur in criminali peccato sine satisfactione et potest satisfacere et non satisfecit, diabolus rapit animam eius de corpore suo cum tanta angustia et tribulatione, quantam nullus scire potest, nisi qui recipit. [83]Et omnia talenta et potestas et scientia, quam putabat habere (Lk 8:18), auferetur ab eo (Mk 4:25). [84]Et propinquis et amicis relinquit et ipsi tollent et divident substantiam eius et dicent postea: "Maledicta sit anima eius, quia potuit plus dare nobis et acquirere quam non acquisivit." [85]Corpus comedunt vermes; et ita perdit corpus et animam in isto brevi sæculo et ibit in inferno, ubi cruciabitur sine fine.

[5]Et ubicumque, quandocumque, qualitercumque moritur homo in criminali peccato sine pœnitentia et satisfactione, si potest satisfacere et non satisfacit, diabolus rapit animam suam de corpore eius cum tanta angustia et tribulatione, quod nemo potest scire, nisi qui recipit. [16]Et omnia talenta et potestatem et scientiam et sapientiam (2 Chr 1:12), quæ putabant habere (Lk 8:18), auferetur ab eis (Lk 8:18; Mk 4, 25). [17]Et propinquis et amicis relinquunt et ipsi tulerunt et diviserunt substantiam eius et dixerunt postea: Maledicta sit anima sua, quia potuit plus dare nobis et acquirere quam non acquisivit. [18]Corpus comedunt vermes, et ita perdiderunt corpus et animam in

confides and entrusts his soul and body and all he has to such hands. [76]That is why God says through the prophet: Doomed the man who trusts in a man (Jer 17:5).

[77]And immediately they make a priest come. The priest says to him: Do you want to receive penance for all your sins? [78]He answers: I do. Do you want to make satisfaction, as much as you can, out of your fortune, for what you have done and the ways you have defrauded and deceived people? [79]He answers: "No." [80]And the priest says: "Why not?" "Because I have disposed of all I have in the hands of my relatives and friends." [81]And he begins to lose his speech, and so does that wretch die.

and so does one die a bitter death.

[82]But let everyone know that wherever and however a man dies in criminal sin without satisfaction, who could make amends and did not, the devil snatches his soul from his body in anguish and torment such as one cannot know if he does not get it. [83]And all the talents and power and knowledge which he thought he had (Lk 8:18) will be taken from him (Mk 4:25). [84]And he leaves his fortune to relatives and friends, and they will take and divide his fortune and say afterwards: Doomed be his soul! He could have given us more and acquired more than he had acquired! [85]Worms eat his body, and so he loses body and soul in this brief age and goes to hell where he will be tortured without end.

[15]And wherever, whenever, however a man dies in criminal sin without penance and satisfaction, if he can make satisfaction and does not make satisfaction, the devil snatches his soul from his body with anguish and torment such that no one can know if he does not get it. [16]And all the talents and power and knowledge and wisdom (2 Chr 1:12), which they thought they had (Lk 8:18), will be taken from them (Mk 4:25). [17]And they leave their fortune to relatives and friends, and they take and divide his fortune, and said afterwards: Doomed be his soul! He could have given us more and acquired more than he had acquired. [18]Worms eat the body, and so they lose body and soul in this brief age

isto brevi sæculo et ibunt in inferno, ubi cruciabuntur sine fine.

[86]In nomine Patris et Filii et Spiritus Sancti. Amen. [87]Ego frater Franciscus, minor servus vester, rogo et obsecro vos in caritate, quæ Deus est (Jn 4:16), et cum voluntate osculandi vestros pedes, quod hæc verba et alia Domini nostri Iesu Christi cum humilitate et caritate debeatis recipere et operari et observare. [88]Et omnes illi et illæ, qui ea benigne recipient, intelligent et mittent aliis in exemplum, et si in ea perseveraverint usque in finem (Mt 24:13), benedicat eis Pater et Filius et Spiritus Sanctus. Amen.

[19]Omnes illos quibus litteræ istæ pervenerint, rogamus in caritate quæ Deus est (1 Jn 4:16), ut ista supradicta odorifera verba Domini nostri Iesu Christi cum divino amore benigne recipiant. [20]Et qui nesciunt legere, sæpe legere faciant; [21]et apud se retineant cum sancta operatione usque in finem, quia spiritus et vita sunt (Jn 6:64). [22]Et qui hoc non fecerint, tenebuntur reddere rationem in die iudicii (Mt 12:36) ante tribunal Domini nostri Iesu Christi (Rm 14:10).

[86]In the name of the Father and the Son and the Holy Spirit. Amen. [87]I, Brother Francis, your lesser servant, I ask and beseech you in the charity which God is (1 Jn 4:16), and with the will to kiss your feet, that you receive and put in action and observe these words and the others of our Lord Jesus Christ, with humility and charity. [88]And all men and women who receive them kindly, understand them and send copies of them to others: if they have persevered to the end in them (Mt 24:13), may the Father and the Son and the Holy Spirit bless them. Amen.

and they shall go to hell where they will be tortured without end.

[19]All those to whom these letters will have come, we ask in the charity which God is (1 Jn 4:16), that they receive kindly with divine love those fragrant words of our Lord Jesus Christ written above. [20]And let those who do not know how to read, have them read often; [21]and let them keep them with them with a holy activity until the end, because they are spirit and life (Jn 6:64). [22]And those who will not have done this, will be bound to render an account on the day of judgment (Mt 12:36) before the tribunal of our Lord Jesus Christ (Rm 14:10).

## Memoriale propositi (1221)

ln nomine patris et filii et spiritus sancti, amen. Memoriale propositi fratrum et sororum de penitentia in domibus propriis existentium, inceptum anno domini MCCXXI, tale est :

1. Viri qui huius fraternitatis fuerint de panno humili sine colore induantur, cuius brachium VI sol. ravegna. pretium non excedat, nisi propter causam evidentem et necessariam ad tempus cum aliquo dispensetur. Et consideretur panni latitudo et artitudo circa predictum pretium.

2. Clamides et pelles habeant sine scollatura, fixas vel integras, tamen affibulatas, non apertas ut portant seculares, et manicas portent clausas.

3. Sorores vero de eiusdem pretii et humilitatis panno clamidem induantur et tunicam, vel saltim cum clamide habeant guarnellum sive placentinum album vel nigrum aut paludellum lineum amplum sine crispaturis, cuius brachii pretium non excedat XII den. pisanorum; de quo tamen pretio et de pellitionibus ipsarum dispensari poterit secundum conditionem mulieris et loci consuetudinem. Bindas et ligaturas sericas sive coloratas non portent.

4. Et tam fratres quam sorores pelles habeant agninas tantum. Bursias de corio et corigias sinpliciter sine serico consutas et non alias habere licet. Et alia vana ornamenta visitatoris arbitrio deponant.

5. Ad convivia inhonesta vel ad spectacula vel coreas non vadant; instrionibus non donent, et donari a familia sua prohibeant.

6. Omnes abstineant a carnibus, exceptis diebus dominicis et III et V feria, nisi propter infirmitatem, debilitatem, minutionem tribus diebus, et in itinere, vel propter precipuam solempnitatem intervenientem, scilicet natalis per III dies, anni novi, epyphanie, pasche resurrectionis per III dies, apostolorum petri et pauli, sancti iohannis batiste, assumptionis gloriose virginis marie, solempnitatis omnium sanctorum et sancti martini. Aliis vero diebus non ieiunandis liceat eis conmedere caseum et ova. Sed cum religiosis in eorum domibus conventualibus de appositis ab eis conmedere licebit; et sint contenti prandio et cena, exceptis languidis, infirmis et viatoribus. Sanis cibus et potus sit temperatus.

## Memorial (1221)

In the name of the Father and of the Son and of the Holy Spirit. Amen.

The memorial of what is proposed for the Brothers and Sisters of Penance living in their own houses, begun in the year of our Lord 1221, is as follows.

1. Let the men of this fraternity wear garments of ordinary colorless cloth the price of which shall not exceed six soldi of Ravenna money per yard, unless from this they shall be dispensed for a time because of an evident and necessary cause. The width and length of the cloth shall be included in the said price.

2. Let them have cloaks and furred outer garments without any opening at the neck, fastened or in one piece, and not buckled as the seculars wear, and with closed sleeves.

3. Let the sisters wear cloaks and tunics of ordinary cloth of the same price, or at least with the cloak let them have black or white skirts or dresses or a roomy linen robe without pleats whose cost is not more than 12 Pisan denarii per yard. According to the state of each woman and the local custom they may be dispensed from the price and manner of outer garments. Let them not wear silk or colored ribbons or cords.

4. And let the brothers as well as the sisters have furs of lambskin only. It is unlawful to have other than leather purses and the thongs sewn without silk. Other ornaments let them put away at the judgment of the visitor.

5. Let them not attend shameful entertainments, theatres, or dances, and let them give nothing to actors and prohibit that anything be given by their family.

6. Let all abstain from meat except on Sundays, Tuesdays, and Thursdays, unless because they are ill, weak, have been bled for three days (in which case they are excused), or on a journey, or because of a special solemnity occurring, namely, for three days at the Nativity of our Lord, the new year, Epiphany, for three days at Easter, the apostles Peter and Paul, the nativity of John the Baptist, the glorious Assumption of the Virgin Mary, the feast of All Saints and St. Martin. On the other days of non-fasting it is lawful to eat cheese and eggs. But when with the religious in their convents it shall be lawful for them to eat what is set before them. And let them be content with dinner and supper,

7. Ante prandium et cenam disant semel orationem dominicam, et post conmestionem similiter, et gratias agant deo. Alioquin dicant III *pater noster*.

8. A pascha resurrectionis usque ad festum omnium sanctorum ieiunent VI feriam. A festo omnium sanctorum usque ad pascha III et VI ferian ieiunabunt, observantes nichilominus alia ieiunia que ab ecclesia indicuntur generaliter facienda.

9. Quadragesimam sancti martini post eamdem diem incipiendam usque ad natale, et quadragesimam maiorem a dominica carnisprivii usque ad pascha coctidie ieiunent, nisi propter infirmitatem vel aliam necessitatem.

10. Sorores gravide usque ad suam purificationem a corporalibus exercitationibus, exceptis vestibus et orationibus, poterunt abstinere.

11. Laborantibus in fatigatione a pascha resurrectionis usque ad sancti michaelis dedicationem in die ter cibus sumere liceat. Et quando aliis laborant, de omnibus appositis conmedere, excepta VI feria et ieiuniis ab ecclesia generaliter indictis, licebit.

12. Omnes dicant coctidie VII canonicas horas, videlicet matutinum, primam, tertiam, sextam, nonam, vesperas, completorium; clerici secundum ordinem clericorum; sciences psalterium dicant pro prima *deus in nomine tuo* et *beati immaculati* usque ad *legem pone*, et alios psalmos horarum cum *gloria patri* dicant. Sed cum ad ecclesiam non vadunt, dicant pro matutino psalmos quos dicit ecclesia, vel alios quoscumque XVIII psalmos, vel saltim *pater noster* cum *gloria patri* post unumquemque ut ilicterati in omnibus horis. Alii pro matutino XII *pater noster* et pro unaquaque alia hora VII *pater noster* cum *gloria patri* post unumquemque. Et qui sciunt *credi in deum* et *miserere mei deus*, in prima et completorio dicant. Si non dixerint horis constitutis, dicant III *pater noster*.

13. Infirmi non dicant horas nisi velint.

14. Omnes ad matutinum vadant in quadragesima sancti martini et maiori, nisi personarum vel rerum inconmoditas immineat.

15. Confessionem de peccatis faciant ter in anno. Conmunionem in natale domini et pascha resurrectionis et pentecosten recipiant. Reconcilient se proximis et aliena restituant. De decimis preteritis satisfaciant et futuras prestent.

excepting the sick, weak and those traveling. Let the healthy be moderate in food and drink.

7. Before dinner and supper let them say once an Our Father and after eating, one Our Father and give thanks to the Lord. Other times let them say three Our Fathers.

8. From Easter to All Saints let them fast on Fridays. From All Saints to Easter they shall fast on Wednesdays and Fridays, observing notwithstanding other fasts which may be indicated by the Church in general observance.

9. During the Lent from the feast of St. Martin to Christmas and during the greater Lent from Sunday of Carnival to Easter let them fast continually unless dispensed because of illness or some other necessity.

10. Until their purification, pregnant sisters may abstain from all bodily mortifications except those pertaining to dress and prayer.

11. It is lawful for those who perform hard work to eat three times a day from Easter to the feast of St. Michael. It shall be lawful for those who work for others to eat of all things set before them except on Fridays and fast days generally appointed by the Church.

12. Daily let all say the seven canonical hours, that is Matins, Prime, Terce, Sext, None, Vespers, and Compline. The clerics according to the order of the clerics; let those who know the psalter say for prime *Deus in nomine tuo* (Ps 53) and *Beati immaculati* as far as *Legem pone* (Ps 118:1-32), and the other psalms of the hours with the Glorys. But when they do not go to church, let them say for Matins the psalms said by the Church, or at least some other 18 psalms or at least the Our Fathers, just as the illiterate. All the others must say for the hours: 12 Our Fathers for Matins, and 7 Our Fathers for each of the other hours together with the Glory after each one. Let those who know the Creed and *Miserere mei Deus* (Ps 50), say them at Prime and Compline. If they have not said them at the constituted hours, let them say three Our Fathers.

13. Let the infirm not say the hours unless they wish to.

14. Let all go for Matins during the Lent of St. Martin and the greater Lent, unless an inconvenience of persons or things would result.

15. Let them confess their sins three times a year and receive Communion on the Nativity of the Lord, Resurrection Sunday and Pentecost. Let them make satisfaction for past tithes and make ready for the future.

16. Arma mortalia contra quempiam non accipiant vel secum deferant.

17. Omnes a iuramentis solempnibus abstineant, nisi necessitate cogente in casibus a summo pontifice exceptis in sua indulgentia, vedelicet pace, fide, calumpnia et testimonio.

18. Et in comuni loquela, sicut poteront, vitabunt iuramenta. Et qui incaute iuraverit lapsu lingue, ut in multiloquio contingit, eadem die in sero, cum recogitare debet quid fecerit, dicat pro talibus iuramentis III *pater noster*. Suam familiam quisque confortet ad serviendum deo.

19. Omnes fratres et sorores cuiusque civitatis et loci quolibet mense, quando videbitur ministris, conveniant apud ecclesiam quam ministri nuntiaverint, ibique audiant divina.

20. Et quilibet det massario I denarium usualem, quos idem massarius colligat et ministrorum consilio distribuat inter fratres et sorores pauperes et maxime infirmos et eos qui non habuerint funeris exequias, deinde inter alios pauperes; et eidem ecclesie de eadem pecunia offerant.

21. Et, si tunc conmode possit, habeant unum virum religiosum instructum verbo dei, qui eos moneat et confortet ad penitientie perseverantiam et opera misercordie facienda. Et sint sub silentio in missa et predicatione, intenti officio, orationi et predicationi, exceptis officialibus.

22. Cum aliquem fratrem vel sororem contigerit infirmari, ministri per se vel per alios, si infirmus eis fecerit nunciari, semel in ebdomada visitent infirmantem et ad penitentiam moneant et, sicut viderint expedire, necessaria corporis quibus indiguerit de comuni administrent.

23. Et si de hac vita migraverit infirmatus, nuntietur fratribus et sororibus qui fuerint in civitate vel loco presentes, ut ad ipsius conveniant sepulturam; nec recedant donec missa fuerit celebrata et corpus traditum sepulture. Et postea quilibet, infra VIII dies defunctionis ipsius, dicat pro anima defuncti: presbiter missam; sciens psalterium L psalmos; alii L *pater noster* cum *requiem eternam* in fine cuiusque.

24. Preter hec infra annum pro salute fratrum et sororum vivorum et mortuorum dicat: presbiter III missas; sciens psalterium dicat ipsum; alii dicant C *pater noster* cum *requiem eternam* in fine cuiusque. Alioquin duplicent.

16. Let them not take up lethal arms against anyone or carry them with themselves.

17. Let all refrain from solemn oaths unless forced by necessity in the cases excepted by the Sovereign Pontiff in his indulgence, namely, for peace, faith, calumny and testimony.

18. And in their speech as much as possible let them avoid oaths. Those who by a slip of the tongue shall unwarily have taken oath, as it happens in much talking, that same day at evening when they must recall what they did, let them say three Our Fathers for such oaths. Let everyone encourage his family in serving God.

19. Let all the brothers and sisters in every city and locality gather each month whenever it shall appear expedient in a church announced by the ministers and there hear the divine word.

20. And let each one give to the treasurer one of the usual denari which he shall collect and on the advice of the ministers distribute among the poor brothers and sisters, and mostly to the infirm and those who would not have funeral services. Finally let him offer of that money to the other poor and to the Church.

21. And then, if they conveniently can, let them have one religious, instructed in the word of God, who would admonish and encourage them to penance, perseverance and the performance of works of mercy. And, except the officials, let them be silent during the Mass and preaching, attentive to the Office, prayer, and sermon.

22. When any of the brothers and sisters might happen to take ill, let the ministers, if informed of this by the sick one, either themselves or through others visit the sick, excite him to penance and provide from the common fund for his bodily needs as they shall see fit.

23. And if any sick brother or sister shall depart from this life, let it be announced to the brothers and sisters who are present in the city or locality, so that they gather at his funeral and let them not depart until Mass has been celebrated and the body given burial. And after that let each one, within eight days of the death itself, say for the soul of the departed, the priest a Mass, those who know how, fifty psalms; and the others fifty Our Fathers together with the Eternal Rest after each.

24. Besides this during the year let a priest say three Masses for the welfare of the brothers and sisters, living and dead; he who knows the psalter let him say it, and let the rest say a hundred Our Fathers together with the Eternal Rest at the end of each. Otherwise let them double the number.

25. Omnes qui possunt de iure, testamentum faciant et de rebus suis infra III menses post promissionem disponant, ne quis ipsorum intestatus decedat.

26. De pace inter fratres et sorores aut extraneos discordes facienda, sicut ministris videbitur sic fiat; habito etiam, si expedierit, consilio domini episcopi.

27. Si contra ius vel privilegia a potestatibus vel rectoribus locorum, in quibus habitant, fratres vel sorores vexentur, ministri loci quod viderint expedire cum consilio domini episcopi faciant.

28. Ministerium et alia officia sibi imposita quilibet suscipiat et fideliter exerceat, dum tamen per annum ab officio vacare quilibet possit.

29. Cum aliquis fraternitatem hanc intrare voluerit, ministri diligenter eius conditionem et officium inquirant, et onera fraternitatis huius et maxime restitutionis alienorum ei exponant. Et si ei placuerit, secundum predictum modum induatur, et de alienis satisfaciat numerata pecunia secundum cautionem pignoris datam. Proximis se reconcilient, et de decimis satisfaciant.

30. Quibus impletis, post annum cum consilio aliquorum discretorum fratrum, si eis ydoneus vedebitur, recipiatur hoc modo. Quod promictat se observare omnia que hic sunt scripta vel scribenda vel minuenda secundum consilium fratrum, toto tempore vite sue, nisi aliquando de licentia steterit ministrorum; et satisfacere, si quid contra hunc modum fecerit, interpellatus a ministris, ad voluntatem visitatoris. Et per manum publicam promissio in scriptis redigatur ibidem. Nemo tamen aliter recipiatur, nisi eis aliter visum fuerit, considerata persone conditione et eius instantia.

31. De hac fraternitate et de hiis que continentur hic nullus exire possit nisi religionem ingrediatur.

32. Nullus hereticus aut de heresi diffamatus recipiatur. Si autem suspectus fuerit, purgatus coram episcopo, si alias ydoneus fuerit admictatur.

33. Mulieres viros habentes non recipiantur, nisi de consensu et licentia maritorum.

25. Let all who by right can do so, make a testament and dispose of their things within three months after their profession so that none of them die intestate.

26. Let it be as it shall appear to the ministers concerning peace among the brothers and sisters or outsiders causing discord; counsel also may be had of the diocesan bishop if it appears necessary.

27. If the right or privileges of the brothers and sisters are harrassed by the authorities or governors of the places in which they live, let the local ministers, with the counsel of the Lord Bishop, do what shall appear necessary.

28. Let everyone on whom the office of minister or the other offices here mentioned fall, accept and faithfully perform them, though anyone may vacate an office after a year.

29. When anyone shall petition to enter this fraternity, let the ministers inquire into his condition and office and let them explain to him the duties of this fraternity and most of all the restitution of the goods of others. And if he shall be pleased with the aforementioned rule, let him be vested, and let him satisfy his creditors either by money or by a given security. Let him be reconciled with his neighbors and pay his tithes.

30. A year after this is fulfilled, he may, on the advice of some discreet brother, if he shall appear fit to them, be received in this manner: That he promise to observe all that is here written or should be written or taken away, according to the Council of the brothers, all the time of his life, unless some time it should occur by the permission of the minister. And that if he do any anything against this manner of life, questioned by the minister he shall make satisfaction according to the will of the visitor. And let him make a public promise in writing thereto. Let no one be received in any other way, unless it shall appear otherwise to them, considering the condition and dignity of the person.

31. Let no one depart from this fraternity or from what is here contained unless to enter into religion.

32. Let no heretic or one accused of heresy be received. If, however, he was only suspected of it, he may be admitted if, cleared before the bishop, he is fit in other respects.

33. Women having husbands shall not be received unless with the consent and permission of their spouses.

34. Fratres et sorores incorigibiles a fraternitate eiecti, in ea iterum non recipiantur, nisi saniori parti fratrum placuerit.

35. Ministri cuiuslibet civitatis et loci culpas fratrum et sororum manifestas nuntient visitatori puniendas. Et si aliquis incorigibilis extiterit, habito consilio aliquorum discretorum fratrum, eidem visitatori intimetur, ab ipso de fraternitate abiciendus, et in congregatione postea publicetur. Insuper, si est frater, potestati loci vel rectori denuntietur.

36. Si quis sciverit de fratribus et sororibus scandalum facere, ministris nuntiet et visitatori valeat nuntiare; quod inter virum et uxorem non teneatur.

37. Visitator cum fratribus et sororibus universis in hiis omnibus potestatem habeant dispensandi, cum viderint expedire.

38. Ministri post annum cum consilio fratrum eligant duos alios ministros et fidelem massarium, qui necessitati fratrum et sororum et aliorum pauperum provideat, et nuntios, qui dicta factaque fraternitatis de mandato ipsorum nuntient.

39. In supradictis omnibus nemo obligetur ad culpam sed ad penam, ita tamen quod, si penam a visitatore impositam vel imponendam bis admonitus a ministris exsolvere neglexerit, tanquam contumax obligetur ad culpam.

34. Incorrigible brothers and sisters expelled from the fraternity shall in no wise be again received, unless it should so please the more prudent part of the brothers.

35. Let the ministers of each city and place declare the manifest faults of the brothers and sisters to the visitor for punishment. And if anyone show himself incorrigible, let the visitor be informed of him through the ministers on the advice of some discreet brothers and expel him from the fraternity and let it be announced in the congregation. Furthermore, if it is a brother, let him be denounced to the local authority or governor.

36. If one should know of some scandal concerning the brothers or sisters let him make it known to the ministers and he ought to inform the visitor, but they are not bound to denounce anything between husband and wife.

37. The visitor has the power to dispense all the brothers in all these things when he shall see fit.

38. Let the ministers with the counsel of their brothers after a year elect two other ministers, and a faithful treasurer who would provide for the necessities of the brothers and sisters and the other poor, and messengers who, at their bidding, should announce the things said and done by the fraternity.

39. In all the aforesaid let none be obliged under sin but to the punishment, so that if twice admonished by the minister he neglects to perform the imposed punishment or that which must be imposed, let him be obliged under sin as one who is contumacious.

## REGULA *SUPRA MONTEM* (1289)

Nicholaus episcopus servus servorum dei dilectis filiis fratribus et dilectis in cristo filiabus sororibus ordinis fratrum de penitentia tam presentibus quam futuris, salutem et apostolicam benedictionem.

Supra montem catholice fidei, quam populis gentium, qui ambulabant in tenebris, discipulorum cristi sincera devotio igne caritatis exestuans verbo sollicite predicationis edocuit, quamque romana tenet et servat ecclesia, solidum cristiane religionis noscitur fundamentum, nullis unquam concutiendum turbinibus, nullis quassandum fluctibus tempestatum. Hec est etenim vera doctaque fides, absque cuius consortio nemo in conspectu altissimi acceptus redditur, nemo gratiosus occurrit. Hec est que salutis semitam preparat, et felicitatis eterne premia grandia pollicetur. Ideoque gloriosus cristi confessor beatus franciscus, huius ordinis institutor, viam accendendi ad deum verbo pariter et exemplo demonstrans, in ipsius sinceritate fidei suos filios erudivit, eosque illam profiteri, constanter tenere firmiter ac opere voluit adimplere, ut per eius semitam salubriter incedentes, mereantur post vite presentis ergastulum eterne beatitudinis effici possessores.

### [I]

[1]Nos igitur ordinem ipsum oportunis favoribus prosequi, et ad eius augmentum benignius attendentes, [2]statuimus, ut omnes quos ad servandum huiusmodi vite formam assumi contigerint, ante assumptionem seu receptionem ipsorum, de fide catholica et obedientia erga prefatam ecclesiam diligenti examinationi subdantur. [3]Et si eas professi firmiter fuerint, vereque crediderint, admitti seu recipi tute poterunt ad eandem. [4]Precavendum est tamen sollicite, ne quis hereticus vel suspectus de heresi, aut etiam infamatus, ad vite observationem ipsius quomodolibet admittatur. [5]Et si talem inveniri contigerit exstitisse receptum, assignetur ille quantocitius inquisitoribus pravitatis heretice puniendus.

### [II]

[1]Cum autem fraternitatem huiusmodi quis intrare voluerit, [2]ministri ad receptionem talium deputati, eius officium, statum et conditionem solerter explorent, [3]sibi fraternitatis eiudem onera, et precipue alienorum restitutionem apertius exponentes. [4]Quibus premissis, si eidem placuerit, iuxta modum huiusmodi induatur, [5]et de alienis si qua fuerint apud eum satisfacere studeat in pecunia numerata, vel secundum exhibitam

## RULE *SUPRA MONTEM* (1289)

Nicholas, bishop, servant of the servants of God, to our beloved sons the brothers and our beloved daughters in Christ, the brothers and sisters of the Order of Penance, present and to come, health and apostolic benediction.

Not to be shaken by any storms or shattered by any waves of tempests, the solid foundation of the Christian religion is known to be placed on the rock of the Catholic faith which the sincere devotion, glowing with the fire of charity, of the disciples of Christ taught by solicitous preaching to the nations walking in darkness, and which the Roman Church holds and preserves. For, this is the right and true faith without which no one is rendered acceptable, no one appears pleasing in the eyes of the Most High. It is this faith which prepares the way to salvation and promises the rewards and joys of an eternal happiness. Wherefore the glorious confessor of Christ, blessed Francis, the founder of this Order, showing by words as well as by example the way leading to God, instructed his children in the sincerity of the same faith, and wished them to confess it boldly, retain it firmly and fulfill it in deed, so that as they profitably advanced along its path, they might merit, after the imprisonment of the present life, to be made possessors of eternal beatitude.

### [I]

[1]We, therefore, honoring this Order with fitting favors and very readily attending its growth, [2]decree that all who may happen to take upon themselves the observance of this form of life, before the undertaking of their reception, be subjected to a diligent examination on the Catholic faith and their obedience to the aforesaid Church. [3]And if they have firmly professed their faith and obedience and truly believe in them, they may safely be admitted or received to it. [4]Solicitous precautions must be taken, however, lest any heretic or one suspected of heresy, or even one of ill-repute be in any way admitted to the observance of this life. [5]And if it happens that such a one was found to have been admitted, he should be turned over to the inquisitors as quickly as possible, to be punished for heretical depravity.

### [II]

[1]When anyone, however, wishes to enter such a fraternity, [2]let the ministers assigned for the reception of such, diligently investigate his office, state and condition, [3]explaining to him very clearly the duties of this fraternity and especially the restitution of goods of others. [4]After this, if he so wishes, he may be clothed after the manner of the fraternity, [5]and let him strive to make satisfaction for the goods of others, should

pignoris cautionem: [6]seque nichilominus proximis reconciliare procuret. [7]Quibus omnibus ad effectum perductis, post unius anni spatium, cum aliquorum discretorum fratrem consilio, ut is videbitur ipsis ydoneus, recipiatur hoc modo, [8]videlicet ut promittat se divina precepta omnia servaturum, [9]ac etiam satisfacturum ut convenit de transgressionibus, quas contra hunc vivendi modum commiserit, cum interpellatus ad visitatoris extiterit voluntatem. [10]Et huiusmodi ab eo facta promissio, per manum publicam in scriptis inibi redigatur. [11]Alio autem modo nullus a ministris recipiatur, nisi visum eis aliter fuerit conditione persone, ac ipius instantia, sollicita consideratione discussis. [12]Ordinamus preterea statuentes, ut nullus post ipsius fraternitatis ingressum, eandem egredi valeat ad seculum reversurus. [13]Possit tamen habere transitum liberum ad religionem aliam approbatam. [14]Mulieribus vero viros habentibus, nisi de ipsorum licentia et consensu, non pateat ad consortium dicte fraternitatis ingressus.


## [III]

[1]Fratres insuper ipsius fraternitatis de humili panno in pretio et colore improrsus albo vel nigro communiter vestiantur, [2]nisi fuerint ad tempus in pretio per visitatores de consilio ministrorum ob causam legitimam et apertam, cum aliquo dispensatum. [3]Clamides quoque ac pelles absque scollatura, scissas vel integras, affibulatas tamen non patulas, ut congruit honestati, clausasque manicas fratres habeant supradicti. [4]Sorores etiam clamide induantur et tunica, de huiusmodi humili panno factis, [5]vel saltim cum clamide habeant guarnellum seu placentinum coloris albi vel nigri, aut paludellum amplum de canape sive lino, absque ulla crispatura consutum. [6]Circa humilitatem vero panni et pelliciones sororum ipsarum, iuxta conditionem cuiuslibet earundum ac loci consuetudinem poterit dispensari. [7]Bindis et ligaturis sericis non utantur. [8]Pelles dumtaxat agninas, bursias de corio, et corrigias simpliciter absque serico ullo factas, et non alias, tam fratres habeant quam sorores, depositis ceteris, iuxta beati petri apostolorum principis salubre consilium, vanis huius seculi ornamentis.


## [IV]

[1]Sit eis ad inhonesta convivia, vel spectacula, sive curias, seu choreas, accessus penitus interdictus. [2]Hystrionibus, seu vanitatis intuitu nichil donent, et ne quiquam illis a propria donetur familia prohibere procurent.

any be in his possession, in money or by giving a pledge of security, [6]and let him take no less care to reconcile himself with his neighbors. [7]A year after all these things had been done, he may, on the advice of some discreet brothers, if he shall appear fit to them, be received in this manner, [8]namely, that he promise to keep all the divine precepts, [9]and also to appear when summoned at the will of the visitor to make satisfaction, as it behooves, for all transgressions which he might commit against this manner of life. [10]After having been made, let this promise be set down in writing there by a notary public. [11]Let no one be received by these ministers in any other manner unless it should appear otherwise to them after having discussed with solicitous consideration the condition and dignity of the person. [12]Moreover, we ordain and decree that after entering this fraternity, no one may leave it to return to the world; [13]he may, however, freely transfer to another approved religious order. [14]Married women may not be admitted to membership in this fraternity without the permission and consent of their husbands.

## [III]

[1]Let the brothers of this fraternity be clothed alike in cloth of low price and of a color neither entirely white nor entirely black, [2]unless, for a legitimate and apparent reason the visitors, upon the advice of their ministers, have temporarily dispensed someone with regard to the price. [3]Let the above mentioned brothers also have cloaks and furred outer garments without an opening at the neck, divided or in one piece, and not open but fastened together as becomes modesty, and let the sleeves be closed. [4]Let the sisters also wear a cloak and tunic made of the same common cloth, [5]or at least with the cloak let them have a black or white skirt or dress or an ample robe of hemp or linen, sewn without any pleats. [6]According to the condition of each of them and the local custom, a dispensation may be granted to the sisters concerning the quality of the cloth and the furred outer garments. [7]Let the brothers and sisters, however, not use ribbons or silk cords. [8]Let them have furs only of lambskin, purses of leather and the thongs made without any silk, and none other shall they have. Other ornaments of the world are to be set aside according to the salutary counsel of saint Peter, prince of the apostles.

## [IV]

[1]Let attendance at unseemly banquets, or shows or public festivals and dances be absolutely forbidden to them. [2]They should give nothing to actors or for the sake of vanity, and let them take care to prohibit that anything be given by their own family.

## [V]

[1]Ab esu autem carnium, secunda, quarta et sexta feria, dieque sabbati abstineant universi, nisi aliud infirmitatis vel debilitatis instantia suaderet. [2]Minutis vero per triduum carnes dentur, nec subtrahantur in itinere constitutis. [3]Sit quoque ipsarum comestio licita singulis, cum solempnitatem precipuam intervenire contigerit in qua ceteri cristiani ab antiquo epulis carneis vesci solent. [4]Aliis autem diebus, in quibus ieiunium non servatur, ova et caseus non negentur. [5]Sed et cum religiosis ceteris in eorum conventualibus domibus licite sumere valeant de appositis ab eisdem. [6]Sintque prandii ceneque refectione contenti, exceptis languidis, et viatoribus, ac infirmis. [7]Sit sanis cibus moderatus et potus, cum textus evangelicus habeat: Attendite ne corda vestra crapula et ebrietate graventur. [8]Prandium autem vel cena, nonnisi premissa semel dominica oratione sumatur, post sumptionem cuiuslibet cum deo gratias iteranda. [9]Quod si obmitti contigerit, dicatur tribus vicibus pater noster. [10]Qualibet vero sexta feria totius anni ieiunium celebrent, nisi forte infirmitate aut alia causa legitima excusentur, vel nisi festum natalis domini feria ipsa occurreret observandum. [11]Sed a festo omnium sanctorum usque pasca, quarta et sexta feria ieiunabunt, alia que ab ecclesia sunt statuta vel ordinariis ex causa communiter indicta ieiunia nichilominus servaturi. [12]In quadragesima vero beati martini usque ad diem natalis domini, et a dominica quadragesime aut quinquagesime usque pasca, diebus singulis, exceptis dominicis, ieiunare procurent, nisi aliud fortassis infirmitas vel necessitas alia suaderent. [13]Sorores gravide, usque ad sue purificationis diem, ab exercitatione quamqualibet corporali, orationibus dumtaxat exceptis, poterunt si voluerint abstinere. [14]Laborantes autem propter fatigationis afficientis instantiam a dominice resurrectionis festo usque ad festivitatem beati francisci predicti ter in die qua exercitationi laboris incumbent, licite sumere cibum possunt. [15]Cum vero illos contigerit aliorum imminere laboribus, de cunctis appositis die qualibet sumere licebit eisdem, nisi sexta feria vel dies sit aliqua alia in qua ab ecclesia generaliter ieiunium noscitur institutum.

## [VI]

[1]Singuli autem fraturm et sororum ipsorum, ter in anno, videlicet in natali domini, et resurrectionis ipsius, et pentecostes festivitatibus peccata propria confiteri, [2]et eucharistiam devote suscipere non postponant, [3]reconciliando se proximis, et restituendo etiam aliena. [4]Impugnationis arma secum fratres non ferant, nisi pro defensione romane ecclesie, cristiane fidei, vel etiam terre ipsorum, aut de suorum licentia ministrorum.

## [V]

[1]Let all abstain from meat on Monday, Wednesday and Saturday, unless a condition of sickness or weakness would suggest otherwise. [2]Let meat, however, be given on three successive days to those who have been bled, and it should not be denied to those making a journey. [3]Let the eating of meat be lawful for all when a special solemnity occurs on which all other Christians, from ancient times, are wont to eat flesh foods; [4]on other days, however, when fast is not observed, eggs and cheese should not be denied. [5]When they are with other religious in their convents they may licitly eat what is placed before them. [6]They should be content with dinner and supper, unless they are weak, sick or on a journey. [7]Let the food and drink of the healthy be moderate, for the Gospel text has: But take heed to yourselves, lest your hearts be overburdened with self-indulgence and drunkenness (Lk 2:34). [8]Dinner or supper should not be eaten until the Lord's Prayer has been said once; after the meal it should be repeated together with "Thanks to God." [9]But if it is omitted, then let three Our Fathers be said. [10]Let them fast on every Friday throughout the year unless the feast of the Nativity of our Lord fall on that day; [11]but from the feast of All Saints until Easter they shall fast on Wednesdays and Fridays. No less shall they observe the other fasts prescribed by the Church or imposed by the Ordinaries for common cause. [12]During the Lent from the feast of blessed Martin until Christmas and from Quinquagesima Sunday until Easter, except Sundays, they should take care to fast every day, unless perhaps sickness or another necessity suggest otherwise. [13]Pregnant sisters may abstain, if they wish, from all bodily mortification, except prayer, until the day of their purification. [14]Workers, on account of the demands brought on by fatigue, may licitly take food three times a day on any day they are engaged in labor from Easter until the feast of saint Francis. [15]When it happens that they are engaged in labor for others, they are allowed every day to eat of all things placed before them except on Friday or a day on which it is known that a fast for all has been instituted by the Church.

## [VI]

[1]Let each of the brothers and sisters not neglect to confess their sins [2]and devoutly receive the Eucharist three times a year, namely, on the feasts of the Nativity of the Lord, the Resurrection of the Lord and Pentecost, [3]reconciling themselves with their neighbors and restoring the goods of others.

[4]Let the brothers not carry offensive weapons with themselves, unless in defense of the Roman Church, the Christian faith, or their country, or with the permission of their ministers.

## [VII]

[1]Dicant universi cotidie septem horas canonicas, videlicet matutinum, primam, tertiam, sextam, nonam, vesperas et completorium. [2]Clerici videlicet scientes psalterium, pro prima deus in nomine tuo et beati inmaculati usque ad legem pone, ac alios horarum psalmos iuxta clericorum ordinem, cum gloria patri dicant. [3]Cum vero ad ecclesiam non accedunt, pro matutino psalmos dicere studeant quos dicunt clerici, vel ecclesia cathedralis, vel saltim, ut illitterati pro matutino duodecim, et pro alia qualibet hora septem vicibus pater noster, cum gloria patri dicere non obmittant. [4]Quibus videlicet prime ac completorii horis, minorem simbolum et miserere mei deus adiciant qui noverunt. [5]Sed si horis non dixerint constitutis, dicant tribus vicibus pater noster. [6]Infirmi autem horas huiusmodi non teneantur dicere, nisi velint. [7]In quadragesima vero sancti martini et etiam in maiori, ecclesias in quarum parochiis habitant matutinalibus horis personaliter adire procurent, nisi causa rationabili excusentur.

## [VIII]

[1]Omnes preterea, quibus de iure facultas affuerit, condant seu faciant testamentum, [2]et de bonis suis intra tres menses post eorum ingressum immediate sequentes, ordinent et disponant, [3]ne quenquam illorum contingat decedere intestatum.

## [IX]

[1]De pace vero inter fratres et sorores, aut etiam exteros in discordia positos facienda, sicut ministris videbitur ita fiat, [2]adhibito si facultas affuerit episcopi diocesani consilio in hac parte.

## [X]

[1]Si vero fratres vel sorores contra ius vel eorum privilegia per potestates seu rectores locorum, ubi domicilum obtinent, vexationibus impetantur, [2]ministri loci ad episcopos et alios locorum ordinarios studeant habere recursum, iuxta consilium et ordinationem ipsorum in tabulis processuri.

## [XI]

[1]A iuramentis autem sollempnibus omnes abstineant, [2]nisi necessitate cogente, in casibus per indulgentiam apostolice sedis exceptis, videlicet pro pace, fide, calumpnia, et testimonio perhibendo, [3]ac etiam in contractu emptionis et venditionis, ubi videbitur expedire. [4]In communi quoque loquela vitent prout poterunt iuramenta, [5]et qui de aliquo

## [VII]

[1]Let all say the seven canonical hours daily, namely, Matins, Prime, Terce, Sext, None, Vespers, and Compline. [2]The clerics, namely, knowing the psalter, should say for Prime *Deus in nomine tuo* (Ps 53) and *Beati immaculati* up to *Legem pone* (Ps 118:1-32), and also the older psalms of the hours with the Glorys according to the rite of clerics. [3]However, when they do not come to church, they should strive to say the psalms for Matins which are said by the clerics or the Cathedral Church, or at least, like the illiterate others, let them not neglect to say for Matins twelve Our Fathers and Glorys, and for each other hour, seven Our Fathers and Glorys. [4]Those who know the minor Creed and the *Miserere mei Deus* (Ps 50) should add it for the hours of Prime and Compline. [5]But if they have not said them at the appointed hours let them say three Our Fathers. [6]The infirm, however, unless they wish to, shall not be obliged to say these hours. [7]In the Lent of blessed Martin and also during the Greater Lent, let them see to it that they be present in their parish churches for morning hours unless they are excused by a reasonable cause.

## [VIII]

[1]Besides, let all who have the right by law, draw up or make a testament, [2]and arrange and dispose of their goods within the three months immediately following their admission, [3]lest any of them die intestate.

## [IX]

[1]Let the peace which must be made among the brothers and sisters or even among outsiders who are in dissension, be brought about as it shall seem proper to the ministers, [2]on the advice, if possible, of the diocesan bishop in this matter.

## [X]

[1]If, contrary to law, the brothers or sisters or their privileges are assailed with molestations by those having authority or the magistrates of the places where they dwell, [2]let the ministers try to have recourse to the bishops and other local ordinaries, and proceed according to their counsel and disposition in such matters.

## [XI]

[1]Let all abstain from solemn oaths [2]unless forced by necessity in the cases excepted through the indulgence of the Apostolic See, namely, for peace, faith, calumny, and affirming a testimony, [3]and also when it shall seem expedient in a contract of buying, selling, or giving. [4]Furthermore, in their ordinary conversation, let them avoid oaths as much as they are

minus caute iuraverit lapsu lingue prout contingere in multiloquio con-
suevit, [6]die ipso in sero cum debet recogitare quid fecerit, dicat tribus
vicibus orationem dominicam propter incaute facta huiusmodi iuramenta. [7]Memor autem sit quilibet, ut ad divina obsequia familiam propriam exhortetur.

## [XII]

[1]Universi sani fratres et sorores cuiuscunque civitatis aut loci, diebus
singulis si commode poterunt misse officium audiant, [2]et mense quolibet ad ecclesiam sive locum ad quam vel quem ministri curaverint in-
timare, conveniant, missarum sollempnia inibi audituri. [3]Unusquisque
autem usualis monete denarium masario tribuat, [4]qui pecuniam huiusmodi colligat, [5]et eam de consilio ministrorum inter fratres et sorores
paupertate gravatos, et precipuse infirmantes, [6]ac eos, qui funeris carere
dignoscuntur exequiis, [7]et deinde inter pauperes alios dividant congru-
enter. [8]Offerant insuper de dicta pecunia ecclesie memorate. [9]Tuncque,
si commode poterunt, virum religiosum et in verbo dei competenter
instructum habere procurent, qui eos ad penitentiam et misericordie
opera exercenda hortetur, sollicite moneat et inducat. [10]Studeat quilibet, dum misse celebratur officium, et predicationis verbum proponitur,
servare silentium, orationi et officio sit intentus, nisi eum communis
utilitas fraternitatis impediat.

## [XIII]

[1]Cum autem quemquam ex fratribus infirmari contigerit, [2]ministri per
se vel per alium seu alios, si hoc eis infirmus fecerit intimari, semel in
hebdomada visitare teneantur egrotum, [3]ipsum sollicite ad recipiendam
penitentiam prout melius et efficaciter expedire potuerit inducentes,
[4]necessaria illi de bonis communibus ministrando.

## [XIV]

[1]Et si prefatus infirmus de presenti luce migraverit, [2]fratribus et sororibus tunc in civitate vel loco ubi eum contigerit mori presentibus nuntietur, [3]ut defuncti exequiis procurent personaliter interesse; [4]a quibus
donec missarum fuerint celebrata sollempnia, et corpus tumulo condi-
tum, non recedant. [5]Hoc quoque circa sorores infirmas decedentesque
volumus observari. [6]Preterea, intra octo dies post ipsius sepulti obitum
immediate sequentes, quilibet fratrum et sororum ipsorum dicat pro
anima eius, sacerdos videlicet missam unam, sciens psalterium quinquaginta psalmos, et illitterati totidem pater noster, et in fine cuiuslibet requiem eternam adiciant. [7]Et preter hec, infra annum, pro fratrum
et sororum earum tam vivorum quam defunctorum salute, tres missa

able, [5]and whoever on any day carelessly swears by a slip of the tongue, as it usually happens in much talking, [6]that evening when he must reflect on what he had done, let him say the Lord's Prayer three times for having taken such oaths carelessly. [7]And let everyone remember to encourage his own family to serve God.

## [XII]

[1]Let all healthy brothers and sisters of every city or locality hear Mass daily if they conveniently are able to do so, [2]and every month let them assemble at a church or place which the ministers have been careful to announce in order to hear Mass there. [3]Let each member give a piece of the usual money to the treasurer [4]who shall collect such money [5]and, on the advice of the ministers, suitably divide it among the brothers and sisters oppressed by poverty, and especially among the infirm [6]and those who are known to lack the means for a funeral service, [7]and finally the other poor. [8]Let them also offer some of this money to the aforesaid church. [9]And then, if they can do so conveniently, they should have a religious, one ably instructed in the word of God, who will earnestly exhort, admonish and arouse them to penance and the exercise of the works of mercy. [10]Let everyone strive to observe silence while the Mass is being celebrated and the sermon preached, and be intent upon the prayer and office, unless the common good of the fraternity impede.

## [XIII]

[1]When any of the brothers happens to take ill, [2]the ministers either themselves or through another or others, are bound if the sick person has notified them of the illness, [3]to visit him once a week and earnestly urge him, as they shall judge it to be of greater advantage and profit, to receive penance, [4]and provide for the necessities of the sick person from the common fund.

## [XIV]

[1]If the aforementioned sick person should depart from the present life, [2]it should be announced to the brothers and sisters then present in the city or locality where he happened to die, [3]that they might be sure to attend  personally the obsequies of the deceased [4]from which let them not depart until after the Mass has been celebrated and the body placed in the grave. [5]We wish that this be observed also with regard to sick and deceased sisters. [6]Moreover, during the eight days immediately following the death of the one interred, let each of the brothers and sisters say for his soul, namely: a priest, one Mass; one who knows the psalter, fifty psalms; and the illiterate, Our Father fifty times, and let them add at the end of each the Eternal Rest. [7]And after this, during the year they

faciant celebrari. [8]Qui vero psalterium sciverit, illud dicat, [9]et ceteri orationem dominicam centies dicere non obmittant, requiem eternam cui-
libet addituri.

## [XV]

[1]Ministeria quoque et alia officia, que presentis formule series exprimit,
imposita sibi quisque devote suscipiat, [2]curetque fideliter exercere. [3]Of-
ficium autem cuiuslibet certi temporis spatio limitetur. [4]Nullus minister instituatur ad vitam, et eius ministerium certus terminus compre-
hendat.

## [XVI]

[1]Ad hec ministri et fratres ac sorores civitatis et loci cuiuslibet, ad vis-
itationem communem in aliquo loco religioso vel ecclesia ubi locum
contigerit deesse conveniant, [2]et visitatorem habeant sacerdotem, qui
alicuius approbate religionis existat, quique illis iniungat penitentiam
de commissis excessibus salutarem, [3]nec quis alius possit eis huiusmodi
visitationis officium exhibere. [4]Quia vero presens vivendi forma institu-
tionem a beato francisco prelibato suscepit, [5]consuliumus ut visitatores
et informatores de fratrum minorum ordine assumantur, quos custodes
vel guardiani eiusdem ordinis, cum supra hoc requisiti fuerint, duxerint
assignandos. [6]Nolumus tamen congregationem huiusmodi a laico visi-
tari. [7]Huiusmodi autem visitationis officium semel exerceatur in anno,
nisi necessitate aliqua suadente fuerit pluries facienda. [8]Incorrigibiles
vero et inobedientes monitio trina preveniat; [9]qui sese corrigere non
curaverint, de ipsius congregationis consortio expellantur omnino, de
consilio discretorum.

## [XVII]

[1]Vitent insuper fratres et sorores iuxta posse litigia inter se, illa si susci-
tari contigerit sollicite dirimendo. [2]Alioquin de iure coram illo respon-
deant, apud quem potestas residet iudicandi.

## [XVIII]

[1]Ordinarii autem locorum, vel visitator, cum fratribus et sororibus universis, in abstinentiis, ieiuniis, et austeritatibus aliis, ex causa legitima
cum expedire viderint poterunt dispensare.

should have three Masses celebrated for the welfare of the brothers and sisters, living and dead. [8]Let those who know the psalter say it, and the rest should not fail to say the Our Father one hundred times, adding at the end of each the Eternal Rest.

## [XV]

[1]Also let everyone on whom the ministerial or other offices mentioned in the contents of this present document are imposed, [2]undertake them devoutly and take care to exercise faithfully. [3]Let each office be limited to a definite period of time [4]and let no minister be installed for life, but let his ministry extend over a definite time.

## [XVI]

[1]For these things, let the ministers, brothers and sisters of every city and locality convene for a visitation in common at some religious place, or in a church when it happens that a place of this kind is lacking, [2]and they should have as visitor a priest who belongs to some approved religious order and who shall impose a salutary penance on those who have committed digressions. [3]Nor may any other perform this office of visitation for them. [4]Because this present form of life took its origin from the aforementioned blessed Francis, [5]we counsel that the visitors and instructors should be taken from the Order of Friars Minor, whom the custodes or guardians of the same Order shall appoint, when they have been requested in the matter. [6]However, we do not want a congregation of this kind to be visited by a lay person. [7]Let such an office of visitation be exercised once a year, unless some necessity urges that it be made more often. [8]Let the incorrigible and disobedient be forewarned three times, [9]and if they should not try to correct themselves, then, on the counsel of the discreets, let them be totally deprived of membership in this congregation.

## [XVII]

[1]Moreover, as far as they are able, let the brothers and sisters avoid quarrels among themselves, suppressing those which might happen to arise, [2]otherwise, let them answer to the law before one vested with judicial power.

## [XVIII]

[1]Local ordinaries or the visitor may dispense all the brothers and sisters from abstinences, fasts and other austerities, when for a legitimate cause it shall seem expedient.

## [XIX]

[1]Ministri vero manifestas fratrum et sororum culpas visitatori denuntient puniendas. [2]Et si quisquam incorrigibilis fuerit, post trine admonitionis instantiam, a ministris de discretorum aliquorum fratrum consilio, visitatori nuntietur eidem, de fraternitatis consortio abiiciendus ab ipso, et in congregatione postmodum publicandus.

## [XX]

[1]Ceterum in premissis omnibus, ad que fratres et sorores vestri ordinis non ex divinis preceptis vel statutis tenentur ecclesie, nullum ipsorum ad mortalem culpam volumus obligari, [2]sed impositam sibi penitentiam, pro transgressionis excessu, prompta humilitate recipiat et efficaciter studeat adimplere.

[3]Nulli ergo omnino hominum liceat hanc paginam nostri statuti et ordinationis infringere, vel ei ausu temerario contraire. [4]Si quis autem hoc attentare presumpserit, indignationem omnipotentis dei et beatorum petri et pauli apostolorum eius se noverit incursurum.

Data reate, XVI kalendas septembris, pontificatus nostri anno secundo.

## [XIX]

[1]Let the ministers denounce the manifest faults of the brothers and sisters to the visitor that they may be punished. [2]And if any one might be incorrigible, after a third admonition, the ministers, on the advice of some of the discreet brothers, should report him to the visitor that he deprive him of membership in the fraternity. Afterwards, this fact must be made known to the congregation.

## [XX]

[1]Finally, we wish that none of the brothers and sisters be obliged under pain of mortal sin to all the foregoing, except where they are bound by divine precepts and statutes of the Church. [2]However, let them promptly and humbly receive the penance imposed upon them according to the gravity of the transgression, and effectively strive to fulfill it.

[3]To no one, therefore, be it allowed to infringe on this page of our statute and confirmation or to oppose it with rash temerity. [4]But if anyone shall have presumed to attempt this, let him know that he will incur the wrath of Almighty God and of his holy apostles Peter and Paul.

Given at Rieti, on the sixteenth of the calends of September, and the second year of our pontificate (17 August 1289).

## Regula *Inter Cetera* (1521)

Leo Papa X dilectis filiis fratribus et sororibus Tertii Ordinis beati Francisci sub tribus votis essentialibus in congregatione viventibus, salutem et apostolicam benedictionem.

Inter cetera nostro regimini credita, ea nos potissime sollicitos reddunt, per quae frenatis mundi carnisque concupiscientiis, innocentiae primaeque pacis coelitus tranquillus status ad suam primaevam reduci cognoscitur originem. Dudum siquidem huius gratia Nicholaus Papa quartus, praedecessor noster, Tertiam Regulam beati Francisci quam de poenitentia appellant per quam almus Confessor omnes utriusque sexus fideles Spiritu Dei plenus salvare contendebat, confirmavit et approbavit. Verum quia temporis decursu spirante illo Spiritu Sancto, non solum viri conjugati mundique huius incolae pro quibus a beato Francisco praefata Tertia Regulla edita fuerat, verum tamen innumerarum Virginum chori, tribus essentialibus, et a quibusdam etiam clausurae nostra auctoritate assumptae, votis, constructisque monasteriis quam pluribus non sine militantis ecclesiae fructu multiplici, et aedificatione praefati Tertii Ordinis iugo sua colla subdiderunt. Et quoniam in dicta Tertia Regula, quaedam maritatis accommoda, caelibi vero virgineoque statui sub huiusmodi Tertia Regula Domino famulantibus nullatenus decentia innectuntur, ob quod castorum animorum nitidi affectus ac iuxta Domini voluntatem, pretiosum a vili separantes, eamdem Tertiam Regulam in modum qui sequitur distinctam, de novo confirmamus et approbamus, ac vobis et successoribus vestris servandam transmittimus, cuius tenor sequitur et est talis.

**Caput primum: De novitiorum seu novitiarum ingressu**
Fratres seu sorores ad hunc Tertium Ordinem recipiendi debent esse fideles catholici, de haeresi non suspecti, in obedientia Romanae Ecclesiae firmi, matrimonio non ligati, debitis expediti, corpore sani, animo prompti, nulla vulgari infamia maculati, cum proximis reconciliati. Et de iis omnibus, antequam recipiantur, ab eo qui recipiendi habet facultatem, sunt diligenter examinandi.

**Caput secundum: De his quae debent promittere fratres et sorores in professione huius Tertiae Regulae**
Fratres et sorores, postquam per unum integrum annum habitum probationis detulerint, qui de vili panno arbitrio visitatoris esse debet, si conversio laudabilis fuerit, apud conventum in quo quis vel quae habitum probationis portaverit, de consilio discretorum dicti conventus

## Rule *Inter Cetera* (1521)

Leo X, Pope, to Our beloved sons, the brothers, and daughters, the sisters, of the Third Order of blessed Francis living in congregation under the three essential vows, health and apostolic benediction.

Among other things committed to our charge and government, those in a special way make us solicitous by which the concupiscences of the world and the flesh being restrained, the quiet state of innocence and first peace given us from heaven may be brought back to its primeval perfection. Long since, indeed, for this reason, Pope Nicholas IV, our predecessor, confirmed and approved the Third Rule of blessed Francis, which he termed "Of Penance," by which the holy confessor, full of the Spirit of God, endeavored to further the salvation of all faithful Christians. But whereas in course of time, through the inspiration of the Holy Ghost, not only married persons and such as dwell in the world, for whom the aforesaid Third Rule was made by blessed Francis, but also choirs of innumerable virgins taking upon themselves the three essential vows, and some also that of enclosure, by our authority, and having built very many monasteries, not without manifold fruit and edification to the militant Church, have subdued their necks under the yoke of the aforesaid Third Order. And whereas in the said Third Rule some things accommodated to married persons are inserted, which are by no means adapted to those who serve the Lord, according to this Third Rule, in celibacy and virginity, and to which the pure affections of chaste minds are averse: We, according to the will of our Lord, separating the more precious from what is of less value, do confirm anew and approve the same Third Rule, and deliver it to be kept by you and your successors, distinguished in the manner which follows, and the tenor of which is:

### Chapter I: The entrance of novices

The brothers or sisters to be received into this Order should be faithful Catholics, unsuspected of heresy, firm in obedience to the Roman Church, not tied in marriage, free of debts, sound in body, docile in mind, of stainless character, reconciled with their neighbor: and of all these things, before they are received, they are diligently to be examined by him who has faculty to admit them.

### Chapter II: The things the brothers and sisters must promise in the profession of this third Rule

After the brothers and sisters have for a whole year borne the habit of probation (which ought to be of coarse cloth, according to the judgment of the Visitor), if their conversation shall be thought laudable in the Convent wherein they have borne the habit of probation, by the

ad professionem dicti conventus recipiatur, in qua professione promittat servare mandata Dei, ac satisfacturum de transgressionibus quas facere posset in futurum contra hanc Tertiam Regulam, ubi a praelatis requisitus fuerat, vivendo in obedientia, sine proprio et in castitate.

### Caput tertium: De ieiunio

Fratres et sorores perpetuis temporibus, feria secunda, quarta, sexta et sabbato, excepto Dominicae Nativitatis festo, carnes non comedant. Et a festo omnium Sanctorum usque ad Resurrectionem Domini omni feria quarta et sexta ieiunare teneantur. Ac similiter qualibet sexta feria totius anni. Item a festo beati Martini usque ad Nativitatem Domini ieiunent quotidie, iniuncta Quadragesima universalis Ecclesiae, usque ad Resurrectionem Domini, quam tamen a Quinquagesima incipere debent. Diebus vero quibus non ieiunatur, bis tantum die dumtaxat comedant. Excepto quod a festo Paschae usque ad mensem Octobris, laborantes poenoso seu gravi labore, ter in die refici poterunt, ieiuniorum semper diebus exceptis. Poterunt autem itinerantes, infirmi, debiles, tempore necessitatis ieiunium solvere.

### Caput quartum: De divino officio et oratione

Fratres et sorores in ecclesia servent silentium, praesertim quando missa celebratur vel sermo Dei proponitur. In aliis vero locis servent quod per suos superiores circa silentium illis fuerit ordinatum. Debent etiam quolibet die in sero intra se et Deum cogitare quod fecerint, dixerint vel cogitaverint. Quolibet autem die, si potuerint commode, debent audire missam. Et procurare debent quod habeant virum religiosum qui illis verbum Dei certis diebus proponat et eos ad poenitentiam et virtutes inducat. Illi autem vel illae, qui vel quae horas canonicas sciunt per se dicere, debent horas canonicas secundum usum sanctae Romanae Ecclesiae persolvere. Qui vero horas canonicas nesciunt dicere, dicant duodecim *Pater noster* pro matutino, et pro qualibet aliarum horarum septem, addito *Gloria Patri* in fine cuiuslibet *Pater noster*, addito etiam *Credo* et *Miserere mei Deus* in principio Primae et Completorii. Et qui praemissa nescierit, ter *Pater noster* pro poenitentia dicere debeat. Quoties autem prandium vel cibum sumunt, gratias Deo reddere debent. De confessione vero sacramentali et sacra communione sumenda, servabunt ordinationem Nicholai Papae quarti quod ter in anno confiteantur atque communicent vel etiam statuta a suis superioribus super hoc ordinata.

council of the said Convent, let them be received to the profession of the said Order. In which profession let them promise to keep the commandments of God, and to make satisfaction for the transgressions which in future they may commit against this Third Rule, when they shall be required to do so by their prelates, living in obedience, without property, and in chastity.

## CHAPTER III: THE FAST

The brothers and sisters perpetually on the second, fourth and sixth ferias, and on the Sabbath, must abstain from flesh meat—except on the feast of the Nativity of our Lord. And from the feast of All Saints unto the Resurrection of our Lord, every fourth and sixth feria they shall be bound to fast; and in like manner, every sixth feria of the whole year. Also from the feast of St. Martin unto the Nativity of our Lord let them fast every day; adjoining thereunto the Lent of the Universal Church, which, however, they must begin from Quinquagesima. But on those days on which they are not bound to fast they shall eat only twice a day; except that from the Feast of Easter until the month of October those who are employed in hard or painful labor may eat three times in the day—the days of fast always excepted. Travellers, however, and infirm and weak persons, in time of necessity are exempt from the fast.

## CHAPTER IV: THE DIVINE OFFICE AND PRAYER

The brothers and sisters must in the church observe silence especially when Mass is celebrated, or the word of God proposed. But in other places let them observe what their Superiors shall have ordained concerning silence. They ought every day, in the evening, between themselves and God, to think over what they have done, said, or thought. And every day (if they can conveniently) they ought to hear Mass. And, they ought to procure that they have a religious who on certain days may propose to them the Word of God, and induce them to penance and virtues.

They who by themselves know how to perform the canonical Hours ought to fulfil the Canonical Hours according to the usage of the Holy Roman Church. But they who do not know how to receive the Canonical Hours, let them say twelve *Pater nosters* for Matins, and for each of the other hours seven, adding *Gloria Patri* at the end of every *Pater noster*; adding also the *Credo*, and the psalm *Miserere mei Deus* at the beginning of Prime and Compline and who know not these aforesaid things must say three times *Pater noster* for penance. And as often as they take dinner or meals they ought to give thanks to God. But of sacramental Confession and receiving the Holy Communion they shall observe the ordinance of Pope Nicholas IV, that thrice in the year they confess and

CAPUT QUINTUM: DE PRAELATORUM ET OFFICIORUM ORDINATIONE

Quaelibet domus, si monasterium virorum fuerit, habebit superiorem istius fraternitatis, qui minister localis appellabitur. Si vero mulierum, mater dicetur. Et eligentur per suos conventus, vel instituemtur per suos provinciales superiores seu Visitatorem generalem. Ita tamen quod nullus sit perpetuus, sed certi temporis. Qui ministri et matres obedient per omnia quae ad praesentem Regulam spectant provincialibus ministris Ordinis Minorum beati Francisci et visitatoribus deputatis ab ipsis ministris, quamdiu in dictis officiis fuerint. Quo vero ad alia officia intra domum servabunt statuta sua.

CAPUT SEXTUM: DE MODO INTERIUS EXTERIUSQUE SERVANDO

Cum fratres et sorores huius fraternitatis dicantur de poenitentia, oportet eos ab omni curiositate, tam in vestibus quam in aliis quibuscumque abstinere. Et iuxta apostolicum principis beati Petri salubre consilium, depositis certis vanis huius saeculi ornamentis, nullum ornamentum corporale portare debent, nisi solum humile et necessarium tegumentum corporis sui. Debent etiam ab accessu curiarum principum, dominorum seu dominarum, ubi mollia huius mundi, Domino testante, habentur, omnino cavere. Nec ullo unquam tempore choreis, ludis, iocis et aliis histrionum vanitatibus interesse. Debent quoque esse parci in verbis et locutionibus, quae raro sine peccato multiplicantur. Et super omnia ab omni mendatio et iuramento quocumque iuxta mandatum Domini, nisi pro pace, fide, calumnia, et testimonio perhibendo, cavere debent. Et omni die in sero, inter cetera, debent examinare se si vel mendacium vel iuramentum aliquod fecerint, et pro quolibet ter Pater Noster dicere debent.

CAPUT SEPTIMUM: DE VISITATIONE ET CURA INFIRMORUM

Si quis frater vel soror huius fraternitatis in infirmitate ceciderit, minister domus vel mater semel quotidie per se vel per aliam personam visitare teneatur. Et de bonis communibus  omnia necessaria diligenter faciat illi ministrare. Teneatur quoque infirmum vel infirmam monere ad poenitentiam acceptandam veramque conversionem ad Deum faciendam, mortis proprinquitatem, iudicii divini districtionem simulque divinam misericordiam proponendo.

communicate; or else they shall keep the statutes of their Superiors ordained hereupon.

### CHAPTER V: THE ORDAINING OF PRELATES AND OFFICERS

Every house, if it be a monastery of men, shall have a Superior of this fraternity, who shall be called the Local Minister; but if it be women the Superioress shall be called the Mother. And they shall be elected by their Convents or instituted by their Provincial Superiors or General Visitor; so, however, that none be perpetual, but for a certain time. Which Ministers and Mothers shall obey, in all things pertaining to this present Rule, the Provincial Ministers of the Order of Minors of St. Francis, and the Visitors deputed by the same Ministers, as long as they shall be in the said offices. But as regards other offices within the house they shall keep their own statutes.

### CHAPTER VI: THE MANNER OF BEHAVING ONESELF IN AND OUTSIDE

Whereas the brothers and sisters of this fraternity are called "Of Penance," it behoveth them to abstain from all luxury, as well in vesture as in other things whatsoever, and according to the salutary counsel of the Prince of the Apostles, Saint Peter, having laid aside certain vain ornaments of this world, they ought to carry no corporal ornament, but only a humble and necessary tegument of their body. They ought to avoid by all means access to the courts of Princes, Lords or Ladies, where the luxuries of this world are found, as the Lord doth testify: nor should they ever be present at dances, plays or other vanities of actors. They ought also be sparing in words and in conversations, which seldom are multiplied without sin. And above all they must abstain from every lie, and avoid every oath whatsoever, according to the commandment of our Lord, unless it be for the sake of peace or faith, for refuting a calumny or for giving testimony. And every day, at evening, they ought to examine themselves whether they have told a lie or taken an oath; and for each one they must say three times the Pater Noster.

### CHAPTER VII: THE VISITATION AND CARE OF THE SICK

If any brother or sister of this fraternity shall fall into infirmity the Minister of the House or the Mother, once every day, by themselves or by another person, shall be bound to visit them. And of the common goods they shall cause all things necessary to be ministered unto them. They shall also be bound to move the sick person to accept penance and to make a true conversion to God, by proposing the nearness of death, the rigor of divine justice, and at the same time, divine mercy.

CAPUT OCTAVUM: DE VISITATIONE QUAM PRAELATI DEBENT FACERE CIRCA
FRATRES ET SORORES

Minister provincialis Fratrum Minorum vel visitator eiusdem Ordinis, cui ipse commiserit, visitabit quolibet anno, cum praesentia seniorum. Et facta visitatione, non debet intrare officinas nec alia interiora sororum. Ipse autem visitator numquam solus maneat et separatus cum aliqua sorore. Debent autem ministri et matres dicere visitatori defectus qui correctione indigent. Similiter et alii fratres et sorores. Et si aliqui fuerint incorrigibiles, iudicio discretorum vel discretarum domus, tamquam morbida pecora eiiciantur de congregatione.

CAPUT NONUM: DE OFFICIO MORTUORUM

Postquam aliquis frater vel soror ab hac luce migraverit, curabit minister seu mater quod eius exequiae solemniter celebrentur. Quibus exequiis omnes fratres vel sorores alicuius domus, ubi ipsum mori contigerit, personaliter interesse debent, nec recedere debent, donec corpus traditum sit sepulturae. Et pro anima cuiuslibet defuncti vel defunctae, infra octo dies, quilibet sacerdos unam missam; scientes autem psalterium, quinquaginta psalmos; nescientes vero psalterium, quinquaginta *Pater noster*, et in fine cuiuslibet *Requiem aeternam* dicere teneantur. In fine autem cuiuslibet anni, seu infra quemlibet annum, quilibet sacerdos tres missas pro defunctis; scientes psalterium, unum psalterium; nescientes vero psalterium, centum *Pater noster* cum *Requiem aeternam* in fine cuiuslibet dicere debeant. Et circa ista officia pro defunctis et alia officia divina in praesenti serie annexa, cura imponitur ministris et matribus ut fideliter persolvantur.

CAPUT DECIMUM: DE OBLIGATIONE CONTENTORUM IN REGULA

Omnia et singula in praesenti Regula contenta sunt consilia ad facilius salvandas animas viatorum, et nulla sunt obligatoria ad peccatum mortale vel veniale, nisi humano vel divino iure aliquis alias esset obligatus. Obligantur tamen fratres et sorores facere poenitentias sibi a superioribus impositas, quando super hoc requiruntur. Obligantur etiam ad tria vota essentialia, paupertatem, nihil habendo in speciali, castitatem, quia post votum non possunt matrimonium contrahere nec sine transgressione vitiis carnis se immiscere, et obedientiam, quantum ad illa sine quibus non potest commode ista fraternitas manuteneri. Tenentur etiam ad clausuram servandam illae quae ipsam expresse servare voluerint. Quod omnibus et singulis conventibus concedimus, dummodo hospitalitas et charitas quam exercere solent apud infirmos nullum cum honestate patiatur detrimentum.

## CHAPTER VIII: THE VISITATION THE PRELATES OUGHT TO MAKE OF THE BROTHERS AND SISTERS

The Provincial Minister of the Friars Minor, or the Visitor of the same Order to whom he shall commit it, shall visit every year once only in every house with the presence of the senior members. And the Visitation being ended he ought not to enter into the offices or other inward places of the sisters, and let the Visitor himself never remain alone and separate with any sister. And the Ministers and Mothers shall tell the Visitor the defects which need correction; and likewise also the other brothers and sisters. And if any shall be found incorrigible by the judgment of the discreets of the house, as infectious sheep let them be cast out of the congregation.

## CHAPTER IX: THE OFFICES FOR THE DEAD

After a brother or sister shall have departed out of this world, the Minister or Mother shall take care that their obsequies be solemnly celebrated, at which all the brothers or sisters of the house wherein the death took place ought to be personally present, nor ought they to depart until the body be consigned to the grave. And for the soul of every one departed, within eight days every priest shall be bound to say one Mass, and they who know the psalter, fifty psalms; and they who know not the psalter, fifty *Pater nosters*; and at the end of every one, *Requiem aeternam*. And at the end of every year, or within every year, every priest ought to say three Masses for the dead, those who know the psalter, one psalter; but those who know not the psalter, a hundred *Pater nosters*, with *Requiem aeternam* at the end of every one. And concerning these Offices for the Dead and other Divine Offices in this present Rule annexed, the care is imposed on the Ministers and Mothers that they be faithfully discharged.

## CHAPTER X: THE OBLIGATION OF THE THINGS CONTAINED IN THE RULE

All and every thing contained in this present Rule are counsels the more easily to save the souls of the wayfaring, and none of them obliges under sin, mortal or venial, unless one should be by human or divine law otherwise obliged thereto. The brothers and sisters are, however, obliged to do the penances imposed upon them by their Superiors when required. They are obliged also to the three essential vows—poverty, by having nothing not held in common; chastity, because after the vow they cannot contract matrimony nor without transgression involve themselves in vices of the flesh; and obedience, inasmuch as regards those things without which this fraternity cannot be conveniently maintained. Those sisters, also, are bound to keep enclosure, who have expressly vowed to keep it; which we grant to all and every Convent, provided that the hospitality and charity which they are wont to exercise towards the infirm suffers no detriment.

Datum Romae apud Sanctum Petrum, sub annulo Piscatoris, die vigesima ianuarii, millesimo quingentesimo vigesimo primo, pontificatus nostri anno octavo.

Given at Rome, at Saint Peter's, under the ring of the Fisherman, the 20th day of January 1521, in the eighth year of our Pontificate.

## Regula *Rerum Condicio* (1927)

Pius episcopus, servus servorum Dei, ad perpetuam memoriam.

    Rerum condicio ea erat, in Italia praesertim, sub exitum saeculi duodecimi aliquantoque serius, ut, quamvis universa christiana societas in fide consisteret, homines tamen nimis multi, fluxarum rerum cupiditate distenti vitaeque superbia elati, in omnem morum pravitatem erumperent; atque, elanguescente iam caritate Christi, odia usquequaque foverent et civitates ad intestina bella calamitose impellerent. Nihil igitur optatius tum esse poterat quam ut singularis vir a Deo excitaretur qui, virtutum omnium laude praecellens, et opportuna remedia his malis afferret et populos ad christianos spiritus revocaret. Iamvero nemo ignorat societatis eorum temporum emendandae munus praecipue Francisco Assisiensi divinitus demandatum esse, qui effrenatis vitiis studium opponens christianae humilitatis et paupertatis, mutua omnes caritate coniungere studuit. Itaque cum plurimi unidque ad tantum virum confluerent discipuli, in immensum sane succrevit Franciscalium Familia, cum ex sodalibus trium Ordinum quos Franciscus ipse constituit, tum deinceps ex iis tertiariis qui, perfectioris vitae cupidi, communem vitam agentes, *sodales Tertii Ordinis Regularis* nuncupati sunt. Merito igitur hi quoque Seraphici Patris memoriam, septimo exeunte saeculo ab obitu eius sanctissimo, non solum piis supplicationibus sollemnibusque sacris publice habitis, sed etiam actuosioris pietatis propositis laeto animo per hunc annum celebrarunt. Etenim omnes norunt quam diligenter, inde ab instituti sui initio, tertiarii regulares sanctum Francisci spiritum induere contenderint, eundemque in multa religionis et caritatis opera traducere consueverint. Quapropter factum est ut Decessor Noster Leo PP. X, Constitutione data Inter cetera, eorum Regulam comprobaret. Atqui, ut in humanis rebus contingit, plura quidem, decursu temporum, quae a Leone PP. X decreta fuerant, vel prorsus obsolevere vel cum quibusdam Codicis iuris canonici praescriptis non omnino consentiunt. Quamobrem necesse fuit ut illa Leonis X lex ad nostra haec tempora itemque ad recentiora Ecclesiae decreta accommodaretur, ut Tertiarii Regulares, aliaeque multiplices votorum simplicium religiosae familiae quae, cum in suum ipsarum institutum Francisci spiritum induxerint et franciscali nomine utantur, Franciscum Patrem quodam modo habent, novum inde incrementum capientes, alacritate vel maiore optime de christiana civilique re mereri pergerent. Itaque legis huiusmodi emendandae munus Sacrae Congregationi negotiis Religiosorum praepositae plenius imbutam et hodierno Ecclesiae iuri congruentem confecisset, eam ipsam Nobis approbandam pro officio subiecit; cuius quidem Legis ea sunt capita quae hic referuntur.

## RULE *RERUM CONDICIO* (1927)

Pius, bishop, servant of the servants of God, as a perpetual memorial.

At the close of the twelfth century and somewhat later, especially in Italy, such was the condition, that, although Christian society generally remained firm in the faith, too many, filled with lust for the passing things of time and with the pride of life, fell into a lamentable decadence of morals; and as the charity of Christ decreased, hate everywhere grew stronger and incited States to direful civil wars. Nothing, therefore, was more to be desired than that a man excelling in the praise of all virtues should be raised up by God to bring a remedy for these evils and to recall the people to the spirit of the Christian life. All know that the work of recreating society in those days was divinely given to Francis of Assisi, who, opposing the love of Christian humility and poverty to the unbridled vices of the day, endeavored to unite all in mutual charity. When, therefore, very many disciples come to this great man from all sides, the Franciscan family increased very greatly, both from the members of the three Orders which he had instituted, and afterward, from those tertiaries, who, in the desire of a more perfect life, led the common life and are termed the members of the Third Order Regular. Rightly, therefore, on the seventh centenary of his most holy death, these tertiaries are during this year joyfully celebrating the memory of their Seraphic Father not only with solemn public services but also with the desire for greater holiness. It is known to all, with what diligence the Regular Tertiaries, even from the very foundation of their institute, have striven after the holy spirit of Francis and have carried that spirit into manifold works of religion and charity. Hence it was, that our predecessor, Pope Leo, in his constitution *Inter cetera*, approved their Rule. But, as happens in all human affairs, in the course of time many things which were decreed by Pope Leo became obsolete or did not accord entirely with certain prescriptions of Canon Law. Therefore, it became necessary to accommodate the law of Pope Leo X to our times and to the more recent echoes of the Church, so that the Regular Tertiaries and the very many other religious families of simple vows which have taken the spirit of Francis as their foundation, use the Franciscan name and recognize saint Francis as their Father, might continue to merit from the Church and the State laudable recognition of their works. Hence we committed to the Sacred Congregation in charge of the affairs of Religious the work of emending this law, and when it had completed the new Rule, fully developed and in accord with the present-day law of the Church, it presented this Rule to Us for our official approbation. The chapters of this law follow:

## Regula Tertii Ordinis Regularis Seraphici Patris S. Francisci

### Caput I – Summa vitae religiosae

1. Forma vitae Fratrum et Sororum Tertii Ordinis regularis sancti Francisci, haec est: Domini nostri Iesu Christi santum Evangelium observare, vivendo in obedientia, castitate et paupertate.

2. Fratres et Sorores, ad imitationem Patris Seraphici, promittunt obedientiam et reverentiam Domino Papae et Ecclesiae Romanae. Tenentur etiam obedire Superioribus suis canonice institutis, in omnibus quae respiciunt finem generalem et specialem proprii Instituti (Ex Reg. I et II Ordinis, cap. I).

### Caput II – De novitiatu et professione

3. Fratres et Sorores ad hunc Tertium Ordinem recipiendi debent esse fideles catholici, de haeresi non suspecti, in obedientia Romanae Ecclesiae firmi, matrimonio non ligati, debitis expediti, corpore sani, animo prompti, nulla vulgari infamia maculati, cum proximis reconciliati. Et de iis omnibus, antequem recipiantur, ab eo qui recipiendi habet facultatem, sunt diligenter examinandi (Regula III Ord. a Leone X approbata, cap. I), sacris canonibus Constitutionibusque propriis servatis.

4. Annus novitiatus debet sub disciplina Magistri hoc habere propositum, ut informetur alumni animus studio regulae et constitutionum, piis meditationibus assiduaque prece, iis perdiscendis quae ad vota et ad virtutes pertinent, exercitationibus opportunis ad vitiorum semina radicitus exstirpanda, ad compescendos animi motus, ad virtutes acquirendas. Conversi praeterea diligenter in christiana doctrina institutantur, speciali collatione ad eos habita semel saltem in hebdomada (can. 565 § 1 et 2).

5. Expleto tempore probationis, qui idonei inveniuntur, ad professionem admittantur.

RULE OF THE THIRD ORDER REGULAR OF THE SERAPHIC FATHER SAINT FRANCIS

## CHAPTER 1: SUM AND SUBSTANCE OF THE RELIGIOUS LIFE

1. The form of life of the brothers and sisters of the Third Order Regular of Saint Francis is this: To observe the holy Gospel of our Lord Jesus Christ by living in obedience, chastity and poverty.

2. The brothers and sisters, following the example of their Seraphic Father, promise obedience and reverence to the Lord Pope and the Roman Church. They are bound also to obey their canonically established superiors in all things that pertain to the general and particular aim of their respective Institute.[1]

## CHAPTER 2: NOVITIATE AND PROFESSION

3. The brothers and sisters to be received in the Third Order must be faithful Catholics, not suspect of heresy, firm in obedience to the Roman Church, unmarried, free of debt, sound of body, ready of mind, of clean reputation, and at peace with their neighbors. On all these matters they shall be carefully examined before reception by him who has the faculty to receive them,[2] with due observance of the sacred Canons and the Constitutions of their Institute.

4. The year of the novitiate must, under the discipline of a Master, have as its purpose to train the mind of the novice in the study of the Rule and Constitutions, in pious meditation and the love of prayer, in mastering all that pertains to the vows and the virtues, in suitable exercises calculated to root out the germs of vice, to curb the passions and to acquire virtues. Lay novices should moreover be carefully instructed in Christian doctrine, a special conference being given to them at least once a week.[3]

5. At the end of the time of probation, those who are found fit should be admitted to profession.

---

[1] LR 1; FLCl 1.
[2] Rule of the III Order of Leo X, ch. I.
[3] Canon 565,1 and 2.

### Caput III – De caritate erga Deum et proximum

6. Remotis per tria sacra vota obstaculis, quae sanctimoniam impediunt, Fratres et Sorores contendant legem divinam implere, quae tota pendet in caritate erga Deum et proximum. Caritas est omnium virtutum forma et vinculum perfectionis. Ad mortificanda vitia, ad proficiendum in gratia, ad consequendam virtutum omnium summam, nihil melius, nihil validius caritate.

7. Magnum signum et adiumentum dilectionis in Christum est frequens, imo quotidianus accessus ad SS. Eucharistiam, quae simul est et sacrum convivium et memoria Passionis eius. Sit quoque religiosarum animarum cura Dominum Iesum, sub mirabili mysterio nobiscum manentem, frequenter visitare ac devote venerari: hoc enim maximum est Sacramentum in Ecclesia et fons inexhaustus bonorum omnium.

8. Probatio autem dilectionis in Deum est exercitium caritatis erga proximum; ideo in vero Christi discipulo caritas in proximum maxime eluceat; omnis locutio sit ordinata, utilis et honesta: ut caritas abundet in opere, necesse est eam in corde prius abundare.

### Caput IV – De divino officio, oratione et ieiunio

9. Fratres et Sorores, prout propriae Constitutiones ferunt, digne, attente ac devote divinum officium persolvant. Conversi vero et Conversae dicant duodecim Pater pro Matutino et Laudibus, pro qualibet alia hora canonica quinque.

10. Quolibet autem die, nisi legitime impediantur, debent Missam audire, et procurare quod habeant pium sacerdotem ab Ordinario loci probatum, qui illis verbum Dei certis diebus proponat et eos ad poenitentiam et virtutes inducat (Reg. III Ord. cit., cap. IV).

11. Debent etiam quolibet die intra se et Deum, cogitare quid fecerint, dixerint et cogitaverint, seu conscientiae examen peragere; de propriis culpis veniam humiliter petere ac emendationis proposita Deo offere et commendare (Reg. cit., cap. IV).

## CHAPTER 3: LOVE OF GOD AND NEIGHBOR

6. The obstacles to sanctity being removed by the three holy vows, the brothers and sisters should strive to fulfill the divine Law, which depends wholly on the love of God and neighbor. Charity is the soul of all virtues and the bond of perfection. Nothing is better, nothing more effective than charity to mortify the vices, to advance in grace and to attain to the height of all virtues.

7. A great sign and aid of the love of Christ is the frequent and even daily approach to the Holy Eucharist, which is at once a sacred banquet and a memorial of His passion. It should also be the endeavor of religious souls frequently to visit and devoutly to venerate our Lord Jesus abiding with us in this admirable mystery, for this is the greatest sacrament of the church and an inexhaustible fountain of all blessings.

8. But the test of the love of God is the practice of charity toward our neighbor. Wherefore charity toward others should appear above all in the true follower of Christ. All his conversation should be guarded, useful and proper; that charity may abound in deed, it must first abound in the heart.

## CHAPTER 4: DIVINE OFFICE, PRAYER AND FASTING

9. The brothers and sisters should perform the Divine Office worthily, attentively and devoutly, according to their Constitutions. Lay members, however, shall say twelve Our Fathers for Matins and Lauds, and five each for the remaining canonical hours.

10 They must attend Mass daily unless they are legitimately prevented; and they must see to it that they have a pious priest approved by the Ordinary to preach the word of God to them on certain days and instruct them in penance and virtue.[4]

11. They should also daily examine themselves before God on what they have done, said and thought, that is examine their conscience, humbly seeking pardon for their faults, and offering and commending to God their purpose of amendment.[5]

[4]Rule of the III Order, ch. IV.
[5]Rule, ch. IV.

12. Curent omnes per frequentem Christi Passionis meditationem devotionis fervorem quotidie nutrire et fovere; Seraphicum Patriarcham sequantur et imitentur, ut valeant et ipsi cum S. Paulo exclamare: "Christo confixus sum cruci, vivo autem iam non ego: vivit in me Christus" (Gal 2:19-20).

13. Praeter abstinentias et ieiunia quibus omnes fideles adstringuntur, ea observent quae in propriis Constitutionibus ordinantur, praesertim vigilias solemnitatum Immaculatae Conceptionis et Seraphicis P. Francisci.

## Caput V – De modo interius exteriusque conversandi

14. Cum Fratres et Sorores huius Fraternitatis dicantur *de Poenitentia*, mortificationis crucem quotidie ferant, sicut vere poenitentibus congruit.

15. Oportet insuper eos ab omni curiositate, tam in vestimentis quam in aliis quibuscumque abstinere. Et iuxta Apostolorum principis beati Petri salubre consilium, depositis ceteris vanis huius saeculi ornamentis, nullum ornamentum corporale portare debent, nisi proprium religionsum habitum (Reg. cit., cap. VI). Tenentur etiam ad clausuram servandam iuxta sacros canones et proprias Constitutiones.

16. Debent quoque esse parci in verbis et locutionibus, quae raro sine peccato multiplicantur. Talis sit Fratrum et Sororum conversatio, ut omnes verbo et exemplo aedificent ac memores sint Dominum dixisse: "Sic luceat lux vestra coram hominibus: ut videant opera vestra bona, et glorificent Patrem vestrum, qui in caelis est" (Mt 5:16). Pacem annuncient omnibus humili et devota salutatione utentes: et pacem non in ore tantum, sed et in corde semper secum deferant (Reg. cit., cap. VI).

## Caput VI – De cura infirmorum

17. Si quis Frater vel Soror in infirmitatem ceciderit, nemo sit qui operam suam adiutricem neget; sed Superiorum erit congruum pro infirmo servitium disponere. Ceteros, tali servitio non addictos, infirmum visitare non pigeat, et consolatoriis verbis confortare. Non tantum infirmis sed et senibus, aut alio modo indigentibus, caritatis officia omnes laeto animo praestent sicut decet seraphici Patris filios.

12. All should try by frequent meditation on the Passion of Christ to nourish and increase day by day the fervor of their devotion; to follow and imitate their Seraphic Father so that also they can say with St. Paul: "With Christ I am nailed to the cross, I live, now not I, but Christ lives in me" (Gal 2:19-20).

13. Beside the fasts and abstinences to which all the faithful are obliged, they should also observe those which are prescribed in their respective Constitutions, notably on the vigils of the Immaculate Conception and of their Seraphic Father Francis.

## CHAPTER 5: INTERIOR AND EXTERIOR CONDUCT

14. Since the brothers and sisters of this Fraternity are called the Order of Penance, they should daily carry the cross of mortification, as becomes true penitents.

15. It behooves them likewise to refrain from all that is choice in apparel as well as in everything else. And according to the salutary advice of St. Peter, the Prince of the apostles, they should, after laying aside the other vain ornaments of this world, wear no other bodily ornament but their religious garb.[6] They are, furthermore, bound to observe the enclosure according to the sacred Canons and their respective Constitutions.

16. They must also be sparing of words and conversations which cannot be indulged in freely without sin. Let the conduct of the brothers and sisters be such that they may edify all by word and example, remembering that our Lord has said: "So let your light shine before men, that they may see your good works and glorify your Father who is in Heaven" (Mt 5:16). Let them approach everybody with humble and pious greeting of peace, and bear peace with them not only on their lips but also in their heart.[7]

## CHAPTER 6: CARE OF THE SICK

17. If a brother or sister falls ill, no one should refuse to offer his help; but it shall be the duty of the Superiors to provide for the proper care of the patient. The others who are not assigned to this duty should not hesitate to visit the patient and comfort him with consoling words. Not only to the sick, however, but also to the aged and the otherwise needy should all gladly tender the office of charity, as becomes the children of the Seraphic Father.

---

[6]Rule, ch. VI.
[7]Rule, ch. VI.

18. Teneantur potissimum Superiores infirmum vel infirmam monere de infirmitatis poenitentia acceptanda, de vera conversione ad Deum facienda, mortis quoque propinquitatem proponant et iudicii divini districtionem simulque divinam misericordiam (Reg. cit., cap. VII).

19. Postquam aliquis Frater vel Soror ab hac luce migraverit, Superiores curabunt quod eius exsequiae magna cum pietate celebrentur (Reg. cit., cap. IX). Pro anima vero cuiusque defuncti statuta suffragia fideliter persolvantur.

## Caput VII – De labore et modo laborandi

20. Qui Dei servitio, Spiritus Sancti adiuvante gratia, sese manciparunt, otium fugiant, et divinis laudibus, vel religiositatis aut caritatis operibus fideliter et devote incumbant (cf. Reg. II Ord., cap. VII).

21. Religiosi ideo officia sua propter Deum adimpleant, et quidquid ab eis Superiores exquisierint, prout vires ferunt, devote et fideliter, ut dictum est, perficiant. Viliora etiam, si quae facienda sint, ne recusent; imo libentius quam alia peragant, Seraphici Patris vestigia sequentes.

22. Omnia in caritate fiant, et sanctus Dei amor animos religiosorum ad opera perficienda ita impellat, ut nonnisi pro eius gloria et honore operari eos contigat: et Sancti Pauli Apostoli monitum adimpleant: "Sive manducatis, sive bibitis, sive aliud quid facitis: omnia in gloriam Dei" (1 Cor 10:31).

## Caput VIII – De obligatione servandi quae in Regula continentur

23. Omnia et singula in praesenti Regula contenta sunt consilia ad facilius salvandas animas viatorum, et nulla sunt obligatoria ad peccatum, mortale et veniale, nisi humano vel divino iure aliquis esset obligatus (Reg. cit., cap. X).

18. The Superiors especially are bound to admonish the sick brother or sister to accept the penance of illness and to be truly reconciled with God, reminding the patient also of the nearness of death, and of the severity of divine judgment, as well as of the divine mercy.[8]

19. When a brother or sister has departed this life, the Superiors shall see to it that the obsequies are held with great piety.[9] The prescribed suffrages should be faithfully performed for the soul of every deceased member.

## CHAPTER 7: NATURE AND MANNER OF WORK

20. Those who, inspired by the grace of the Holy Spirit, have dedicated themselves to the service of God, should avoid idleness, and give their efforts faithfully and devoutly to the divine praises or the various works of piety and charity.[10]

21. The religious should, therefore, comply with their duties for the love of God, and perform what their Superiors require of them, to the best of their ability, devoutly and faithfully, as has been said. Nor should they refuse to perform the humbler tasks that may be imposed on them; on the contrary following the footsteps of their Seraphic Father, they should perform them more willingly than other tasks.

22. Let all things be done in charity, and let the holy love of God so animate the sentiments of the religious in doing their work that they may labor only for his honor and glory, and fulfill the admonition of St. Paul the Apostle: "Whether you eat or drink, or whatsoever else you do, do all to the glory of God" (1 Cor 10:31).

## CHAPTER 8: OBLIGATIONS OF THE RULE

23. Each and all the articles contained in the present Rule are counsels to help the wayfarers save their soul the more easily, none of them obliges under sin, either mortal or venial, except where one were otherwise obliged to them by human or divine law.[11]

---

[8]Rule, ch. VI.
[9]Rule, ch. IX.
[10]Rule of the III Order, ch. VII.
[11]Rule, ch. X.

24. Obligantur tamen Fratres et Sorores facere poenitentias sibi a Superioribus impositas, quando super hoc requiruntur. Obligantur etiam ad tria vota essentialia: ad paupertatem, iuxta terminos propriorum statutorum; ad castitatem, se adstringendo ad servandum caelibatum et insuper novo titulo, id est ipsius voti, ad abstinendum a quocumque actu, tum externo, tum interno castitati opposito; ad obedientiam, assumendo obligationem obediendi mandato legitimi Superioris ad normam propriarum Constitutionum (cf. Reg. cit., cap. X).

25. Omnes tam Fratres quam Sorores ad religiosi status quem professi sunt praescriptum, vitam instituant et componant, atque in primis, quae ad suorum votorum perfectionem pertinent, fideliter observent. Ea praesertim maximi faciant, quae ad Seraphici Patris caritatem et paupertatem sectandas inducunt: filium enim maxime decet Parentis sui et imaginem et virtutes referre.

## Conclusio – Sancti Patris Francisci Benedictio

Quicumque haec observaverint, in caelo repleantur benedictione altissimi Patris caelestis, et in terra repleantur benedictione dilecti Filii sui, cum sanctissimo Spiritu Paraclito et omnibus Virtutibus caelorum et omnibus Sanctis. Et ego Frater Franciscus, parvulus vester et servus, quantumcumque possum, confirmo vobis intus et foris istam sanctissimam benedictionem, quam habeatis cum omnibus Virtutibus caelorum et omnibus Sanctis nunc et in saecula saeculorum. Amen.

Nos quidem, veterem legem Leonis PP. prorsus abrogantes, libenter, saeculo a Francisci obitu septimo exeunte, hanc *Regulam Tertii Ordinis Regularis Seraphicis Patris Francisci* apostolica auctoritate Nostra approbamus et confirmamus: id fore plane confisi ut Tertiarii Regulares, iique omnes qui, etsi vota sollemnia ex instituto non habent, religiosam tamen vitam, duce Francisco, agunt, spiritu novae Legis roborati, quemadmodum egregie scribebat Decessor Noster Benedictus PP. XV, *ceteris sodalibus Tertiariis, qui mundi negotiis curisque impliciti remaneant, in christiana perfectione colenda sint exemplo, eisque tamquam duces ad sempiternam salutem quaerendam* praeire pergant.[1]

Haec mandamus, decernentes, praesentes Litteras et Statuta in eas inserta atque inclusa, firma, valida atque efficacia semper exstare ac permanere, suosque plenos atque integros effectus sortiri et obtinere, illisque, ad quos spectant aut in posterum spectare poterunt, nunc et pro tempore amplissime suffragari; sicque rite iudicandum esse ac definien-

---

[1]Cf. *Acta Apostolicae Sedis*, vol. XIII, p. 131 (N. M.).

24. The brothers and sisters are, however, obliged to perform the penances imposed on them by their Superiors when required to do so. They are also obliged to keep the three essential vows: Poverty, within the limits of their respective constitutions; Chastity, binding themselves to observe celibacy and to refrain under an additional title, namely, that of the vow itself, from every act whatsoever, be it external or internal, that is opposed to Chastity, and Obedience, assuming the obligation to obey the command of their lawful Superior according to the tenor of their respective Constitutions.[12]

25. All, both brothers and sisters, should guide and govern their life according to the law of the religious state which they have professed, and above all faithfully observe what pertains to the perfect fulfillment of their vows. They should have the highest regard especially for those points which direct them to follow the charity and poverty of their Seraphic Father, for it becomes the child most of all to reproduce in itself the image and virtues of its parents.

## CONCLUSION: BLESSING OF OUR HOLY FATHER SAINT FRANCIS

And whosoever will observe these things, may they be filled in heaven with the blessing of the most high heavenly Father, and may they be filled on earth with the blessing of His beloved Son, together with the most Holy Spirit, the Paraclete, and all the virtues of the heavens and all the saints. And I, brother Francis, your little one and servant, so far as ever I am able, confirm unto you within and without this most holy blessing, which may you enjoy with all the virtues of the heavens and all the saints now and forevermore. Amen.[13]

On our part, abrogating altogether the old Rule of Pope Leo, we gladly, at the close of the seventh centenary of the death of Francis, approve and confirm by Our apostolic authority, this Rule of the Third Order Regular of the Seraphic Father St. Francis; trusting that Tertiaries Regular, as also all those who, though they do not have solemn vows according to their Institute, yet lead a religious life under the guidance of Francis, will find strength in the spirit of the new Rule to be models in the pursuit of Christian perfection for those of their Tertiary brethren who remain involved in the business and cares of the world – as Our Predecessor Pope Benedict XV so beautifully wrote – continuing to go before them as leaders in the quest of eternal salvation.

This We command, decreeing that the present document and the laws inserted and included in it shall be and remain ever firm, valid and

---

[12]Rule, ch. X.
[13]Test 41-42.

dum, irritumque ex nunc et inane fieri, si quidquam secus super his, a quovis, auctoritate qualibet, scienter vel ignoranter attentari contigerit. Non obstantibus contrariis quibuslibet, etiam speciali atque individua mentione dignis. Volumus autem, ut harum Litterarum exemplis atque excerptis, etiam impressis, manu alicuius Notarii publici subscriptis et sigillo viri in ecclesiastica dignitate constituti munitis, eadem prorsus fides adhibeatur, quae haberetur ipsis praesentibus, si forent exhibitae vel ostensae.

Datum Romae apud Sanctum Petrum, die IV mensis Octobris, in festo Sancti Francisci Assisiensis, anno MDCCCCXXVII, Pontificatus Nostri sexto.

effective, acquiring and keeping their full and entire force, and redounding to the fullest benefit of those who are or shall hereafter be concerned in them; and thus shall all daily judge and define; and whatsoever may be attempted otherwise by whomsoever, under whatever authority, wittingly or unwittingly, in the matter, shall be henceforth null and void. Anything to the contrary notwithstanding, worthy though it be even of special and individual mention. We want however that copies and excerpts of this document, also printed ones, so far as they bear the signature of a notary public and are armed with the seal of an ecclesiastical dignity, shall fully enjoy the same respect as should be given to these presents were they produced or displayed.

Given at Rome, at St. Peter's, the fourth day of the month of October, on the feast of St. Francis of Assisi, in the year 1927, the sixth of Our Pontificate.

# CONTEMPORARY SOURCES

# 2

## Contemporary Sources

In the aftermath of the Vatican II Council, the congregations of the Third Order Regular returned to their origins. In the 1960s and 1970s, it became clear that the Rule of Pius XI was no longer adequate. Projects of renewal appeared: in the German-speaking area, *Lebensregel der Franziskanerinnen des klösterlichen Dritten Ordens*[1]; in the Dutch-speaking area, *Franciscaanse Leefregel*; and in the French-speaking area, *Règle de Vie des Soeurs de l'Ordre de Saint François*. An inter-obediential congress of the Third Order Regular gathered in Madrid, Spain, in 1974, produced a *Statement of Understanding of Franciscan Penitential Life*.

Those movements of renewal converged during the 1970s, and in 1980 an international Work Group was appointed to draft a new text of the Rule. The Work Group produced a first draft during their initial meeting in Reute, Germany, in 1980 and a second draft during their second meeting in Brussels, Belgium, in 1981. The Brussels text is the text that the General Assembly examined, amended and voted in Rome in 1982.

---

[1]Since the purpose of this lengthy document was only to help the congregations with the drafting of new, post-concilliar constitutions, we have only reproduced its outline.

# TWENTIETH-CENTURY FRANCISCAN RENEWAL PROJECTS

## LEBENSREGEL DER FRANZISKANERINNEN DES KLÖSTERLICHEN DRITTEN ORDENS

### FRANZISKANISCHE ARBEITSGEMEINSCHAFT, 1967

#### ZUR EINFÜHRUNG

Die Zentralkommission der Franziskanischen Arbeitsgemeinschaft legt den Genossenschaften, die sie mit der Vorbereitung neuer Generalkonstitutionen beauftragt haben, nachstehend einen Textentwurf für diese Konstitutionen vor. Dabei ist sich die Zentralkommission bewußt, daß sie keine Rechtsinstanz ist, die in irgendeiner Weise die wirkliche Annahme dieses Textes erzwingen könnte. Der Text hat den Charakter eines Vorschlages, über den die Generalkapitel der einzelnen Genossenschaften befinden werden. Doch glaubt die Zentralkommission, darauf hinweisen zu dürfen, daß sie mit aller Sorgfalt geprüft hat, ob sie diesen Text vorschlagen kann.

Gemünden/Main, den 30. November 1967

#### 1. KAPITEL
##### DIE GRUNDLAGEN UNSERER ORDENSGEMEINSCHAFT

I. Quellgründe und Eigenart unseres Ordenslebens

II. Unsere Profeß

III. Unser Leben in Ehelosigkeit um des Himmelreiches willen

IV. Unser Leben in Armut

V. Unser Leben in Gehorsam

#### 2. KAPITEL
##### UNSER LEBEN VOR GOTT

Liturgie und Leben
Unser Leben in Buße

## RULE AND LIFE OF THE FRANCISCAN SISTERS OF THE THIRD ORDER REGULAR

## CENTRAL COMMITTEE OF THE FRANCISCAN WORKGROUP

INTRODUCTION

The Central Committee of the Franciscan Workgroup presents, below, a text draft for these Constitutions to the Congregations that entrusted them with the preparation of new General Constitutions. The Central Committee is aware that it has no legal authority that could force the real acceptance of this text in any way. The text has the character of a suggestion, which the General Chapters of the individual Congregations will consider. But the Central Committee thinks it may point out that it has very diligently examined whether it can suggest this text.

Gemuenden/Main, November 30, 1967.

CHAPTER 1
THE FOUNDATIONS OF OUR RELIGIOUS COMMUNITY

I. Sources and character of our religious life

II. Our profession

III. Our life in celibacy for the sake of the Kingdom

IV. Our life in poverty

V. Our life in obedience

CHAPTER 2
OUR LIFE BEFORE GOD

Liturgy and life
Our life in penance

## 3. Kapitel
### Unser Leben in Schwesterlicher Gemeinschaft

Entlassung und Austritt
Unsere Beziehungen zu anderen franziskanischen Gemeinschaften
Unsere Beziehungen zu denen, die im weiteren Sinne zu unserer
Gemeinschaft gehören

## 4. Kapitel
### Unser Leben in franziskanischer Armut und Demut

Das Erbe der Schwester
  A. Regelung ohne Verzicht
  B. Regelung mit Verzicht
Verwaltung der Güter

## 5. Kapitel
### Unser Lebenszeugnis in der Tätigkeit

Mission (*für alle Genossenschaften*)
Sonderbeslimmungen für die Missionstätigkeit
Oder (*bei ungegliederten Genossenschaften*)

## 6. Kapitel
### Unsere Ausbildung zum Leben und Wirken

Ausbildung im allgemeinen
Ausbildung im besonderen
  Die Aufnahme der Kandidatinnen
  Das Postulat
  Das kanonische Noviziat
    (*Erste Möglichkeit:* ein Jahr Noviziat)
    (*Zweite Möglichkeit:* zwei Jahre Noviziat)

Ist das Noviziat beendet, wird die Novizin zur Ablegung der
  zeitlichen Gelübde zugelassen.
Die Zulassung zu den ewigen Gelübden

CHAPTER 3
OUR LIFE IN SISTERLY COMMUNITY

Dismissal and leaving
Our interrelationships with other Franciscan communities
Our interrelationships with those who belong to our community in
    a wider sense

CHAPTER 4
OUR LIFE IN FRANCISCAN POVERTY AND HUMILITY

The inheritance of the sister
        A. regulation without renunciation
        B. regulation with renunciation
Administration of temporal goods

CHAPTER 5
OUR LIFE OF WITNESS IN APOSTOLIC ACTIVITY

Mission (*for all entities*)
Special provisions for the missionary work
Other provisions (*for entities non-canonically established*)

CHAPTER 6
OUR FORMATION FOR LIFE AND APOSTOLIC WORK

Formation in general
Formation in particular
        The reception of candidates
        The postulancy
        The canonical novitiate
                (First possibility: novitiate of one year)
                (Second possibility: novitiate of two years)

After finishing the novitiate, the novice is admitted to make
    temporary profession
Admission to perpetual vows

**7. KAPITEL (SCHEMA 1)**

**AUFBAU UND LEITUNG BEI GENOSSENSCHAFTEN, DIE IN PROVINZEN GEGLIEDERT SIND**

I. Grundsätzliches zur rechtlichen Struktur

II. Die Generalleitung
1. Das Generalkapilel
   a) Grundsätzliches
   b) Teilnehmerinnen des Generalkapitels
   c) Vorbereitung des Generalkapitels
   d) Die Wahl der Generalleitung
   e) Das Sachkapitel
2. Die Generaloberin
3. Die Generalvikarin
4. Der Generalrat
5. Ämter im Generalat
6. Der Ordensrat

III. Provinzleitung
1. Das Provinzkapitel
   a) Grundsätzliches
   b) Teilnehmerinnen
   c) Vorbereitung
   d) Das Wahlkapitel
   e) Das Provinz-Sachkapitel
   f) Der Kapitelskongreß
2. Die Provinzoberin
3. Die Provinzvikarin
4. Der Provinzrat
5. Ämter im Provinzialat
6. Der Schwesternrat

IV. Gebiete, die noch nicht selbständig sind

V. Die Niederlassungen
1. Die Hausoberin
2. Die Konventsvikarin
3. Die Konventsrätinnen und die Hausökonomin
4. Das Konventskapitel

CHAPTER 7 (SCHEME 1)
STRUCTURE AND ADMINISTRATION OF CONGREGATIONS THAT ARE DIVIDED
INTO PROVINCES

I. Fundamental of the legal structure

II. The General Administration
    1. The General Chapter
        a) Principles
        b) Members of the General Chapter
        c) Preparation of the General Chapter
        d) Election of the General Administration
        e) Chapter of Affairs
    2. Superior General
    3. Vicar General
    4. General Council
    5. Official duties in the Generalate
    6. Congregational Council

III. Provincial Administration
    1. The Provincial Chapter
        a) Principles
        b) Members
        c) Preparation
        d) The Chapter of Elections
        e) The Chapter of Affairs
        f) The Chapter Congress
    2. The Provincial Superior
    3. The Provincial Vicar
    4. The Provincial Council
    5. Official duties in the Provincialate
    6. The Council of Sisters

IV. Areas that are not yet independent

V. Local Convents
    1. The Local Superior
    2. The Local Vicar
    3. The Convent Council and the Treasurer
    4. The Convent Chapter

**7. Kapitel (Schema 2)**
**Aufbau und Leitung bei Genossenschaften ohne Provinzen**

I. Grundsätzliches zur rechtlichen Struktur

II. Die Generalleitung
  1. Das Generalkapitel
    a) Grundsätzliches
    b) Teilnehmerinnen des Generalkapitels
    c) Vorbereitung des Generalkapitels
    d) Die Wahl der Generalleitung
    e) Das Sachkapitel
  2. Die Generaloberin
  3. Die Generalvikarin
  4. Der Generalrat
  5. Ämter im Generalat
  6. Der Schwesternrat

III. Gebiete, die noch nicht selbständig sind

IV. Die Niederlassungen
  1. Die Hausoberin
  2. Die Konventsvikarin
  3. Die Konventsrätinnen und die Hausökonomin
  4. Das Konventskapitel

**Schlusswort**

Legt nichts fest, sondern lebt!

Das ist eigentliches Anliegen unserer Lebensregel. In einer Welt, in der das Wort viel von seiner Bedeutung verloren hat, muß die Tat sprechen, damit "der Glaube durch die Liebe wirksam wird" (Gal 5, 6). Unser Leben findet seine verpflichtenden Normen im Evangelium. Es ist Fundament dieser Lebensregel, sie selbst eine Hilfe, gleich Franziskus den Lehren und Fußspuren unseres Herrn Jesus Christus beharrlich zu folgen.

"Denn dazu hat er euch in alle Welt gesandt, daß ihr durch Wort und Werk von seiner Stimme Zeugnis gebt" (Franziskus).

*Die auf den Werkwochen in Olpe (10.-17. 12. 1967), in Vöcklabruck (9.-16. 1. 1968) und in Reute (20.-27. 1. 1968) erarbeiteten Alternativvorschläge zu den einzelnen Artikeln werden allen Kongregationen gesammelt zur Verfügung gestellt, damit die jeweiligen Generalkapitel auswählen und entscheiden können.*

CHAPTER 7 (SCHEME 2)
STRUCTURE AND ADMINISTRATION OF CONGREGATIONS WITHOUT PROVINCES

I. Principles of the legal structure

II. The General Administration
    1. The General Chapter
        a) Principles
        b) Members of the General Chapter
        c) Preparation of the General Chapter
        d) The Election of the General Administration
        e) The Chapter of Affairs
    2. The Superior General
    3. The Vicar General
    4. The General Council
    5. Official duties in the Generalate
    6. The Council of the Sisters

III. Areas that are not yet independent

IV. Local Convents
    1. The Local Superior
    2. The Local Vicar
    3. The Conventual Council and the Treasurer
    4. The Conventual Chapter

CLOSING WORDS

Do not lay down anything but live!
That is the actual concern of our rule of life. In a world in which the word has lost much of its importance, the act must speak so that "faith becomes effective through love" (Gal 5:6). Our life finds its obligating norms in the Gospel. It is the foundation of this rule of life, it itself helps us, like Francis, to persistently follow the teachings and the footsteps of our Lord Jesus Christ. "For this reason he has sent you into the whole world that you may bear witness to His voice in word and deed."[1]

*The alternative proposals to the individual articles compiled at the workshops in Olpe (December 10-17, 1967), in Voecklabruck (January 9-16, 1968) and in Reute (January 20-27, 1968), are made available to all Congregations, so that the respective General Chapters may select and decide.*

---

[1]LtOrd 9; FA:ED I, 117.

## Franciscaanse Leefregel

## Franciscaanse Samenwerking, 1969

### Verklaring

1. Voor allen die in Christus geloven (Rm 13:10; Col 3:12-15),
is het evangelie de eerste en hoogste levensnorm
en de liefde de volheid van de wet.
Hen riep de Vader samen als zijn volk (1Pt 2:9-10),[1]

5. opdat zij één zouden zijn in Jezus Christus, zijn Zoon,
en deel hebben aan zijn zending:
de voltooiing van de wereld.
Door zijn Geest geleid zullen zij (Eph 4:4-17; 1 Cor 12),[2]
naar de verschillende gaven hun geschonken,

10. elkaar en alle mensen dienstbaar zijn.
Zo verwerkelijken zij Gods bedoeling
met de mens en de wereld.

De ene Geest,
die zijn gaven uitdeelt zoals Hij het wil (1 Cor 12:11),

15. schenkt óns de genade,
omwille van het evangelie te kiezen
voor een ongehuwd leven binnen een gemeenschap (Mt 19:12),[3]
die deel uitmaakt van de gehele franciscaanse orde.
Omwille van Gods aanwezigheid onder de mensen

20. en tot opbouw van het lichaam van Christus (Eph 4:12)
wijden wij ons zo toe aan elkaar en aan alle mensen.

---

[1]*Ecclesia Docens* 9.

[2]*Ecclesia Docens* 41.

[3]*Ecclesia Docens* 42.

## FRANCISCAN RULE OF LIFE

## FRANCISCAN COMMISSION, 1969

### Declaration

1.To all who believe in Christ (Rm 13:10; Col 3:12-15)
the Gospel is the first and highest rule of life
and love is the summation of the law.
The Father called them together as his people (1Pt 2:9-10)

5. that they might be one in Jesus Christ, his Son,
and might partake of his mission:
the completion of the world.
Led by his Spirit, they shall (Eph 4:4-17; 1 Cor 12),
according to the diverse gifts granted them,

10. be of service to one another and to all men.[1]
Thus they shall realize God's purpose
for men and for the world.

The one spirit,
who parcels out his gifts at will (1 Cor 12:11),

15. grants us the grace,
to choose for the sake of the gospel (Mt 19:12)
the unmarried life within a community
which forms a part of the whole Franciscan Order.
For the sake of God's presence among us

20. and for the edification of the body of Christ (Eph 4:12)
we devote ourselves to one another and to all people.

---

[1]ER 5:6; FA:ED I, 67.

In dit leven vinden wij vrijheid en ruimte
om de woorden en voetstappen van onze Heer Jezus Chrlstus
zo volkomen mogelijk te volgen

25. en de Geest des Heren levend in ons te dragen.
Deze navolging van Christus bindt ons samen
tot een gemeenschap van zusters en broeders.
leder van ons is hiertoe persoonlijk geroepen,
draagt verantwoordelijkheid voor het geheel

30. en heeft zijn bijzondere waarde en persoonlijke taak.
In deze gemeenschap willen wij

"elkaar van harte dienen en gehoorzamen,
want dit is de echte en heilige gehoorzaamheid
van onze Heer Jezus Christus."

35. Dit vraagt de moed
de mindere van de ander te willen zijn
en hierin Jezus te volgen, die omwille van ons
niets heeft vastgehouden van zijn goddelijke rijkdom (Phil 2:5-8),
maar geheel aan ons gelijk is geworden.

40. Praktisch betekent dit,
dat wij werkelijk arm voor God, onthecht en sober willen leven
en geen onnodige eisen stellen aan het leven.
Volgens deze wet van het evangelie,
ons bijzonder voorgehouden door Franciscus,

45. moeten wij onze liefde allereerst richten op de hulpbehoevenden,
zoals onze tijd en situatie dit vragen.
Ons onderling verkeer en onze komst bij anderen
en al ons dienstbetoon hun gewijd
zalsteeds gericht zijn op de vrede van Christus (Jn 14:27)

50. en de eenheid onder de mensen.

In this life we find the freedom and the scope
to follow as fully as possible
the words and in the footprints of our Lord Jesus Christ[2]

> 25. and to bear in ourselves the living Spirit of the Lord.
> This imitation of Christ binds us together
> into a community of Sisters and Brothers.
> Each one of us is personally called to this,
> bears responsibility for the whole

> 30. and has his or her particular worth and personal task.
> In this community we want

"to serve and obey each other willingly
for this is the true and holy obedience
of our Lord Jesus Christ."[3]

> 35. This requires the courage
> always to be prepared to be the lesser to the other
> to follow Jesus Christ who for our sake
> did not cling to his equality with God
> so as to assume totally our condition (Phil. 2:5-8).

> 40. In practice this means
> that truly poor before God, we shall live detachedly and frugally
> without making unnecessary demands of life.
> According to this law of the Gospel,
> proposed to us in particular by Francis,[4]

> 45. we ought to direct our lives first of all to the needy
> according to the demands of time and circumstance.
> Our community fellowship and our encounter with others
> and all gestures of service to them
> shall constantly intend the peace of Christ (Jn 14:27)

> 50. and unity among men.

---

[2]ER 1; FA:ED I, 63-64.
[3]ER 5; FA:ED I, 67-68.
[4]ER 9; FA:ED I, 70-71.

Het leven in gemeenschap vraagt,
dat de zusters en broeders uit hun midden
iemand kiezen en aanvaarden
die hen in Chrlstus' naam zal dienen en leiden (Rm 12:8).

> 55. Ons dagelijks samenleven en onze arbeid
> eisen een voortdurende geest van inkeer en gebed
> en worden gedragen door woord en sacrament.

Zij die tot deze gemeenschap wensen toe te treden
zullen, als zij geschikt worden bevonden,

> 60. beloven deze leefregel te onderhouden.
> Zij die hierin volharden, zullen gezegend zijn door de Heer.

The life in community demands
that the sisters and brothers shall choose
and accept someone out of their midst
who shall serve and lead them in the name of Christ (Rom 12:8).

> 55. Our daily communal life and our work
> require a continual spirit of reflection and prayer[5]
> and should be supported by word and sacrament.

Those who wish to enter this community shall,
when they are found to be suitable,

> 60. promise to keep this Rule of life.
> Those who will stand fast till the end shall be blessed by the Lord.

---

[5]Test 4; FA:ED I, 124.

HOOFDSTUK I: Onze toewijding aan God in de geest van Franciscus

1. Wij allen, die deze leefregel aanvaarden,
willen het evangelie van onze Heer Jezus Christus beleven
in een gemeenschap waarvan Franclscus het inspirerend voorbeeld is.

Hier hopen wij het evangelie te ervaren als een kracht Gods (Rm 1:16)

5. tot voortdurende heiliging en innerlijke vernieuwing
van onszelf en van heel de Kerk.
Met zijn scheppend en verlossend woord
verblijft de Heer in ons midden
en zo nodigt Hij ons steeds weer uit

10. het Rijk Gods gestalte te geven
in onze gemeenschap en onder allen met wie wij verkeren.

Deze uitgesproken aandacht voor het evangelie
en de eerlijke beleving ervan binnen de Kerk
was de oorspronkelijke roeping van Franciscus.

15. Door Gods Geest liet hij zich in alles inspireren.
Op profetische wijze maakte hij met zijn broeders en zusters
de boodschap van Gods mensenliefde weer verstaanbaar.
Onvoorwaardelijke trouw aan de Kerk heeft hij haar
naar de maatstaf van het evangelie vernieuwd en omgevormd.

20. In Franciscus spreekt ons aan:
zijn ervaring van de onuitsprekelijke God,
in een grondig besef van eigen geringheid en zondigheid,
zijn liefdevolle aandacht
voor de menselijkheid en het lijden van Jezus Christus

25. en voor zijn moeder Maria,
zijn eerbied voor de eucharistie,
zijn trouw en apostolische vrijmoedigheid,

CHAPTER I: OUR DEDICATION TO GOD IN THE SPIRIT OF FRANCIS

1. All of us who accept this Rule of life
want to live according to the Gospel of our Lord Jesus Christ
in a community of which St. Francis is the inspiring example.

Here we hope to experience the gospel as a power of God (Rm 1:16)

5. calling for the constant sanctification and inner renewal
of ourselves and of the whole church.
In his creative redemptive word
the Lord remains in our midst
and invites us time and again

10. to give form to God's reign
in our community and among those with whom we live.

This explicit attention to the Gospel
and its authentic realization in the Church
was the original calling of Francis.

15. He permitted God's spirit to be his inspiration in everything.
In a prophetic manner, with his brothers and sisters,
he made the message of God's love for men once more
     understandable.
Unconditionally faithful to the Church, yet, he renewed and
     transformed her
according to the standards of the Gospel.

20. Francis attracts us
because of his experience of the inexpressible God
in a radical realization of his own nothingness and sinfulness,
his loving attention
to the humanity and the suffering of Jesus Christ

25. and to his mother Mary,
his respect for the Eucharist,
his fidelity and apostolic frankness,

zijn persoonlijke inzet voor de vrede
en de broederschap van alle mensen.

30. In hem zien wij op bijzondere wijze verpersoonlijkt
de verwondering over Gods schepping,
de lofprijzing van Hem om al het goede en mooie daarin
en tegelijk een radicale onthechting en armoede
naar het voorbeeld van Jezus Christus, zijn moeder en zijn
    apostelen.

35. In deze geest van Franciscus willen ook wij het evangelie
    volgen.
Zo hopen wij in onze tijd
de vrede en de universele broederschap te mogen dienen
en Gods huis te helpen herstellen.
Daarbij voelen wij ons in dankbaarheid verbonden (Heb 12:1)

40. met allen die vóór ons en onder ons
hiervan een voorbeeld waren en zijn.
De binding van ons leven aan het evangelie
binnen de gemeenschap die wij kiezen en die ons opneemt,
brengen wij tot uitdrukking in onze professie.

45. Deze toewijding aan God en aan elkaar
spreken wij uit voor degene die onze gemeenschap leidt
en daarom op bijzondere wijze de Kerk vertegenwoordigt.

Ieder van ons doet dit met deze woorden:
Ik . . . . beloof aan U, God, mijn almachtige Vader.

50. het evangelie van Uw Zoon, onze Heer Jezus Christus,
te zullen volgen, in een ongehuwd leven
samen met de zusters (broeders) die U mij gegeven hebt
en die mij in hun midden opnemen.
Ik beloof dit voor geheel mijn leven;

55. in de geest en naar het voorbeeld van Franciscus,
volgens de leefregel van onze gemeenschap,
in onthechting en soberheid, in dienstbaarheid en
    gehoorzaamheid.

his personal effort for peace
and for brotherhood among mankind.

30. In him we see embodied in an exceptional manner
the marvel of God's creation,
the praise of God for all the good and beautiful
and yet at the same time a radical detachment and poverty
according to the example of Jesus Christ, his mother and his
apostles.

35. According to this spirit of Francis we wish to follow
the Gospel.
Accordingly we hope to be able
to serve the peace and universal brotherhood
and help build God's house in our time.[6]
We consider ourselves united in thankfulness (Heb 12:1)

40. with all those past or present
who exemplify this.
The bond of our life to the Gospel
will be expressed in our profession within the community,
which we choose and which accepts us in her midst.

45. This dedication to God and to one another
we shall pronounce before the one who leads our community
and for that reason represents the Church in a special manner.

Each one shall do this using the following words:
I . . . . promise to you, God, my Father allmighty,

50. to always observe the Gospel of your Son, our Lord Jesus
Christ,
in an unmarried life
together with the sisters (brothers) that you gave me
and who receive me among them.
I promise this for all my life;

55. in the spirit and after the example of Francis,
according to the rule of life of our community,
in detachment and frugality, in service and obedience.

[6]2C; FA:ED II, 249.

HOOFDSTUK II: ZUSTERS EN BROEDERS VAN ALLEN

1. Dit is het beeld dat Franciscus
in Christus heeft gezien en dat hij volgde:
"Wie onder u groot wil worden, moet dienaar onder u zijn,
en wie de eerste wil zijn, moet aller slaaf wezen,

5. want ook de Mensenzoon is niet gekomen om gediend te
    worden,
maar om te dienen en zijn leven te geven als losprijs voor velen"
    (Mk 10:43-45).
Hij werd bijzonder getroffen door onze Heer Jezus Christus,
die ons aller dienaar en broeder werd
en zich niet ontzien heeft aan het kruis voor ons te sterven
    (Phil 2:8).

10. Dit moet ook ons ertoe brengen
voor allen beschikbaar te zijn.
Daarvoor is nodig
dat wij de anderen aanvaarden zoals zij zijn,
respecteren en ons vertrouwen schenken.

15. Wij moeten er niet naar streven boven anderen te staan,
maar veeleer ons in dienst stellen van allen (Phil 2:3),
mild, vredelievend en doorzichtig.
Wanneer wij op deze wijze trachten arm voor God te zijn,
zullen wij als blijmoedige en onbezorgde mensen kunnen leven,

20. bereid aan allen onze zorg en liefde te geven.
Zo zullen wij als vrije mensen
ons actief kunnen inzetten voor vrede en gerechtigheid.

*ongehuwd leven omwille van het Rijk Gods*

In Christus' liefde voor God en alle mensen

25. is het Rijk Gods definitief en overtuigend op aarde verschenen,
als een goddelijk zaad, een alles doordesemend gist (Mt 13:1-46)
en als een kostbare schat,
waaraan al het andere ondergeschikt moet zijn.
Overal waar ware vrijheid en broederlijkheid gaan heersen,

CHAPTER II: SISTERS AND BROTHERS TO ALL

1.This is the image that Francis
saw and followed in Christ:
"Among you, whoever wants to be great must be your servant,
and whoever wants to be first must be the willing slave of all.

5. For even the Son of Man did not come to be served but to serve,
and to surrender his life as a ransom for many." (Mk 10:43-45)
He was particularly affected by our Lord Jesus Christ,
who became brother and servant to us all,[7]
and who humbled himself even to accepting death on a cross.
    (Phil 2:8)

10. This should induce us
to be of service to all.[8]
For this it is necessary
that we accept others as they are,
that we respect them and have confidence in them.

15. We ought not to strive for superior positions
but rather to be at the service of all, (Phil 2:3)
to be gentle, peaceable and transparent.[9]
If we are poor before God in this manner
we shall be able to live as joyful and carefree human beings

20. prepared to extend our care and our love to all.
Then we shall be free human beings
able to engage ourselves actively for peace and justice.

*unmarried life for the sake of the Reign of God*

In Christ's love for God and all men

25. God's Reign as hade its definitive and decisive appearance
upon earth
as a divine seed, as a yeast that leavens all (Mt 13:1-46)
and like a treasure
to which all the rest must remain subject.
Wherever true freedom and brotherhood reign,

---

[7]ER 9; FA:ED I, 70-71.
[8]Test 4; FA:ED I, 124.
[9]LR 3; FA:ED I, 101-02.

30. komt dit Rijk Gods en groeit de schepping naar haar
    voltooiing:
de nieuwe hemel en de nieuwe aarde,
waarvan de Schrift zegt:
"Ziehier Gods woning onder de mensen!
Hij zal bij hen wonen.

35. Zij zullen zijn volk zijn en Hij, God-met-hen,
zal hun God zijn.
En Hij zal alle tranen van hun ogen afwissen,
en de dood zal niet meer zijn;
geen rouw, geen geween, geen smart zal er zijn.

40. want al het oude is voorbij.
En Hij die op de troon is gezeten sprak:
Zie, Ik maak alles nieuw" (Rev 21:3-5).
Van deze belofte
en van deze hoopvolle verwachting

45. is de keuze voor het ongehuwde leven een bijzonder teken,
echter alleen dan, wanneer hierin werkelijk
ware vrijheid en broederlijkheid zichtbaar worden.

In onderlinge verbondenheid zullen wij daarom trachten
een zo doorzichtig mogelijke verwerkelijking te zijn

50. van de Kerk als mensengemeenschap in Christus.
Waar wij ook verblijven of elkaar treffen,
moeten wij ons metterdaad elkaars huisgenoten tonen.
Dit vraagt een menselijke liefde
en bezorgdheid voor ieders welzijn

55. In een sfeer van vrijheid en vertrouwen.
Zieke en bejaarde huisgenoten
gaan ons bijzonder ter harte.
Een hartelijke gemeenschap helpt ons
het ongehuwd-zijn zinvol te beleven.

30. God's Reign becomes present and creation grows to its
    completion:
the new heaven and the new earth,
of which scripture says:
"Here God has his dwelling among men.
He will make his home among them."

35. They shall be his people and he will be their God;
His name is God-with-them.
He will wipe away all tears from their eyes;
there will be no more death,
and no more mourning and sadness.

40. The world of the past has gone.
Then the One sitting on the throne spoke:
"Now I am making the whole of creation new." (Rev 21:3-5)
Of this promise
and of this hopeful expectation

45. the choice for unmarried life is a special sign,
but only when herein becomes truly visible
real liberty and brotherhood.

In our mutual relationships we shall attempt
to be as palpable a realization as possible

50. of the Church, of the fellowship of men in Christ.
Wherever we may reside or meet each other
we ought to behave as real members of one family.[10]
This requires a human love
and solicitude for each other's well being

55. in an atmosphere of freedom and trust.
The sick and the aged among us
shall receive particular care.
A spirited community helps us[11]
to live our celibacy meaningfully.

---

[10]ER9; FA:ED I, 70-71.
[11]*Perfectae Caritatis* 12.

60. Wij behoren in ons samenzijn elkaar te steunen in het geloof,
dat de Heer in ons midden verblijft (Mt 18:20),
zodat wij trouw kunnen blijven aan onze roeping.
Deze onderlinge verbondenheid in lief en leed
zal ons sterken in de omgang met anderen,

65. In onze arbeid en geheel ons verkeer in de wereld.
Wanneer een zuster of broeder onze bijzondere hulp nodig heeft
in moeilijkheden, in zwakheid, bij ontrouw,
zullen wij ons bereid tonen die hulp van harte te verlenen (Gal 6:1-2).
Overeenkomstig Franciscus' uitdrukkelijke wens:

70. moeten wij er ons voor wachten
kwaad te worden om iemands zwakheden of zonden,
want dit is een belemmering voor de waarachtige liefde.

*evangelische armoede*

Als franciscaanse gemeenschap hopen wij ook in onze tijd

75. een profetische getuigenis af te leggen van de evangelische
armoede.
Wij zullen ons metterdaad tonen als mensen (1 Pt 2:11)
die op weg zijn naar hetgeen wij hopen,
nergens gevestigd en aan niets vastzittend.
Graag moeten wij bereid zijn van hetgeen wij hebben

80. royaal mee te delen aan anderen (Mt 25:40)
en gastvrij te ontvangen hen die ons bezoeken.
In dankbaarheid aanvaarden wij de aardse goederen
om ze te benutten tot vervulling van onze opdracht in de wereld.

Ons bezit mag niet meer omvatten dan wij nodig hebben

85. voor ons leven, onze behuizing en arbeid.
Er worden geen grotere reserves aangelegd dan noodzakelijk is.
Onze behuizing en wijze van wonen
moeten het kenmerk dragen van levenseenvoud.
Hetzelfde geldt voor onze kleding,

60. In our fellowship we ought to support one another in the belief
that the Lord dwells in our midst (Mt 18:20),
so that we may remain faithful to our calling.
This mutual concern in good and adverse times
will strengthen us in our relationships with others,

65. in our work and in all our contacts in the world.
Whenever a sister or brother requires our special help
in difficulties, in weakness, in fidelity,
we shall be prepared to render help if at all possible (Gal 6:1-2).
According to the express wish of Francis

70. we must avoid getting angry
at anyone's weaknesses or sins,
for this is a hindrance to true love.

*evangelical poverty*

As Franciscan community we hope to give

75. a prophetic witness also in our time to evangelical poverty.
We shall show ourselves to be men,
pilgrims on their way to the object of our hope (1Pt 2:11),
having no permanent home or attachment.[12]
We should be prepared to share gladly

80. with others what we ourselves possess (Mt 25:40)[13]
and to show hospitality to all who visit us.[14]
We accept earthly goods with gratitude
that we may use them in fulfillment of our earthly task.

Our possessions may not comprise more than we need

85. for our lives, our housing and our work.
Our reserves ought not to exceed the strictly necessary.
Our dwellings and way of living
must be characterized by simplicity.[15]
The same holds true for clothing,

---

[12]LR 6: FA:ED I, 103.
[13]*Perfectae Caritatis*, 13.
[14]*Perfectae Caritatis* 13.
[15]ER 2; LR 2; Test 4; FA:ED I, 64, 100, 124.

90. de middelen van vervoer,
de wijze waarop wij onze vakanties doorbrengen,
en voor geheel onze omgang met mensen van allerlei slag.

Voortdurend moeten wij er ook individueel op bedacht zijn,
hoe wij in onze tijd de evangelische armoede kunnen beleven.

95. In persoonlijke verantwoordelijkheid moet ieder
rekenschap kunnen afleggen van eigen geldgebruik.
Iedere aanwending en reservering
van inkomens, geschenken en erfenissen tot eigen baat
is uit den boze.

100. Want onze verbondenheid met elkaar
willen wij tot uitdrukking brengen
in gemeenschap van goederen
en zorg voor elkaar in het materiële.
Hierin volgen wij de leerlingenkring van Jezus na (Lk 8:1-3),

105. de eerste gemeente van Jeruzalem (Acts 4:32)
en de oorspronkelijke broederschap van Franciscus.


*belijdenis van de hoop*

Wij zijn ons ervan bewust dat dit leven
hoge eisen stelt aan onze gemeenschap

110. en aan ieder van ons afzonderlijk,
maar de aanwezigheid van de Heer, in wiens naam wij bijeen zijn,
schenkt ons het vertrouwen
dit leven met elkaar tot een goed einde te brengen.
"Want Hij die de belofte deed is betrouwbaar;


115. laten wij naar elkaar zien om te worden aangevuurd
tot liefde en goede werken,
en ons niet onttrekken aan de eigen gemeenschap,
zoals sommigen plegen te doen,
maar elkaar bemoedigen

120. en wel des te meer naarmate gij de dag des Heren ziet
naderen" (Heb 10:23-25).

90. the means of transportation,
the manner in which we spend our holidays,
and actualize our relationships with all types of people.

Also individually, we ought to be constantly mindful
how we can practice evangelical poverty in our times.

95. With our personal responsibility everyone should
give an account of the money spent.
Any appropriation or investment
of income, gifts or inheritance for one's own benefit
is to be rejected,

100. since our mutual bond
must find its expression
in the commonality of goods
and the material care for each other.
In this respect we imitate the circle of disciples around Jesus
    (Lk 8:1-3),

105. the first community of Jerusalem (Acts 4:32)
and the original brotherhood of Francis.[16]

*confession of hope*

We are aware that this life
makes strenuous demands upon our community

110. and upon each one of us individually,
but the presence of the Lord in whose name we are together
gives us the confidence
that we shall be able to bring this life with one another to a good
    conclusion.
"Because the one who made the promise is faithful,

115. let us be concerned for each other, to stir a response
in love and good works.
Do not stay away from the meetings of the community
as some do
but encourage each other to go:

120. the moreso as you see the day of the Lord drawing near"
    (Heb 10:23-25).

---

[16]ER 9; FA:ED I, 70-71.

Hoofdstuk III: Opbouw van onze gemeenschap

1. Samen dragen wij de verantwoordelijkheid[4]
voor de trouw aan onze evangelische levenswijze.
Ieder van ons wordt op goddelijke ingeving
tot dit leven geroepen

5. en door de Geest onderwezen tot opbouw van onze
    gemeenschap.
Elkaar respecterend en aanvullend
behartigen wij allen de gemeenschappelijke belangen.

*het kapittel*

Deze gezamenlijke verantwoordelijkheid

10. komt tot een duidelijk hoogtepunt
tijdens het kapittel,
dat bijeenkomt om onze idealen en belangen te bespreken.
Onze allereerste zorg daarbij moet zijn
de Geest, die waait waar Hij wil,

15. ruim de kans te geven
zijn woord tot ons te richten.
Daarom dient heel de gemeenschap zodanig
in de voorbereiding en de uitwerking
van het kapittel betrokken te worden,

20. dat werkelijk allen aan het beraad deelnemen.[5]

*leden van het kapittel*

Waar dit mogelijk is, wordt het kapittel gevormd
door allen die tot de gemeenschap behoren.
Een kapittel kan alleen dan zinvol zijn taak verrichten,

26. als het aantal deelnemers niet te groot is.
In grotere gemeenschappen wordt het kapittel daarom gevormd
door de leden van het bestuur
en door een in de statuten omschreven aantal gekozen leden.
Ook andere personen kunnen krachtens eigen statuten

---

[4]*Perfectae Caritatis* 14; *Ecclesiae Sanctae* 11, 18.
[5]*Ecclesiae Sanctae* 11, 2.

CHAPTER III: CONSTITUTION OF OUR COMMUNITY

1. Together we bear the responsibility
for the fidelity to our evangelical style of life.
Each one of us is called to this life
inspired by God

5. and taught by the Spirit to build up our community.[17]
Respecting and completing each other
we promote and are responsible for the communal interests.

*the chapter*

This communal responsibility

10. comes to a clear apogee
during chapter,
which gathers us to discuss our ideals and interests.
Our very first concern on that occasion should be
to give the Spirit, who blows where He wants,

15. ample chance
to direct his word to us.
Therefore the whole community
has to be enlisted in the preparation and execution
of the chapter in such a way,

20. that really all take part in the deliberations.

*members of the chapter*

Where possible, the chapter is formed
by all who belong to the community.
A chapter can only then fulfill its task meaningfully

26. when the number of participants is not too great.
In larger communities, the chapter therefore consists
of the members of the leadership body,
and by a number of chosen members as described in the statutes.
Also, other people can, by virtue of their own statutes

---

[17]2C 192; FA:ED II, 370-71.

30. rechtens aan het kapittel deelnemen,
maar steeds zó, dat toch tenminste de helft van het totaal
gekozen leden zijn.
Elke zuster en broeder, die professie gedaan heeft,
bezit het recht afgevaardigden voor het kapittel te kiezen

35. en kan als afgevaardigde gekozen worden.
Omtrent het actief en passief stemrecht
van de nog niet geprofeste leden
beslist het eigen kapittel of de statuten.
De keuze moet vrij en onbevooroordeeld zijn.

40. Men mag alleen letten op geschiktheid en bekwaamheid,
met uitsluiting van ieder ander motief.
De statuten geven aan op welke wijze de keuze zal geschieden.
Hierbij moet zoveel mogelijk rekening worden gehouden
met de opbouw en de spreiding van de gemeenschap.

45. De gekozen afgevaardigden blijven in functie
tot aan de dag waarop de leden van het nieuwe kapittel
bekend worden gemaakt.
Zo kunnen zij steeds in kapittel bijeenkomen,
wanneer het bestuur of een derde van het aantal kapittelleden

50. dit wenselijk acht.
De deelname van de kapittelleden uit het buitenland
wordt dan door hen in overleg met het bestuur geregeld.
Uiterlijk drie maanden voordat er een nieuw bestuur gekozen wordt,
vindt de keuze van de nieuwe afgevaardigden plaats.

55. Wanneer het kapittel nieuwe bestuursleden kiest,
worden deze aanstonds rechtens lid van het kapittel.
De aftredende bestuursleden blijven lid van het kapittel
tot aan de dag waarop de leden van het volgend kapittel
bekend worden gemaakt.


60. Waarnemers en deskundigen kunnen bij het kapittel
    aanwezig zijn,
uitgenodigd door het bestuur
of door het kapittel, met absolute meerderheid van stemmen.

30. take part in the chapter by right,
but always in such a way that at least half of participants
are chosen members.
Each sister or brother, who has made profession
has the right to choose representatives for the chapter,

35. and can be chosen as representative.
Concerning active and passive voting rights
of not-yet professed community members,
the decision lies with the community chapter or the statutes.
The choice has to be free and without prejudice.

40. One should pay attention only to suitability and capability,
to the exclusion of all other motives.
The statutes indicate in which way votes shall be cast.
In this, the composition and distribution of the community
should be taken into acount as much as possible.

45. The chosen representatives continue to function
until the day on which the new members of the new chapter
are proclaimed.
Thus they can always gather in chapter
when the leadership body or a third of the chapter members

50. think it wise to do so.
The participation of chapter members from foreign countries
will then be arranged in consultation with the leadership body.
At least three months before the new leadership body is chosen,
the choice of the new representatives takes place.

55. When the chapter chooses new members for the membership
     body,
these become by right immediately members of the chapter.
The retiring members of the leadership body remain members of
     the chapter
until the day on which the members of the new chapter
are proclaimed.

60. Observers and experts can be present at the chapter,
by invitation of the leadership body,
or by the chapter, with an absolute majority of votes.

*taak van het kapittel*

De trouw aan onze evangelische levenswijze vraagt, dat wij steeds

65. het ideaal en de feitelijkheid van ons leven aan elkaar toetsen.
Dit is de eerste en voornaamste taak van het kapittel.
Bovendien komt het aan het kapittel toe
zaken van algemeen belang te bespreken,
op basis van deze leefregel eigen statuten goed te keuren

70. en een bestuur te kiezen.
De leiding van het kapittel berust bij de overste.
Maar om vrijer aan de discussie te kunnen deelnemen
kan deze de leiding van het gesprek aan een ander toevertrouwen.
Het bestuur stelt de te volgen werkwijze en de agenda voor,


75. doch ook de kapittelleden kunnen hierover voorstellen doen.
Met absolute meerderheid van stemmen
neemt het kapittel dan een beslissing.
Eigen statuten worden op het kapittel van kracht.
wanneer met tweederde meerderheid van stemmen

80. de tekst of veranderingen hierin worden aanvaard.
Over andere zaken van algemeen belang kan het kapittel,
binnen de mogelijkheden van de leefregel en de eigen statuten,
met tweederde meerderheid van stemmen
bindende beslissingen nemen.

85. Het kapittel kan zich echter ook beperken
tot het bespreken van problemen en plannen
zonder bindende beslissingen te nemen,
maar met absolute meerderheid van stemmen
bepaalde aanbevelingen doen voor het bestuur,

90. waaraan de beslissing en concretisering wordt overgelaten.
De stemming over zaken zal als regel openbaar zijn.
tenzij de leiding van het kapittel een geheime stemming
    wenselijk acht
of deze door tenminste eenvierde deel van de leden wordt
    gevraagd.

*task of the chapters*

Fidelity to our evangelical way of life asks that we always

65. examine amongst each other the ideal and manifestation of
    our life.
This is the first and most important task of the chapter.
On top of this, it is for the chapter
to discuss matters of common interest,
to approve its own statutes on the basis of this rule of life,

70. and to elect a leadership body.
The direction of the chapter rests with the superior.
But to take part more freely in the discussion,
s/he can entrust the guidance of the discussion to another.
The leadership body proposes the operating procedure and the
    agenda,

75. yet the chapter members can also make proposals in this regard.
The decision is then taken by the chapter
with an absolute majority of votes.
Specific statutes become valid in chapter
when, with two-third majority of the votes,

80. the text or changes therein are accepted.
On other matters of common interest, the chapter,
within the possibilities of the rule of life and its own statutes,
can make binding decisions
with a two-third majority of the votes.

85. However, the chapter can also limit itself
to discussing problems and plans
without making binding decisions,
but with an absolute majority of votes
may make recommendations to the leadership body,

90. to which it leaves the decision and further implementation.
The vote on matters shall as a rule be public,
unless the leadership of the chapter deems it advisable to hold a
    secret ballot,
or when this is demanded by at least a quarter of the members.

*het bestuur*

95. De gemeenschap wordt geleid door het bestuur,
bestaande uit de overste en tenminste vier andere leden.
Zij worden door het kapittel gekozen voor drie jaar
en kunnen telkens voor drie jaar herkozen worden,
tenzij eigen statuten anders bepalen.

100. In hun keuze moeten alle kapittelleden
uitsluitend het welzijn der gemeenschap voor ogen hebben.
Tot overste en bestuurslid kunnen gekozen worden
zij die door professie tot de gemeenschap zijn toegetreden.
De keuze geschiedt door geheime stemming

105. en bij absolute meerderheid van stemmen,
volgens de gewone normen van het kerkelijk recht.
Wanneer bij de tweede stemming door geen kandidaat
de absolute meerderheid van stemmen is bereikt
wordt een derde stemming gehouden, waarin degene gekozen is,

110. die het grootste aantal stemmen behaalt.
Wanneer dit grootste aantal stemmen
door meer personen tegelijk wordt behaald,
is de jongste in leeftijd gekozen.
Het bestuurslid dat als eerste wordt gekozen

115. vervangt de overste bij diens afwezigheid.

De voornaamste taak van het bestuur is de zorg
voor de evangelische levenswijze van de gemeenschap.
Het zal daarom bijzondere aandacht schenken
aan de onderlinge verstandhouding van de zusters en broeders

120. en aan de samenstelling van de communiteiten.
Bovendien behartigt het, volgens de normen van de leefregel
en de statuten,
alle bestuurszaken van groter belang
en beslist daarover met meerderheid van stemmen.
Bij dit alles houdt het bestuur zich

125. aan de richtlijnen en beslissingen van het kapittel,
Het brengt ook verslag uit aan het kapittel
over het gevoerde beleid,
de stand van zaken en de plannen voor de toekomst.

*the leadership*

95. The community is guided by the leadership body,
consisting of a prior/superior and at least four other members.
They are chosen by the chapter for three years
and can each time be re-elected for three years,
unless its own statutes determine otherwise.

100. In their choice all chapter members should only
be concerned with the well-being of the community.
Those can be chosen to be prior or member of the leadership body
who have entered the community by making profession.
The choice takes place with a secret ballot

105. and with an absolute majority of votes,
in accordance with the normal rules of canon law.
When, with the second ballot, no candidate
has obtained an absolute majority of votes,
a third ballot is held, in which the candidate is chosen

110. who has received the largest number of votes.
When this highest number is obtained
by two or more persons at the same time,
the youngest in age is chosen.
The member of the leadership body who is chosen first

115. will replace the prior/superior during the absence of the latter.

The main task of the leadership body is the care
for the evangelical way of life of the community.
Hence it will pay special attention
to the mutual relationship between the sisters and brothers,

120. and to the composition of the communities.
In addition, it takes care of all governing issues of higher import,
in accordance with the norms of the rule of life
and the statutes,
and decides on those things with a majority vote.
In all of this, the leadership body adheres

125. to the guidelines and decisions of the chapter.
It also reports to the chapter
about its course of action,
the state of affairs and the plans for the future.

Wanneer werkzaamheden verdeeld worden

130. over de leden van het bestuur
berust de verantwoordelijkheid toch bij het gehele bestuur.
Het is raadzaam, dat het bestuur zich laat bijstaan
door deskundigen en commissies
die echter geen beslissingsbevoegdheid bezitten.

135. Het bestuur zal ook vergaderen
bijvoorbeeld met hen die de leiding hebben in de communiteiten
of met vertegenwoordigers van bepaalde werkzaamheden.
Deze bijeenkomsten kunnen dienen tot advies
bij het te voeren beleid.

140. De eventuele verhouding tussen
provinciaal en generaal kapittel en bestuur
wordt in eigen statuten geregeld.
Een norm hierbij dient te zijn
dat elke provincie voldoende zelfstandigheid heeft.


*de overste*


De overste staat aan het hoofd van het bestuur
en heeft als zodanig de hoogste verantwoordelijkheid
voor heel de gemeenschap.
Dit vraagt een grote mate van dienstbaarheid (Lk 22:26-27).

150. Alle zusters en broeders zullen
een welwillende openheid aan de dag leggen
voor de concrete beslissingen die door de overste
genomen worden in dienst van de gemeenschap.
Zij moeten daarom hun overste gehoorzamen

155. in alles wat niet in strijd is met hun geweten.
De zin van een voorschrift of besluit
zal de overste zo goed mogelijk verklaren,
tenzij er strikt persoonlijke factoren in het spel zijn
waaraan de overste geen ruchtbaarheid mag geven.

When tasks are divided

130. among the members of the leadership body,
the responsibility lies nevertheless
with the leadership body as a whole.It is advisable
that the leadership body takes counsel of experts
and committees,who will not have power of decision, however.

135. The leadership body will also hold meetings,
for instance with those who lead the communities,
or with representatives of specific activities.
These meetings can serve to obtain advice
regarding the policy direction.

140. The eventual relationship between the provincial and the general chapter and the leadership body is regulated in separate statutes. A guideline in this should be that each province has sufficient independence.

*the superior*

The Superior presides over the leadership body
and as such bears the highest responsibility
for the whole community (Lk 22:26-27).
This requires a high disposition for service.[18]

150. All sisters and brothers shall show an eager acceptance
of the concrete decisions of the Superior
made in the interest of the community.
Therefore they ought to obey their superiors

155. in everything not contrary to their conscience.[19]
The superior will explain the reason behind an obligation
or a decision to the best of his abilities,
unless strictly personal factors are at play
which the superior cannot divulge.

---

[18]ER 4; LR 10; FA:ED I, 66-67; 105.
[19]LR 10; FA:ED I, 105.

160. Tot de voornaamste taken van de overste behoort
de behartiging van de persoonlijke belangen
van de zusters of broeders.
Allen moeten, vooral in ernstige persoonlijke aangelegenheden,
hun toevlucht kunnen nemen tot hun overste.

165. Aan belangrijke beslissingen hen betreffende zal,
indien enigszins mogelijk, een gesprek voorafgaan.
De overste zal regelmatig alle huizen bezoeken
en persoonlijk contact hebben met alle zusters of broeders,
zich op de hoogte stellen van hun situatie en arbeid

170. en hun zoveel mogelijk belangstelling en hulp geven.
Ook zal de overste bijzondere zorg besteden
aan degenen die in andere landen werken
en hen regelmatig bezoeken.

Bovendien heeft de overste tot taak te zorgen[6]

175. dat de nodige contacten worden onderhouden
met andere religieuze groeperingen.

*vergadering van de oversten*

Regelmatig komen de oversten van de franciscaanse gemeenschap
in vergadering bijeen.

180. Het streven hierbij is
tot grotere samenwerking en eenheid te geraken.
Samen zullen zij zich bezinnen
op de beleving en vormgeving van ons evangelisch leven.
Wanneer de goedkeuring van de leefregel

185. of van veranderingen in de tekst aan de orde is,
bezitten alleen de stemgerechtigde oversten
een beslissende stem.
De overste kan alleen dan in naam van de eigen gemeenschap
aan deze beslissende stemming deelnemen

190. wanneer het kapittel zich over de tekst heeft uitgesproken,
of tenminste aan de overste volmacht heeft verleend zich
bij de tweederde meerderheid van de vergadering aan te sluiten.
Wanneer echter een groepering in provincies is verdeeld,
heeft het kapittel bovendien de instemming nodig

---

[6]*Perfectae Caritatis* 22-23.

160. Among most important tasks of the superior
pertain the promotion of the personal interests
of the sisters and the brothers.
All should be able, especially in serious personal matters,
to seek refuge with their superior.

165. Important decisions concerning them will,
if possible, take place after their consultation.
The superior shall visit all the houses regularly
and have personal contact with all sisters and brothers.
The superior ought to be informed of their situation and work,

170. and give them attention and aid whenever possible.
The superior shall also show particular care
to those who work in other countries
and visit them regularly.

In addition, the superior has the task to provide

175. for the maintenance of sufficient contacts
with other religious groups.

*meeting of the superiors*

The superiors of the franciscan communities
regularly come together in meetings.

180. The aspiration in this is
to reach higher levels of collaboration and unity.
Together they will reflect
on the experience and the expression of our evangelical life.
When the approval of the rule

185. or changes of the text are at play,
only superiors qualified to vote
have a deciding voice.
The superior can only then, in name of his own community,
take part in this deciding vote,

190. when the chapter has voiced its opinion on the text,
or at least has given the superior permission
to join the two-third majority of the meeting.
When, however, a group is divided in provinces,
the chapter also needs the permission

195. van het generaal kapittel of bestuur.
Wanneer de leefregel of latere veranderingen hierin
door tweederde meerderheid van stemgerechtigde oversten
zijn aanvaard en bekrachtigd,
en voor zover nodig door de kerkelijke leiding zijn bevestigd,

200. worden de herders van de Kerk
in het gebied waar men woont en werkt
hiervan op de hoogte gesteld.

*de communiteiten*

De plaatselijke communiteiten bestaan uit

205. tenminste drie zusters of broeders.
Daar waar meer kleinere groepen
in dezelfde streek of stad gevestigd zijn,
of waar personen afzonderlijk wonen,
verdient het aanbeveling regionale communiteiten te vormen.

210. De leden van deze regionale communiteiten
zullen regelmatig contact met elkaar onderhouden.
Tenminste éénmaal per maand moeten allen
gedurende één volle dag samenkomen
voor gebed en eucharistieviering,

215. voor gesprek en gezellig samenzijn.
Er kunnen ook communiteiten worden gevormd
van zusters of broeders van verschillende congregaties,
wanneer de onderlinge verbondenheid
en de vruchtbaarheid van het werk daarmee zijn gediend.

220. De zusters of broeders die de leiding hebben van de
      communiteiten,
worden door het bestuur voor drie jaar benoemd.
Zij kunnen meermalen voor drie jaar worden herbenoemd,
indien het bestuur dit, in overleg met de communiteit,
      wenselijk acht.
In grotere communiteiten, nader te omschrijven door het bestuur,

225. wordt door het huiskapittel,
waarvan alle huisgenoten deel uitmaken,
een plaatselijke raad gekozen
volgens de gewone normen van het kerkelijk recht en deze
      leefregel.
Deze keuze vindt plaats

195. of the general chapter or the leadership body.
When the rule of life or later changes therein
are accepted and confirmed with a two-third majority
of superiors qualified to vote,
and, if necessary, is reconfirmed by the ecclesiastical leadership,

200. the sheperds of the Church
in the region in which one lives and works
are notified.

*the communities*

The local communities consist of

205. at least three sisters or brothers.
Where more smaller communities exist
in the same region or town,
or where persons live separately,
it is advisable to create regional communities.

210. The members of these regional communities
will stay in touch on a regular basis.
At least once a month they must all come together
one full day
for prayer and the celebration of the eucharist,

215. for conversation and companionship.
It is also possible to form communities
of sisters or brothers of different congregations,
when the mutual connectedness
and the effectiveness of labor is served by it.

220. The sisters or brothers who lead the communities
will be appointed by the leadership body for three years.
They can be re-appointed for three years multiple times,
when the leadership body considers this advisable, in consultation
    with the community.
In larger communities, to be described more specifically by the
    leadership body,

225. the house chapter,
in which all house members participate,
chooses a local council,
in accordance with the normal guidelines of canon law and this
    rule of life.
This choice takes place

230. telkens wanneer de plaatselijke leiding is benoemd of
    herbenoemd.
Degene die de leiding heeft van de communiteit
moet aandacht hebben voor de persoonlijke belangen
van de zusters of broeders,
voor de goede sfeer in huis

235. en is verantwoordelijk voor de dagelijkse gang van zaken.
Bij meer gewichtige aangelegenheden
en in zaken in de eigen statuten vastgesteld,
zal deze het advies inwinnen van de communiteit
en, in grotere communiteiten, van de plaatselijke raad.

240. Tenminste éénmaal in de drie maanden
worden alle leden in huiskapittel bijeengeroepen
ter bespreking van het wel en wee van de communiteit.
Ieder kan hier voorstellen doen.
Alleen bij ingrijpende vragen

245. moet het bestuur geraadpleegd worden.

230. each time the local leadership is appointed or
    reappointed.
Those who leads the community
must pay attention to the personal interests
of the sisters or brothers,
to the good atmosphere in the house,

235. and is responsible for the daily affairs.
In more weighty issues,
and in cases called for in the community statutes,
s/he will ask the advice of the community
and, in larger communities, of the local council.

240. At least once every three months
all members are convened in a house chapter,
to discuss the situation of the community.
At these meetings everyone can make proposals.
However, in fundamental questions

245. the leadership must be consulted.

## Hoofdstuk IV: Arbeid en vrijetijdsbesteding

1. Ieders leven houdt van Godswege een opdracht in
om te werken aan eigen geluk,
zo te komen tot ontplooiing van zichzelf
en mee te werken aan de vooruitgang van de gehele mensheid.[7]

*5. arbeid*

Gezamenlijke arbeid,
waarbij men verwachtingen en teleurstellingen,
verlangens en vreugden samen deelt,
brengt de mensen tot elkaar.

10. Bij het samen verrichten van het werk
leren zij elkaar zien als zusters en broeders.[8]

Degenen van ons aan wie de Heer de genade geeft om te werken,
moeten trouw en toegewijd hun taak verrichten.
De arbeid is bij uitstek geschikt

15. om ons in te zetten voor het geluk van de medemens,
de ons geschonken talenten te benutten
en hierin echte levensvreugde te ervaren.
Bij alles wat wij doen,
zal attentie en zorg voor anderen voorop moeten staan,

20. en zullen wij bedacht moeten zijn
op een goede verstandhouding met al degenen, met wie wij
samenwerken.
Ieder van ons moet bereid zijn,
overeenkomstig deskundigheid en geschiktheid
en volgens het oordeel van de overste,

25. elke taak binnen onze gemeenschap of daarbuiten
op zich te nemen.
Om deze taak zo goed mogelijk te kunnen verrichten,
moeten wij ons hierop degelijk voorbereiden
en door voortdurende aandacht, studie en vorming

---

[7]*Populorum Progressio* 15.
[8]*Populorum Progressio* 17, 27.

CHAPTER IV: WORK AND LEISURE

1. Everyone's life contains the God-given task
to work for one's own happiness,
in order to arrive at the development of self
and to collaborate in the progress of the whole of humanity.

5. *work*

Communal work
in which we share with one another our expectations and
disappointments, desires and joys,
brings people together.

10. In the common effort of the work
they learn to regard one another as sisters and brothers.

Those to whom the Lord has given the grace to work,
must perform their work faithfully and with devotion.[20]
Labor is the pre-eminent way to engage[21]

15. ourselves for the happiness of our fellowmen,
to make use of the talents given us
and to experience authentic joy of life in this.
In all that we do,
attention and concern for others should be primary.

20. It should be our constant care
to remain on good terms with those with whom we work.
Each one of us must be prepared
according to his expertise and aptitude
and the judgment of the superior

25. to accept every task
both within and without our community.
In order to accomplish this task as well as possible
we must receive a thorough preparation
and through a constant attention, study and education

---

[18]ER 4; LR 10; FA:ED I, 66-67; 105.

[19]LR 10; FA:ED I, 105.

30. op de hoogte blijven van de eisen welke deze aan ons stelt.
Het is wenselijk dat leef- en werkmilieu gescheiden zijn.
Wat de arbeidstijd en arbeidsvoorwaarden betreft
zal men zich aanpassen aan het maatschappelijk arbeidsbestel.
Wij zullen elkaar zoveel mogelijk helpen

35. bij de noodzakelijk werkzaamheden binnen onze gemeenschap.

De besturen zowel als de leden zullen ervoor zorgen,
dat er tussen de verschillende congregaties
een gezonde samenwerking bestaat.

Wanneer de herders van de Kerk ons vragen

40. voor bepaalde werkzaamheden op charitatief of pastoraal
    terrein
zullen wij hierop naar ons beste vermogen antwoorden.[9]
Ofschoon in beginsel alle arbeid geschikt is,
zullen wij toch uitzien naar die werkterreinen
waar het sterkst een beroep op ons wordt gedaan

45. en waar wij het best van dienst kunnen zijn.
Daarom dienen wij ons voortdurend te bezinnen op de arbeid
die wij op ons genomen hebben,
steeds bereid bepaalde taken op te geven
en nieuwe aan te nemen als de veranderde situatie dat vraagt.

50. Wanneer voor onverwachte en kortstondige noden
onze hulp wordt ingeroepen,
zullen wij zo goed mogelijk hieraan beantwoorden.
Bij dit alles zullen wij de woorden van Jezus Chrlstus ter
    harte nemen:
"Wanneer ge alles hebt gedaan wat u opgedragen werd,

55. zegt dan: wij zijn maar armzalige knechten,
want we hebben alleen maar onze plicht gedaan" (Lk 7:10).

---

[9]*Ecclesiae Sanctae* 1, 36.

30. keep in touch with the demands which this task imposes
    upon us.
It is desirable that work and living quarters be separate.
As far as the time and conditions of work are concerned,
the communities shall adapt themselves to the current social
    norms for labor.
We shall help each other as much as possible

35. with the necessary work within our own communities.

The leadership as well as the members shall take care
that a healthy cooperation shall exist
among the various congregations.

When the pastors of the Church ask us

40. for particular activities of a charitable or pastoral nature
we shall fulfill this request to the best of our ability.
Although in principle any work is suitable,
we shall be on the lookout for those fields of activity
where the need is greatest

45. and where we can best render our services.
For that reason we ought to reflect constantly upon the work
that we have taken upon ourselves,
and take on other work
as the changing situation demands.

50. When our help is requested
for unexpected and short-term needs
we shall respond if possible.
And in all this we shall keep in mind the words of Jesus Christ:
"When you have done all you have been told to do

55. say, we are merely servants:
we have done no more than our duty" (Lk 17:10).[22]

---

[22]ER 11; FA:ED I, 72-73.

*vrijetijdsbesteding*

85. Ieder van ons moet kunnen beschikken
over voldoende vrije tijd en vakantie.[12]
Hierbij moet ruimte geboden worden
aan persoonlijke interesse en ontwikkeling,
eenvoudig en sober zoals ons past.

90. Deze vrije tijd is bij uitstek geschikt
om zich te ontspannen en op krachten te komen,
voor het gezellig samenzijn met elkaar,
voor contacten met familie en kennissen.

---

[12]*Ecclesiae Sanctae* 11, 26.

*leisure time*

85. Each one of us should have
sufficient leisure time and holidays.
In this respect there must be room
for personal interests and development,
but with the simplicity and frugality that befits us.

90. Leisure time is pre-eminently suitable
to relax and restore our energies,
to find conviviality with one another,
to renew contacts with the family and acquaintances.

HOOFDSTUK V: GEBEDSGEMEENSCHAP

1. Naar het voorbeeld van de Kerk uit de eerste tijd,
waarin de velen één van hart en één van ziel waren (Acts 4:32),
moeten ook wij volharden in het geloof,
in het breken van het brood en in het gebed (Acts 2:42).

5. Zo ervaren wij ons als Kerk van Christus.
Hij heeft immers gezegd:
"Waar twee of drie in mijn naam samenkomen
daar ben Ik in hun midden" (Mt 18:20).
Ons geloof hierin maken wij ons vooral bewust door te bidden.

10. De bruidsverhouding van de Kerk tot haar Heer
vindt daarin haar uitdrukking en haar kracht.

Het middelpunt van ons leven en bidden
is de viering van de eucharistie.
Daarin stellen wij ons alledaagse leven

15. in het teken van Christus,
bereid de wil van de Vader te volbrengen (Jn 6:38).
Wij komen samen rond de tafel des Heren (Phil 2:8)
om het woord Gods te horen en te beamen
en het lichaam en bloed van Christus te ontvangen (Mk 14:36)

20. tot vergeving van zonden (Mt 26:28),
versterking van levenskracht (Jn 6:35).
en als voorschot op het eeuwig leven (Eph 1:14; 1 Cor 11:26).
Al ons bidden gedurende de dag,
vooral het gemeenschappelijk verrichte gebed,

25. sluit hierop aan en bereidt ons erop voor.
Het gemeenschappelijk gebed moet zo geregeld worden,
dat allen er regelmatig aan kunnen deelnemen.
Het is waardevol voor onze gehele orde,
dat in bepaalde communiteiten

30. aan gebed en beschouwing
zeer bijzondere aandacht wordt besteed.

CHAPTER V: COMMUNITY OF PRAYER

1. After the example of the primitive Church
in which all were of one heart and one mind (Acts 4:32),
also we must persevere in the faith,
in the breaking of the bread and in prayer (Acts 2:42).

5. Thus we experience ourselves as the Church of Christ.
For he has said:
"Where two or three meet in my name,
I shall be there with them" (Mt 18:20).
Our faith in this we make conscious in us through prayer.

10. The bridal relationship of the Church with the Lord
finds there its expression and its force.

The heart of our life and prayer
is the celebration of the Eucharist.
Through this we put our daily life

15. in union with Christ,
ready to fulfill the will of the Father (Jn 6:38).
We gather round the table of the Lord (Phil 2:8)
to listen to the Word of God and to give our assent to it,
and to receive the body and blood of Christ (Mk 14:36)

20. for the forgiveness of sins (Mt 26:28),
for the reinforcement of our vital strength (Jn 6:35),
and as a foretaste of eternal life (Eph 1:14; 1 Cor 11:26).
All our prayers during the day,
especially our communal prayers,

25. ensue from it and prepare us for it.
Our communal prayer should be arranged in such a way
that all can regularly take part in it.
It is of great value to our entire Order
that in certain communities

30. special attention should be paid
to prayer and contemplation.

Samen met de heiligen en met allen die op God vertrouwen,
zeggen wij Hem dank voor zijn grote daden
en leggen wij Hem onze noden en die van alle mensen voor.

35. Onze omgang met elkaar, onze arbeid, ons verkeer met
    de mensen
en heel het wereldgebeuren
zullen wij in ons gebed betrekken.
Ook onze gestorven medezusters en -broeders,
familieleden en alle overledenen

40. gedenken wij in onze gebeden.
Maria, de moeder van de Heer (Lk 1:38; 46),
is voor ons een volmaakt voorbeeld van overgave en trouw;
wij willen haar bijzonder vereren.
Gemeenschappelijk en persoonlijk gebed ondersteunen elkaar

45. en putten beide uit de heilige schrift[13]
en de volheid van het christelijk mysterie.
Daarom moet de bijbellezing een vaste gewoonte zijn
en de liturgische beleving van het kerkelijk jaar alle aandacht
    krijgen.
Om de geest van gebed,

50. waaraan al het overige dienstbaar moet zijn,
in onze arbeid en in onze gebedsoefeningen te bewaren,
moet de persoonlijke bezinning ons bijzonder ter harte gaan.[14]
Wij moeten elkaar hierin helpen en sterken.
Daarom is het goed dat we zo nu en dan hierover spreken

55. en elkaar tot gebed opwekken.
Dit contact met elkaar kan ons helpen
om persoonlijk te blijven bidden
en zal ook het gemeenschappelijk gebed ten goede komen.
Door deze bezinning op ons leven

---

[13] Perfectae Caritatis 6.
[14] Ecclesiae Sanctae 11, 21.

Together with the saints and with those who put their trust in God
we express our thanks to Him for His mighty deeds
and place before Him our needs and those of all men.

35. Our mutual association, our work, our relationships
        with people
and the totality of world events—
all this shall be drawn into our prayer.
We remember in our prayers
also our deceased fellow sisters and brothers,

40. members of our family and all the dead.
Mary, the mother of the Lord (Lk 1:38; 46),
is for us the perfect example of surrender and fidelity;
we want, therefore, to honor her in particular.
Communal and personal prayer support one another

45. and both find their source in Sacred Scripture
and the fullness of the Christian Mystery.
Therefore, reading of scripture should be an established custom
and the liturgical celebration of the ecclesiastical year should
        receive full attention.
In order to retain the spirit of prayer,

50. to which all the rest ought to be subservient,[25]
in our labor and in our prayer,
personal reflection must also receive an appropriate place.
Herein we ought to help and strengthen one another.
Therefore, it would seem a good practice to bring the topic
        of prayer
into our discussions from time to time,

55. and to stimulate one another to prayer.
This contact with one another can help us
to keep up the practice of personal prayer.
This will be for the good of communal life as well.
In our reflection upon our life

---

[25]LR 10; FA:ED I, 105.

60. zullen wij ons ook bewust blijven
van onze ontoereikendheid en zondigheid (Lk 17:10).
Daarom erkennen wij de noodzaak
van een voortdurende bekering en vernieuwing (Eph 4:23)
en zullen wij regelmatig het sacrament van boetvaardigheid
    ontvangen.

65. Het gemeenschappelijk gebed en de persoonlijk bezinning
vragen om een sfeer van rust en stilte
waarin ieder tot zichzelf kan komen (Mt 6:6).
Rust en stilte zoeke men niet enkel voor zichzelf,
maar moet men ook aan anderen gunnen

70. en voor hen mogelijk maken.
Aparte dagen en tijden van bezinning zijn eveneens nodig
om gevoelig te blijven voor de heilige Geest.

60. we shall also remain conscious
of our shortcomings and our sinfulness (Lk 17:10).
For that reason we recognize the necessity
of constant conversion and renewal (Eph 4:23)
and we shall regularly receive the sacrament of penance.[26]

65. Our communal prayer and personal reflection
demand an atmosphere of peace and quiet
in which everyone can find her or himself (Mt 6:6).
Peace and quiet are not to be sought for oneself alone,
but others are entitled to it as well

70. and we should make it possible for them.
Days and times set aside for reflection are also necessary
in order to remain sensitive to the inspiration of the Holy Spirit.

---

[26]1C 103; FA:ED I, 272-73.

## Hoofdstuk VI: Inleiding in onze gemeenschap

1. Wanneer iemand zich tot onze gemeenschap aangetrokken voelt
en zich bij ons meldt,
zal men de nodige informaties inwinnen en
als deze voldoen, de kandidaat de gelegenheid bieden

5. ons leven nader te leren kennen.
De duur van deze wederzijdse kennismaking
kan van persoon tot persoon verschillen,
maar zal als regel niet langer zijn dan één jaar.
Men kan de kandidaat over eigen geld en goederen laten
     beschikken

10. en deze zal, als het gewenst is,
beroepsopleiding of taak in de maatschappij voortzetten.
Als de kandidaat het verlangen uit
ons leven geheel te delen,
zal het bestuur hierover beslissen

15. na advies van de communiteit gevraagd te hebben.

De toetreding tot onze gemeenschap vindt plaats
in een kerkelijke viering,
waarin de kandidaten uiting geven aan hun wil
zich voor te bereiden op de professie

20. en waarin zij als nieuwe leden worden aanvaard.
In deze tijd van voorbereiding
moeten zij voldoende gelegenheid krijgen
door bezinning op eigen leven en taak,
door gebed en studie,

25. zich hun levensroeping in onze gemeenschap eigen te maken.
Naast godsdienstige vorming is ook ontwikkeling wenselijk
op cultureel, sociaal en huishoudelijk gebied.
In alles zullen zij zich aansluiten
bij de geldende normen van onze gemeenschap.

30. De bijzondere verantwoordelijkheid voor henberust bij degene,
     die hiertoe door het bestuur is aangewezen.

## CHAPTER VI: ENTRANCE IN OUR COMMUNITY

1. When someone feels attracted to our community
and asks to be accepted,
the necessary information shall be obtained and
if this is satisfactory, the candidate will be offered the opportunity

5. to become acquainted with our way of life.
The duration of this mutual acquaintance
can differ from person to person,
but will, as a rule, take no longer than one year.
The candidate will be allowed to dispose of his or his own money
and property

10. and if it is desirable
she or he will continue in vocational training or activity in society.
If the candidate expresses the desire
to share our life completely,
the leadership body shall make the final decision

15. after consulting the community.

The entrance into our community takes place
in an ecclesiastical celebration,
in which the candidates express their will
to form themselves in our way of life

20. and in which they are accepted as new members.
In this time of preparation,
they must receive sufficient opportunity,
through reflection on their own life and task,
through prayer and study,

25. to appropriate for themselves their calling in our community.
Aside from religious formation, development is also desirable
in cultural, social and domestic areas.
In everything they will adhere
to the current norms of our community.

30. A special responsibility for them lies with the person
appointed to this task by the leadership body.

Wanneer zij door hun professie
definitief tot de gemeenschap wensen toe te treden,
zal het bestuur hierover beslissen

35. na het advies gevraagd te hebben
van degene die speciaal verantwoordelijk is voor hun vorming
en van de betreffende communiteiten.
Deze definitieve binding zal als regel
op zijn vroegst vier jaar en op zijn laatst acht jaar

40. na de toetreding tot de gemeenschap plaatsvinden.

Ook aan personen die zich niet vast aan de gemeenschap wensen
te binden,
kan gelegenheid gegeven worden voor enige tijd
het leven van de gemeenschap te delen
en met ons samen te werken.

45. Tevoren moet een overeenkomst zijn aangegaan
waarin wederzijdse rechten en plichten staan omschreven.
Wij allen die beloofd hebben deze leefregel te onderhouden
zullen ons daarop niet beroemen,
maar de woorden van Paulus indachtig zijn:

50. "Niet dat ik het reeds bereikt heb
of al volmaakt zou zijn,
maar met alle macht streef ik ernaar het te grijpen,
gegrepen als ik ben door Jezus Christus.
Heus. broeders, ik beeld mij niet in het al gegrepen te hebben;

55. alleen dit:
zonder te tellen wat achter mij ligt,
werp ik mij voorwaarts en ijl naar het doel:
de kampprijs van Gods hemelse roeping.
Laten wij, als volwassenen in het geloof, er zo over denken;

60 en als gij op een of ander punt anders denkt,
zal God u ook daarin zijn licht geven.
Laten wij in ieder geval op de ingeslagen weg voortgaan"
(Phil 3:12-16).

De Heer zegene en beware u,
Hij tone u zijn aanschijn
en ontferme zich over u
en geve u vrede.

When they, through making their profession,
want to join our community permanently,
the leadership body will make a decision

35. after asking advice
of the person who is particularly responsible for their formation,
and of the communities in question.
This permanent bond will, as a rule,
take place at the earliest four years and at the latest eight years

40. after joining the community.


To people who do not want to bind themselves
permanently to the community,
the opportunity for some time
to share community life,
and to collaborate with us can be given.

45. In advance, an agreement must be made
in which mutual rights and obligations are described.
All of us who have promised to observe this rule of life
shall not take pride in it,
but shall remember the words of Paul:

50. "Not that I have already succeeded
or am already made perfect,
but I keep striving to win the prize
for which Jesus Christ has already won me to himself.
Brothers, I do not consider myself as having already won it;

55. but keep only this in mind:
forgetting what is behind me,
I strain forward to the things ahead and race to the goal:
God's heavenly call.
Let us, as adults in the faith, think of it like that;

60. but if you think differently on one or another point,
God will make this clear to you.
In any case, let us go forward on the road we have taken"
        (Phil 3:12-16).


May the Lord bless and guard you,
May He show you his face
And have mercy of you
And give you peace.

### Règle de Vie des Soeurs de l'Ordre de Saint François Comité Franciscain, France-Belgique, 1972

**I. Au nom du Seigneur commence la vie des soeurs de l'Ordre de Saint François**

1. La forme de vie des Soeurs de l'Ordre de S. François est la suivante: observer le saint Évangile de notre Seigneur Jésus-Christ en vivant en obéissance, "sans propre" et en chasteté.[1]

2. Les Soeurs promettent obéissance et respect à l'Église en la personne du Pape et des Évêques. Elles sont tenues d'obéir aux Soeurs à qui l'Église confie le service de la Fraternité.[2]

3. Afin de rester fidèles à la grâce de leur vocation, les Soeurs maintiendront vivant le lien fraternel qui les rattache à toute la famille franciscaine.

**II. De celles qui veulent partager cette vie et de la manière de les recevoir**

4. Celle qui, sous l'inspiration du Seigneur, vient à nous dans l'intention de partager cette vie, sera accueillie avec bonté.[3] En temps voulu, elle sera présentée aux Supérieures qui, seules, ont le pouvoir d'admettre dans la Fraternité.[4]

5. Les Supérieures s'assureront qu'elle adhère véritablement à la foi et à la vie de l'Église. Si elle croit tout cela et qu'elle soit décidée à le professer fidèlement et à l'observer courageusement jusqu'au bout; si par ailleurs, étant libre de tout empêchement, elle est reconnue apte à mener cette vie, on lui exposera avec soin à quoi celle-ci nous engage. Si elle persévère dans son désir, on lui dira la parole du saint Évangile: *Va, vends tout ce que tu as, distribue-le aux pauvres et tu auras un trésor aux cieux; puis viens, suis-moi* (Mt 19:21). Si elle ne peut le faire, l'intention vraie suffira.[5]

---

[1]LR 1:1.
[2]LR 1:2-3.
[3]ER 2:1.
[4]LR 2:1.
[5]LR 2:2-6; FLCl 2.

## RULE AND LIFE OF THE SISTERS OF THE ORDER OF SAINT FRANCIS
### FRANCISCAN COMMITTEE, FRANCE-BELGIUM, 1972

### I. IN THE NAME OF THE LORD HERE BEGINS THE LIFE OF THE SISTERS OF THE ORDER OF ST. FRANCIS.

1. The form of life of the Sisters of the Order of St. Francis is as follows to observe the holy Gospel of our Lord Jesus Christ through living in obedience without property and in chastity.[1]

2. The Sisters promise obedience and reverence to the Church in the Person of the Pope and of the Bishops. They are bound to obey the Sisters on whom the Church has bestowed the service of the Fraternity.[2]

3. In order to remain faithful to the grace of their vocation, the Sisters will keep living the fraternal bond which makes them members of the Franciscan family.

### II. FOR THOSE WHO WANT TO SHARE THIS LIFE AND HOW THEY SHOULD BE RECEIVED

4. She, who through the Lord's inspiration, comes to us with the intention of sharing this life, will be welcomed with kindness.[3] When the time comes, she will be presented to the superiors who alone have the power to admit to the Fraternity.[4]

5. The superiors must take pains to find out whether or not she really holds fast to faith and to the life of the Church. If she believes and is determined to profess this faithfully and to observe it resolutely to the end; if, in addition, being free from every impediment, she is considered apt for this way of life, then the tenor and the content of it must be clearly explained to her. Should she persevere in her desire, then let the words of the Gospel be told her: "Go sell all that you own and distribute the money to the poor, and you will have treasure in Heaven: then come follow me" (Mt 19:21). If she is unable to do this, it shall suffice if she has the right intention to do so.[5]

---

[1] LR 1:1. FA:ED I, 100.
[2] LR 1:2-3; FA:ED I, 100.
[3] ER 2:1; FA:ED I, 64.
[4] LR 2:1; FA:ED I, 100.
[5] LR 2:2-6; FA:ED I, 100. FLCl 2; CA:ED, 110-12.

6. Pour ce qui regarde la disposition de ses biens, les Supérieures et les Soeurs la laisseront faire librement ce que le Seigneur lui inspirera. Si toutefois elle demande conseil, les Supérieures pourront l'envoyer à quelques personnes ayant le sens des choses de Dieu, d'après l'avis desquelles elle pourra distribuer ses biens aux pauvres.[6]

7. Après le temps de probation, elle sera reçue à l'obéissance, promettant, sans esprit de retour, d'observer cette vie et cette règle, puisque, selon le saint Évangile, *celui qui met la main à la charrue et regarde en arrière n'est pas apte au royaume de Dieu* (Lk 9:62).[7]

8. Ne cherchant plus les habits coûteux de ce monde afin d'avoir un vêtement dans le royaume des cieux,[8] elle ne portera désormais, en signe de conversion à la vie évangélique, que des vêtements simples et pauvres, sans recherche, adaptés aux lieux et aux temps, car le Seigneur a dit: "*Ceux qui portent de somptueux vêtements et vivent dans le luxe* (Lk 7:25) *sont dans les maisons des rois*" (Mt 11:8).[9]

9. Et les Soeurs se souviendront de l'exhortation de François à ses Frères: "Je les avertis et les exhorte de ne pas mépriser et de ne pas juger ceux qu'ils voient porter des vêtements de luxe et user de boissons et de mets recherchés; mais plutôt que chacun se juge et se méprise soi-même".[10]

**III. De la louange divine, du jeûne, et comment les soeurs doivent aller par le monde**

10. S'attachant aux paroles, à la vie, à la doctrine et au saint Évangile de Celui qui a daigné prier pour nous son Père et nous révéler son Nom,[11] les Soeurs célébreront l'Office divin selon l'usage et les directives de la sainte Église. Partout, en tout lieu, à toute heure et en tout temps, qu'elles croient d'une foi véritable et humble et qu'elles gardent en leur coeur, aiment, honorent, servent, louent, bénissent et glorifient le Très-Haut et Souverain Dieu Éternel, Père, Fils et Saint-Esprit.[12]

---

[6]LR 2:7-8.

[7]LR 2:11-13.

[8]ER 2:17.

[9]ER 2:15.

[10]LR 2:17.

[11]ER 22:38.

[12]ER 23:11.

6. The Superiors and the Sisters will leave her free to dispose of her goods as the Lord may inspire her. If, however, she asks for advice, the superiors may direct her to some persons who have an understanding of the things of God, according to whose counsel she may distribute her goods to the poor.[6]

7. When the time of probation is ended, she is to be received to obedience, promising, with no reservations, to observe this life and this Rule because according to the holy Gospel: "Once the hand is laid to the plow, no one who looks back is fit for the reign of God" (Lk 9:62).[7]

8. "She will no longer seek to have costly garments in this world" so as "to have them in the Kingdom of heaven."[8] Because of her conversion to the evangelical life her clothing henceforth will be modest, simple and poor; in keeping with (or adapted to) times and places, for the Lord said: "Those who go in for fine clothes and live luxuriously (Lk 7:28) are to be found in royal courts" (Mt 11:8).[9]

9. On the other hand, the Sisters would do well to keep in mind Francis's admonition to his brothers: "I caution the friars and beg them not to look down upon or pass judgment on those whom they see wearing luxurious clothes and enjoying the choicest food and drink, but rather let each one judge and despise himself."[10]

**III. THE LITURGY OF THE HOURS AND OF FASTING: AND OF THE WAY THE SISTERS SHOULD GO ABOUT IN THE WORLD.**

10. Holding fast to the words, the life, the teaching and to the holy Gospel of Him who deigned to pray for us to His Father and revealed to us His Name,[11] the Sisters will celebrate the Divine Office according to the usages and directions of the Holy Church.

Everywhere in every place, at every hour, at every time they must have a true and humble faith, guarding their hearts, loving, honoring, serving, praising blessing and glorifying the Most High, Sovereign and Eternal God, Father, Son and Holy Spirit.[12]

---

[6]LR 2:7-8; FA:ED I, 100-101.

[7]LR 2:11-13; FA:ED I, 101.

[8]ER 2:15; FA:ED I, 65.

[9]ER 2:15; FA:ED I, 65.

[10]LR 2:17; FA:ED I, 101.

[11]ER 22:38; FA:ED I, 81.

[12]ER 23:11; FA:ED I, 85 .

11. Que les Soeurs témoignent aussi profond respect et grand honneur qu'elles pourront au Corps et au Sang très saints de notre Seigneur Jésus-Christ, en qui tout ce qu'il y a dans le ciel et sur la terre a été pacifié et réconcilié (Col 1:21) au Dieu Tout-Puissant.[13]

12. C'est pourquoi elles participeront au véritable sacrifice de notre Seigneur Jésus-Christ dans une intention sainte et pure. Que toute leur volonté, soutenue par la grâce du Tout-Puissant, se tende vers Lui, ne désirant plaire qu'à Lui seul, le Souverain Seigneur, puisque Lui seul opère dans ce mystère comme il Lui plaît et que Lui-même a dit: "Faites ceci en mémoire de Moi" (Lk 22:19).[14] C'est pourquoi aussi, elles recevront le Corps et le Sang de notre Seigneur Jésus-Christ avec grande humilité et vénération, se souvenant que le Seigneur Lui-même a dit: "Celui qui mange ma Chair et boit mon Sang a la vie éternelle" (Jn 6:55).[15]

13. Prenant bien garde de se montrer tristes comme les hypocrites (Mt 6:16),[16] les Soeurs observeront les jeûnes prescrits par l'Église. Celles qui, sous la conduite de l'Esprit, voudront suivre le Seigneur en d'autres jeûnes et renoncements, qu'elles soient bénies du Seigneur. En cas de manifeste nécessité, les Soeurs ne seront pas tenues au jeûne corporel.[17]

14. Lorsqu'elles vont par le monde, qu'elles évitent toute querelle et contestation (1 Tm 2:14) et ne jugent pas les autres; mais qu'elles soient douces, pacifiques et sereines, bienveillantes et humbles, parlant honnêtement à tous, comme il convient. En quelque lieu qu'elles aillent, qu'elles apportent la paix; car le Seigneur a dit dans l'Évangile: "En toute maison où vous entrerez, dites d'abord: paix à cette maison" (Lk 10:5).[18]

---

[13]LtOrd 12-13.
[14]LtOrd 14-17.
[15]ER 20:5-6.
[16]ER 3:2.
[17]LR 3:9.
[18]LR 3:10-13.

11. Let the Sisters show the greatest possible reverence and honor to the most holy Body and Blood of our Lord Jesus Christ through whom all things, whether on earth or in the heavens, have been brought to peace and reconciled with Almighty God.[13]

12. Therefore, they will participate in the true sacrifice of our Lord Jesus Christ with a pure and holy intention. With the help of God's grace, their whole attention should be fixed on Him, with a will to please the most high Lord alone, because it is He alone who accomplishes this mystery in his own way. He told us, "Do this in remembrance of Me" (Lk 22:19).[14]
When they receive the Body and Blood of our Lord Jesus Christ, they should do so with great humility and reverence, remembering the words of Our Lord Himself, "He who eats My flesh and drinks My blood has life everlasting" (Jn 6:54).[15]

13. Taking care not to look sad like hypocrites (Mt 6:16)[16] the Sisters will observe the fasts prescribed by the Church. Those who, guided by the Spirit wish to imitate the Lord in other fasts and renunciations, may do so, and may the Lord bless them for it. But whenever there is a clear necessity, the Sisters need not do any corporal fasting.[17]

14. When they go out into the world they should avoid quarrels and contests, and judging others. Rather they should be meek, peaceful and serene, kind and humble, speaking honestly to all as becomes them. Wherever they go, let them bring peace, for in the Gospel the Lord says: "into whatever house you enter first say: Peace to this house" (Lk 10:5-9).[18]

---

[13]LtOrd 12-13; FA:ED I, 117.

[14]LtOrd 14-17; FA:ED I, 117.

[15]ER 20:5-6; FA:Ed I, 78 .

[16]ER 3:2; FA:ED I, 65.

[17]LR 3:9; FA:ED I, 102.

[18]LR 3:10; FA:ED I, 102.

## IV. De l'attitude des soeurs devant les biens de ce monde

15. Toutes les Soeurs s'appliqueront à suivre l'humilité et la pauvreté de notre Seigneur Jésus-Christ. Elles se rappelleront que de tous les biens de ce monde elles ne doivent avoir rien d'autre que ce qu'indique l'Apôtre: *Lors donc que nous avons nourriture et vêtement, sachons nous en contenter* (1 Tm 6:8).[19]

16. Le Seigneur ordonne dans l'Évangile: *Attention, gardez-vous de toute* malice et de toute *cupidité* (Lk 12:15) et *évitez soigneusement* les préoccupations de ce siècle et *les soucis de cette vie* (Lk 24:34).[20]

17. Aussi, où qu'elles soient, où qu'elles aillent, les Soeurs seront toutes très vigilantes pour que l'attrait d'une récompense, d'un travail ou d'un avantage quelconque, ne détourne pas de Dieu leur esprit et leur cœur.[21] "Le diable, dit Frère François, s'emploie à aveugler ceux qui convoitent l'argent ou l'estiment plus que les pierres. Nous qui avons tout quitté (Mt 19:27) n'allons donc pas perdre pour si peu le Royaume des cieux".[22]

18. Cependant, que les Supérieures aient grand soin de pourvoir aux besoins des malades et de chacune des Soeurs, en tenant compte des lieux, des saisons, des pays, selon ce qu'elles jugeront nécessaire.[23]

19. Mais que toutes restent bien sur leurs gardes au sujet de l'argent.[24]

## V. De la manière de travailler

20. Les Soeurs à qui le Seigneur a fait la grâce de travailler, travailleront consciencieusement et avec foi, de telle sorte que, une fois écartée l'oisiveté, ennemie de l'âme, elles n'éteignent pas en elles l'esprit de prière et de dévotion, que doivent servir toutes les choses temporelles.[25]

---

[19] ER 9:1-2.
[20] ER 8:1.
[21] ER 22-25.
[22] ER8:4-5.
[23] LR 4:2.
[24] ER 8:11.
[25] LR 5:1-2.

## IV. HOW THE SISTERS ARE TO LOOK UPON THE GOODS OF THIS WORLD

15. All the Sisters strive to imitate the humility and poverty of Our Lord Jesus Christ. They must keep in mind that of all the goods of this world, they may have nothing more than what the Apostle mentions: "Having food and clothing, with these let us be content" (1 Tm 6:8).[19]

16. The Lord says in the Gospel: "Take heed and beware of all the malice and avarice" (Lk 12:15) and "carefully avoid the anxieties of the world and the cares of this life" (Lk 24:34).[20]

17. Wherever they are, the Sisters shall be very much on their guard that under the guise of some reward, work or benefit they do not take their spirit and their heart away from God.[21] "The devil, says Brother Francis, wants to blind those who desire money or consider it better than stones. May we who have left all things (Mt 19:27) be careful of not losing the Kingdom of heaven for so little."[22]

18. The superiors will carefully provide for the needs of the sick and for each one of the Sisters; taking into account the diversity of places, seasons, and countries, they will judge what is necessary.[23]

19. However, all must be on their guard against money.[24]

## V. THE MANNER OF WORK

20. The Sisters to whom God has given the grace of working, will work conscientiously and with faith, in such a manner that while avoiding idleness, the enemy of the soul, they will not extinguish in themselves the spirit of prayer and devotion, which all temporal things must serve.[25]

---

[19]ER 9:1-2; FA:ED I, 70.
[20]ER 8:1; FA:ED I, 69.
[21]ER 22:25; FA;ED I, 80.
[22]ER 8:4-5; FA:ED I, 70.
[23]LR 4:2; FA:ED I, 102.
[24]ER 8:11; FA:ED I, 70.
[25]LR 5:1-2; FA:ED I, 102.

21. En échange de leur travail, elles peuvent recevoir ce qui est néces-saire pour elles et pour leurs Soeurs, et cela humblement, comme il convient à des servantes de Dieu et à des disciples de la Très Sainte Pauvreté.[26]

## VI. De la vie fraternelle dans la pauvreté

22. Que les Soeurs ne s'approprient rien, ni maison, ni lieu, ni quoi que ce soit. *Comme des pèlerins et des étrangers* (1 P 2:11) en ce siè-cle, qu'elles servent le Seigneur dans la pauvreté et l'humilité, car le Seigneur pour nous s'est fait pauvre en ce monde (2 Cor 8:9). "C'est là, dit Frère François, l'excellence de la très haute pauvreté qui vous a établis, vous mes frères très chers, héritiers et rois du Royaume des cieux, vous a faits pauvres en biens terrestres, mais élevés en vertus (Jas 2:5). Qu'elle soit *votre partage*, elle qui conduit *à la terre des vivants* (Ps 141:6). Attachez-vous-y totalement, frères bien-aimés, et pour le Nom de notre Seigneur Jesus-Christ, refusez à jamais d'avoir rien d'autre sous le ciel".[27]

23. Où que soient les Soeurs et partout où elles se rencontreront, elles se montreront les unes aux autres qu'elles sont de la même famille. Qu'elles se fassent connaître l'une à l'autre en toute confiance leurs besoins, car si une mère nourrit et aime sa fille (1 Thes 2:7) selon la chair, avec combien plus d'affection chacune doit-elle aimer et nourrir sa Soeur selon l'esprit.[28] Toutes sont tenues de prendre soin de leurs Soeurs malades et de les servir comme elles voudraient elles-mêmes être servies (Mt 7:12), si elles étaient à leur tour éprouvées par la ma-ladie.[29] Les Soeurs malades se souviendront de l'exhortation de Frère François: "Je prie le Frère malade de rendre grâces au Créateur de tout ce qui lui arrive et de désirer être dans l'état où Dieu le veut, bien por-tant ou malade."[30]

---

[26]LR 5:3-4.

[27]LR 6:1-6.

[28]LR6:7-8.

[29]FlCl 8.

[30]ER 10:3.

21. As remuneration for their work, they may receive for themselves and for their fellow Sisters what is necessary, and accept it humbly as is becoming for servants of God and disciples of the most holy poverty.[26]

## VI. FRATERNAL LIFE IN POVERTY

22. Let the Sisters make nothing their own: neither house, nor place, nor anything whatsoever. "As pilgrims and strangers" (1 P 2:11) "in this world, let them serve the Lord in poverty and humility because for us the Lord made himself poor in this world" (2 Cor 8:9). Such, said St. Francis, "is the excellence of most high poverty, that it makes you, my dearest brothers heirs and kings of the kingdom of heaven, poor in earthly goods, but rich in virtue (Jas 2:5). This should be your portion because it leads to the land of the living (Ps 141:6). And to this poverty, my beloved brothers, you must cling with all your heart, and wish never to have anything else under heaven, for the name of our Lord Jesus Christ."[27]

23. Wherever the Sisters are and wherever they meet one another, they will show mutually that they are of the same family. They should have no hesitation in making known their needs to one another, for if a mother nurtures and cherishes her daughter in the flesh (1 Thes 2:7) with how much more affection must not each one love and nourish her Sister according to the spirit.[28] All are bound to take care of their Sisters who are ill, and to serve them as they themselves would like to be served (Mt 7:12) if they were in turn affected by illness.[29] And the Sisters who are ill should keep in mind the exhortation of St. Francis. I beg the friar who is sick to thank the Creator for everything; he should be content to be as God wishes him to be, in sickness or in health.[30]

---

[26]LR 5:3-4; FA:ED I, 102-103.

[27]LR 6:1-6; FA:ED I, 103.

[28]LR 6:7-8; FA:ED I, 103.

[29]FLCl 8; CA:ED, 119-121.

[30]ER 10:3-4; FA:ED I, 71-72.

## VII. De l'aide fraternelle et du pardon

24. Si une Soeur, à l'instigation de l'ennemi, vient à manquer grave-
ment à la forme de vie dont elle a fait profession, elle sera avertie par
la Supérieure ou par les autres Soeurs qui connaîtraient sa faute. Celles-ci ne lui feront ni honte, ni reproche; elles lui témoigneront au
contraire beaucoup de miséricorde et tiendront soigneusement cachée
la faute de leur Sœur.[31] Elles prieront le Seigneur d'éclairer son coeur
pour l'amener à la pénitence.[32] Mais toutes doivent prendre bien garde
de s'irriter ou de se troubler à cause de la faute de l'une d'elles; car
la colère et le trouble sont un obstacle à la charité en soi et dans les
autres.[33]

25. S'il arrive qu'entre deux Soeurs une parole ou un geste donne occasion d'irritation ou de trouble, celle qui en est la cause ira sans tarder,
avant même de présenter à Dieu l'offrande de sa prière (Mt 5:23-24),
demander humblement pardon à sa compagne. Bien mieux, elle la
priera d'intercéder pour elle auprès du Seigneur, afin qu'Il lui fasse
miséricorde.[34] Et l'autre Soeur, se souvenant de la parole du Seigneur:
*Si ce n'est pas du fond du coeur que vous pardonnez*, votre Père céleste
ne vous pardonnera pas non plus (Mt 18:35), oubliera de grand coeur
ce que sa Soeur lui a fait.[35]

## VIII. Des soeurs servantes de la fraternité

26. Toutes les Soeurs sont tenues d'avoir toujours l'une d'entre elles
comme Supérieure et Servante de la Fraternité et elles sont tenues fermement de lui obéir.[36]

27. En ce qui concerne son élection et celle des autres Supérieures, elles
suivront les prescriptions de l'Église.

---

[31]LtMin 15.

[32]FlCl 9.

[33]LR 7:3.

[34]FlCl9.

[35]FlCl 9.

[36]LR 8:1.

## VII. FRATERNAL ASSISTANCE AND PARDON

24. Should any Sister, at the instigation of the enemy, commit a serious fault against the form of life, which she has professed, the superior or the other Sisters who are aware of what she has done must warn her. They may not put her to shame nor reproach her; but on the contrary they will show great mercy and keep her fault secret.[31] They must pray that God may enlighten her heart to do penance.[32] Let all be on their guard against irritation or annoyance because of the fault of one of their Sisters for anger and annoyance hinder charity in one's self and in others.[33]

25. Should it happen that between two Sisters a word or gesture give rise to irritation or trouble, the one who caused it, shall without delay even before she offers her prayer (Mt 5:23-23) before God – humbly asks pardon of her Sister. Better still she will implore her intercession that God may be merciful to her.[34] And the other Sister, mindful of that word of the Lord: "If you do not forgive with all your heart, your Father will not forgive you either" (Mt 18:35) will, with all her heart, forgive her Sister whatever she has done to her.[35]

## VIII. THE SISTERS WHO ARE SERVANTS OF THE FRATERNITY

26. All the Sisters are always bound to have one from among them as superior and servant of the fraternity, and they are firmly bound to obey her.[36]

27. For her election and that of the other superiors, they will follow the prescriptions of the Church.

---

[31]LtMin 15; FA:ED I, 98.

[32]FLCl 9; CA:ED, 121-122.

[33]LR 7:3; FA:ED I, 104.

[34]FLCl 9; CA:ED, 121-122.

[35]FLCl 9; CA:ED, 121-122.

[36]LR 8:1; FA:ED I, 104.

28. Celle qui sera ainsi élue aura soin de convoquer au temps fixé par les Constitutions, Chapitres généraux et Conseils. En outre, chacune des responsables des Provinces et des Fraternités, réunira régulièrement ses Soeurs pour s'entretenir avec toutes de tout ce qui regarde la vie et le bien de la Fraternité, tel que l'exige leur forme de vie évangélique.[37]

29. Toutes celles des Soeurs qui ont reçu une charge se souviendront que le Seigneur dit: "Je suis venu *non pour être servi, mais pour servir*" (Mt 20:28), et que l'âme de leurs Soeurs leur est confiée. Si quelqu'une se perdait par leur faute et par leur mauvais exemple, elles auraient à en *rendre compte au jour du jugement* (Mt 12:36) devant le Seigneur Jésus-Christ.[38]

30. Elles penseront à la grandeur de la charge qu'elles ont acceptée et s'emploieront au service des Soeurs et, avec toutes, rechercheront le bien de la Fraternité. S'appliquant à être les premières par leur fidélité plutôt que par leur charge, elles observeront elles-mêmes en toutes choses la vie commune, en sorte que, entraînées par leur exemple, les Soeurs obéissent par amour plutôt que par crainte.[39] Elles réconforteront celles qui sont dans la peine ou dans l'épreuve. Que nulle de leurs Soeurs ne soit accablée par le mal du désespoir pour n'avoir pas trouvé auprès d'elles le soutien qui l'aurait sauvée.[40] Cependant, elles éviteront de manifester des préférences, de peur que ce qu'elles donnent à quelques-unes en affection ne tourne à la ruine de la Fraternité.[41] Elles seront, au contraire, attentives à ce que toutes gardent entre elles l'unité en s'aimant les unes les autres, car la charité *est le lien de la perfection* (Col 3:14).[42]

31. Aucune Supérieure ne considérera comme son bien propre le service qu'elle exerce auprès de ses Soeurs; mais le moment venu, elle remettra volontiers sa charge.[43]

---

[37]FlCl 4.

[38]ER 4:6.

[39]FlCl 4.

[40]FlCl 4.

[41]FlCl 4.

[42]FlCl 10.

[43]ER 17:4.

28. The Sister thus elected must convoke the general Chapters and councils at the time fixed by the Constitutions. The Sisters in charge of the Provinces and of the communities must regularly convene all the Sisters to discuss with them all that concerns the life and the good of the fraternity, and in the way prescribed by their evangelical form of life.[37]

29. Every Sister who has received such a charge must keep in mind these words of the Lord: "I came to serve and not to be served" (Mt 20:28). Let her remember that she has been entrusted with the souls of her Sisters. Should any of them be lost through her fault and her bad example, she must give an account of it on the day of judgment (Mt 12:36) before our Lord Jesus Christ.[38]

30. Each must be ever mindful of the charge she has accepted and spend herself in the service of the Sisters and, together with them, seek the good of the fraternity. She will strive to be first by her fidelity rather than by her office: observing the common life in all things in such a way that, led by her example the Sisters obey out of love rather than out of fear.[39] Let her encourage and console those who may be troubled or going through a trial. May none of her Sisters ever give way to despair for not having found in her the support which would have been their salvation.[40] However she must have no favorites lest the affection she has for a few lead to the ruin of the community.[41] Rather she will strive to preserve among all the Sisters the unity of mutual love, for charity is the bond of perfection (Col 3:14).[42]

31. No superior shall look upon her service to the Sisters as her personal right, but shall willingly relinquish it when the time comes.[43]

---

[37]FLCl 4; CA:ED, 114-116.

[38]ER 4:6; FA:ED I, 66-67.

[39]FLCl 4; CA:ED, 114-116.

[40]FLCl 4; CA:ED, 114-116.

[41]FLCl 4; CA:ED, 114-116.

[42]FLCl 10; CA:ED, 122-123.

[43]ER 17:4; FA:ED I, 75.

**IX. DE LA VIE APOSTOLIQUE DES SOEURS ET DE L'ENVOI EN MISSION**

32. D'un coeur totalement docile aux volontés du Seigneur et dans un esprit soucieux d'accomplir ses désirs, les Soeurs proclameront qu'Il est bon (Ps 135:1) et L'exalteront dans leurs oeuvres (Tb 13:6); car, si le Seigneur les envoie par le monde, c'est pour que, de parole et d'action, elles lui rendent témoignage et fassent savoir à tous *qu'il n'y a de Tout-Puissant que Lui* (Tb 13:4).[44]

33. Les Soeurs peuvent envisager leur rôle spirituel de deux manières: ou bien, s'abstenir de toute dispute ou chicane, se soumettre *à toute créature humaine à cause de Dieu* (1 P 2:13) et reconnaître simplement qu'elles sont chrétiennes; ou bien, lorsqu'elles voient que c'est le bon plaisir de Dieu, annoncer la Parole, afin que tous les hommes croient au Dieu Tout-Puissant, Père, Fils et Saint-Esprit, Créateur de toutes choses, au Fils Rédempteur et Sauveur, qu'ils reçoivent le baptême et qu'ils deviennent chrétiens: car *si quelqu'un ne renaît de l'eau et de l'Esprit-Saint, il ne peut entrer au Royaume de Dieu* (Jn 3:5). De cela et d'autres choses qui plairaient au Seigneur, elles pourront parler à toute personne qu'elles rencontreront.[45]

34. Celles qui, sous l'inspiration de Dieu, voudraient aller annoncer l'Évangile chez les non-croyants, en demanderont l'autorisation à leurs Supérieures. Celles-ci l'accorderont aux Soeurs qu'elles reconnaîtront aptes à être envoyées,[46] se souvenant qu'elles devront rendre compte au Seigneur (Lk 12:6), si en cette occasion comme en d'autres, elles ont agi sans discernement.[47]

35. De même, toutes celles qui exercent quelque ministère le feront en dépendance de leurs Supérieures et de la Sainte Église. Cependant toutes les Soeurs feront de leur vie une annonce de l'Évangile.[48]

36. Dans l'amour qu'est Dieu (1 Jn 4:16), que toutes les Soeurs, celles qui prient, celles qui annoncent la Parole, celles qui travaillent, s'appliquent à s'humilier en tout, à ne pas se glorifier, ni se complaire en elles-mêmes, ni s'enorgueillir intérieurement des bonnes paroles et des bonnes oeuvres, ni même d'aucun bien que Dieu dit, fait ou accomplit parfois en elles ou par elles.[49] En tout lieu, en toutes circonstances, que

---

44LtOrd 7-9.

45ER 16:6-9.

46LR 12:1-2.

47ER 16:4.

48ER 17:1-3.

49ER 17:5-6.

## IX. THE APOSTOLIC LIFE OF THE SISTERS AND THEIR MISSIONING

32. By their whole-hearted observance of the Lord's will and with a spirit anxious to accomplish His desire, the Sisters will proclaim that the Lord is good (Ps 135:1) and extol Him in all they do (Tb 13:6). Thus, He sends them all over the world so that by word and by deed they may bear witness to His message and make known to all that He alone is the Almighty One (Tb 13:4).[44]

33. The Sisters may see their spiritual role in two ways: either avoiding every occasion of strife and controversy, being subject to every human creature for God's sake, and simply acknowledging that they are Christians; or proclaiming the Word of God openly, when they see that such is the will of God, and calling on their hearers to believe in Almighty God, Creator of all things, Father, Son and Holy Spirit, and in the Son, the Redeemer and Savior, so that they may be baptized and become Christians, because "unless one is born through water and the spirit he cannot enter into the Kingdom of God" (Jn 3:5). They may tell them all that and more, as God inspires them.[45]

34. Those who, under divine inspiration wish to teach the gospel to unbelievers, must ask the permission of their superiors who will grant it to those Sisters whom they judge apt for such a mission.[46] The superiors must remember that they shall be held to render an account to the Lord (Lk 16:2) should they act indiscreetly in this or in other things.[47]

35. Likewise, all to whom some charge has been entrusted, should exercise it in dependence on their superiors and on the Holy Church. Nevertheless, all the Sisters will announce the Gospel by their lives.[48]

36. In that love which God is, let all the Sisters, whether they are engaged in prayer or in apostolic works, or in announcing the word or in work, strive to humble themselves in all things. Let them not boast or be self-satisfied or inwardly puffed up over the good words and deeds or any good whatever which God may sometimes say or do or work in them or through them.[49] In all places and circumstances, the Sisters must refer every good to the Lord God and sovereign of all

---

[44]LtOrd 7-9; FA:ED I, 117.

[45]ER 16:6-7; FA:ED I, 74.

[46]LR 12:1-2; FA:ED I, 106.

[47]ER 16:4; FA:ED I, 74.

[48]ER 17:1-3; FA:ED I, 75.

[49]ER 17:5-6; FA:ED I, 75.

les Soeurs reconnaissent que tous les biens appartiennent au Seigneur Dieu Très-Haut et Souverain de toutes choses; qu'elles Lui rendent grâces, à Lui de qui procèdent tous les biens. Et quand elles verront ou entendront dire ou faire le mal ou blasphémer Dieu, alors qu'elles le bénissent, fassent le bien et louent le Seigneur (Rm 12:21), *qui est béni dans les siècles* (Rm 1:25).[50]

## X. De la vie fraternelle dans l'obéissance

37. Les Soeurs qui sont Supérieures et Servantes de leurs Soeurs, les visiteront, les avertiront, les reprendront avec humilité et charité sans leur prescrire jamais rien qui soit contre leur âme et contre la Règle.[51]

38. Les autres Soeurs, à l'exemple du Seigneur Jésus, qui mit sa volonté dans la volonté de son Père,[52] se rappelleront que pour Dieu elles ont renoncé à leur volonté propre. Elles sont donc tenues d'obéir à leurs Supérieures en tout ce qu'elles ont promis au Seigneur d'observer et qui n'est pas contraire à leur âme et à la Règle.[53] Bien plus, dans l'Amour qu'est Dieu (1 Jn 4:16), que toutes les Soeurs se rendent volontiers service et s'obéissent mutuellement (Gal 5:13): telle est la vraie et sainte obéissance de notre Seigneur Jésus-Christ.[54]

39. Et en quelqu'endroit que se trouvent les Soeurs, s'il en est qui savent et reconnaissent ne pouvoir observer spirituellement la Règle, elles devront et pourront recourir à leurs Supérieures. Celles-ci alors les recevront avec amour et bonté; elles seront d'un abord si familier que les Soeurs puissent leur parler et agir avec elles comme des maîtresses avec leurs servantes; car il doit en être ainsi, les Supérieures sont au service de toutes les Sœurs.[55]

40. Que les Soeurs, elles, pour le Seigneur Jésus-Christ, se gardent de tout orgueil, vaine gloire, envie, *de tout avarice* (Lk 12:15), soucis et sollicitudes de ce monde, détraction et murmure.[56]

---

[50]ER17:17-19.

[51]LR 10:1.

[52]2LtF 10.

[53]LR 10:2-3.

[54]ER 5:13-15.

[55]LR 10:4-6.

[56]LR 10:7.

things, acknowledging that all good belongs to Him; and they must thank Him for it all, because all good comes from Him. And when they see or hear people speaking or doing evil or blaspheming God, they must say and do good, praising God (Rm 12:21) who is blessed forever (Rm 1:25).[50]

## X. FRATERNAL LIFE IN OBEDIENCE

37. The Sisters who are superiors and servants of their Sisters shall visit them, admonish the, and correct them in humility and charity. They shall never prescribe for the Sisters anything that is against their conscience or against the Rule.[51]

38. Following the example of the Lord Jesus who made His own the will of his Father,[52] the other Sisters will always bear in mind that they have renounced their own will for God's sake. They are therefore bound to obey their superiors in all those things which they have promised the Lord to observe and which are not against their conscience or their Rule.[53] Moreover, in that love, which is God (1 Jn 4:16), let all the Sisters gladly serve and obey one another (Gal 5:13). this is the true and holy obedience of our Lord Jesus Christ.[54]

39. And should there be Sisters anywhere who know and recognize that they cannot observe their Rule according to its true spirit, it is their duty and their right to have recourse to their superiors. The superiors must receive them with love and goodness so that the Sisters may speak and act with them as mistresses with their servants; for thus it should be that the superiors be at the service of their Sisters.[55]

40. Let the Sisters for the sake of our Lord Jesus Christ beware of all pride, vainglory, envy, avarice (Lk 12:15), the cares and worries of this world, detraction and complaining.[56]

---

[50]ER 17:17-19; FA:ED I, 76.

[51]LR 10:1; FA:ED I, 105.

[52]2LtF 10; FA:ED I, 46.

[53]LR 10:2-3; FA:ED I, 105.

[54]ER 5:13-15; FA:ED I, 67-68.

[55]LR 10:4-6; FA:ED I, 105.

[56]LR 10:7; FA:ED I, 105.

41. Les unes et les autres considéreront que, par-dessus tout, ce qu'elles doivent désirer, c'est d'avoir l'Esprit du Seigneur et sa sainte opération; prier toujours Dieu d'un coeur pur; avoir l'humilité, la patience dans l'épreuve et la maladie; aimer ceux qui les persécutent, les reprennent et les blâment, car le Seigneur dit: *"Aimez vos ennemis et priez pour ceux qui vous persécutent et vous calomnient* (Mt 5:44). *Bienheureux ceux qui souffrent persécution pour la justice, car le Royaume des cieux leur appartient* (Mt 5:10). *Celui qui persévérera jusqu'à la fin sera sauvé"* (Mt 10:20).[57]

## XI. Comment les soeurs rechercheront par-dessus tout l'amour du Seigneur

42. Que toutes les Soeurs considèrent attentivement ce que dit le Seigneur: *"Si quelqu'un veut venir à Moi et qu'il ne hait pas son père et sa mère et son épouse et ses fils et ses frères et ses soeurs et jusqu'à sa propre vie, il ne peut être mon disciple"* (Lk 14:26).[58]

43. Maintenant qu'elles ont quitté le monde, elles n'ont rien d'autre à faire que de s'appliquer à suivre la volonté du Seigneur et à Lui plaire.[59] Ayant donc écarté tout empêchement et rejeté tout souci et inquiétude de la meilleure manière qu'elles pourront, qu'elles se mettent en devoir de servir, aimer, adorer et honorer le Seigneur Dieu, dans la pureté du coeur et de l'esprit; car c'est là ce qu'Il cherche par-dessus tout.[60]

44. Qu'elles lui fassent toujours en elles un temple et une demeure (Jn 14:23), à Lui, le Seigneur Tout-Puissant, Père, Fils et Saint-Esprit.[61]

---

[57]LR 10:8-12.

[58]ER 1:4.

[59]ER 22:9.

[60]ER 22:26.

[61]ER 22:27.

41. What each one must desire above all and earnestly strive for is to have the spirit of the Lord and His holy workings, to pray always with a pure heart, to have humility, patience in tribulation and illness, to love those who persecute, accuse and blame them, for the Lord says: "Love your enemies and pray for those who persecute and calumniate you (Mt 5:44). Blessed are they who suffer persecution for justice sake, for theirs is the Kingdom of Heaven (Mt 5:10). He who will persevere to the end will be saved" (Mt 10:20).[57]

## XI. HOW THE SISTERS ARE TO SEEK TO LOVE THE LORD ABOVE ALL ELSE

42. Let every Sister weigh carefully these words of the Lord: "If anyone comes to me does not hate father, mother, wife, children, brothers, Sisters, yes, and even one's own life that one cannot be my disciple" (Lk 14:26).[58]

43. They have left the world now, and all they have to do is to be careful to follow God's will and please Him.[59] Having removed all hindrances and put aside all cares and worries, with all their might, as best they can, they will serve, love, adore and honor the Lord God with a clean heart and a pure mind; for this He asks above all else.[60]

44. And they will make within themselves a temple and dwelling for Him (Jn 14:23) who is the Lord God Almighty, Father, Son and Holy Spirit.[61]

---

[57]LR 10:8; FA:ED I, 105.
[58]ER 1:4; FA:ED I, 64.
[59]ER 22:9; FA:ED I, 79.
[60]ER 22:26; FA:ED I, 80.
[61]ER 22:27; FA:ED I, 80.

## XII. Que les soeurs persévèrent jusqu'à la fin à la suite du Seigneur Jésus, humble et pauvre

45. Puisque, par inspiration divine, les Soeurs se sont faites filles et servantes du Très-Haut et Souverain Roi, le Père Céleste, et qu'elles se sont données comme épouses à l'Esprit-Saint en choisissant de vivre selon la perfection du saint Évangile, elles persévéreront jusqu'à la fin dans cette volonté.[62]

46. Refusant d'être sages et prudentes selon la chair, qu'elles soient simples, humbles et pures, ne désirant jamais être au-dessus des autres, mais plutôt servantes et soumises *à toute humaine créature à cause de Dieu* (1 Pt 2:13).[63]

47. Aussi, en constante soumission à l'Église, stables dans la foi catholique, elles observeront la pauvreté et l'humilité de notre Seigneur Jésus-Christ et de sa très Sainte Mère, ainsi que le saint Évangile, comme elles l'ont fermement promis.[64] Toutes celles qui agiront de la sorte, *l'Esprit du Seigneur reposera sur elles* (Is 11:2) *et fera en elles habitation et demeure* (Jn 14:23).[65]

---

[62]FlCl 6.

[63]2LtF 45-47.

[64]LR 12:4; FlCl 12.

[65]2LtF 48.

## XII. THE SISTERS WILL PERSEVERE UNTIL THE END IN FOLLOWING THE LORD JESUS, HUMBLE AND POOR

45. Since by divine inspiration the Sisters have made themselves daughters and handmaids of the Most High and Sovereign King, the Heavenly Father, and have espoused themselves to the Holy Spirit by the choice of a life according to the perfection of the Holy Gospel, they should persevere therein until the end.[62]

46. Refusing to be wise and prudent according to the flesh, they will strive to be simple, humble, and pure; nor will they desire to be over others, but seek rather to be the servants and subjects of all human creatures for God's sake (1 Pt 2:13).[63]

47. Thus, in constant submission to the Church, steadfast in the Catholic faith, they will observe the poverty and humility of our Lord Jesus Christ and of his Holy Mother and the Holy Gospel as they have firmly promised.[64] On all those who do this "the Spirit of the Lord will rest" (Is 11:2) and will make in them a home and a dwelling (Jn 14:23).[65]

---

[62]FLCl 6; CA:ED, 110.

[63]2LtF 45-47; FA:ED I, 48.

[64]LR 12:4; FA:ED I, 106; FlCl 12; CA:ED, 124-26.

[65]2LtF 48: FA:ED I, 48.

# A STATEMENT OF UNDERSTANDING OF FRANCISCAN PENITENTIAL LIFE

## INTER-OBEDIENTIAL CONGRESS, MADRID, 1974

### CHAPTER I: THE NATURE AND PURPOSE OF THE ORDER

1. In the plan of God the Father, realized through the action of the Holy Spirit in the Church, the Regular Order of Penance of St. Francis of Assisi has this form and life: to observe the Holy Gospel of our Lord Jesus Christ living poverty, obedience, and consecrated chastity in community.[1]

2. The specific character of the Order is the commitment of its members to live the Gospel message of a penitential life. After the life and example of St. Francis, the friars and sisters are called to serve God and the People of God in holiness. Their aim is the continual building up of the Body of Christ (Eph 4:12).

3. Through a shared life of prayer and work the friars and sisters strive to realize total and continuous conversion to God (Mk 1:15).

In daily bearing the cross (Lk 9:23) they participate in the saving work of Christ who is the center and source of their lives.

As a community they are committed to a constant renewal of life which is not only interior and individual but external and social as well.[2]

### CHAPTER II: THE LIFE OF PRAYER

4. The life of penance is directed toward an ever more intense union with the Lord (Jn 15:1-5).

It is therefore inseparable from the life of prayer (Jn 15:7.16), with its reflection on the mystery of Christ, especially as expressed in the Sacred Liturgy with the Eucharist as its center.[3]

5. The prayerful reading of the Word of God is at the heart of Franciscan life.[4]

---

[1]Cf. ER 1; FA:ED I, 63; *Regula T.O.R. Sancti Francisci* (1927), n. 1; *Lumen Gentium* 42; *Perfectae Caritatis* 2a.

[2]Cf. *Constitutio Apostolica, Paenitemini, Proemium.*

[3]Cf. *Eucharisticum Mysterium, Proemium.*

[4]Cf. 2C 102; FA:ED II, 314-15.

In the Scriptures the religious meet their Divine Master in His life and teaching and draw inspiration from the life and virtues of God's chosen ones, especially Mary, the Virgin Mother of the Lord.

6. In the tradition of Franciscan prayer, the friars and sisters reflect, as well, on the marvels of God in creation. This, along with a Christian consciousness in their daily service to the Church and in their relations with their fellow man gives substance to their daily lives. As the Seraphic Father exhorts: "…give him praise and prayer by day and night, saying 'Our Father' because it is necessary to pray and never cease."[1]

## CHAPTER III: THE LIFE OF POVERTY

7. With a joyful spirit, the religious of the Order of Penance accept their life of ongoing conversion as an expression of their love for Christ.[2]

It is the central aspect of their witness to the world because the grain of wheat must die to bring forth fruit (Jn 12:24).

In this Franciscan life of penance is rooted the practice of evangelical poverty (Mt 19:21).[3]

8. By their poverty, the friars and sisters conform themselves intimately to Christ (2 Cor 8:9) who emptied himself for our sake (Phil 2:5).

They dedicate themselves to joyful service to the Church and mankind, desiring only what will lead them and those they serve to the Lord. They recognize the sacred character of the world and by their lives show the proper use of this world's goods (Lk 12:15ff.).[4]

9. Evangelical poverty is likewise expressed in the friars' and sisters' love for the poor. It obliges them to share themselves and their goods with those in need and to defend the rights of the poor.[5]

This, together with their moderation in the use of material things, constitutes an authentic witness to human and Christian brotherhood.

---

[1] 2LtF 21; FA:ED I, 47; *Perfectae Caritatis*, n. 6.

[2] Cf. 1C 44: *Nihil volebat proprietatis habere, ut omnia posset in Domino plenius possidere.* FA:ED I, 222.

[3] Cf. *Perfectae Caritatis*, n. 13.

[4] Cf. *Paenitemini, Proemium.*

[5] Cf. *Perfectae Caritatis*, n. 13, par. 5.

Chapter IV: Obedience in the Order of Penance

10. The obedience professed by the friars and sisters of the Regular Order of Penance likewise proceeds from their life of conversion to God. United with Christ, and in His spirit, they always seek to respond to the Father's will (Jn 4:34) in their daily living of the Gospel (Jn 5:30; 6:38).

They freely pledge themselves to respond also to the voice of Christ alive in the Church (Mt 28:20; Lk 10:16; Jn 14:20-21).[6]

After the example of St. Francis, they are obedient, in a special way, to the Holy Father, to the duly authorized Shepherds of the Church,[7] and to those who, within the community, serve in the exercise of authority.

11. Since Christ is present in the entire Church, religious communities within the Order of Penance are each committed to serve the needs of God's people (Mt 25:34-40) according to their particular purpose.

In this way, the variety of apostolic witness and service of these various communities will continue. Fidelity to a life of conversion requires that both the life and the work of the friars and sisters be constantly maintained in a state of religious and apostolic renewal.

12. Those in authority should exercise their service in an atmosphere of fraternal dialogue so that the life and work of each distinct community may be truly an expression of Franciscan fidelity.[8]

Let them serve keeping in mind the Seraphic Father's admonition: "Woe to that religious who is elevated by his fellow religious and is of no mind to step down from his rank of his own accord. And blessed is that servant who is elevated through no will of his own and who is always minded to stay at the feet of the rest."[9]

13. Each distinct community, according to the norms of its Constitutions and the established norms of the Church, shall provide its members, especially the younger religious, with that guidance necessary for growth in Franciscan religious life and spirit.[10]

---

[6]Cf. *Perfectae Caritatis*, n. 14.

[7]ER Prologue; FA:ED I, 63.

[8]Cf. *Perfectae. Caritatis*, n. 14, par. 3.

[9]Adm 20; FA:ED I, 135.

[10]Cf. *Renovationis Causam*, I, 4, 5; II, 10-32.

## CHAPTER V: CONSECRATED CHASTITY IN SERVICE

14. The friars and sisters inspired by the love of God and following the example of Christ embrace a life of consecrated chastity for the sake of the Kingdom of God. With undivided hearts they are freed for a universal love expressed in a life of conversion and dedication to God and work among the People of God (1 Cor 7:32-35).[11]

15. The religious dedicate themselves to serve their fellow men out of love. Let them especially bring to those in sorrow the joy of God and to broken humanity the healing of Christ.[12]

As true penitents, they live no longer for themselves but with faith in the Son of God who loved them and gave Himself for all (Gal 2:19-20).

They rejoice in suffering, filling up in their own flesh that which is lacking in the sufferings of Christ for His Body which is the Church (Col 1:24).

## CHAPTER VI: MESSENGERS OF PEACE

16. The friars and sisters of this Order of Penance are called to be messengers of peace. As their Seraphic Father says: "...go two by two about the several parts of the world proclaiming peace to the people, and repentance for the forgiveness of their sins. And be patient under trial, assured that the Lord will fulfill His intention and promise. To people who question you, give a humble reply, bless those who persecute you, thank those who insult you and slander you, because for such things an eternal Kingdom is being prepared for you".[13]

17. Not only shall the friars and sisters esteem their calling to be messengers of that peace with which Christ endowed His disciples (Jn 14:27; 16:33). They shall strive for that harmony in their community life which reflects their own interior harmony with God.[14]

They shall remain simple in their lifestyle as a witness to that interior calm which flows from trust in Providence (Lk 12:22-34).

---

[11]*Perfectae Caritatis*, n. 12; *Lumen Gentium* n. 42.

[12]*Lumen Gentium* n. 46.

[13]1C 29; FA:ED I, 207.

[14]*Perfectae Caritatis*, n. 15.

18. They are to share each other's sorrows and joys and by prayer and work are to support one another in fraternity as an expression of their love. They are to trust and respect each other and all men, so that their lives may witness to the futility of every form of contention (Col 3:12-15).[15]

19. Their words and deeds should always be marked by charity and joy. Let them announce to all men the peace and goodness of God, But always in the spirit of the Seraphic man of peace: "While you are proclaiming peace with your lips, be careful to have it even more in your heart. Nobody should be roused to wrath or insult on your account. Everyone should be moved rather to peace, goodwill and mercy as a result of your self restraint. For we are called for the purpose of healing the wounded, binding up those who are bruised, and reclaiming the erring."[16]

---

[15]L. Temperini, "La Regola degli Ordini Francescani," in *Analecta T.O.R*, II (1968): 43, 51, 55-57.

[16]L3C 14; FA:ED II, 76.

RULE PROJECT: OFFICIAL WORKING DRAFTS

## Regula et Vita Fratrum et Sororum
## Ordinis Franciscani Regularis
(Reute, September 1980)

### I. In nomine Domini! Incipit regula et vita fratrum et sororum ordinis franciscani regularis

1. Forma vitae fratrum et sororum Ordinis Franciscani Regularis haec est: Domini nostri Iesu Christi sanctum Evangelium observare, vivendo in obedientia, in paupertate et in castitate.[1] Secundum vitam et exemplum sancti Francisci fratres et sorores evangelicum poenitantiae nuntium vivant in servitium Dei et hominum.

2. Fratres et sorores promittunt obedientiam et reverentiam Domino Papae et Ecclesiae Romanae.[2] Eodem spiritu his qui in eorum fraternitate ad servitium auctoritatis canonice instituti sunt, secundum Regulam et Constitutiones obediant.[3]

3. Fratres et sorores secundum propriam vocationem fideliter viventes unitatem et vitalem mutuam communionem cum omnibus familiae franciscanae membris foveant ut charisma peculiare sancti Francisci in Ecclesia incarnent, amorem Christi erga omnes homines manifestantes.

### II. De his qui volunt vitam istam accipere et qualiter recipi debeant

4. Illi qui divina inspiratione veniunt ad nos volentes hanc vitam accipere benigne recipiantur.[4] Statuto tempore ministris praesentabuntur quibus potestas est in Fraternitatem admittendi.[5]

---

[1] LR 1:1.

[2] LR 1:2.

[3] LR 1:3.

[4] ER 2:1.

[5] LR 2:1.

### RULE AND LIFE OF THE THE BROTHERS AND SISTERS OF THE FRANCISCAN ORDER REGULAR
### (Reute, September 1980)

**I. IN THE NAME OF THE LORD! BEGINS THE RULE AND LIFE OF THE BROTHERS AND SISTERS OF THE FRANCISCAN ORDER REGULAR**

1. The way of life of the brothers and sisters of the Franciscan Order Regular is this: To observe the holy Gospel of our Lord Jesus Christ by living in obedience, poverty and chastity.[1] The brothers and sisters shall live the Gospel message of penance through serving God and man, following the life and example of Saint Francis.

2. The brothers and sisters promise obedience and reverence to the Lord Pope and to the holy Roman Church.[2] They shall also obey in the same spirit those who are canonically placed in authority within their own fraternity in keeping with the Rule and Constitutions.[3]

3. The brothers and sisters, while remaining faithful to the vocation proper to them, shall foster unity and a living, mutual communion within all the members of the Franciscan family. By showing in this way the love of Christ for all men, they will give substance within the Church to the special charism of Saint Francis.

**II. OF THOSE WHO WISH TO TAKE UP THIS LIFE AND HOW THEY ARE TO BE RECEIVED**

4. Those who through divine inspiration come to us wishing to take on this life should be received kindly.[4] At a set time they are to be presented to the ministers to whom the power belongs of admitting into the fraternity.[5]

---

[1] LR 1:1; FA:ED I, 100.
[2] LR 1:2: FA:ED I, 100.
[3] LR 1:3; FA:ED I, 100.
[4] ER 2:1; FA:ED I, 64.
[5] LR 2:1; FA:ED I, 100.

5. Ministri certiores fiant aspirantes vere fidei catholicae adhaerere vitaeque Ecclesiae Romanae.[6] Si illi idonei sint, recipiantur ad probationis tempus et vitae fraternitatis initientur. Et omnia ad hanc vitam evangelicam pertinentia eis diligenter exponantur. Si in desiderio suo perseverent, dicatur eis verbum sancti Evangelii: *Si vis perfectus esse, vade* (Mt 19:21) *et vende omnia* (Lk 18:22) *quae habes, et da pauperibus et habebis thesaurum in caelo, et veni, sequere me* (Mt 19:21). Et: *Si quis vult post me venire abneget semetipsum et tollat crucem suam et sequatur me* (Mt 16:24).[7]

6. Sic a Domino ducti incipiant vitam poenitentiae scientes quod omnes continuo converti debemus, memores verborum sancti Francisci : *Incipiamus fratres servire Domino Deo.*[8]

7. Finito tempore probationis, recipiantur ad obedientiam promittentes vitam istam semper et regulam observare, quia, secundum sanctum Evangelium, *nemo mittens manum ad aratrum et aspiciens retro aptus est regno Dei* (Lk 9:62).[9]

8. In signum conversionis ad vitam evangelicam non induant in posterum nisi vestimenta simplicia et vilia, sine affectatione.[10]

### III. De spiritu orationis, de officio divino et de eucharistia

9. Ubique, omni loco, omni hora et omni tempore fratres et sorores credant veraciter et humiliter et in corde teneant et ament, honorent, serviant, laudent, benedicant et glorificent altissimum et summum Deum aeternum Patrem et Filium et Spiritum sanctum.[11] Fratres et sorores in mente considerent et servent verba Domini nostri Iesu Christi, qui est Verbum Patris, et verba Spiritus sancti, quae *spiritus et vita sunt* (Jn 6:63).[12] Tenentes ergo verba, vitam et doctrinam et sanctum eius Evangelium qui dignatus est pro nobis rogare Patrem sum et nobis eius Nomen manifestare,[13] liturgiam horarum celebrent in unione cum universali Ecclesia.

---

[6]R 2:2.

[7]ER 1:2-3.

[8]1C 103.

[9]ER 2:11-13.

[10]ER 2:14.

[11]ER 23:11.

[12]2LtF 3.

[13]ER 22, 41.

5. The ministers are to make sure that the aspirants truly adhere to the Catholic faith and the life of the Roman Church.[6] If they are suitable they are to be admitted to a time of probation and introduced into the life of the fraternity. All that goes to make up this gospel way of life is to be explained to them with care. If they persevere in their desire, then let the words of the holy Gospel be proclaimed to them: If you would be perfect, go (Mt 19:21) and sell all (Lk 18:22) you possess and give to the poor, and you will have treasure in heaven, and come, follow me (Mt 19: 21). And: if anyone wishes to come after me let him deny himself, take up his cross and follow me (Mt 16:24).[7]

6. Thus, led by the Lord, let them begin a life of penance knowing that we all must continually be converted, mindful of the words of Saint Francis: "Brothers, let us begin to serve the Lord God."[8]

7. When the period of probation is complete, let them be received to obedience as they promise to observe this life and rule always. For according to the holy Gospel no one putting a hand to the plow and looking back is fit for the kingdom of God (Lk 9:62).[9]

8. From now on, as a sign of conversion to the gospel way of life they should only wear clothes that are simple, plain and unostentatious.[10]

### III. OF THE SPIRIT OF PRAYER, THE DIVINE OFFICE AND THE EUCHARIST

9. Everywhere and in every place, every day and all day the brothers and sisters must have a true and humble faith and keep him in their hearts and love, honor, adore, serve, praise, bless and glorify the most high, supreme and eternal God, the Father, Son and Holy Spirit.[11] The brothers and sisters should consider and keep in their hearts the words of our Lord Jesus Christ who is the Word of the Father, and the words of the Holy Spirit which are spirit and life (Jn 6:63).[12] They shall celebrate the Liturgy of the Hours in union with the whole Church, holding fast to the words, the life, the teaching and the holy Gospel of our

---

[6]LR 2:2; FA:ED I, 100.

[7]ER1:2-3; FA:ED I, 64.

[8]1C 103; FA:ED I, 272.

[9]LR 2:11-13; FA:ED I, 101.

[10]ER 2:14; FA:ED I, 101.

[11]ER 23:11; FA:ED I, 85.

[12]2LtF 3; FA:ED I, 45.

10. Exhibeant omnem reverentiam et omnem honorem, quantumcumque poterint, sanctissimo Corpori et Sanguini Domini nostri Iesu Christi, in quo quae in caelis et quae in terris sunt, pacificata sunt et reconciliata omnipotenti Deo (Col 1:20).[14]

11. Participent sacrificium Domini nostri Iesu Christi et recipiant Corpus et Sanguinem eius cum magna humilitate et veneratione, recordantes quod Dominus dicit: *Qui manducat* carnem meam *et bibit* sanguinem meum *habet vitam aeternam* (Jn 6:54).[15]

12. In spiritu orationis et laetitiae studeant sensum mortis et resurrectionis in Christo acquirere.

Et ieiunent diebus ab Ecclesia constitutis et aliis diebus in communitate vel propria decisione stabilitis, nisi ab infirmitate vel aliis causis impediantur.

13. Fratres et sorores Deum grati laudent propter eius mirabilia in creaturis. In labore et servitio erga homines Dominum Deum benedicant et amorem et benignitatem eius manifestent.

#### IV. Quomodo debeant ire per mundum

14. Omnes fratres et sorores, ubicumque sunt vel vadunt per mundum, non litigent neque contendant verbis, nec alios iudicent.[16] Et memores sint verborum sancti Francisci: Quos moneo et exhortor ne despiciant neque iudicent homines, quos vident mollibus vestimentis et coloratis indutos, uti cibis et potibus delicatis, sed magis unusquisque iudicet et despiciat semetipsum.[17]

Sed sint mites, pacifici et modesti, mansueti et humiles, honeste loquentes omnibus, sicut decet. *In quacumque domum intraverint, primum* dicant: *Pax huic domui* (Lk 10:5).[18]

---

[14]LtOrd 12-13.

[15]ER 20:5.

[16]LR 3:10.

[17]LR 2:17.

[18]LR 3:11-13.

Lord Jesus Christ. Of His own goodness He prayed for us to His Father and made His Father's name known to us.[13]

10. Let them show all reverence and all honor as much as lies in their power towards the most Sacred Body and Blood of our Lord Jesus Christ, in whom all things, whether in heaven or on earth, are brought to peace with and reconciled to Almighty God (Col 1:20).[14]

11. Let them take part in the sacrifice of Our Lord Jesus Christ and receive His Body and Blood with deep humility and veneration, calling to mind what the Lord says: he who eats My flesh and drinks My blood has eternal life (Jn 6:54).[15]

12. In a spirit of prayer and joy let them strive to acquire a sense of being united with Christ in His death and resurrection. And let them fast on the days prescribed by the Church and on other days decided in community or by their own decision, unless they are prevented from fasting because of sickness or some other reason.

13. The brothers and sisters shall praise God with thankfulness for His wonders in creation. Let them bless the Lord God in their work and service towards men; let them show forth His love and kindness.

### IV. OF HOW THEY ARE TO TRAVEL ABOUT THE WORLD

14. All the brothers and sisters wherever they may be or wherever they may travel about the world should not be quarrelsome or take part in disputes with words or criticize others.[16] Let them remember the words of Saint Francis: I warn and exhort them not to condemn or look down on people whom they see wearing soft or gaudy clothes and enjoying luxuries in food or drink; each one should rather condemn and despise himself.[17] Let them be gentle, peaceful, and unassuming, courteous and humble, speaking respectfully to everyone as is expected of them. Whatever house they enter, they should first say: Peace to this house (Lk 10:5).[18]

---

[13]ER 22:41; FA:ED I, 81.

[14]LtOrd 12-13; FA:ED I, 117.

[15]ER 20:5; FA:ED I, 78.

[16]LR 3:10; FA:ED I, 102.

[17]LR 2:17; FA:ED I, 101.

[18]LR 3:11-13; FA:ED I, 102.

## V. De modo serviendi et laborandi

15. Fratres et sorores quibus gratiam dedit Dominus serviendi vel laborandi serviant et laborent fideliter et devote, ita quod, excluso otio animae inimico, sanctae orationis et devotionis spiritum non exstinguant, cui debent cetera temporalia deservire.[19] Studeant bonis operibus insudare, quia scriptum est: Semper facito aliquid boni.[20] Numquam debent desiderare esse super alios, sed magis debent esse servi et subditi omni humanae creaturae propter Deum (1 Pt 2:13).[21]

16. Sicut pauperes de fructu manuum suarum manducabunt. Et pro labore possint recipere omnia necessaria eis et servitio hominum.[22]

Cupiditatem accumulandi repellentes, omnia quae supersunt pauperibus studeant erogare.[23]

## VI. De vita in paupertate

17. Omnes fratres et sorores studeant sequi humilitatem et paupertatem Domini nostri Iesu Christi qui, cum dives esset (2 Cor 8:9) super omnia, voluit ipse in mundo cum beatissima Virgine, matre sua, eligere paupertatem et semetipsum exinanivit (Phil 2:5).[24]

Et recordentur quod nihil aliud oportet nos habere de toto mundo nisi, sicut dixit apostolus, habentes alimenta et quibus tegamur, his contenti sumus (1 Tm 6:8).[25]

Et debent gaudere quando conversantur inter viles et despectas personas, inter pauperes et debiles et infirmos et leprosos et iuxta viam mendicantes.[26]

---

[19]LR 5:1-2.

[20]ER 7:10.

[21]2LtF 47.

[22]ER7:7.

[23]ER 2:4.

[24]ER 9:1; 2LtF 5.

[25]ER9:1.

[26]ER 9:2.

## V. OF THE MANNER OF SERVING AND OF WORKING

15. The brothers and sisters to whom God has given the grace of serving or working should serve and work in a spirit of faith and devotion and avoid idleness which is the enemy of the soul, without, however, extinguishing the spirit of prayer to which every temporal consideration must be subordinate.[19] Let them strive to exert themselves in doing good works, for it is written: Always do something good.[20] They must never desire to be over others, but they should prefer to serve and be subject to every human creature for God's sake (1 Pt 2:13).[21]

16. Let them labor for the food that they eat, as poor people do. From their labors they may receive all that is necessary for themselves and for their ministry to others.[22]

They must always resist the temptation to accumulate goods for themselves; rather let them be eager to give to the poor whatever is superfluous to their own needs.[23]

## VI. OF THE LIFE OF POVERTY

17. All the brothers and sisters should be eager to follow the humility and poverty of our Lord Jesus Christ. Although He was rich above all things (2 Cor 8:9), He emptied Himself (Phil 2:5), and together with the Holy Virgin His Mother, He chose poverty in this world.[24]

Let them remember that of the whole world we must own nothing; but having food and sufficient clothing, with these let us be content, as the Apostle says (1 Tm 6:8).[25]

They should be glad to live among social outcasts, among the poor and helpless, the infirm and the lepers and those who beg by the wayside.[26]

---

[19]LR 5:1-2; FA:ED I, 102.

[20]ER 7:10; FA:ED I, 69.

[21]2LtF 47; FA:ED I, 48.

[22]ER 7:7; FA:ED I, 69.

[23]ER 2:4; 64.

[24]ER 9:1; 2LtF 5; FA:ED I, 70:46.

[25]ER 9:1; FA:ED I, 70.

[26]ER 9:2; FA:ED I, 70.

18. Et nihil sibi approprient nec alicui defendant, nec domum nec locum nec aliquam rem.

Et tanquam peregrini et advenae (1 Pt 2:11) in hoc saeculo, in paupertate et humilitate Domino famulentur. Haec est illa celsitudo altissimae paupertatis, quae nos heredes et reges regni caelorum instituit, pauperes rebus fecit, virtutibus sublimavit (Jas 2:5).

Haec sit portio nostra quae perducit in terram viventium (Ps 141:6). Cui totaliter inhaerentes nihil aliud pro nomine Domini nostri Iesu Christi in perpetuum sub caelo habere velimus.[27]

19. Et ubicumque sunt et se invenerint, ostendant se domesticos inter se. Et secure manifestet unus alteri necessitatem suam, quia si mater nutrit et diligit filium sum (1 Thes 2:7) carnalem, quanto diligentius debet unusquisque diligere et nutrire fratrem sum spiritualem. Et, si quis eorum in infirmitate ceciderit, alii debent ei servire, sicut *vellent sibi serviri* (Mt 7:12).[28] Et de omnibus quae ipsis accidunt referant gratias Creatori, et quales vult eos Dominus, tales se esse desiderent sive sanos sive infirmos.[29]

## VII. De vita apostolica

20. Toto corde servantes mandata Domini et consilia eius perfecta mente implentes fratres et sorores confiteantur ei quoniam bonus (Ps 135:1) et exaltent eum in operibus suis (Tb 13:6) quoniam ideo misit eis in universo mundo, ut verbo et opere dent testimonium ei et faciant scire omnes, quoniam non est omnipotens praeter eum (Tb 13:4).[30]

21. Pacem et benignitatem Dei omnibus annuntient modo sancti Francisci: Sicut pacem annuntiatis ore, sic in cordibus vestris et amplius habeatis. Nullus per vos provocetur ad iram vel scandalum, sed omnes per mansuetudinem vestram ad pacem benignitatem et concordiam provocentur. Nam ad hoc vocati sumus ut vulneratos curemus, alligemus confractos et erroneos revocemus.[31]

---

[27]LR 6:1-2, 4-6.

[28]LR 6:7-9.

[29]ER 10:3.

[30]LtOrd 7-9.

[31]L3C 58.

18. Let them appropriate nothing to themselves, neither house, place nor anything else, nor defend them from anyone. As pilgrims and strangers (1 Pt 2:11) in this world let them serve the Lord in poverty and humility. This is the pinnacle of the most exalted poverty which has made us heirs and kings of the kingdom of heaven and poor in temporal things but rich in virtue (Jas 2:5).

This should be our portion which leads us to the land of the living (Ps 141:6). And to this we must cling with all our heart, and wish never to have anything else under heaven for the sake of our Lord Jesus Christ.[27]

19. Wherever they meet one another they should show that they are members of the same family. They should have no hesitation in making known their needs to one another. For if a mother loves and cares for her child (1 Thes 2:7) in the flesh, each one should certainly love and care for his or her spiritual brother or sister all the more tenderly. And if any of them falls ill, the others are bound to look after them as they would like to be looked after themselves (Mt 7:12).[28] And whatever may befall them let them give thanks to the Creator for it; let them be content to be as the Lord wishes them to be, in sickness or in health.[29]

## VII. OF THE LIFE OF THE APOSTOLATE

20. As they put their whole heart into keeping the precepts of the Lord and their whole mind into practicing His counsels, let the brothers and sisters bless the Lord for He is good (Ps 135:1), and exalt Him in their work (Tb 13:6) because for this reason He sent them into the whole world: to give witness to Him by word and deed and make known to all that there is no other God but Him (Tb 13:4).[30]

21. Let them proclaim the peace and goodness of God to everyone after the manner of Saint Francis: "Since you speak of peace, all the more must you have it in your hearts. Let none be provoked to anger or scandal by you, but rather may they be drawn to peace and good will, to kindness and concord through your gentleness. We have been called to heal wounds, to unite what has fallen apart, and to bring home those who have lost their way."[31]

---

[27]LR 6:1-2, 4-6; FA:ED I, 103.

[28]LR 6:7-9; FA:ED I, 103.

[29]ER 10:3; FA:ED I, 71-72.

[30]LtOrd 7-9; FA:ED I, 117.

[31]L3C 58; FA:ED II, 101.

22. Unde in caritate quae Deus est (1 Jn 4:16) omnes fratres et sorores, sive orantes sive verbum Dei annuntiantes sive laborantes, studeant se humiliare in omnibus, non gloriari nec in se gaudere nec interius se exaltare de bonis verbis et operibus, immo de nullo bono quod Deus facit vel dicit et operatur in eis aliquando et per ipsos.[32]

In omni loco et in omnibus adiunctis, agnoscant omnia bona esse Domini Dei altissimi et dominatoris omnium rerum; et ipsi gratias referant, a quo bona cuncta procedunt. Et quando viderint vel audierint malum dicere vel facere vel blasphemare Deum, ipsi bene dicant et bene faciant et laudent Deum (Rm 12:21) qui est benedictus in saecula (Rm 1:25).[33]

## VIII. De correctione fraterna

23. Fratres et sorores ostendant inter se tantam domesticam familiaritatem ut filii eiusdem matris esse videantur, sicut sanctus Franciscus desiderabat.[34] Si quis graviter neglexerit formam vitae quam professus est, admoneatur a ministro vel ab aliis qui eius culpam cognoverint. Et illi non faciant ei verecundiam neque detractionem, sed magnam misericordiam habeant circa ipsum.[35] Sed omnes attente cavere debent ne irascantur vel conturbentur propter peccatum alicuius, quia ira et conturbatio in se et in aliis impediunt caritatem.[36]

24. Si contingeret inter fratrem et fratrem vel inter sororem et sororem verbo vel signo occasionem turbationis vel scandali aliquando suboriri, qui turbationis causam dederit, statim, antequam offerat munus orationis suae coram Domino (Mt 5:24), alteri humiliter veniam petat. Et ille memor sit illius verbi Domini: *Nisi ex corde dimiseritis, nec pater vester caelestis dimittet vobis* (Mt 18:35).

---

[32]ER 17:5-6.

[33]ER 17:17-19.

[34]2C 180.

[35]LtMin 15.

[36]LR 7:3.

22. In that love which is God (1 Jn 4:16) let all the brothers and sisters, whether they are given to praying, or preaching the word of God, or manual labor, do their best to humble themselves at every opportunity; not to boast nor be self-satisfied nor to take pride in any good work which God says or does or accomplishes in them or by them.[32]

In every place and circumstance they must acknowledge that all good belongs to the most high supreme God and Master of all things, and let them give thanks to him, for all good comes from him. And when they see or hear people speaking or doing evil or blaspheming God, they must say and do good, praising God (Rm 12:21) who is blessed for ever (Rm 1:25).[33]

### VIII. OF FRATERNAL CORRECTION

23. The brothers and sisters should show to one another the familiarity of family life, so much so that they might appear to be the children of the same mother, as Saint Francis desired.[34] If any of them neglects in a serious way the form of life they have professed, let them be warned by the minister or by others who have come to know of their fault. These should not cause them embarrassment nor speak about it to others, but rather should show the greatest sympathy towards them.[35] Rather all must be careful not to be angry or upset because of another's sin, because anger or annoyance in themselves or in others makes it difficult to be charitable.[36]

24. If it should happen between one brother and another or between one sister and another, that an occasion of discord or scandal be given by word or sign, let the one who gave rise to the discord humbly seek forgiveness from the other as soon as possible, and before he or she comes before the Lord to make his or her offering of prayer (Mt 5:24). Let the other remember this saying of the Lord: If you do not forgive from your heart, your heavenly Father will not forgive you (Mt 18:35).

---

[32]ER 17:5-6; FA:ED 1, 75.

[33]ER 17:17-19; FA:ED I, 75.

[34]2C 180; FA:ED II, 362.

[35]LtMin 15; FA:ED I, 98.

[36]LR 7:3; FA:ED I, 104.

## IX. De vita in obedientia

25. Fratres et sorores, exemplo Domini Iesu qui posuit voluntatem-suam in voluntate Patris,[37] recordentur quod propter Deum abne-gaverunt proprias voluntates. Non habeant potestatem vel domina-tionemmaxime inter se. Nullus malum faciat vel malum dicat alteri; immomagis per caritatem spiritus voluntarie serviant et obediant invicem(Gal 5:13). Et haec est vera et sancta obedientia Domini nostri Iesu Christi.[38]

## X. De capitulis et ministris

26. In omnibus capitulis quae faciunt, fratres et sorores primum quaer-ant regnum Dei et iustitiam eius (Mt 6:33)[39] et sese exhortentur ut pos-sint regulam quam promiserunt melius observare[40] et fideliter sequi vestigia Domini nostri Iesu Christi.

27. Unum teneantur semper habere ministrum et servum fraternitatis et ei teneantur firmiter obedire.[41]

28. Illi qui sunt ministri et servi aliorum visitent et moneant eos, ethu-militer et caritative corrigant eos, non praecipientes eis aliquid, quod sit contra animam suam et regulam.[42]

29. Et ubicumque sunt fratres et sorores, qui scirent et cognoscerent se non posse regulam spiritualiter observare, ad suos ministros debeant et possint recurrere. Ministri vero caritative et benigne eos recipiant et tantam familiaritatem habeant circa ipsos, ut dicere possint eis et facere sicut domini servis suis; nam ita esse debet quod ministri sint servi omnium.[43]

30. Et nullus sibi appropriet aliquod ministerium; tempore statuto ipse libenter munus suum dimittat.[44]

---

[37]2LtF 10.
[38]ER 5:9, 13-15.
[39]RH 3.
[40]Test 34.
[41]LR 8:1.
[42]LR 10:1.
[43]LR 10:4-6.
[44]ER 17:4.

## IX. OF THE LIFE OF OBEDIENCE

25. Let the brothers and sisters remember that for God they have renounced their own free will, after the example of the Lord Jesus who placed His own will into the will of the Father.[37] Let them not have power or authority, especially over one another. Far from doing or speaking evil to one another, they should be glad to serve and obey one another in a spirit of charity (Gal 5:13). This is the true and holy obedience of our Lord Jesus Christ.[38]

## X. OF CHAPTERS AND MINISTERS

26. In all the chapters that they hold the brothers and sisters should seek first the kingdom of God and His justice (Mt 6:33).[39] Let them exhort one another as to how they can observe better the Rule which they have promised to keep,[40] and follow in the footsteps of our Lord Jesus Christ.

27. They must always have as minister and servant of the fraternity, one whom they are firmly bound to obey.[41]

28. Those who are ministers and servants of the others must visit them and admonish them, correcting them humbly and charitably, without commanding them anything that is against their conscience and Rule.[42]

29. Wherever they may be, the brothers and sisters who know and are convinced that they cannot observe the Rule spiritually can and must have recourse to their ministers. The ministers for their part are bound to receive them kindly and charitably, and be so sympathetic towards them that these may speak and deal with them as employers with their servants. Indeed this is the way it ought to be: the ministers should be servants of all.[43]

30. No one is to appropriate any office; and this office must be relinquished willingly at the appointed time.[44]

---

[37] 2LtF, 10; FA:ED I, 42.

[38] ER 5:9, 13-15; FA:ED I, 67-68.

[39] RH 3; FA:ED I, 61.

[40] Test 34; FA:ED I, 127.

[41] LR 8:1; FA:ED I, 104.

[42] LR 10:1; FA:ED I, 105.

[43] LR 10:4-6; FA:ED I, 105.

[44] ER 17:4; FA:ED I, 75.

## XI. De vita in castitate

31. Omni impedimento remoto et omni cura et sollicitudine postposita satagant, quocumque modo melius possunt, servire, amare, honorare et adorare Dominum Deum mundo corde et pura mente, in castitate viventes.[45]

32. Et semper in seipsis faciant habitaculum et mansionem (Jn 14:23) ipsi qui est Dominus Deus omnipotens, Pater et Filius et Spiritus sanctus,[46] ita ut in amorem universalem cum cordibus indivisis crescant, sese continuo convertentes ad Deum et proximum.

## XII. De admonitione fratrum et sororum

33. Attendant omnes fratres et sorores quod super omnia desiderare debent habere spiritum Domini et sanctam eius operationem, orare semper ad eum puro corde et habere humilitatem, patientiam in persecutione et infirmitate et diligere eos qui nos persequuntur et reprehendunt et arguunt, quia dicit Dominus: Diligite inimicos vestros et orate pro persequentibus et calumniantibus vos (Mt 5:44). Beati qui persecutionem patiuntur propter iustitiam, quoniam ipsorum est regnum caelorum (Mt 5:10). Qui autem perseveraverit usque in finem hic salvus erit (Mt 10:22).[47]

34. Et semper subditi sanctae Ecclesiae stabiles in fide catholica paupertatem et humilitatem et sanctum Evangelium Domini nostri Iesu Christi quod firmiter promiserunt observent.[48]

35. Et quicumque haec observaverit in caelo repleatur benedictione dilecti Filii sui cum sanctissimo Spiritu Paraclito et omnibus virtutibus caelorum et omnibus sanctis. Et ego frater Franciscus parvulus vester servus, quantumcumque possum, confirmo vobis intus et foris istam sanctissimam benedictionem.[49]

---

[45]ER 22:26.
[46]ER 22:27.
[47]LR 10:8-12.
[48]LR 12:4.
[49]Test 40-41.

## XI. OF THE LIFE OF CHASTITY

31. Let them put away every attachment and leave aside all care and solicitude, and through a life of chastity let them occupy themselves to the best of their ability in serving, loving, honoring and adoring the Lord God with a pure heart and unsullied mind.[45]

32. They should always have a dwelling place and home within themselves (Jn 14:23) for Him who is the Lord God Almighty, Father, Son and Holy Spirit,[46] so that while their heart remains undivided, they may grow in an all-embracing love for both God and their neighbor, to whom they should always be attentive.

## XII. ON ADMONISHING THE BROTHERS AND SISTERS

33. Let the brothers and sisters realize that the only thing they should desire is to have the Spirit of God at work within them, while they pray to Him unceasingly with a heart free from self-interest. They must be humble, too, and patient in persecution or illness, loving those who persecute us by blaming us or bringing charges against us, as our Lord tells us: Love your enemies, pray for those who persecute and calumniate you (Mt 5:44). Blessed are those who suffer persecution for justice sake for theirs is the kingdom of heaven (Mt 5:10). He who has persevered to the end will be saved (Mt 10:22).[47]

34. Let them be submissive to the Holy Church; firmly established in the Catholic faith, may they live always according to the poverty and the humility and the Gospel of our Lord Jesus Christ as they have firmly promised.[48]

35. And may whoever observes all this be filled in heaven with the blessing of the most high Father, and on earth with that of His beloved Son, together with the Holy Spirit, the Comforter, and all the powers of heaven and all the saints. And I, brother Francis, your poor worthless servant, add my share internally and externally to that most holy blessing.[49]

---

[45]ER 22:26; FA:ED I, 80.

[46]ER 22:27; FA:ED I, 80.

[47]LR 10:8-12; FA:ED I, 105.

[48]LR 12:4; FA:ED I, 106.

[49]Test 40-41; FA:ED I, 127.

## REGULA ET VITA FRATRUM ET SORORUM ORDINIS REGULARIS
## SANCTI FRANCISCI
### (Brussels, May 1981)

PROLOGUS[1]

In nomine Domini!

Omnes qui Dominum diligunt ex toto corde, ex tota anima et mente, ex tota virtute (Mk 12:30) et diligunt proximos suos sicut se ipsos (Mt 22:39), et odio habent corpora eorum cum vitiis et peccatis, et recipiunt corpus et sanguinem Domini nostri Iesu Christi, et faciunt fructus dignos poenitentiae: O quam beati et benedicti sunt illi et illae, dum talia faciunt et in talibus perseverant, qui requiescet super eos spiritus Domini (Is 11:2) et faciet apud eos habitaculum et mansionem (Jn 14:23), et sunt filii patris caelestis (Mt 5:45), cuis opera faciunt, et sunt sponsi, fratres et matres Domini nostri Iesu Christi (Mt 12:50).

Sponsi sumus, quando Spiritu Sancto coniungitur fidelis anima Domino nostro Iesu Christo. Fratres ei sumus, quando facimus voluntatem patris qui in caelis est (Mt 12:50); matres, quando portamus eum in corde et corpore nostro (1 Cor 6:20) per divinum amorem et puram et sinceram conscientiam; parturimus eum per sanctam operationem, quae lucere debet aliis in exemplum (Mt 5:16).

O quam gloriosum est, sanctum et magnum in caelis habere patrem! O quam sanctum, paraclitum, pulchrum et admirabilem talem habere sponsum! O quam sanctum et quam dilectum, beneplacitum, humilem, pacificum, dulcem, amabilem et super omnia desiderabilem habere talem fratrem et talem filium: Dominum nostrum Iesum Christum, qui posuit animam pro ovibus suis (Jn 10:15) et oravit patri dicens: Pater sancte, serva eos in nomine tuo (Jn 17:11), quos dedisti mihi in mundo; tui erant et mihi dedisti eos (Jn 17:6). Et verba quae mihi dedisti, dedi eis, et ipsi acceperunt et crediderunt vere, quia a te exivi et cognoverunt, quia tu me misisti (Jn 17:8). Rogo pro eis et non pro mundo (Jn 17:9). Benedic et sanctifica (Jn 17:17) et pro eis sanctifico me ipsum (Jn 17:19). Non pro eis rogo tantum, sed et pro eis qui credituri sunt per verbum illorum in me (Jn 17:20), ut sint sanctificati in unum (Jn 17:23) sicut et nos (Jn 17:11). Et volo, pater, ut ubi ego sum et illi sint mecum, ut videant claritatem meam (Jn 17:24) in regno tuo (Mt 20:21). Amen.

---

[1]1LtF I.

# RULE AND LIFE OF THE BROTHERS AND SISTERS OF THE REGULAR ORDER OF SAINT FRANCIS
(Brussels, May 1981)

## PROLOGUE[1]
In the Name of the Lord!

All men and women who love the Lord with their whole heart, with their whole soul and mind, and with their whole strength (Mk 12:30) and love their neighbor as themselves (Mt 22:39); who hate the source of evil in themselves and the vices and sins which come from it; who receive the Body and Blood of our Lord Jesus Christ, and bring forth worthy fruits of penance – how fortunate and blessed they are in doing these things and persevering in them. For the Spirit of the Lord shall rest upon them (Is 11:2), and He will make his home and dwelling place with them (Jn 14:23); they are children of the Father in heaven (Mt 5:45), whose works they do. They are the spouses, brothers and mothers of our Lord Jesus Christ (Mt 12:50).

We are His spouses, when the faithful soul is joined to our Lord Jesus Christ by the Holy Spirit. We are His brothers, when we do the will of the Father who is in heaven (Mt 12:5); we are mothers to Him, when we carry Him in our heart and body (1 Cor 6:20), through divine love and by a pure and sincere conscience. We give birth to Him by our good works, which should shine out as an example for others (Mt 5:16).

O how glorious it is to have a Father in heaven, holy and great! O how holy it is to have such a Spouse, comforting, beautiful and wonderful! O how holy and delightful it is to have such a Brother and Son, well pleasing, humble and peaceful, sweet, lovable and desirable above everything: our Lord Jesus Christ, who laid down His life for His sheep (Jn 10:15); He prayed to the Father, saying: Holy Father, keep them in your name (Jn 17:11), whom You have given to Me in the world. They were Yours and You have given them to Me (Jn 17:6). I have given them the words which You gave to Me, and they have received them and believe in truth that I came from You, and they know that You did send Me (Jn 17:8). I am praying for them, not for the world (Jn 17:9). Bless and sanctify them (Jn 17:17), for their sake I consecrate Myself (Jn 17:19). I do not pray for these only, but also for those who believe in Me through their word (Jn 17:20), that they may be consecrated in unity (Jn 17:23), even as We are (Jn 17:11). And I wish, Father, that where I am, they may be with Me, to behold my glory (Jn 17:24) in Your kingdom (Mt 20:21). Amen.

---

[1]1LtF1; FA:ED I, 41-42.

**I. In nomine Domini! Incipit regula et vita fratrum et sororum Ordinis Regularis sancti Francisci.**

1. Forma vitae fratrum et sororum Ordinis Regularis sancti Francisci haec est: Domini nostri Iesu Christi sanctum Evangelium observare, vivendo in obedientia, in paupertate et in castitate.[2] Attendentes vitam et exemplum sancti Francisci[3] tenentur plura et maiora facere observantes praecepta et consilia Domini nostri Iesu Christi et debent semetipsos abnegare (Mt 16:24) sicut unusquisque promisit Deo.[4]

2. Fratres et sorores istius Ordinis cum universis qui Domino Deo intra sanctam Ecclesiam catholicam et apostolicam servire volunt in vera fide et poenitentia perseverent quia aliter nullus salvari potest.[5] Et abstineant ab omni malo et perseverent usque in finem in bono[6] quia ipse Filius Dei venturus est in gloria et dicet omnibus qui eum cognoverunt et adoraverunt et ei servierunt in poenitentia: *Venite, benedicti Patris mei*, percipite *regnum* quod *vobis paratum* est ab origine *mundi* (Mt 25:34).[7]

3. Fratres et sorores promittunt obedientiam et reverentiam Papae et Ecclesiae catholicae. Eodem spiritu his qui ad servitium fraternitatis instituti sunt obediant.[8] Et ubicumque sunt et in quocumque loco se invenerint, spiritualiter et diligenter debeant se revidere et honorare ad invicem.[9] Et unitatem et communionem cum omnibus familiae franciscanae membris foveant.

**II. De vita ista accipienda**

4. Illi qui Domino inspirante veniunt ad nos volentes hanc vitam accipere benigne recipiantur. Et opportuno tempore ministris praesentabuntur quibus potestas est in fraternitatem admittendi.[10]

---

[2] LR 1:1; ER 1:1; FLCl 1:2.

[3] FLCl 6:1.

[4] 2LtF 36-40.

[5] ER 23:7.

[6] ER 21:9.

[7] ER 23:4.

[8] LR 1:2-3; FLCl 1:3-5.

[9] ER 7:15; LR 6:7-8.

[10] Test 1; ER 2:1-3; LR 2:1; FLCl 2:1.

**I. IN THE NAME OF THE LORD! HERE BEGINS THE RULE AND LIFE OF THE BROTHERS AND SISTERS OF THE REGULAR ORDER OF SAINT FRANCIS**

1. This is the form of life of the brothers and sisters of the Regular Order of Saint Francis: to observe the Holy Gospel of our Lord Jesus Christ, by living in obedience, poverty and chastity.[2] As followers of the life and example of Saint Francis,[3] they are obliged to make more and greater efforts in observing the precepts and counsels of our Lord Jesus Christ. They are bound to deny themselves (Mt 16:24) as each has promised to God.[4]

2. The brothers and sisters of this Order, like everyone who desires to serve the Lord in the holy, catholic and apostolic Church, must persevere in true faith and penance, because there is no other way to be saved.[5] Therefore, they must keep away from all evil and go on doing good to the end.[6] For the Son of God will come again in glory, and He will say to all who have acknowledged and worshipped Him, and served Him in penance: Come, you whom my Father has blessed, take for your heritage the kingdom prepared for you since the foundation of the world (Mt 25:34).[7]

3. The brothers and sisters promise obedience and reverence to the Pope and to the Catholic Church. In the same spirit they are to obey those who have been entrusted with the service of authority in the fraternity.[8] Wherever they are and in whatever place they meet, the brothers and sisters should greet and honor one another fervently and from the heart.[9] They should foster unity and fellowship with all the members of the Franciscan family.

**II. RECEPTION INTO THIS WAY OF LIFE**

4. Those who come to us, under the Lord's inspiration, wishing to take up this way of life, are to be received with kindness. At the appropriate

---

[2]LR 1:1; FA:ED I, 100; ER 1:1; FA:ED I, 63; FLCl 1:2; CA:ED, 108.
[3]FLCl 6:1; CA:ED, 117.
[4]2LtF 36-40; FA:ED I, 48.
[5]ER 23:7; FA:ED I, 84.
[6]ER 21:9; FA:ED I, 78.
[7]ER 23:4; FA:ED I, 82.
[8]LR 1:2-3; FA:ED I, 100; FLCl 1:3-5; CA:ED, 109.
[9]ER 7:15; FA:ED I, 69; LR 6:7-8; FA:ED I, 103.

5. Ministri certiores fiant aspirantes vere fidei catholicae adhaerere sacramentisque ecclesiasticis. Si illi idonei sint, vitae fraternitatis initientur. Et omnia ad hanc vitam evangelicam pertinentia eis diligenter exponantur, praesertim haec verba Domini: *Si vis perfectus esse, vade et vende omnia quae habes, et da pauperibus* (Mt 19:21; Lk 18:22) *et habebis thesaurum in caelo, et veni, sequere me. Et si quis vult post me venire, abneget semetipsum et tollat crucem suam et sequatur me* (Mt 16:24).[11]

6. Sic Domino ducente incipiant vitam poenitentiae scientes quod omnes continuo convertendi sumus. Conversionem et consecrationem ad vitam evangelicam significantes vilibus vestibus induantur et simpliciter conversentur.[12]

7. Finito vero tempore probationis recipiantur ad obedientiam promittentes vitam istam semper et regulam observare.[13] Et omni cura et sollicitudine postposita satagant, quocumque modo melius possunt, servire, amare, honorare et adorare Dominum Deum mundo corde et pura mente.[14]

8. Et semper in seipsis faciant habitaculum et mansionem ipsi qui est Dominus Deus omnipotens, Pater et Filius et Spiritus sanctus,[15] ita ut in amorem universalem cum cordibus indivisis crescant, sese continuo convertentes ad Deum et proximum (Jn 14:23).

## III. De spiritu orationis

9. Ubique, omni loco, omni hora et omni tempore fratres et sorores credant veraciter et humiliter et in corde teneant et ament, honorent, adorent, serviant, laudent, benedicant et glorificent altissimum et summum Deum aeternum Patrem et Filium et Spiritum sanctum.[16] Et adorent eum puro corde, *quoniam oportet semper orare et non*

---

[11]LR 2:2-6; FLCl 2:2-4; ER 1:1-3.

[12]ER 2:14.

[13]LR 2:11; FLCl 2:8.

[14]ER 22:26; Adm 16.

[15]ER 22:27; 1LtF 1:5-10; 2LtF 48-53.

[16]ER 23:11.

time they are to be presented to the ministers, who have the authority to admit them.[10]

5. The ministers must make sure that aspirants truly adhere to the Catholic faith and the sacraments of the Church. If they have the qualities, they are to be introduced to the life of the fraternity. Then, everything about this Gospel way of life is to be carefully explained to them, especially these words of the Lord: if you wish to be perfect go and sell all that you own and give the money to the poor (Mt 19:21; Lk 18:22), and you will have treasure in heaven; then come, follow Me; and if anyone wants to be a follower of mine, let him renounce himself and take up his cross and follow Me (Mt 16:24).[11]

6. So, under the Lord's guidance, let them set out on a life of penance, knowing that we are all obliged to constant conversion of heart. As a sign of their conversion and consecration to the Gospel life, they are to wear inexpensive clothes and lead a simple life.[12]

7. At the end of the period of formation they are to be received into obedience, promising to observe this rule and life always.[13] They should cast away all cares and anxiety and be concerned how best to serve, love, reverence and adore the Lord God, with an honest heart and a devout mind.[14]

8. Let them always make a home and dwelling place in themselves for Him who is the Lord God almighty, Father, Son and Holy Spirit.[15] So, with undivided hearts, they may grow in all-embracing love, as they turn without ceasing towards God and their neighbor (Jn 14:23).

## III. THE SPIRIT OF PRAYER

9. All over the world, in every place, at every hour and every moment, the brothers and sisters should believe truly and humbly. In their heart they should cherish, love, reverence, adore, serve, praise, bless and glorify the most high and supreme, eternal God, Father, Son and Holy Spirit.[16] They should adore Him with all their heart because we ought always to pray and not lose heart (Lk 18:1). The Father seeks such

---

[10]Test 1; FA:ED I, 124; ER 2:1; FA:ED I, 64; LR 2:1; FA:ED I, 100.

[11]LR 2:2-6; FA:ED I, 100; FLCl 2:-4; CA:ED, 110; ER 1:2-3; FA:ED I, 64.

[12]ER 2:14; FA:ED I, 65.

[13]LR 2:11; FA:ED I, 101; FLCl 2:8; CA:ED, 110.

[14]ER 22:26; FA:ED I, 80; Adm 16; FAED, 134.

[15]ER 22:27; FA:ED I, 80; 1LtF 1:5-10; FA:ED I, 41-42; 2LtF 48-53; FA:ED I, 49-49.

[16]ER 23:11; FA:ED I, 85-86.

*deficere* (Lk 18:11); nam Pater tales quaerit adoratores.[17] Itaque officium divinum in unione cum universali Ecclesia celebrent.

10. Dominum regem caeli et terrae (Mt 11:25) fratres et sorores laudent cum universis creaturis eius et gratias ei agant quod per sanctam voluntatem suam et per unicum Filium suum cum Spiritu sancto creavit omnia spiritualia et corporalia et nos ad imaginem suam et simimilitudinem.[18]

11. Sancto Evangelio se totaliter conformantes fratres et sorores in mente considerent et servent verba Domini nostri Iesu Christi qui est verbum Patris, et verba Spiritus sancti quae *spiritus et vita sunt* (Jn 6:63).[19]

12. Participent sacrificium Domini nostri Iesu Christi et recipiant Corpus et Sanguinem eius cum magna humilitate et veneratione, recordantes quod Dominus dicit: *Qui manducat* carnem meam *et bibit* sanguinem meum *habet vitam aeternam* (Jn 6:54).[20]

Exhibeant omnem reverentiam et omnem honorem, quantumcumque poterint, sanctissimo Corpori et Sanguini Domini nostri Iesu Christi in quo quae in caelis et quae in terris sunt pacificata sunt et reconciliata omnipotenti Deo (Col 1:20).[21]

13. Et in omnibus suis offensis fratres et sorores non tardant interius punire per contritionem et exterius per confessionem et faciant fructus dignos poenitentiae.[22] Debent etiam ieiunare, sed studeant semper esse simplices et humiles.[23] Nihil ergo aliquid aliud desiderent nisi Salvatorem nostrum qui se ipsum per proprium sanguinem suum sacrificium et hostiam in ara crucis obtulit pro peccatis nostris, relinquens nobis exemplum ut sequamur vestigia eius.[24]

## IV. De modo serviendi et laborandi

14. Sicut pauperes fratres et sorores quibus gratiam dedit Dominus serviendi vel laborandi, serviant et laborent fideliter et devote, ita

---

[17]ER 22:29-30.

[18]ER 23:1; CtC 3.

[19]2LtF 3.

[20]ER 20:5.

[21]LtOrd 12-13; 1LtF 1; Test 12.

[22]Adm 23:3; 2LtF 25.

[23]Adm 19:2; 2LtF 45.

[24]ER 23:9; 2LtF 11-14.

worshippers.[17] Therefore in union with the whole Church, the brothers and sisters should celebrate the Liturgy of the Hours.

10. The brothers and sisters should praise the Lord King of heaven and earth (Mt 11:25), in union with all His creatures. They should give Him thanks because by his own holy will and through His only Son, with the Holy Spirit, He created all things spiritual and material and He made us in His own image and likeness.[18]

11. The brothers and sisters are to conform themselves totally to the Holy Gospel. Therefore they should keep in mind and meditate on the words of our Lord Jesus Christ, who is the Word of the Father, and on the words of the Holy Spirit, which are spirit and life (Jn 6:63).[19]

12. They should take part in the sacrifice of our Lord Jesus Christ and receive His Body and Blood with great humility and reverence, recalling the words of the Lord: Anyone who eats my flesh and drinks my blood has eternal life (Jn 6:54).[20]

They must show all reverence and honor, as much as they are able, for the most holy Body and Blood of our Lord Jesus Christ, in whom all things in heaven and on earth, have been brought to peace and reconciled with Almighty God (Col 1:20).[21]

13. When they sin, the brothers and sisters should do penance without delay, inwardly by sorrow and outwardly by confession, and they should bring forth worthy fruits of penance.[22] They should fast, and strive to be always simple and humble.[23]

They should desire nothing else except our Savior who offered Himself, by his own blood, on the altar of the cross, as a sacrifice and victim for our sins. He left us an example so that we might follow in His footsteps.[24]

## IV. THE WAY TO SERVE AND WORK

14. The brothers and sisters to whom the Lord has given the grace of serving others or working, should serve and work faithfully and de-

---

[17]ER 22:29-30; FA:ED I, 80.

[18]ER 23:1; FA:ED I, 81; CtC 3; FA:ED I, 113.

[19]2LtF 3; FA:ED I, 45.

[20]ER 20:5; FA:ED I, 78.

[21]LtOrd 12-13; FA:ED I, 117; 1LtF 1; FA:ED I, 41-42; Test 12; FA:ED I, 125.

[22]Adm 23:3; FA:ED I, 136; 2LtF 25; FA:ED I, 47.

[23]Adm 19; FA:ED I, 48; 2LtF 45; FA:ED I, 48.

[24]ER 23:9; FA:ED I, 85; 2LtF 11-14; FA:ED I, 46.

quod, excluso otio animae inimico, sanctae orationis et devotionis spiritum non exstinguant, cui debent cetera temporalia deservire.[25]

15. De mercede vero laboris pro se et suis fratribus et sororibus corporis necessaria recipiant et hoc humiliter sicut decet servos Dei et paupertatis sanctissimae sectatores.[26] Et omnia quae supersint pauperibus studeant erogare. Et numquam debent desiderare esse super alios, sed magis debent esse servi et subditi omni humanae creaturae propter Deum (1 Pt 2:13).[27]

16. Fratres et sorores sint mites, pacifici et modest, mansueti et humiles, honeste loquentes omnibus sicut decet. Et ubicumque sunt vel vadunt per mundum, non litigent neque contendant verbis, nec alios iudicent, sed ostendant se *gaudentes in Domino* (Phil 4:4) et *hilares* et convenienter gratiosos.[28] Et salutationem dicant: Dominus det tibi pacem.[29]

## V. DE VITA IN PAUPERTATE

17. Omnes fratres et sorores studeant sequi humilitatem et paupertatem Domini nostri Iesu Christi qui, *cum dives esset super omnia* (2 Cor 8:9), voluit ipse in mundo cum beatissima Virgine matre sua eligere paupertatem et semetipsum exinanivit (Phil 2:7).[30]

Et recordentur quod nihil aliud oportet nos habere de toto mundo nisi, sicut dicit apostolus, *habentes alimenta et quibus tegamur, his contenti sumus* (1 Tm 6:8).[31] Et caveant multum a pecunia.[32]

Et debent gaudere, quando conversantur inter viles et despectas personas, inter pauperes et debilis et infirmos et leprosos et iuxta viam mendicantes.[33]

---

[25]LR 5:1-2; FLCl 7:1-2.

[26]ER 2:4; 9:8.

[27]2LtF 47.

[28]LR 2:17; 3:10; ER 7:16.

[29]Test 23.

[30]ER 9:1; 2LtF 5; FLCl 6:3.

[31]LR 6:3-4.

[32]ER 8:11.

[33]ER 9:2.

votedly, like the poor. Let them beware of idleness which is the enemy of the soul. In their service and work they should not extinguish the spirit of holy prayer and devotion, which all earthly things are meant to foster.[25]

15. In return for their work they may accept what is necessary for their material needs and those of their brothers and sisters. They should accept it humbly as is rightfully expected of God's servants and followers of most high poverty.[26] What they have left over, they should give to the poor. They should never want to be in charge of others. On the contrary, they should be servants and, for the Lord's sake, be subject to human creature. (1 Pt 2:13)[27]

16. The brothers and sisters should be meek, peaceful and unassuming, gentle and humble, speaking courteously to everyone, as it is right. Wherever they are and wherever they go in the world, they are not to quarrel, get into arguments or others. They should show that they are joyful in the Lord (Phil 4:4), good-humored and gracious, as is right.[28] When they greet others they should say: The Lord give you peace.[29]

## V. THE LIFE OF POVERTY

17. All the brothers and sisters must strive to follow the humility and the poverty of our Lord Jesus Christ. Though He was rich beyond measure (2 Cor 8:9), He chose poverty in this world, as did His mother, the Blessed Virgin Mary; and He emptied Himself (Phil 2:7).[30] Let them remember that we are to have nothing of this world except food and clothing; let us be content with that (1 Tm 6:8),[31] as Saint Paul says. They should be profoundly suspicious of money.[32]

Let them rejoice when they live among the outcast and despised, among the poor and the weak, the sick and the lepers and those who beg in the streets.[33]

---

[25]LR 5:1-2; FA:ED I, 102; FLCl 7:1-2; CA:ED, 119.

[26]ER 2:4, 9:8; FA:ED I, 64,71.

[27]2LtF 47; FA:ED I, 48.

[28]LR 2:17; 3:10; FA:ED I, 101-102; ER 7:16; FA:ED I, 69.

[29]Test 23; FA:ED I, 126.

[30]ER 9:1; FA:ED I, 70; 2LtF 5; FA:ED I, 46; FLCl 6:3; CA:ED, 118.

[31]LR 5:3-4; FA:ED I, 102-103.

[32]ER 8:11; FA:ED I, 70.

[33]ER 9:2; FA:ED I, 70.

18. Qui vere pauperes sunt spiritu, exemplum Domini sequentes nihil sibi appropriant nec alicui defendunt, sed tanquam peregrini et advenae (1 Pt 2:1) in hoc saeculo vivunt. Haec est illa celsiduto altissimae paupertatis quae nos heredes et reges regni caelorum instituit, pauperes rebus fecit, virtutibus sublimavit (Jas 2:5).

Haec sit portio nostra quae perducit in terram viventium (Ps 141:6). Cui totaliter inhaerentes nihil aliud pro nomine Domini nostri Iesu Christi in perpetuum sub caelo habere velimus (Mt 10:27-29).[34]

### VI. De vita fraterna

19. Propter amorem Dei fratres et sorores diligant se ad invicem, sicut dicit Dominis: *hoc est praeceptum meum ut diligatis invicem sicut dilexi vos* (Jn 15:12). Et ostendant ex operibus dilectionem quam habent ad invicem (Jn 12:18; 1 Jn 3:18).[35] Et secure manifestet unus alteri necessitatem suam, ut sibi necessaria inveniat et ministret.[36] Et beati sunt qui tantum diligerent alterum quando est infirmus, quod non potest eis satisfacere, quantum quando est sanus, qui potest eis satisfacere.[37]

Et de omnibus quae ipsis accidunt, referant gratias Creatori,[38] et quales sint tales se esse desiderent sive sanos sive infirmos.

20. Si contingeret inter eos verbo vel signo occasionem turbationis aliquando suboriri, statim (Mt 5:24), antequam offerat munus orationis suae coram Domino (Mt 18:35), unus alteri humiliter veniam petat. Si quis graviter neglexerit forman vitae quam professus est, admoneatur a ministro vel ab aliis qui eius culpam cognoverint. Et illi non faciant ei verecundiam neque detractionem, sed magnam misericordiam habeant circa ipsum.[39] Sed omnes attente cavere debent ne irascantur et conturbentur propter peccatum alicuius, quia ira et conturbatio in se et in aliis impediunt caritatem.[40]

---

[34]LR 6:1-2, 4-6; FLCl 8:1-2.

[35]ER 11:5-6; TestCl 18.

[36]ER 9:10.

[37]Adm 24.

[38]ER 10:3.

[39]LtMin 15.

[40]LR 7:3; FLCl 9:3-4.

18. The truly poor in spirit, following the example of the Lord neither possess nor defend anything as their own. They live in this world as pilgrims and strangers (1 Pt 2:1). This is the summit of the most exalted poverty which makes us heirs and kings of the kingdom of heaven. It has made us poor in earthly goods, but has raised us high in virtue (Jas 2:5).

Let this be our heritage which leads into the land of the living (Ps 141:6). Holding fast to this, for the name of our Lord Jesus Christ, may we never want to have anything else under heaven (Mt 10: 27-29).[34]

### VI. FRATERNAL LIFE

19. Because of God's love, the brothers and sisters should love one another, as the Lord says: This is my commandment, that you love one another as I have loved you (Jn 15:12). Let them show by their actions that they love one another (Jn 12:18; 1 Jn 3:18).[35] With confidence let them make their needs known to one another.[36] They are blessed who love their brethren as much when they are sick and cannot repay them, as when they are well and can repay them.[37]

No matter what happens to they should give thanks to the Creator.[38] They should accept willingly the condition in which they themselves, be it sickness or health.

20. If disharmony arises among them because of something said or done, they should ask forgiveness of one another at once with humility, before they offer their gift of prayer to the Lord (Mt 5:24; Mt 18:35). If any brothers or sisters gravely transgress the form of life they have professed, the minister, or others who may know about it, should admonish them. In doing so, they should cause them no shame, nor speak evil about them, but show them great kindness.[39]

They must all be very careful not to be angry or vexed on account of anyone's sin, because anger and vexation hinder love in themselves and in others.[40]

---

[34]LR 6:1-2; 4-6; FA:ED I, 103; FLCl 8: 1-2; CA:ED, 119.

[35]ER 11:5-6; FA:ED I, 72; TestCl 18; CA:ED, 61.

[36]ER 9:10; FA:ED I, 71.

[37]Adm 24; FA:ED I, 136.

[38]ER 10:3; FA:ED I, 71.

[39]LtMin 15; FA:ED I, 98.

[40]LR 7:3; FA:ED I, 104; FLCl 9:3-4; CA:ED, 121.

**VII. DE OBEDIENTIA CARITATIVA**

21. Fratres et sorores, exemplo Domini Iesu qui posuit voluntatem suam in voluntate Patris,[41] recordentur quod propter Deum abnegaverunt proprias voluntates.[42] In omnibus capitulis quae faciunt primum quaerant *regnum Dei et iustitiam eius* (Mt 6:33) et sese exhortentur ut possint regulam quam promiserunt melius observare et fideliter sequi vestigia Domini nostri Iesu Christi.[43] Non habeant potestatem vel dominationem maxime inter se.[44] *Per caritatem spiritus* (Gal 5:13) voluntarie serviant et obediant *invicem*. Et haec est vera et sancta obedientia Domini nostri Iesu Christi.[45]

22. Unum tenantur semper habere ministrum et servum fraternitatis[46] et ei teneantur firmiter obedire in omnibus quae promiserunt Domino observare et non sunt contraria animae et isti regulae.[47]

23. Illi qui sunt ministri et servi aliorum eos visitent et humiliter et caritative moneant et confortent eos.[48] Et ubicumque sunt fratres et sorores qui scirent et cognoscerent se non posse regulam spiritualiter observare, ad suos ministros debeant et possing recurrere. Ministri vero caritative et benigne eos recipiant et tantam familiaritatem habeant circa ipsos ut dicere possint eis et facere sicut domini servis suis: nam ita debet esse quod ministri sint servi omnium.[49]

24. Et nullus sibi appropriet aliquod ministerium; sed statuto tempore ipse libenter munus suum dimittat.[50]

---

[41]2LtF 10.

[42]LR 10:2; FLCl 10:2.

[43]ER 18:1; Test 34.

[44]ER 5:9.

[45]ER 5:14-15.

[46]LR 8:1.

[47]LR 10:3; FLCl 10:2.

[48]ER 4:2; FLCl 10:1.

[49]LR 10:4-6; FLCl 10:3; TestCl 19.

[50]ER 17:4.

## VII. THE OBEDIENCE OF LOVE

21. According to the example of the Lord Jesus, who sacrificed His own will to the will of the Father,[41] the brothers and sisters should remember that they have renounced their own wills for God's sake.[42] In all the chapters they hold let them seek first the kingdom of God and His justice (Mt 6:33), and exhort one another to observe with greater dedication the rule they have professed, and to follow faithfully in the footsteps of our Lord Jesus Christ.[43] No one is to have power or dominate over others.[44] Through love, all should serve and obey one another willingly (Gal 5:13). This is true and holy obedience of our Lord Jesus Christ.[45]

22. They are always bound to have one of their members as ministers and servants of the fraternity,[46] whom they are strictly obliged to obey in everything they have promised the Lord to observe, and which is not against their conscience and this rule.[47]

23. Those who are ministers and servants of the others, should visit them, and with humility and love, advise and encourage them.[48] Wherever there are brothers and sisters who know and acknowledge that they cannot observe the rule spiritually, they can and ought to have recourse to their ministers. The ministers, for their part, should receive them with love and kindness, and show them such friendship that these brothers and sisters can speak and treat with them as would masters with their servants. For so it should be, that the ministers be the servants of everyone.[49]

24. No one is to appropriate any ministry. On the contrary, those who hold any office should relinquish it gladly at the appointed time.[50]

---

[41] 2LtF 10; FA:ED I, 46.

[42] LR 10:2; FA:ED I, 105; FLCl 10:2; CA:ED, 122.

[43] ER 18:1;FA:ED I, 76; Test 24; FA:ED I, 127.

[44] ER 5:9; FA:ED I, 67.

[45] ER 5:14-15; FA:ED I, 67-68.

[46] LR 8:1; FA:ED I, 104.

[47] LR 10:3; FA:ED I, 105; FLCl 10:2; CA:ED, 122.

[48] ER 4:2; FA:ED I, 66; FLCl 10:1; CA:ED, 122.

[49] LR 10:4-6; FA:ED I, 72;FLCl 10:3; TestCl 19; CA:ED, 122, 61.

[50] ER 17:4; FA:ED I, 75.

## VIII. De vita apostolica

25. Fratres et sorores Dominum diligant *ex toto corde, ex tota anima et mente, ex tota virtute* et diligant proximos suos sicut se ipsos (Mt 22:39; Mk 12:30). Et exaltent Dominum in operibus suis (Tb 13:6) quoniam ideo misit eos in universo mundo ut verbo et opere dent testimonium voci eius et faciant scire omnes quoniam non est omnipotens praeter eum (Tb 13:4).[51]

26. Sicut pacem annuntiant voce, sic in cordibus suis et amplius habeant. Nullus per eos provocetur ad iram vel scandalum, sed omnes per mansuetudinem eorum ad pacem, benignitatem et concordiam provocentur.[52] Nam fratres et sorores ad hoc vocati sunt ut vulneratos curent, alligent confractos et erroneos revocent. Et ubicumque sunt recordentur quod dederunt se et reliquerunt corpora sua Domino Iesu Christo. Et pro eius amore debent se exponere inimicis tam visibilibus quam invisibilibus, quia dicit Dominus: *Beati qui persecutionem patiuntur propter iustitiam, quoniam ipsorum est regnum caelorum* (Mt 5:10).[53]

27. In caritate quae Deus est (1 Jn 4:16) omnes fratres et sorores, sive orantes sive servientes sive laborantes, studeant se humiliare in omnibus, non gloriari nec in se gaudere nec interius se exaltare de bonis verbis et operibus, immo de nullo bono quod Deus facit vel dicit et operatur in eis aliquando et per ipsos.[54] In omni loco et in omnibus adiunctis agnoscant omnia bona essa Domini Dei altissimi et dominatoris omnium rerum; et ipsi gratias referant a quo bona cuncta procedunt.[55]

28. Attendant omnes fratres et sorores quod super omnia desiderare debent habere spiritum Domini et sanctam eius operationem.[56]

    Et semper subditi sanctae Ecclesiae stabiles in fide catholica paupertatem et humilitatem et sanctum Evangelium Domini nostri Iesu Christi quod firmiter promiserunt observent.[57]

---

[51] 1LtF 1:1; LtOrd 8-9.

[52] L3C 58.

[53] ER 16:10-12.

[54] ER 17:5-6.

[55] ER 17:17.

[56] LR 10:8; FLCl 10:7.

[57] LR 12:4; FLCl 12:11.

## VIII. THE APOSTOLIC LIFE

25. The brothers and sisters shall love the Lord with all their heart, and with all their soul and mind and with all their strength, and they shall love heir neighbor as themselves (Mk 12:30; Mt 22:39). Let them glorify the Lord in all that they do (Tob 13:6). He has sent them into the world to bear witness by word and deed to His voice and to proclaim to everyone that He alone is the Almighty Lord (Tb 13:4).[51]

26. As they proclaim peace with their lips, they must have it to overflowing in their hearts. No one should be provoked to anger or offended because of them. On the contrary, everyone should be drawn to peace, kindness and friendship, by their gentleness. The brothers and sisters have been called to heal the wounded, mend the broken and bring back those who have gone astray.[52]

Wherever they are, let them remember that they have given themselves to the Lord Jesus Christ and pledged their whole life to Him. For love of Him they must face every enemy, seen and unseen, because the Lord says: Blessed are those who suffer persecution in the cause of right, theirs is the kingdom of heaven (Mt 5:10).[53]

27. In the love which is God (I Jn 4:16), let all the brothers and sisters, whether at prayer, or serving others, or working, strive to have humility in all things. They are not to boast, not to be self-satisfied, and not to pride themselves in their heart for the good they do by word or deed, not even for the good which God sometimes does or speaks and accomplishes in and through them.[54] No matter where they are, in all circumstances, they must acknowledge that every good belongs to the Lord God Almighty, the Ruler of all things; and they must thank Him from whom, all good things come.[55]

28. Let all the brothers and sisters keep in mind, that above everything else, they should desire to have the Spirit of the Lord and His holy operation.[56]

Always obedient to the Holy Church, and steadfast in the Catholic faith, let them observe, as they have firmly promised, the poverty and the humility, and the Gospel of our Lord Jesus Christ.[57]

---

[51] 1LtF 1; FA:ED I, 41; 1LtOrd 8-9; FA:ED I, 117.

[52] L3C 58; FA:ED II, 101.

[53] ER 16:10-12; FA:ED I, 74.

[54] ER 17:5-6; FA:ED I, 75.

[55] ER 17:17; FA:ED I, 76.

[56] LR 10:8; FA:ED I, 105; FLCl 10:7; CA:ED, 123.

[57] LR 12:4; FA:ED I, 106; FLCl 12:11; CA:ED, 125.

## Epilogus

Et quicumque haec observaverit in caelo repleatur benedictione altissimi Patris et in terra repleatur benedictione dilecti Filii sui cum sanctissimo Spiritu Paraclito et omnibus virtutibus caelorum et omnibus sanctis. Et ego frater Franciscus parvulus vester servus, quantumcumque possum, confirmo vobis intus et foris istam sanctissimam benedictionem.[58]

---

[58]Test 40-41.

EPILOGUE

May all who observe these things be filled in heaven with the blessing of the most high Father, and on earth with the blessing of his Beloved Son, with the most Holy Spirit, the Comforter, and with all the powers of heaven, and with all that is holy. And I, Brother Francis, your poor, little servant, as much as I am able, confirm for you, within and without, this most holy blessing.[58]

---

[58]Test 40-41; FA:ED I, 127.

# ROME INTERNATIONAL ASSEMBLY: MATRIX PRESENTATIONS

# 3

## Rome International Assembly: Matrix Presentations

At the close of the meeting in Brussels, the Work Group members were charged with preparing presentations for the Rome Assembly. The design of the text and the program for the Assembly dictated that thirteen separate presentations would be required.

A general presentation of the text that would outline in brief the events that led to the project, the manner in which the consultation was conducted, the contributions of various "fonts" of historical and theological materials, the lessons learned in the consultation and the resulting choices in regard to content and structure of the document. This was the opening presentation given by Thaddeus Horgan. During the next seven days, all members of the Work Group would share the responsibility to present brief introductions to the four fundamental values and the content of each of the eight chapters of the Brussels draft text.

In completing this assignment, members of the Work Group decided to prepare brief outlines for each presentation. The outline format would allow for the most succinct use of language. (There was constant attention to the fact that every word spoken in the Assembly had to be translated simultaneously into five languages.) It also allowed for a skeletal exegesis which could later be used in presentations by all charged with formation. The group recognized early on that these outlines would not only be useful to the Assembly, but they could then be disseminated as a teaching tool to all the congregations. These outlines could, in fact, serve as a universal key to writing commentaries in the different languages of the members. Future teachers of the text could thus develop their materials knowing with precision how the text's authors selected materials and what the original thought process was that guided that selection. Anyone who has struggled with the question of discerning the "true meaning" of different texts from Francis and Clare can appreciate the value of such a tool.

When Scripture scholars work with materials common to the early forms of the Gospel, they often cite the lost, but omnipresent, "Q" source: the *Quelle* or basic words that are the source being transmitted in the material we call the Gospel of Mark, Matthew or Luke. The materials presented in this section are the "Q" source of the Rule commentaries published in Section Six. These short summations were never intended to be the complete "gloss" on the text. They were intended to indicate the mind of the authors while providing freedom to future generations to re-interpret and to add newer insights. Consider, for example, the use of the "early form" of the *Letter to the Faithful* as the Introduction to the text. Much research has added to our knowledge of this text and we now know that it was not an "early" but a later "executive summary" of the longer text now referred to as the *Later Admonition and Exhortation to the Brothers and Sisters of Penance* in the *Francis of Assisi: Early Documents* edition. This is one example of change in understanding over the twenty-five years. However, the foundational insights and explanations continue to serve their purpose for teachers of this material.

One very important explanation must, however, precede this section. How did the final text come to have nine chapters when the Rome Assembly approved the eight chapter draft from Brussels? The reader will note in the introductory lecture by Horgan that a conscious choice was made to avoid writing chapters on the canonical understanding of the vows. The Rule text was intended to serve as an inspirational guide in Franciscan-biblical language. The constitutions of each congregation would set forth the understanding of the obligations of the vows as they have developed over the centuries and in each congregation. However, in respect to the four fundamental values and to the actual writings of Francis in his Rules of 1221 and 1223, there were sections that elaborated an evangelical framework for poverty and obedience. The Assembly members found it difficult to understand why these two chapters could be incorporated and a distinct chapter on chastity omitted. Taking the argument from the paucity of positive affirmations of vowed chastity in Francis's writings, the Work Group cited several elements that were included and intended to denote a commitment to a chaste and celibate life. The persuasive explanations were accepted and the vote approved the text as presented.

When the text was presented for pontifical approval, however, the question emerged again. This time there was insistence on including a specific chapter on chastity. It can be assumed that curial officials – possibly alerted by a minority of Assembly participants unhappy with the vote on this issue – decided that the text with headings on the Life of Poverty and the Obedience of Love needed explicit attention to chastity lest its omission be seen as capitulation to radical changes in social mores regarding sexuality. Regardless of motive, the decision was made to add a chapter and the chapter composition was not requested of the Work Group members. Lothar Hardick, O.F.M., longtime consultant to Germany's Franciscans, wrote the text and it was inserted and the enumeration of the chapters altered. Careful reading of the text conveys a different hand at work in that chapter.

Subsequent experience has shown that for many congregations in developing nations where a tradition of celibate life is virtually unknown, the explicit description of this call serves as an important educational foundation. Further, reflection on the long debate of Francis with the members of his own fraternity and of the Roman Curia regarding what should and should not be included in his *Vita et Regula* allows us to see that the dynamics of the thirteenth century were repeated in the twentieth. As it was in the beginning, is now and ever will be.

The reader should note that the editors made no linguistic changes to these presentations which were written in each speaker's native language and then translated.

## PRESENTATION OF THE TEXT OF THE RULE

### †FR. THADDEUS HORGAN, S.A.

#### PART I – GENESIS OF THE TEXT

Few Christians have been as open and aware of the event of Jesus Christ in their lives as Francis of Assisi. His radical fidelity to the Gospel made this consciousness a continuous experience. This awareness is part of the Franciscan Charism. It is not surprising that the followers of Francis became particularly conscious of the Second Vatican Council's call to all religious. For Franciscans the Council primarily was a renewing event in the life of Christ's body, the Church. Through the Council the Holy Spirit called all the faithful to renewal. Franciscans throughout the world, therefore, had to respond and did so in many ways and at different levels because this was a modern call to live anew their ancient vocation to *rebuild my Church*.

The majority of Franciscan religious looked to their communities' constitutions to formulate their expressions of renewal for our present era. But many also looked to the Rule of 1927. A rule is a statement of shared identity, fundamental values and basic guidelines for religious living. For many of us this was the first time we read the Rule critically. We had the Church's criteria to guide us.[1] After Vatican II the 1927 Rule seemed to be a *timed* document. Somehow it seemed unable to state our identity or shared values inspiringly. Further, it did not reflect the Church's new directives nor project our Gospel life in a biblical fashion or in a style that reflected clearly the spirit of our founder. For some it also did not seem to address the signs of our times. It is no wonder, then, that some of us thought about renewing our Rule as well as renewing our form of Gospel life.

Prompted by the Church's guidelines serious study was undertaken in many places with the purpose of *trying to recapture again the spirit of the founder*. Many within individual congregations rediscovered the *franciscanism* of their particular founders. Others were concerned with the origin of our shared charism, with Francis's influence on it, and its lived historic expression in the Third Order Regular Congregations. Still others concentrated on Francis's inspiration as this is set forth in his authenticated writings. Because the Franciscan movement is eight hundred years old it is only natural that different approaches for the same purpose were taken. Histories, experiences, perceptions are different. Yet, it seems safe to say, these have been all part of God's providence enriching the Franciscan Movement in our day. The differing approach-

---

[1] *Ecclesiae Sanctae* 15.

es to the matter of the "spirit of the founder" resulted in the so-called *French Document* with its emphasis on poverty and minority and on the bonds that unite TOR congregations to the Order of Friar Minor. It also resulted in the *Madrid Statement* with its emphasis on biblical *metanoia* and Francis's conversion experiences and how these speak to the meaning of our vows, fraternal life and ministry. Finally, it resulted in the *Dutch Rule* which emphasized Vatican II's renewal program and related it to Franciscan living. It even resulted in a renewed appreciation for the *Rule of 1927* which, despite its language, does contain the values historically associated with the Third Order Regular.

At first these four paths did not lead to a shared experience of renewal. They caused tension! But by 1980 the Work Group of the International Franciscan Commission was able to come together, to learn from these documents, and to be enriched by them and by those who worked so hard to produce them. None of the values presented in these documents contradicted the other. Rather, they represent various aspects of the same inspiration which the Lord gave to St. Francis. All were important, even essential, to this renewal process. The *Brussels Text* which you have received, we believe, is faithful to Francis's inspiration, to the historic expressions of that inspiration in Third Order Regular Congregations existing throughout the world today, and to its more recent antecedents: *The Rule of 1927,* the *French Document,* the *Madrid Statement* and the *Dutch Rule.*

## PART II – AN INSPIRATIONAL TEXT

Francis wanted his followers to be authentic Gospel people. What comes from the hearts of people make them what they are (Matt 15: 10-20). Inspired by the Lord, Francis proposed to his followers, his basic Gospel values, attitudes so that we could be true disciples and radical followers of Jesus Christ. Only when we have truly assimilated and made these values and attitudes part of ourselves can it be said that we will do the Gospel literally. The *Brussels Text* intent is singular: to state Francis's vision of our life of total and continuous conversion to God and neighbor through the literal living of the Gospel. In doing this it presents us with those basic values and attitudes, which Francis indicated are necessary for radical evangelical living. The text challenges us to grasp these values, to experience their dynamism, and to be truly a Gospel people within the Church and for the Church and world.

What the text does not do is set forth regulations or laws. Each congregation has constitutions for that. According to Church norms, constitutions are to apply canon law, the particular charism of individual founders, cultural circumstances, particular customs, and the Rule to each congregation. With reference to the Rule, constitutions apply its values, attitudes, and principles to a particular congregation. The inspiration of each particular founder is important in this process. The difference between what goes into the Rule or the constitutions can be shown by an example. There is nothing in this Rule text about vows except for the first sentence. In fact apart from mentioning chastity once in each of the Rules of 1221 and of 1223 Francis never cites it directly again. But he speaks several times of the evangelical values that chastity could represent – as does this text – in much the same way as Vatican II did. The canonical objectives of poverty and obedience are material renunciation and doing the legitimate commands of a superior. When Francis speaks of poverty and obedience he does not give us regulations, but the example of the life and deeds of our Lord Jesus Christ who is the incarnation of the attitudes and values that the vows represent. Francis would have us live poverty and obedience maximally. From the Franciscan perspective the canonical vows only express the minimum. For people dedicated to the total surrender of self to God through radical fidelity to the Gospel much more needs to be projected. Francis does this by noting the motive and style of the life of the Lord. This is why this *Brussels Text,* quoting Francis, directs us to *"…hold fast to the words, the life, the teaching and the Holy Gospel of our Lord Jesus Christ."*[2] It is a statement of fundamental Gospel living which highlights the supreme and the only Rule: Our Lord Jesus Christ as Francis was inspired to know, follow and love him.

There is no one exclusive way to live the Gospel. The multiplicity of congregations and Orders in the Church demonstrate this. Therefore, we should recognize that there is also no single style of Franciscan Gospel living either. Rather, inspired by the Lord and influenced by the circumstances of his time, Francis pointed out three ways to live the Gospel. This is why there are three Orders. This, too, is why we say that the Franciscan charism is always inclusive and never exclusive. What differentiates the three Orders are the emphases given by each of our traditions to the values Francis projects for radical Gospel living. The three Orders are distinctive because of the particular emphases given to fundamental Gospel values and because of the purposes and styles of our Gospel living. Yet we are one family, children of one spiritual father.

In the Third Order Regular there are several hundred congregations, some of apostolic life, others contemplative; still others are active-contemplative. Historically we all have had one Rule even though we are in masculine and feminine congregations. This attests to the universality of Gospel life even within our tradition of franciscanism. This is part of our heritage. And each of our congregations has its own proper charac-

---

[2]ER XXII:41; FA:ED I, 81.

teristics (*propria indolis*). Often we are localized and reflect particular cultures. These factors show the richness of our diversity. Yet we are one because we have shared Franciscan values presented in our one Rule. The *Brussels Text*"was composed with all these points in mind. This was possible because we followed the Church's directives and turned to the actual sources of Francis's original inspiration, his own words.

*Spirit, inspiration* and *charism* are all gifts of the Holy Spirit and not dependent on words. Yet the Spirit moves people to express these gifts in words as all of Sacred Scripture manifests. The words of Francis, therefore, have a special significance. They capture his experience of Gospel values and attitudes which the Lord inspired him to live. We felt we could more faithfully project his Gospel way of life for all in the Third Order Regular if we used his own words in the Rule. Moreover, his words could make our text *classic* not time-bound as the present Rule of 1927 is. If this text is adopted, the Rule of the Third Order Regular would be in Francis's words for the first time in history. Our Brothers and Sisters would welcome this. The consultation clearly indicated that.

Using Francis's words also would make the text a source for life-long reflection and on-going formation. To appreciate fully the content of the text, a knowledge of Franciscan sources and history is necessary. Just as Scripture should be constantly studied so too should our Rule Text. This would help us to embrace our heritage more. The words of Francis, we hope, will make this text not just a document, but also an inspiration to share and to hand on to future Franciscans.

### PART III – A TEXT OF FUNDAMENTAL VALUES

With an Order as large and diverse as our Third Order Regular it can be legitimately asked: "How does one determine what the fundamental values of our Franciscan life are?" The Church in General Council has given us the criteria to ascertain these. They are: return to the spirit of the founder; rediscover history because charisms are lived, and consult all in the congregations to learn the living convictions about charism. This, in fact, is what we did. Much resource work had already been completed when the Work-Group convened because of the studies done in preparing the *French Document,* the *Madrid Statement* and the *Dutch Rule.* The Work Group itself experienced a gradual coming to one mind through a process of study, prayer, reflection and sharing. Small but significant discoveries were made. For example, those among us who are especially sensitive to our heritage from the Order of Penance came to realize that, for Francis, total and continuous conversion meant living the Gospel literally. Those of us more oriented to Francis's plan for evangelical life with emphasis on poverty and minority realized that the beginning of all evangelical life is *metanoia.* Our study of the writings of Francis and of the history and spirituality of the Third Order Regular further led us to the shared conclusion that in all there are four fundamental values involved in our Franciscan Gospel living. These must be interiorized before all the manifestations of Gospel life associated with Franciscan living can be called authentic. We learned that simplicity, joy, fraternity, and the ministries of charity and of justice for peace are all manifestations of more fundamental values. Interestingly our studies were done separately. But our discoveries were shared experiences!

As you know we prepared a Rule Text (Reute Draft) a year ago, which was circulated in your congregations. That consultation was the greatest and widest ever undertaken within our Order. But what we felt was truly historic about it were the results. Its conclusions were the same as those of the Work Group, affirming our findings and reflections. Therefore, from the writings of Francis, from a study of the Third Order Regular history, and from the current existential awareness of our brothers and sisters, we can say that *metanoia, prayer, poverty* and *minority* are the four fundamental values of our Third Order Regular Franciscan life. These values are the content of this Rule text making it the spiritual document that it is.

In the past, these values have been variously interpreted. No doubt they will be variously interpreted in the future, too. Since the Spirit is the source of life and never limited, this should not surprise us. For this reason, this text does no more than what Francis did. We simply and directly name our charism, its inherent Gospel values, and point to Christ the Lord as the descriptive definition of our life. The Spirit must always be tested, however. That is why the Church's criteria for authentic renewal must be applied to every interpretation and manifestation of Gospel life that we call *Franciscan*. You are part of that testing of the Spirit here and now because you have come to affirm or deny authoritatively what we propose as our way of life. This is far more important than merely approving a document or not.

## PART IV — THE DOCUMENT ITSELF

Nevertheless, a word about the document itself must be said. As the vehicle you commissioned, you should know that it was developed as you requested: namely, to express briefly, clearly and explicitly the fundamental values of our Franciscan Gospel life. We developed a sequence for these values that generally follows Francis's Rule of 1221. This Rule, along with other writings, but especially this Rule, guided us in giving expression to how Francis reflectively unfolded the implications of Gospel life based on the four fundamental values. This sequence, we feel, helped us to be faithful to Francis's spirit. Besides serving our purposes of presentation, the Rule of 1221, as a guide, also helped us preserve our form of Franciscan Gospel life distinctively within the larger Franciscan movement. This Rule will not be confused with those of the minorite or clarissan traditions. Nevertheless, our proposed text still preserves the unity of the Franciscan family by recognizing the inclusiveness of the overall Franciscan charism (literal Gospel living) and its explicit reference (article 3) to mutual communion with all branches of the Franciscan Movement. No other Franciscan Rule does this.

The text has eight chapters. All eight, even though on specific topics, are permeated with the four fundamental values. The *Reute Text*, the one used in the consultation, had twelve. One result of the consultation was a request for a shorter text. We achieved this by combining four chapters into two, eliminating one chapter and choosing shorter texts from the words of Francis. Yet all that was in the *Reute Text* is contained in the shorter text you have before you. The eliminated chapter was the one on chastity. Since Francis did not write directly about it, neither did we. But the evangelical values that a chaste life represents are stated in articles 7 and 8 (these were the articles on chastity in the *Reute Text*).

Finally, permit me to point out that the proposed text has a Prologue and an Epilogue. Many congregations requested the Epilogue. Because it was the conclusion of the 1927 Rule it is a link to that document and serves to show the continuity of our Order's efforts for its own ongoing renewal. A Prologue is also offered because of its historical linkages. It is the first part of St. Francis's *First Letter To The Brothers and Sisters of Penance* (The *Volterra Letter*). As such it points to the origins of our form of Franciscan Gospel life in the ancient Order of Penance. Moreover, it is the prologue of the already approved Rule for the Secular Franciscan Order. The most ancient branch of our Order, represented here by the Third Order Regular Friars of Sts. Cosmas and Damian had its origin in the *Ordo Penitentiae Sancti Francisci.* Many of our congregations' founders and foundresses were themselves secular Franciscans before establishing their communities. And our modern brothers and sisters in the Secular Franciscan Order share with us the centrality of conversion in our way of Gospel living. The Prologue is intended to point all this out. But it is *ad libitum* as are the citations from the writings of St. Clare in our proposed text. The Work Group suggests that it be chosen for inclusion by those congregations, which find it particularly significant to their own histories and spirit.

We have tried to be faithful to our mandate, to the spirit of St. Francis, and to our brothers and sisters in the Franciscan Third Order Regular. We present you with the results of our work. During these days we will share our reflections on this text's content with you. We will pray with you. We will serve you in your service to all our brothers and sisters in our Franciscan congregations. May the Spirit be with us all so that we may be enlivened by the spirit of St. Francis.

## Fundamental value: *Conversion*

### Sister Margaret Carney, O.S.F.

In order to understand the fundamental value of conversion as we have placed it within our synthesis of Franciscan life, let us reflect for a moment on the experience of conversion in the life of St. Francis.

When we read the description that Francis himself recorded in his *Testament*, we find three elements. First, the initiative of God ("The Lord led me..."). Second, a change of outward behavior ("It seemed exceedingly bitter to me to see lepers..."). Third, an interior transformation ("that which had seemed bitter to me was changed into sweetness.")[3]

In yet another text,[4] Francis describes the life of penance or conversion using three ideas. He speaks of those who know, adore and serve the Lord "in penance." These terms will be a helpful means to explore the qualities of life of continuous conversion, as we must try to understand it today. They will enable us to see how Francis understood the meaning of penance.

Before beginning such a reflection it would be honest to acknowledge the difficulty of using language that is clear on this point. The word used by Francis in his writings is *poenitentia*. Translated today, the word is "penance." However, the word "penance" now creates harsh images of ascetical practices and it suggests an attitude of denial of the world and of legitimate human aspirations and experiences. If we use the term "conversion" we also have the danger of a narrow definition which refers principally to acceptance of faith by an unbeliever, or a single dramatic moment of religious awakening granted to a few charismatic souls. The third term, *metanoia*, is rooted in Greek and provides a possible way of connecting past understandings with new vocabulary, but it is not a word that is easily incorporated into contemporary vocabulary.

So we chose as our term the word "conversion." It is our hope that by investing ourselves in a deep reflection on this word we will eventually reappropriate those qualities of biblical and Franciscan spirituality, which may have suffered some deformation over the centuries. It is our hope that by reflection and by responding to the grace of our charism we will discover the deep riches that are part of the heritage of this Order which in times past was called an order of penitents.

We will try now to grasp the meanings and movements behind the word "conversion." We will do this by focusing on the words of Francis and relating his words and ideas and convictions to the funda-

---

[3]Test 1-2; FA:ED I, 124.
[4]ER XXIII: 8; FA:ED I, 84-85.

mental source of his spirit – the Word of God reflected in the words of Scripture.

### I. *COGNOVERUNT:* KNOWING THE LORD

We cannot know the Lord without knowing as well our sinfulness. This is the first step in the journey of conversion. In the *Later Admonition and Exhortation,* Francis speaks of the darkness and blindness of sin. "All those who refuse to taste and see how good the Lord is and who love the darkness rather than the light are under a curse."[5] Again in the *Later Admonition and Exhortation* he warns of the mistrust we must have of our own sinful tendencies and that we must place ourselves under "the yoke of obedience" in order to break with sin in our lives.[6] So, too, the prophets called to Israel to renounce her sinfulness and return to the Lord (Ez 18:23; Jer 1:16; Hos 3:5).

But it is also true that this break with sin is not the work of the human person. It is God's work in us. Francis insists that it was the Lord alone who led and inspired him, just as Paul would remind his hearers in the Letter to Romans "so it depends not upon man's will, but upon God's mercy" (Rom 9:16). Francis echoes this thought when he reminds us that we must give thanks to God because "the Lord God…through his mercy alone saved us; who did and does every good thing for us, miserable…though we are.…"[7]

And since it is through the Passion and Resurrection of the Lord Jesus that this grace is made possible for us, we must grant him dominion over our lives if we are to be fully turned towards God. Francis in the First Admonition uses the words of Jesus to remind us that he alone is the way to the Father (Jn 13:6-9).[8] And in her Testament, Clare, the most faithful follower of Francis, reminded her sisters that the "Son of God made himself our way" and that Francis taught that way by his word and example. This way, however, is not simply a way of commandments, but a way of union, of relationship. Fully realized, it is a way that leads to the most profound surrender of the person to the Lord. Francis uses the terms of the most intimate human relationships to describe this reality.[9] We are to be brides of the Lord when our soul is united to Him by the Holy Spirit.

Francis thus dares to suggest – to insist, even – that our conversion from sin to obedience and to love will lead us to that union which even

---

[5] LtF 63-71; FA:ED I, 50.
[6] 2LtF 37-41; FA:ED I, 48.
[7] ER XXIII:8; FA:ED I, 84.
[8] Adm I:1; FA:ED I, 128.
[9] 2LtF 40-54; FA:ED I, 48-49.

the prophets described in nuptial terms when they described the espousal of Yahweh with his people, Israel.

## II. *Adoraverunt*: Adoring the Lord

Both Celano and Bonaventure relate that Francis saw that perfect poverty consisted in renunciation of worldly wisdom and he urged his brothers to put aside even the "possession" of learning so as to be able to offer themselves naked to the arms of the Crucified.[10] Francis saw how radical the demands of the Gospel were. Jesus calls for a total gift of self to the Kingdom, for an engagement to God and his interests, which calls for an undivided response and for radical separation from all that would keep us from the Kingdom (Lk 14: 26-27). It is this radical self-donation and separation from the values of the world that Francis puts so clearly before us in the first chapter of the Rule of 1221.

The adoration of the one who knows the grace of conversion is rooted in a purity of heart and mind that keeps our whole attention centered on the Lord "day and night."[11]

We must not think of this adoration simply as the strength of personal or communal prayer and its fruits – however central such intense prayer is to the process of turning continuously towards God. This adoration that reverses the values of our lives by putting the justice of God before earthly considerations also has the power to regenerate the whole of our lives and of our persons. The gifting of the Spirit in us leads to a powerful reorientation. Paul speaks of this eloquently over and over again: "Formerly, when you did not know God, you were in bondage to beings that by nature are no god; but now that you have come to know God, or rather to be known by God, how can you turn back again to the weak and beggarly elemental spirits, whose slaves you want to be once more?"(Gal 4:8-10; cf. Rom 6:33; Col 2:12; 1Cor 6:11).

## III. *Servierunt*: Serving the Lord

The result of the powerful re-direction of the energies of our lives is seen in our life of service of others. In both of the *Letters to the Faithful*, Francis links the love of God and neighbor by placing the Great Commandment before us.[12] The law of love is the yardstick by which we measure the height and depth of our conversion to God. Francis had read and understood well the description of the final judgment in which the Lord rewards the loving acts of those who performed the works of mercy (Mt 25:31-46). This point has a special importance for us as we seek to ar-

---

[10]LMj VII: 2; FA:ED II, 671; 2C CXLIV:192; FA:ED II, 370.
[11]2LtF 19-21; FA:ED I, 46-47.
[12]1LtF 1; FA:ED I, 41.

ticulate the tradition and spirituality of our branch of the Franciscan family. Beginning with the exhortations in the *Letters to the Penitents* and down through the centuries, it is clear that the flowering of conversion is found in works done for the good of our neighbor. In our times when it becomes difficult to discern just how to continue – or in what forms to continue – our services to others, it is important to realize that the dichotomy sometimes posed between "being" and "doing" can be false and create an attitude that our works are not essentially related to our lives and prayer. For the members of the Franciscan Third Order this would be a false conclusion.

When writing to the penitents Francis offers concrete ideas about the forms of good works that they should adopt. They must bring forth the fruits of repentance (Lk 3:8). Those who have the power to judge are to be merciful; charitable almsgiving is encouraged; authorities are to serve sympathetically.[13]

What Francis proposed to these lay followers of his during his lifetime evolved as we know, into a history of works undertaken in the name of the Church in many cultures, in many ages for the needy of every description.

The ultimate work of mercy, of love, is to lay down one's life for the sake of the Gospel. Francis proposed this ideal to his friars in his description of their mission as he envisioned it in the Rule of 1221. Moving from the works that require a generous heart and discerning eye towards the poor, he calls for a courageous encounter with evil in any form and for a willingness to suffer persecution.[14]

Following the call of the Church in our times, we recognize in this text the seed that can grow in our service into a deep commitment to the poor that is also expressed in loving actions and work for justice in the world.

While practices aimed at self-discipline have a proper and necessary place in Christian life, they are not the central meaning of the penitential life if it is truly understood. In fact, we find indications in the Scriptures that the Lord himself rejected such a notion of penance (Matt 11:18-19). And Francis warned his followers not to make the mistake of believing that external works alone would constitute true religious service.[15]

## Conclusion

We know from early biographies that the preaching of Francis was a kind of revolution for the people of his time.[16] He provided an ortho-

---

[13] 2LtF 25-31; FA:ED I, 47.
[14] ER IX:8-9; FA:ED I, 71.
[15] Adm XIV; FA:ED I, 133-34.
[16] 1C X:23, XV:36; FA:ED I, 202-03, 214-15; L3C VIII:25, IX 33; FA:ED II, 84, 87-88.

dox and realizable program of Christian spirituality that captured the
imagination of his hearers and overcame problems encountered by lay
movements that were destroyed by heresy and false directions.

Today a similar need is evident in the Church. The council opened the
Scriptures for us again and restored the liturgy to the people. New forms
of Christian community are growing and there is evidence of a hunger
for God. In view of this work of the Spirit, there is a call to us to once
again "preach penance" – not in the form of sermons but by sharing our
experience of the work of the Spirit within the human person that is at
the heart of conversion.

Our "sermon" can be the hope that is shared when we allow ourselves
to be the clay in the hand of the potter (Jer 18:1-6). By opening ourselves
to be shaped, to be broken and to be re-fashioned, we can be a sign of
encouragement to our brothers and sisters who need to see in human
persons the manifestation of God's goodness and greatness. The question that many agonize over is the same question that Francis used to
ask: "Who are you, my God, and who am I?"

To keep asking the question, to keep accepting the answers that come
at every moment of our existence, is to know the meaning of a life of
penance, of continual conversion.

## FUNDAMENTAL VALUE: *CONTEMPLATION*

### SISTER IGNATIA GOMEZ, MISS. SRS.

*"Him I covet, Him I seek*
*and nothing but Him."*

This paper, my dear Brothers and Sisters, deals with "Prayer" which was a value so dear to Our Father St. Francis and which should likewise be dear to all who call themselves Franciscans.

We look to Francis as a model of contemplation. We see in him a man led by the Holy Spirit. As Francis himself tells us in his *Testament* – God took the initiative and led him by the grace of His Holy Spirit.

Prayer for Francis meant getting lost in love: "My brothers, my sisters" – "My God and my all." Prayer in other words was an expression of that union – between God and Man. For Francis, life itself became a prayer because he was so absorbed in that love. He was lost in admiration for the Father who created the universe and all things therein. Francis loved all creatures because he saw God in them. Being absorbed by love for the Father made Him Christ-like. Because of his burning love for Jesus, Francis was carried away with wonder before the crib at the sight of God becoming a helpless infant. He was beside himself with joy, love and gratitude before the Eucharist at the loving condescension and the most condescending love manifested therein. Francis could never stop weeping at the thought of his crucified Savior as he contemplated there the love of God for Man. He would have loved to express this love for God and men in a thousand ways but he could not find words to express it. This is why he constantly kept repeating these words – "My God and my all."

It is God then who must be primary in our life. In his Second Rule as well as in his *Admonitions*[17] Francis tells us to turn ourselves unceasingly towards God, through prayer in a simple and pure heart, overcoming every obstacle, every care, every preoccupation, in order to discover how to better love, serve and honor the Lord God. Again in his First Rule Francis says: "Therefore let us desire nothing else, let us want nothing else, let nothing else please us and cause us delight except our creator, redeemer and savior, the only true God, who is the fullness of good, all good, every good, the true and supreme good."[18] In all places and all times, we must believe in Him, bless Him and give Him thanks.

We are thus required to have the experience of God, to know Him in faith and to hold ourselves open to the gift of Himself which He wishes

---

[17]LR X:9; FA:ED I, 105; Adm XVI; FA:ED I, 134.
[18]ER XXIII:9; FA:ED I, 85.

to offer us. It is not merely Jesus Christ whom we are expected to know, but the Father, Son and Holy Spirit.

In the Father we admire the source of all good and the author of our salvation. He is at the origin of the work of the Son and of the mission of the Spirit.

Everything returns to Him and we must give Him thanks, first of all for Himself, Him to whom all adoration and all prayer is addressed.

The Son of God, the Lord Jesus Christ, is the only way, truth and life for us, who makes us know the Father.[19] It is to the total knowledge of the mystery of Christ that we are called. We should contemplate Him:

1. First of all in His eternal existence, Him in whom all has been created;[20]

2. In His historical coming into this world when He took the true flesh of our humanity and our fragility in the womb of the holy and glorious Virgin Mary;[21]

3. In His earthly life where, rich as He was, He nevertheless chose poverty and made Himself the servant of all;

4. In His passion and death which He endured to save us, His sheep[22] and to pacify and reconcile with the all-powerful God all that exists in heaven and on earth;[23]

5. We contemplate Him also in His victory over death, when the Father received Him into glory, exalted Him and made Him sit at His right hand;[24]

6. And finally in His last coming when He will come to judge the world.[25]

And since the whole mystery of Christ is rendered present to us in the sacrament of His Body and Blood, there, too, we are invited to see both the humility of God who gives Himself to us in material elements[26] and the glory of Him who no longer dies, but who is eternally victor.[27]

It is Jesus Christ in all His mystery who is our sole master[28] and all the efforts of our life consists in following His teaching and His footsteps,[29]

---

[19] Adm I:1-4; FA:ED I, 128.

[20] ER XXIII:1; FA:ED I, 81-82.

[21] 2LtF 4; FA:ED I, 46.

[22] Adm VI:1-2; FA:ED I, 131.

[23] LtOrd 13; FA:ED I, 117.

[24] OfP None 11-14; Vespers 1-9; FA:ED I, 146-47.

[25] ER XXIII:7; FA:ED I, 83-84.

[26] L3C VIII:28; FA:ED II, 85.

[27] L3C VII:22; FA:ED II, 81-82.

[28] ER XXII:32; FA:ED I, 80.

[29] ER I:1-5; FA:ED I, 63-64; 2LtF 13; FA:ED I, 46.

in clinging to His words, to His life, to His Gospel and in sharing in His sufferings and in His glory.[30]

The Holy Spirit the Paraclete who proceeds from the Father and the Son helps us to call God "Father." It is He who enables us to confess Jesus as Lord and to spiritually receive His Body and His Blood. He gives us life and His words are spirit and life. Through Him alone, in communion with the Son, are we able to offer thanks to the Father as He deserves. We should, therefore, desire above all else to have the Spirit of the Lord and His dynamism[31] to conduct ourselves spiritually under the force of His inspiration, to die to ourselves, to begin again, to take on new forms. It is essential to leave much room for divine inspiration in our lives.

In order to always live in the presence of God, never to turn one's heart and spirit from Him, to remain ready for the Lord's coming, we need to pray without ceasing. As St. Francis tells us in his Second Rule "... while avoiding idleness [through work] ... they do not extinguish the Spirit of holy prayer and devotion to which all temporal things must contribute."[32] Hearing, reading and meditating on the word of God daily as Francis did, will keep us in this constant attitude of prayer.

As we know, Francis and his first disciples made the Gospel their Rule of Life. Paying attention to persons and to events, casting a marveling gaze on fraternal creativity, will help us to read the signs of the times, and maintain a permanent contact with the living God, Father, Son and Holy Spirit.

In order to communicate this message of the Gospel which is a need of the Church, we have to become original responses to the Gospel according to the need of the time. Francis was able to do this because of his deep union with God and we will be able to do our part only if we likewise attain this deep union with Christ.

Contemplative prayer for Francis is the prayer of being always present to the Lord. His praise of God and His creatures draws him to pray in Psalms and thanksgiving. For this reason we pray the Church's prayer of praise – the Liturgy of the Hours.[33] For Francis, saying the Office is also a sign of fidelity to the Church. In the intercessory prayer we pray both for the Church and the world. It is therefore a turning to God and our neighbor.

Francis loved all his brothers and sisters in Christ. For Francis, the robber was not a robber but his brother who happened to rob. He loved the leper not because he was a leper but because he saw in him a brother who happened to have leprosy. Francis did not hesitate to kiss him because

[30]ER XXII:41; FA:ED I, 81.

[31]LR X:8; FA:ED I, 105.

[32]LR V:2; FA:ED I, 102.

[33]ER III:1-2; FA:ED I, 101.

he wanted to make the leper feel he was his brother. Francis identified himself with the poor people. In doing so he did not mean to identify himself with their misery or poverty but rather he went out to them to make them feel that he was their brother – that he was one with them. This Francis did in imitation of Jesus Christ who became like us in all things – in other words he identified himself with us in every respect – except sin. Our work as Franciscans – like our Father St. Francis – is a task of building a kingdom of love. We are to make the people we serve feel that we are one with them in love because they are our brothers and sisters – even though they may be poor, sick, lonely, frustrated, incapacitated, without any hope of life. We have to make them feel through us that God, our Father, loves them as they are.

Because the Eucharist is the greatest prayer of praise and thanksgiving, given to us by the Lord himself, for Francis and for us Franciscans, participation in the Eucharist is the highest expression of prayer (Jn 6:54).[34]

The Word of God we hear and the sacraments we are offered invite us to faith, and if we consent, introduce us into communion with God. To make contemplative prayer possible, each of us must reserve for herself or himself periods of solitude and silence. The possibility of living in hermitages should also be seriously considered.

As we know, the contemplative character of St. Francis is beyond dispute, but few of us realize that perhaps the majority of his early followers were contemplatives. According to the late Fr. Cajetan Esser, O.F.M., a highly respected Franciscan historian, "A tendency towards the contemplative life, towards solitude can be observed in the Franciscan Order from the very beginning. This contemplative dimension is one of Francis's greatest gifts to his followers through the world."

That this contemplative charism is the essence of Franciscan spirituality has been universally recognized even by the Secular Franciscan Order who, although they are called to remain vitally involved in the world as a special Franciscan "leaven," they are reminded in their new Rule: "As Jesus was the true worshipper of the Father, so let prayer and contemplation be the soul of all you are and do."

This was Francis's contemplative charism. Let us now see what Vatican II says about the contemplative dimension of our religious life.

## VATICAN II AND THE CONTEMPLATIVE DIMENSION

As recently as January 1981, the Sacred Congregation for Religious and Secular Institutes issued a document on the *Contemplative Dimension of Religious Life*. With substantial reference to the documents of the Second

---

[34]ER XX:5; FA:ED I, 78.

Vatican Council, the Sacred Congregation reminded us that the "contemplative dimension is the real secret of renewal for every religious life." In the guidelines, the Congregation affirmed the primacy of the contemplative dimension for Institutes of the active life as well as for specifically contemplative Institutes. In their directives, one can almost hear the echo of Francis's voice, as he praises those friars who have been faithful to prayer in these words:

"These friars are my Knights of the Round Table, who remain hidden in deserts and lonely places in order to devote themselves more completely to prayer and meditation, lamenting their own sins and the sin of others, living simply and behaving humbly, whose sanctity is known to God, and at times to other friars, but unknown to the world."[35]

In his second Rule, speaking on their manner of work Francis says: "The friars to whom God has given the grace of working should work in a spirit of faith and devotion and avoid idleness, which is the enemy of the soul, without however extinguishing the spirit of prayer and devotion, to which every temporal consideration must be subordinated."[36]

May we who are trying to recapture the spirit of our Seraphic Father St. Francis open ourselves to the spirit of prayer, which alone can make us attentive to the demands of the Kingdom and help us to see the plan of God with the eyes of faith. If we do anything less than this we will merely be mimicking St. Francis as did the simple Brother John, who repeated and copied every movement that Francis did, e.g. when Francis coughed, he coughed; when Francis sighed, he sighed; when Francis wept, he wept. Francis himself forbade him to act in that way.[37]

Desiring nothing but God and His Holy Will, may God be all to us, so that like our beloved Father Francis we too may be able to say:

"My God and my All."

Him alone may we covet, Him alone may we seek, nothing but Him.

---

[35] 2MP 3:72; FA:ED III, 320.

[36] LR V:1-4; FA:ED I, 102-03.

[37] 2C CXLIII:190; FA:ED II, 369.

## FUNDAMENTAL VALUE: *POVERTY*

### SISTER MARIANNE JUNGBLUTH, F.H.F.

#### INTRODUCTION

When Brother Thaddeus was giving you his presentation of the substance of the Project of the Rule yesterday morning, he drew your attention to the fact that the Franciscan Task Force had been unable to find any better outline to follow than St. Francis's First Rule composed by him in 1221. This text, in fact, had seemed to us the most appropriate guide because St. Francis had devoted so much thought to it. This Rule – like our own Project of the Rule – begins with a few simple words and is the fruit of St. Francis's ponderings and additions over the years. This Rule is the source crystallizing the four fundamental values that we discerned together. In her excellent talk yesterday, Sr. Ignatia showed us how for St. Francis this Rule was nothing else but the Gospel, which was the whole sum and substance of his life.[38] He wanted to live nothing else but the Gospel, to hear no one else but the Lord Jesus Christ who expressed Himself in his heart. This was clearly brought home to us in the presentation of the first chapter of the Project of the Rule. It was becoming clear to us what living the Gospel really means: knowing the Lord, adoring and serving Him in an attitude of prayer, in minority, obedience, purity of heart and poverty.

The name of St. Francis is indissolubly bound up with this last-mentioned attitude: that of poverty – and poverty in its most rigorous form, without any compromise whatsoever. But we must not make the common mistake of drawing the line at material poverty, or exterior poverty: we need to penetrate to the very essence of Francis's idea of poverty, a poverty that is rooted in the very poverty of Christ Himself.

We will therefore concentrate first on the foundations of evangelical poverty.

## I. THE FOUNDATION OF EVANGELICAL POVERTY

### A. THE POVERTY OF CHRIST

In his Second Letter to the Corinthians (2 Cor 8: 9), St. Paul writes: "You are well acquainted with the favor shown you by our Lord Jesus Christ: how for your sake he made himself poor though he was rich, so that you might become rich by his poverty." This is the only time that the Holy Scripture explicitly mentions the poverty of Jesus, His having "become poor." St. Paul declares first of all that Christ had been "rich." He who was rich not only turned towards the poor, but also in addition (and

---

[38]Test 5; FA:ED I, 124-25.

both aspects belong together) appeared among us in poverty. St. Paul does not isolate Christ's material poverty; in these verses he describes Christ's self-abasement, His path to salvation, the way He chose to accomplish our redemption.

Christ does not distribute His gifts from above, like a rich benefactor; no, He shares His riches by becoming poor Himself. Here we are confronted not only with the poverty of death, but also with the poverty of the Incarnation. Before becoming a man who was materially poor, Christ embraced the poverty of being man: He accepted the poverty of our human condition, and hence the poverty of death.

St. Paul describes in similar terms (Phil 2:6-11) the path of salvation: "His state was divine, yet He did not cling to His equality with God, but emptied Himself to assume the condition of a slave, and became as men are." Here once again, the "becoming poor," the self-emptying, are directly linked to Christ's Incarnation and to His death on the Cross. We must therefore conclude that herein lies the real poverty of Christ: His becoming man was so complete and so radical that it encompassed all the consequences that flow from being human: death itself, and even an ignominious death by crucifixion. Christ's poverty, therefore, goes far beyond mere exterior poverty.

Francis understood St Paul's words in their deepest sense, and in his own *Letter to all the Faithful* he echoes the words of the Apostle: "Though he was rich, He wished, together with the most Blessed Virgin, His mother, to choose poverty in the world beyond all else."[39]

## B. THE POVERTY OF ST. FRANCIS

Francis's determination was to live as Christ had lived. He himself acknowledged this in that wonderful Last Will for St. Clare and her sisters: "I, little Brother Francis, wish to follow the life and poverty of our most high Lord Jesus Christ and of His most holy Mother and *to persevere* in this *until the end.*"[40] St. Clare, in her turn, confirms this in her Testament to her daughters: St. Francis, she wrote, in following the example of the Son of God never departed from the path of poverty.

Francis willed to be poor, but not with the attitude of making a virtue of necessity. No, Francis wanted to be poor because Christ, the Lord, had been poor on this earth. Few of Christ's words had made such a deep impression upon Francis as these: "Foxes have lairs, the birds in the sky have nests, but the Son of Man has nowhere to lay His head" (Matt 8:20).

No aspect of the life of Christ made so deep an impression upon him as the poverty of the Incarnate Lord in the crib and His state of utter

---

[39] 2LtF 5; FA:ED I, 46.
[40] FLCl 6:7; CA:ED, 118.

privation upon the Cross: "It is good to read the testimonies of Scripture, and it is good to seek the Lord our God in them. But I have already taken in so much of Scripture that I have more than enough for meditating and reflecting. I do not need more, son; I know Christ, poor and crucified."[41] As we see, "being poor" became for Francis an attitude, a life orientation, a way of living that involves the whole person. The ideal of "the most complete poverty" as understood by Francis, the model for his contemporaries, comprises the renunciation of all earthly possessions, of everything that provides security for human life. Those who make profession of poverty—"Let the brothers not make anything their own, neither house, nor place, nor anything at all."[42] "As strangers and pilgrims" (1 Pt 2:11)—those who are authentically poor must journey through this world without fixed abode, without rights, without protection, without property and without any security, even with respect to God. Francis sums up this ideal in a brief but profound statement in which he provides us with his own most convincing interpretation of "most high poverty": "Hold back nothing of yourselves for yourselves, that He Who gives Himself totally to you may receive you totally."[43]

Francis confronts the un-Christian spirit of selfishness that seeks its security in amassing the goods of this world with a spirit of radical fidelity to the ideals of Christ. He challenges the spirit of materialism and attachment to the world that was gaining around in his time by a totally Christ-like spirit, living by God and for God alone. In a world that hankers after money and possessions, Francis sets aside ideals of this kind and reveals that one can also be happy without any of those things, and even know a happiness far greater than that enjoyed by persons attached to worldly goods. For he who truly possesses nothing in reality possesses everything, since he has God.

So Francis understands poverty in the Biblical sense: that it is primarily the comprehensive attitude of the inner being, with exterior poverty being the mere outward expression of this interior disposition which is far deeper, as well as all-embracing. This poverty, this "being really poor," implies penance, minority, obedience, as well as chastity for Francis. Obedience and chastity are perhaps the most important elements of "being truly poor."

## II. Evangelical Poverty and Material Goods

When we read the first part of the Rule, what cannot fail to strike us most is that Francis speaks of a life of obedience and a life of chastity,

---

[41] 2C LXXI:105, FA:ED II, 316.

[42] LR VI:1; FA:ED I, 103.

[43] LtOrd 29; FA:ED I, 118.

but not of a life of poverty. He speaks rather of a life "without property," *sine proprio*.[44] However the *Regula Bullata* does speak of serving God "in poverty and humility, in *paupertate et humilitate*.[45] *Sine proprio* (without possessing anything whatsoever): here is to be found the very essence of evangelical poverty; it implies incessant effort to maintain an attitude of non-possession. Being poor means not wanting to possess, nor appropriate to oneself anything whatsoever, either one's own will, nor another person, as well as being devoid of aspirations towards any of the things of this world. Total renunciation means never using anything as though one had any "rights" to it. The genuinely poor will not seek to be masters of their own will, or to have dominion over others, or to possess goods. Being poor, in fact, consists in proclaiming that not man, but God, is Lord of all.

We human beings, however, have need of things in order to sustain our life. And not only do we need such things – we depend upon them. Without things, we cannot exist; generally speaking, we require a certain quantity of things in order to function as human beings. So when we apply to this situation the rules established by St. Francis we reach an interesting conclusion. When St. Francis reminded us of the words of St. Paul, "If we have food and clothing we have all that we need" (1 Tm 6:8)[46] he was quite well aware that people need other things as well as food and clothing, within reasonable limits. And these reasonable limits he conceded to his friars without difficulty. Hence in his writings we find him alluding to clothing,[47] breviaries,[48] places,[49] chalices, corporals, adornments for the altar and everything pertaining to the celebration of the Eucharist, for which they should even have precious materials.[50]

The friars therefore are permitted to have all these things; but St. Francis insists that there should never be any question of "having" in the sense of "possessing," but only having freedom to give away.[51]

Francis never made any stipulation in terms of "rights." Each friar must have what is necessary for life, but everything over and beyond this belongs to the poor. Through the poor, all superfluity must be given back to God. It is to God, the Lord and Creator that all that man has belongs; of ourselves, we own nothing. Renunciation of all one possesses, of all superfluity, is nothing more than recognition of the sovereignty of

[44]ER I:1; FA:ED I, 63; LR I:1; FA:ED I, 100.

[45]LR VII:2; FA:ED I, 103-04.

[46]ER IX:1; FA:ED I, 70.

[47]ER II:14; FA:ED I, 65; LR II:13; FA:ED I, 101; Test 16; FA:ED I, 125.

[48]LR III:2, 7; FA:ED I, 101.

[49]Test 24; FA:ED I, 126.

[50]2LtCl 4; FA:ED I, 54.

[51]ER XIV:1-6; FA:ED I, 73.

God on the practical level. Renouncing one's goods in favor of the poor[52] is, moreover, recognition of the grace God grants us of enabling us to encounter God Himself in the poor.

The biographies give abundant illustrations of St. Francis's own liberality towards the poor. It had been a facet of his character, even before his conversion, and it steadily increased together with his love for Christ, until he had made himself completely one with the poor. This concrete solidarity with the distresses of the life of the poor is an obligatory part of any Franciscan's attitude. "They must rejoice when they live among people considered of little value and looked down upon, among the poor and the powerless, the sick and the lepers, and the beggars by the wayside."[53] This attitude urges us towards the fringes of society to share the life of the underprivileged, whatever they may be called.

Sharing the life of the poor means first of all relieving their distress as far as we can, but then going on to give them a sense of their own human dignity, which is even more important and enduring. The poor must be made aware of this truth: I am not loved and esteemed for any of my possessions, but for myself. Such awareness makes it possible for them to live their lives in peace and justice.

This solidarity with the poor, which is our vocation, must be revealed through our life-style, whatever social or cultural context in which we find ourselves. Our life-style and our dress[54] must be simple and poor, and free from all self-seeking; they must clearly denote our interior attitude and make it visible for all to see.

A simple life-style must be unpretentious, satisfied with simple necessities and even aimed at reducing these to a minimum. Authentic poverty requires such unpretentiousness, being satisfied with the bare necessities. We each know through daily experience how easily we can become enslaved by ever increasing "needs." Things exert a magnetic attraction over us, exciting in us the desire to have and possess them. Here clearly can be found a great danger to "living without possessing anything of one's own" – vivere...sine proprio.

For this reason we always need to begin afresh. Only one who keeps the spirit of poverty vibrant and living within his heart can be kept safe from this danger over a long period. "The friars are to appropriate nothing for themselves."[55] Only in this way can we become free for God and open to our neighbor.

But our neighbor is, first and foremost, our Brother or our Sister with whom we live day after day. Francis is well aware of that and he wants

---

[52]LR II:4-9; FA:ED I, 100-101; Test 15-17; FA:ED I, 125.
[53]ER IX:2; FA:ED I, 70.
[54]ER II:14; FA:ED I, 65.
[55]LR VI:1; FA:ED I, 103.

our material poverty to be in harmony with the needs and requirements of the Brothers because, when all is said and done, poverty is determined by and oriented to necessity and brotherly love. Both the *Regula Non Bullata* and the *Regula Bullata* are eloquent on this point, as a few examples will show: "Nevertheless, if the brothers are in need, they can accept, like other poor people, whatever is needed for the body excepting money."[56] "And for their work they can receive whatever is necessary excepting money. And when it is necessary, they may seek alms like other poor people."[57] "Let each one confidently make known his need to another that the other might discover what is needed and minister to him."[58] "Let each one love and care for his brother as a mother loves and cares for her son in those matters in which God has given him the grace."[59] The First Rule concludes its ninth chapter with this magnanimous proclamation: "Similarly, in time of an obvious need, all the brothers may do as the Lord has given them the grace to satisfy their needs, because necessity has no law."[60]

Such statements are extremely daring for inclusion in the Rule of a Religious Order, there is no doubt about that. However, in a certain sense they protect and ensure this life of "most high poverty" through their stress on brotherly love, which exceeds even the love of a mother. Where people looked to Francis for a standard norm, none was provided – there are no rigid definitions or regulations. Obviously each friar must individually discern according to his conscience the decisions to be taken regarding his own needs and those of his Brothers.

Francis trusted his friars to be men who would always "love and be faithful to our Lady, Holy Poverty";[61] he persisted in his idea that each friar should foresee and provide for the needs of his Brother with a love exceeding the love of a mother. Every time they met or came together he wanted them all to be united in a deep communion of mutual giving and receiving. In this way – openness to the needs of others and concern to remedy such needs as best one can – poverty becomes the path to authentic brotherly love lived and expressed concrete terms: the love that is the very foundation of community life.

---

[56]ER II:7; FA:ED I, 64.

[57]ER VII:7-8; FA:ED I, 69.

[58]ER IX:10; FA:ED I, 71.

[59]ER IX:11: FA:ED I, 71; LR VI:8; FA:ED I, 103.

[60]ER IX:16; FA:ED I, 71.

[61]TestS 4, *Francis and Clare: The Complete Works*, Regis Armstrong and Ignatius Brady, trans. (New York: Paulist Press, 1982), 164. The source of this simple blessing is found in LP 17; *St. Francis of Assisi: Writings and Early Biographies*, Marion Habig, ed. (Chicago: Franciscan Herald Press, 1973), 993.

### III. Evangelical Poverty and Interpersonal Relations

Taking such reflections as these as our starting point, we can see that in the mind of St. Francis, poverty was not restricted to the relationship between persons and things; it also played an important role in relationships between one person and another.

According to the example of Jesus and of St. Francis, we are to be unpretentious men and women, without power, without dominion over others, for the will to control or to dominate is but one aspect of the will to possess. Francis makes clear when he says: "Likewise, let all the brothers not have power or control in this instance, especially among themselves...."[62] And this unwillingness to possess leads to the following result: "On the contrary, *through the charity of the Spirit, let them serve* and obey *one another* voluntarily."[63] They may not accept any titles conferring privileges and no one may be called "Prior," but let "everyone in general be called a lesser brother."[64] To drive the point home Francis refers to the Gospel: "Let one wash the feet of another."[65]

It is made clear here that "being poor" entails some important requirements: one must be unpretentious, unmindful of oneself, eager to serve, continually available – as Francis himself says when describing his ideal: We made no claim to learning "and we were simple and subject to all."[66]

These attitudes are also recommended to those who seek to follow Francis. He calls "blessed" the man who "supports his neighbor in his weakness as he would want to be supported were he in a similar situation."[67] Here again it is a question of accepting one's neighbor just as he is and of setting aside selfish requirements and pretensions. To sum it all up, the one who is truly poor stands humbly before God who does all things and who gives all things to all. The poor person receives through other men these gifts that God wants to give him. But this very receiving is an indication to him of the measure of his own giving. Following the example of St. Francis, the one who is poor must be responsive to God's action in the hearts of men – as responsive as it is possible for him to be – and this without any thought of receiving approval or reward and refusing to keep anything for himself: "Blessed is the servant who stores up in heaven the good things which the Lord shows to him and does not wish to reveal them to people under the guise of a reward, because the Most High Himself will reveal His deeds to whomever He wishes."[68] If

---

[62]ER V:9; FA:ED I, 67.
[63]ER V:14; FA:ED I, 67-68.
[64]ER VI:3; FA:ED I, 68.
[65]ER VI:4; FA:ED I, 68.
[66]Test 19; FA:ED I, 125.
[67]Adm XVIII:1; FA:ED I, 134.
[68]Adm XXVIII;1-2; FA:ED I, 137.

we act in this way, then we are living "as strangers and pilgrims in this world, serving the Lord in poverty and humility."[69]

It is, therefore, the spirit of service that must characterize our inter-personal relationships: we are to seek nothing for ourselves, "because of the Lord, be obedient to every human institution…" (1 Pt 2:13).[70]

In the Franciscan Brotherhood the same disinterested spirit of service, free from all self-seeking, characterizes the relations between subjects and superiors. Francis calls the superiors "ministers and servants," and he gives substance to this concept through the warning we have already noted: no wielding of power nor lording it over others but rather the washing of feet: "for so it must be that the ministers are the servants of all the brothers."[71] Francis himself is the model of this art of being a truly poor superior, the servant of all: "I am the servant of all, I am obliged to serve all and to administer the fragrant words of my Lord to them."[72] His attitude is completely natural as he calls himself "the least of your servants, with a wish to kiss your feet…."[73] Such a spirit of service on the part of superiors is seen within the context of total availability on the part of each friar to all the rest: "on the contrary, *through the charity of the Spirit, let them serve* and obey one another voluntarily."[74]

To live without possessions, without owning anything, creates very special bonds of relationship between those who live in this way; bonds such as these, perhaps, can only be forged between those who seek to follow Christ seriously, that Christ Who said, "The Son of Man who has come, not to be served by others, but to serve…" (Matt 20:28).[75] From this it can be seen that "living without property" is one of the essential elements of Gospel life that create bonds of authentic community.

## IV. Evangelical Poverty and Our Relationship with God

Up to this point we have been concerned with Francis's estimation of poverty with respect to material things. But how does he envisage pov-erty with respect to man's relationship to God? The answer is simple: he who wants to be truly poor must realize that he is always poor before God. In God's presence he has neither merits nor good works in which he can glory. One who is truly poor is, like Francis, convinced of man's destitution before God. This highlights a saying of St. Francis's recorded by Celano and which can reliably be considered authentic: "After sin ev-

---

[69]LR VI:2; FA:ED I, 103.
[70]2LtF 47; FA:ED I, 48.
[71]LR X:6; FA:ED I, 105.
[72]2LtF 2;FA:ED I, 45.
[73]2LtF 87; FA:ED I, 51.
[74]ER V:14; FA:ED I, 67-68.
[75]ER IV:6; FA:ED I, 66-67.

erything is bestowed as alms, for the Great Almsgiver gives to the worthy and the unworthy with kind piety."[76] Wherever Francis met with goodness and kindness, wherever he recognized goodness, wherever he experienced benevolence, he attributed it always to God. "Let us refer all good to the Lord, God Almighty and Most High, acknowledge that every good is His, and thank Him, from Whom all good comes, for everything."[77]

Through these words, Francis expressed his fundamental conviction regarding Christian life: God, the Lord, is the Master of all good; man can lay claim to nothing but sin, which is a misuse of the gifts of God. From this fundamental conviction there flows a number of consequences which throw even more light on his thinking: since it is God who distributes His gifts to each one as He wills, and since man has no right to anything whatsoever, man must be careful to avoid the sin of jealousy, for "whoever envies his brother the good that the Lord says or does in him incurs a sin of blasphemy because he envies the Most High Himself Who says and does every good thing."[78]

Jealousy is not only a form of cupidity, of the will to possess, but also an encroachment upon the authority of God: "…are you envious because I am generous?" (Matt 20:15). Francis reveals the remedy for this jealousy: rejoicing at the work of God in the life of one's brother: "Blessed is that servant (Matt 24:46) who no more exalts himself over the good the Lord says or does through him than over what He says or does through another."[79] From these words we learn poverty delivers man from all selfishness and makes him eligible for total self-giving to God. Once this has taken place, man cannot presume to pass harsh and unloving judgments on others. He who knows that he has received from God all that he has, no longer possesses either the right or the power to judge another.

Since God is the proprietor of all good man has no grounds for boasting or for vainglory.

Here lurks one of the dangers of a life of poverty and Francis never wearies of warning his followers about it. The one who is truly poor must beware of appropriating to himself what is really God's work, and hence God's property. Once again Francis provides the remedy: "Blessed is the servant who stores up in heaven the good things which the Lord shows to him and does not wish to reveal them to people under the guise of a reward because the Most High Himself will reveal His deeds to whomever He wishes."[80]

---

[76] 2C XLVII:77; FA:ED II, 298.

[77] ER XVII:17; FA:ED I, 76.

[78] Adm VIII: 3; FA:ED I, 132.

[79] Adm XVII:1; FA:ED I, 134.

[80] Adm XXVIII:1; FA:ED I, 137.

In connection with this point, Francis asks the one seeking to be truly poor to "restore" to God all the good things he has received from Him. This "restitution" is a very basic attitude: the genuinely poor attribute nothing good to themselves, but "brought to life by the spirit of the divine letter who do not attribute every letter they know, or wish to know, to the body but, by word and example, return them to the most high Lord God to Whom every good belongs."[81] For St. Francis it is only natural that all should culminate in boundless thanksgiving: poverty and gratitude to God are inseparable. But "restitution to God" also implies service of our sacred trust, which must be used to the full to the benefit of our neighbor.

A further consequence of living *sine proprio* is that the poor are totally poor, and without security for the future. This is the ultimate degree of poverty. Francis acknowledges in all simplicity "...*the Lord God* Who has given and gives to each one of us our whole body, our whole soul and our whole life...."[82] He recalls all these truths and prays "...by Your grace alone, may we make our way to You, Most High...."[83] By God's grace alone: here we see how radically and seriously Francis understood a life "lived without property." He shows us what is for him the essence of living in poverty – the very heart of the mystery of poverty: to receive everything from God.

## Conclusion

By way of conclusion we can say that poverty, "being poor," is a basic pre-supposition for being religious, for our relationship with God, since poverty is, as it were, the door through which man enters into interior freedom, freedom to give himself to God. Through this door, man attains joy in God. And it is only in this freedom and joy that man becomes capable of love. In such a man the Spirit of the Lord will rest and make its home and dwelling place....[84] He who, like St. Francis, keeps nothing of himself for himself, can be totally possessed by God in a very real way; God can give Himself to him without reserve: "Hold back nothing of yourselves for yourselves, that He Who gives Himself totally to you may receive you totally."[85] Here is to be found the great charism of St. Francis: his ability to open the eyes of the men of his time, and indeed those of men of all ages, to the mystery of poverty.

---

[81]Adm VII:4; FA:ED I, 132.
[82]ER XXIII:8; FA:ED I, 84.
[83]LtOrd 52; FA:ED I, 121.
[84]2LtF 19; FA:ED I, 48.
[85]LtOrd 29; FA:ED I, 118.

Francis cries out to all of us: "Give yourselves totally to this, beloved brothers, never seek anything else under heaven for the name of our Lord Jesus Christ."[86]

---

[86]LR VI:6; FA:ED I, 103; FLCl 8:1-2; CA:ED, 119.

# Fundamental Value: *Minority*

## Sister Maria Luiza Piva, C.F.

### Introduction

In the same way as conversion, contemplation and poverty, minority is considered as a fundamental value in Saint Francis's experience in Gospel life.

In his prayer of praise and thanksgiving,[87] Francis reveals to us how he lived these values, these attitudes, wholly, day after day.[88]

### I. Francis, Minority and the Gospels

Francis wanted to be a Friar "minor" according to that which Jesus had taught us in the Gospel.

1. In his First Rule (1221) he refers all those who adopt this form of Gospel life, to the text of Matthew (Mt 25:31-46) where we meet Jesus Christ:

    a. comparing us to the least (Mt 25:40). "I assure you, as often as you did it for one of my least brothers, you did it for me."

    b. promising the reward of the Kingdom to the least (Mt 25:34). "Come. You have my Father's blessing! Inherit the kingdom prepared for you from the creation of the world."

    c. because of Jesus Christ, Francis chose for himself and his brothers the name of "minor." All, without distinction, are to be known as "Friars Minor."[89] Thereby, he wanted to express a fundamental aspect of the ideals of the Order and the vocation which it is supposed to realize within the Church.

        Francis synthesized rightly this mode of life saying: "The brothers are to appropriate nothing for themselves, but they should live as pilgrims and strangers (1 P 2:11) in this world, serving God in poverty and humility."

    d. in his writings, Francis presents himself: ... "and I, little brother Francis, your servant..."[90]

        —"Brother Francis, the least of the servants of God...."[91]

---

[87]ER XXIII:1-11; FA:ED I, 81-86.

[88]Brussels Rule III:10,

[89]ER VI:3; FA:ED I, 68.

[90]Test 41; FA:ED I, 127.

[91]2Lt Cus 1; FA:ED I, 60.

—"Brother Francis, their servant and subject...."[92]

—"...I wish to know in this way if you love the Lord and me, His servant and yours...."[93]

—"Because I am the servant of all, I am obliged to serve all and to administer the fragrant words of my Lord to them."[94]

—"Kissing your feet, therefore, and with all that love of which I am capable...."[95]

This is the way Francis presents himself: as a brother and a servant. However, the stress is put on the word servant, the least of the servants.

2. The text of the washing of the feet (Jn 13)

Francis loved it much, surely because it calls to actual gestures of welcome, service and mutual help.

"But if I washed your feet – I who am Teacher and Lord – then you must wash each other's feet. What I just did was to give you an example: as I have done, so you must do" (Jn 13:14-15).

This passage of the Gospel, wholly assumed by Saint Francis, reappears under various forms in the Rule. "Let no one be called 'prior,' but let everyone in general be called a lesser brother. Let one wash the feet of the other."[96]

The service of mutual obedience[97] is a concrete way of living this Gospel passage. "...Anyone among you who aspires to greatness must serve the rest, and whoever wants to rank first among you must serve the needs of all" (Mt 20:26-27). "...Let the greater among you be as the junior, the leader as the servant" (Lk 22:26). "Far from doing or speaking evil to one another, the brothers should be glad to serve and obey one another in a spirit of charity. This is the true, holy obedience of our Lord Jesus Christ."

For Francis, to be a friar minor consists in complete self-renunciation, joyful and serene acceptation of the human condition and union with the incarnate Word.

---

[92]2LtF; FA:ED I, 45.
[93]LtMin 9; FA:ED I, 97.
[94]2LtF 2; FA:ED I, 45.
[95]LtOrd 12; FA:ED I, 117.
[96]ER VI:3-4; FA:ED I, 68.
[97]ER V:13-17; FA:ED I, 67-68.

## II. MINORITY, REQUIRED ATTITUDE FOR THE KINGDOM

"Let the children come to me. Do not hinder them. The kingdom of God belongs to such as these" (Mt 19:14).

We receive everything from God. We are as little ones in His presence, like little beggars; we should not keep anything to ourselves, but whatever we have and whatever we are, we should leave it at the disposal and service of others and of the divine plan. This Gospel spirit is an essential condition to enter the Kingdom.

Francis assumed this simple form of life in the everyday happenings and he proposed it to all who follow him.

1. Relationship between the members of the fraternity.[98]

> Minority is not an isolated attitude, but it is always related to something. It is the life and the ferment of our relations, and it makes them fruitful. It is the atmosphere in which the brothers and sisters live.
>
> Francis wanted his brothers to be friars "minor," that is to say, to be obliging to each other, putting all their strength in the common treasury of fraternity.
>
> Because he understood that his brothers were all on an equal footing according to the Gospel, he forbade that anyone should be called "prior" or "superior." "No one is to be called "Prior." They are all to be known as "Friars Minor" without distinction, and they should be prepared to wash one another's feet."[99]
>
> This quotation is quite enlightening: no one is superior, all are "minors" and hence without titles or exigencies or rights over others. And so that this should be well understood, reference is made to the Last Supper: "Let them wash one another's feet."
>
> Let he who presides over the fraternity be called "guardian," "minister," "servant of all." Let the ministers deal with the brothers in need with friendship and such great love that those may speak and treat them as would masters with their servants; "for so it must be that the ministers are the servants of all the brothers."[100]
>
> Only one is our Father who is in heaven and only one our Master, Jesus Christ. Hence, let us call no one on earth our father or our master.[101]
>
> Spurred on by the love that the Spirit arouses and stirs in us, we should serve and obey one another everyday and reject all

---

[98]Brussels Rule VI, 23.
[99]ER VI:3-4; FA:ED I, 68.
[100]LR X:6; FA:ED I, 105.
[101]ER XXII:1-52; FA:ED I, 79-80.

that could look like power, domination, appropriation and intrigue.

Francis started a fraternal life made of spontaneity, respect, mutual care, courtesy, refinement of charity, and wide liberty, and the bonds of mutual love being the cohesive strength of the fraternity.

He understood that with this type of itinerant life, of moneyless and homeless travelers, his brothers needed to feel mutual love and support, in a concrete way. "And let them show by their actions that they love one another."[102]

The members of the fraternity should be at each other's service in confidence and liberty.[103]

This mutual and free service should spread over the whole of the Franciscan family, helping and strengthening communion.[104]

2. Relationship between brothers and sisters and all men

"True love longs to be universal, it desires to unite all men in one friendly interchange."

"That is why the brothers were wandering about the world, working among men, praying, in a really itinerant form of life, to exhort, everywhere, the brothers to do penance, and to announce the Kingdom of God."

a. Work is a concrete way of being at everybody's service; as brothers and sisters "minor," we have to work. After Francis, we should look on work as a grace, a gift of the Lord, and always accomplish it faithfully and with devotion.

This insertion into the reality of work enabled the first brothers – and enables us all today – to become partners with all men, to share the life of the poor and to struggle for a more human, more equitable and more fraternal world.

The brothers and sisters should work so as to provide for themselves and the fraternity; they should do it humbly and with a spirit of service and not to hoard goods or get a better position than others, but for the love of God, they should be servants and subject to every human creature.

b. They should rejoice when they are among the poor, the outcast, the weak, the sick, the lepers and those who beg in the streets.

---

[102]ER XI:5-6; FA:ED I, 72; Brussels Rule VI:19.
[103]Brussels Rule VI:19.
[104]Brussels Rule I:3.

As an expression of minority, they should adopt a simple way of life and their clothes should be poor.

Francis insists also on our attitude towards all men: we should be welcoming, meek, humble and unassuming, speaking courteously to everyone as is right. Wherever we are, we should avoid getting into arguments and we should not provoke anyone to anger nor cause scandal, nor condemn others: instead we should be joyful in the Lord, good humored, gracious. Our greetings should be: "The Lord give you peace."[105]

### c. Mission of peace

Francis leads the whole Order towards a real mission of peace. "As they proclaim peace with their lips, they must have it to overflowing in their hearts. No one should be provoked by anger or offended because of them. On the contrary, everyone should be drawn to peace, kindness and friendship, by their gentleness."[106] This is what we have been called for.[107]

In order to obtain peace, Francis rejects all kinds of violence; himself goes in with the persuasive strength of his words, poetry, and songs. Peace is not only a goal to be reached, it is also a method to be followed. This is why the first biographers tell us – rightly – that Francis always announced the Gospel of peace that he made himself as the "angel of peace" and that he always started his sermons with: "The Lord give you his peace." He admonished his brothers saying: "Go and announce peace to all men."

### 3. Our relationship with God

Our Franciscan life should be a loving answer to God Who is Love Himself. "Love is the atmosphere where our prayer can live, the seal of our spirituality and the fundamental message that we have to give to the world."

Francis was filled with the Spirit of God, elated with the Spirit of God and he proposes instantly to all those who follow this form of Gospel life to desire above all things to have the Spirit of the Lord and His holy operation.[108]

---

[105]Brussels Rule VIII:26.
[106]Brussels Rule VIII:26.
[107]L3C XIV:58; FA:ED II, 101-02.
[108]Brussels Rule IV:14-15.

The crucial point of the Franciscan project is the desire to give oneself to the Spirit of the Lord and to His dynamism in a fundamental fidelity to the Gospel of Jesus Christ.

For this, we should constantly turn ourselves toward God and our neighbor, with humility and submission:[109] "That everywhere they acknowledge that all things belong to the Lord, most High God, Master of all things, giving Him thanks through all and in all, for all things come from Him."[110]

## CONCLUSION

This experience of minority experienced by Francis constitutes a fundamental value in our spirituality. That is why it is present throughout the Rule Project. It is also for us all, Franciscan brothers and sisters, an evangelical claim and a challenge.

---

[109]Brussels Rule III:13.
[110]Brussels Rule III:13.

# Chapter I
## *Incipit regula et vita*

### †Fr. Thaddeus Horgan, S.A.

The title of the opening chapter is a medieval way of stating that this is a spiritual document containing values, attitudes and principles necessary for a way of living. *Regula et Vita* are not regulations for our lives. The opening words of the text reiterate this point by using the words *forma vitae*. St. Francis was concerned with his and his follower's living "... according to the pattern of the holy Gospel."[111] The Rule's purpose is to have us grasp again and again the dynamism of those evangelical values and attitudes, which Francis's life, example, and writings propose to us. It is our responsibility to give them concrete and practical expression in our day.

This first chapter summarizes the whole Rule and specifically identifies who we are in the Church. The first article says we are religious Franciscans in the Third Order, or as the text says, we are members of "The Regular Order of St. Francis." In this name there is a whole unwritten history that goes back to the ancient Order of Penance. It includes the history of the Third Order Regular and its sense of rootedness in St. Francis. The histories of many congregations and of founders who chose to follow Christ after the example of St. Francis is also intended by the name. But above all it points out that we are Franciscans in a particular way. We are not one of the Orders of friars minor, nor one of the branches of the Poor Clares and not Secular Franciscans either. Francis projected three ways in his day for his followers "to observe the Holy Gospel." We follow the path of the third way and share that with our secular brothers and sisters with significant distinctiveness. We publicly profess the evangelical counsels and live in religious fraternity. Within a lifetime after Francis's death his followers in the Order of Penance began living this style of Gospel life. This was the origin of our present day heritage and tradition as Third Order Regular religious both in individual congregations and in the Order of friars whose General House is at Saints Cosmos and Damian in Rome.

Nevertheless the unity of the whole Franciscan movement is expressed in the opening article. With our brothers and sisters in the other branches of the Franciscan movement who are religious, we share the overall Franciscan charism of Gospel life through the profession of the counsels of obedience, poverty and chastity. With our secular Franciscan brothers and sisters we share the tradition of the Penitents of Francis's day who

---

[111]Test 14; FA:ED I, 125.

asked him to give them guidelines so they could follow his example. This is why the text calls us to be "aware of the life" of Francis. If the Lord calls us to be Franciscan the example of Francis becomes significant for our living.

Using his own words to the religious of his day[112] our text presents us with Vatican II's teaching on religious life. We are not different from all the faithful who are called to holiness rather we are called to live more and more intensely the percepts and counsels of Our Lord Jesus Christ. The very last sentence of the article points out the canonical object of the Church's public vows for religious (renunciation) and uses Francis's own terms to express religious profession itself *promisit Deo*.

In summary article 1 states the following:

    a. this is a spiritual document about our

    b. identity and life which is centered in the charism of

    c. observing the Gospel. It notes that we are

    d religious who profess the Church's

    e. canonical vows.

### Article 2:

The characteristic of Franciscan Third Order Regular spirituality is its emphasis that turning to God and being conformed to the Christ of the Gospel is never accomplished all at once. These are on-going religious experiences. To be faithful to the Gospel, as Francis's experience shows,[113]we always have to do penance (*metanoia*) in our Order's spirituality. It is the most basic of the four fundamental Franciscan values which are set forth in this Rule. Because this is so, some refer to this article as the charism statement of the Third Order Regular.

Francis's own words are used to explain *metanoia* or biblical penance. Unfortunately today, many misunderstand even Francis's use of "... *in vera fide et poeitentia....*" Since this is so, Francis's words from both the Rules of 1221 and 1223 are employed. As a form of Gospel living *metanoia/penitentia* is a style of Gospel life, which has three basic elements according to Francis:[114]

    a. to acknowledge the Lord, in the creation, in the word of the scripture, in the manifest goodness of God, and especially in the words, life, deed and teachings of the Lord Jesus Christ. This is what persevering in true faith means. To persevere further implies

---

[112]2LtF 36-40; FA:ED I, 48.

[113]Test 1-26; FA:ED I, 124-26.

[114]ER XXIII; FA:ED I, 81-86.

b. to adore the Lord concretely with one's whole life by living prayer-fully in a child-like way with purity of heart, in poverty and in loving obedience which impels the true Gospel person:

c. to serve the Lord in one's neighbor by doing charity for the sake of justice and peace (Mt 25:34).

The rest of this Rule will now spell out in detail a whole style of Gospel living, which has been summarized here.

## ARTICLE 3:

Begins by expanding that part of Article 2 which is concerned with *vera fide*. The Church is the guardian of the truth of revelation as well as responsible for its transmission. In this light fidelity to the Church becomes one of the ways to "persevere in true faith." Specifically, this article refers to fidelity to the leaders of the Church: the Pope and Bishops. They are responsible for leading God's people in fulfilling the mission of the Church. In this they will have our support and cooperation. We are to be of service to them particularly by living our Gospel way of life as a witness within the Church, as well as by announcing "penance and peace" to all. This article calls us to deep fraternity, not only in the larger Church or within our local diocesan Church, but especially within our communities or fraternities which should be microcosms of the Church itself. The Church is the community of God's new people in Jesus Christ. It should be the community of Gospel people. We are called to be turned totally to God and manifest this by living the Gospel intensely after the example of St. Francis.

The place "where" we are to do this primarily is within our fraternities and congregations. Like the Church itself our communities need structure and leadership. A sign of our fidelity to fraternity, then, is our obedience to our Ministers. But not this alone. Of equal importance is our recognition and reverence for each other. And since we are all spiritual sons and daughters of one Father, anybody who is in a Franciscan movement is equally in relationship with us. First, because we are all in Christ and secondly because all of us share the same vocation to live the Gospel. How we love one another, even beyond the limits of our Orders and our congregations, will or will not be the witness to the authenticity of our Gospel life.

## CHAPTER II
## ACCEPTANCE INTO THIS LIFE

### †FR. THADDEUS HORGAN, S.A.

This chapter primarily considers the formation and the ongoing process of *metanoia*. It should be noted that all four fundamental values
(*metanoia*, prayer, poverty and minority) of our Franciscan life will now
begin to appear in each chapter. Each chapter may refer to specific values
but, because Gospel life is one, all four will constitute the fabric of the
Rule text in each of its parts. This chapter obviously deals with formation. But a closer look at the text shows that what is said of the process
of formation is also the process for on-going conversion (*metanoia*) in
all our lives. In Francis's life conversion resulted from the Lord's inspiration. To follow this Gospel way of life whose beginning is conversion one
must be inspired by the Lord. Only in this way can conversion be total
and continuous. The purpose and formation is to incorporate a person
fully into the company of others who share the same calling to be totally
and continually turned to God. *Metanoia* is manifested in our tradition
of Franciscanism by our living the Gospel literally after the example of
St. Francis. This form of Gospel life includes poverty (article 5), humble
service (article 7) and prayerfulness (article 8). Our Franciscan commitment and consecration is a life-long process and experience (article 6).

**Articles 4 and 5** reflect the initial conversion experience of Francis as
much as they reflect his instruction about formation. From this perspective we can see that for Francis it is essential that one be convinced
that his or her call is from the Lord. This implies discernment, which
is carried out through dialogue between the individual and the fraternity's representatives. The fraternity through its ministers has particular
responsibilities to itself and to its candidates. The minister is to ascertain that the one called is "truly catholic" and genuinely faithful to the
Church. The sign of this is not in mere words but in the Candidate's
deeds. If this is so then two things are to follow. The candidate is to be
initiated into the life of the fraternity. This statement is this Rule's text's
first explicit reference to the essentially formative character (on-going
conversion) of Franciscan living. As Francis experienced and reflected in
the Testament the textbook of our religious formation are the Gospels.
They are explained to the candidate, especially those parts which express
the radical and complete giving of self to God. For Francis divesting self
or all that could hinder one's total conversion is a requisite if one would
walk in Christ's footsteps.

**Article 6** is among the most direct in the Rule Text. It is addressed to the novice: "Let them begin..." It is addressed to all in the fraternity: "Let them begin." The life of penance is always begun anew and is continuous. It is an on-going commitment. It is our religious commitment. That is why the word "consecration" is used in the second sentence. With Francis everything must be concrete, not ideal. Therefore if one is to surrender self to God, then one must manifest this by giving possessions to God's poor people (article 5). If one begins and continually pursues a life of evangelical conversion than the simplicity of Christ's life should characterize the Franciscan's total living, beginning with the very clothes on one's back. Conversion to God implies being counter-cultural. To be such is not merely a matter of clothing, but of total life style.

**Article 7** refers to life-profession and the attitudes Francis says are necessary once one has begun a life of penance. The expression "to be received into obedience" has a special meaning. It means profession into a type of religious life that is not monastic. Instead of a commitment to live an enclosed life, one binds oneself to live the bond of fraternal relationship with others equally committed to total conversion and the observance of the Holy Gospel. The living link for all in the fraternity is the minister whom all are to obey and who is to encourage the others to do "...all they have promised the Lord to observe (Article 22). Mutual and shared responsibility for our Gospel living and for one another is a principle found in Francis's writings. It is not something new since Vatican II for Franciscans.

The fundamental attitudes and evangelical values of poverty and minority (the second sentence) are presented by Francis as characteristics we should develop in our on-going observance of "...this life and rule." They will be treated in subsequent chapters. What perhaps needs to be pointed out here is the final sentence. It at once summarizes Vatican II's general teaching about religious life as well as that Council's specific teaching about consecrated chastity. It does so in the words of Francis. Here, too, is a summary of Francis's understanding of continuous conversion through Gospel living. For Francis and for us it is the positive surrender of one's whole being to God and God's service.

**Article 8** spells out more concretely what article 7 indicates. In the first place it notes that our turning to the Lord is to be so complete that nothing less than union with God in Christ by the Spirit is to be our life's objective. At the same time it points out that being filled with God's life and love is to be continually manifested by love for your neighbor. Doing the works of charity has been a consistent characteristic of the histories of our congregations and fraternities. This article situates this tradition squarely within our life of conversion.

# Chapter III
## The Spirit of Prayer

### Sr. Maria Luiza Piva, C.F.

This chapter deals with the spirit of prayer and defines it as a fundamental value in our form of life, as the marrow of our Franciscan spirituality.

In developing this chapter we shall follow the following order:

1. Contemplative prayer – Church prayer;
2. Praise and thanksgiving;
3. Meditation on the Holy Scriptures;
4. Eucharist;
5. The mystery of the Cross and of reconciliation.

These five points coincide with the articles of this chapter.

### Article 9: Franciscan and contemplative prayer

a. According to Francis, we should be saturated with the love of God to such a point that, at every moment and at every place, we should adore the Lord with a pure and sincere heart, with joy and thanksgiving.

Our Franciscan prayer should be a permanent endeavor to answer God's free love by our own love.

In his First Rule (1221), Francis expresses eloquently our vocation to thanksgiving and love of God in everything.

Contemplating the Lord in His greatness and His boundless love for us, our attitude is that of prayer.

b. The prayer of the Church, the Liturgy of the Hours, should sanctify every moment of our day.

Francis enjoins us to pray this office devoutly before God, not concentrating on the melody of the chant, but being cheerful that our hearts be in harmony so that our words may be in harmony with our hearts and our hearts with God.[115]

---

[115]LtOrd 1-52; FA:ED I, 116-122.

## ARTICLE 10:

Francis does not lay stress so much on petition as on praise. In his transparency, he unites himself to all creatures and is able to love them all without excluding the leper, the sinner, nor the robber who ill-treats him.... Entirely free, he can pray "My God and my All" and sing lovingly the Canticle of the Sun, hymn of love to the God of beauty present in every creature: "Be praised, my Lord, with all your creatures."

## ARTICLE 11:

As Francis's love proves, total conformity to the Gospel is possible only through a constant meditation on the words of our Lord Jesus Christ and the whole of the Holy Scriptures.

Our only Master is Jesus Christ, in His whole Mystery. Our sole endeavor is to follow his doctrine and his footsteps,[116] to adhere to his words and his life, and to share his sorrowful and glorious destiny.[117] In this consists the "following of Christ."

To succeed in this way, our main source of Franciscan meditation is the Holy Scriptures, although all creatures and events are also, for a Franciscan soul, a constant book of meditation.

All that reveals God's love is a subject for Franciscan meditation.

## ARTICLE 12: THE EUCHARIST

a. The Eucharist is the highest thanksgiving that we could offer to God. That is why we must take part in its celebration.

b. We must revere the Blessed Sacrament, because Jesus is peace and reconciliation for all.

In the Eucharist, Christ achieves the reconciliation of all creatures with God: it is the sign and the cause of harmony and unity.

We live and honor the Eucharist when, transformed into Christ, we live in union with our brothers....

And so the Eucharist gives its fruit....

If Jesus Christ has lowered himself to the point of making himself our food, we must after his example, serve our brothers, becoming for them a gift, a blessing.

Jesus Christ gave himself as a free gift, so we must act after his example, so that "He who has given himself wholly to you may receive you wholly."

---

[116]1LtF 1-19; FA:ED I, 41-42.
[117]ER XXII:1-51; FA:ED I, 81.

## Article 13: reconciliation with God and with all

The life of prayer expresses our conversion to God and to others. Conversion being a method to maintain in us the dispositions of the reconciled, we must when necessary, have recourse to confession.

"Good and faithful servant (Mt. 24:21) – says Francis – who, for all sins, does penance without delay, inwardly by sorrow and outwardly by confession."

For Francis, confession has an ecclesial and community dimension and must be full of a spirit of conversion.

In the same article, we are invited to bring forth worthy fruits of penance, to live in availability and humility.

In this way, we shall live in permanent reconciliation.

We should desire nothing else except our Savior who has reconciled us in offering Himself on the altar of the Cross.

CHAPTER IV
HOW TO SERVE AND WORK

SR. MARIANNE JUNGBLUTH, F.H.F.

This chapter deals with the fundamental value of "minority" – service and work are the expression of this fundamental attitude – a conversion, an expression used by Francis himself.

As we have already seen, all Francis's efforts tend towards the imitation of Jesus Christ, whom we see living in the Gospel and an imitation as faithful as possible. Besides the poverty of Christ, there is precisely "above all, the humility of the Incarnation…which so occupied Francis's thoughts that he was barely able to think of anything else." But the humility manifested in the Incarnation is the manifestation of the "minority" of annihilation to the extreme which made of Christ, the Son of the living God, the servant of His creatures, and even the servant of sinners. "The Son of Man did not come to be served but to serve and to give His life in ransom for many" (Mt 20:28).[118]

St. Francis admires the humility of Christ, His disposition to serve; though He is Lord, He has a special love for the poor, the little ones, the despised and the exiled. He has pity on the sick and the wretched, serving them humbly because the Father sent Him for that. Francis shows us how we can realize this way of being "minor" in daily life, in interpersonal relationships, and in our dealings with all men.

ARTICLE 14:

*The Brothers and Sisters to whom the Lord has given the grace of working…*

St. Francis places these words at the beginning of the 5th chapter of the Second Rule. He sees the possibility of being able to serve and to work as a grace given by God. It is a grace because we can give back to God all He has given us – restore them to God who has given to each one of us our body, soul and life, and who gives them to us every day. It is a grace because in all that we do we accomplish a mission for which each one has been destined and of which each is capable. Thus we contribute our part to the realization of God's plan for the salvation of mankind. Through us, the Providence of God must be seen and implemented for our neighbor. This imitation of God, this being able to serve and to work, is a divine service; it is the glorification of God.

---

[118]ER V:12, Adm IV:1; FA:ED I, 67, 130.

*They should serve and work faithfully and devotedly, like the poor.*

These words of St. Francis have special meaning in our day when work can become an end in itself, and even the supreme value to which everything else is subordinated. A person is often esteemed by the amount of work he does and for his capacity for work. We know, too, that service and work today are often just a means of escape from self and from God.

Francis, on the contrary, lays down as a principle that work exists in relation to God. If I work "faithfully and devotedly," it presupposes that I have received a mission (here I mean the mission of God addressed to me), a mission to which I am completely devoted. By this fidelity and devotedness, a poor person realizes his obedience to the Lord, because, through this service and work, he submits himself always anew to the domination of God and thus co-operates in the fulfillment of the Kingdom of God.

*Let them beware of idleness, which is the enemy of the soul. In their service and work they should not extinguish the spirit of holy prayer and devotion, which all earthly things are meant to foster.*

Francis wants the basic contemplative structure of which we spoke yesterday to condition our work also: work only on condition that the spirit of prayer and devotion is not extinguished in you. Idleness, the source of so much evil, is avoided when there is service and work. Why? Self-indulgence triumphs in the lazy, indolent person who fears work. Such a person does not use his talents but buries them. He refuses to serve God and becomes his own slave. That is why Francis insists on warning against idleness, so harmful to the soul.

In addition to the extreme case of idleness, there is another one: a person is in some way obsessed by his work; it literally devours him. This is very dangerous because work no longer leaves him any time for his neighbor and "the spirit of prayer and devotion is extinguished." Work can also become a passion; a person seeks his own satisfaction in it. This is defecting from the service of God in order to serve oneself.

## ARTICLE 15:

*In return for their work they may accept what is necessary for their material needs and those of their Brothers and Sisters.*

Many things are said on this subject: work must not lead to the accumulation of a fortune obtaining more profit than is necessary for one's livelihood. We should earn, and we have the permission to earn and keep what is necessary for our livelihood. But in our different situations we must seriously reflect anew and find out if we are obeying, not only what Francis asks of us, but also what the Second Vatican Council asks, namely "to possess whatever they need for their temporal life and work, they should avoid any semblance of luxury, excessive wealth and accumulation of property."[119] The Council adds that we should live by the work of our hands and not from our fortune and its interest.

It also says that the salary we earn from our work is for our subsistence and that of our Brothers and Sisters, as well as for the upkeep of the community. A person who lives in community gives everything to the community and keeps nothing for himself; he shares everything with his Brothers and Sisters. By his work he is entirely at the service of the community.

*And this, humbly, as it befits servants of God and followers of the most high poverty....*

In this simple phrase we rediscover the center of "minority": to be minor. This is how the grace of work is protected. The "minor" is ready to serve all men, as the servant of God and the disciple of holy poverty, for the coming of the Kingdom and also in the domain of his work, which he accepts as a grace from God, which he tries to live out in conformity with grace.

*What they have left over, they should give to the poor.*

We have been told that we should never work for ourselves, but always for the community. Francis said so very clearly in the context of his times: "In recompense for their work they many receive what is necessary for the life of the body." Everything we earn, everything we acquire in one way or another, everything that is given to us, must be for the community and the Church, for the subsistence of the poor. Here also the decree *Perfectae Caritatis* says, "They should willingly contribute part of what they possess for the other needs of the Church and for the support of the poor, whom all religious should love with the deep yearning of Christ."[120]

*They should never want to be in charge of others. On the contrary, they should be servants, and for the Lord's sake be subject to every human creature.*

---

[119]Austin Flannery, ed., "Perfectae Caritatis" *Vatican Council II: The Conciliar and Post Conciliar Documents.* (Northport: Costello Publishing Company, 1975), 618-19.
    [120]Ibid., 618.

Once again, it is clear that Francis means to be below others: "minor." The man who is truly so, possesses neither material goods, nor authority, nor power. Others can dispose of those who are ready to serve all, as masters dispose of their servants.

ARTICLE 16:

*The Brothers and Sisters should be meek, humble, gentle, peaceful and unassuming, speaking courteously to everyone, as is right. Wherever they are, and wherever they go in the world....*

Being minor, we indicate that we imitate the poor and humble Jesus. As is shown in the Project of the Rule, this attitude has many forms of expression. Francis sees in this the possibility of serving for the extension of the Kingdom of God. He is convinced of the silent apostolate of "being minor," which he ranks as equal to, if not above, the apostolate of preaching and catechesis. To be kind, peaceful, modest, meek and humble is to bear living witness to the fact that we are "Christians," convincing proof of the message of Christ. This witness is the element that will perhaps make preaching efficacious. For this reason we must make it visible in our milieu.

*...they should show that they are joyful in the Lord, good-humored and gracious, as is right. When they greet others, they should say, 'The Lord give you peace.'*

Joy, gaiety, amiability are also living signs that we are "Christians." Francis followed the Lord's way with a joyful heart, though it was not always easy. In this way he conducted himself as a messenger of peace. This desire for peace animated him throughout his life. He proves this in his Testament and greets everyone: "May the Lord give you His peace." At every doorstep he says, "Peace to this house."

We, too, are called to be messengers of peace, but we will only be able to lead others to peace, as St. Francis did, if we ourselves have peace, and live in peace. By our lives and our activity we must help others to realize their dream of peace, and their ardent desire to establish concord among men. We are called to "seek out, the strayed I will bring back, the injured I will bind up, the sick I will heal, shepherding them rightly." (Ez 34:16).

CHAPTER V
THE LIFE OF POVERTY

SR. IGNATIA GOMEZ, MISS. SRS.

Chapter 5 of the proposed text talks about one of the most important values of Franciscanism, namely poverty.

Our Father Saint Francis chose poverty as his way of life because Jesus himself chose a life of humility and poverty. As St. Paul in his Second Letter to the Corinthians, Chapter 8 tells us "...shown you by our Lord Jesus Christ; how for your sake he made himself poor though he was rich so that you might become rich by his poverty" (2 Cor 8:9). And quoting the same Saint again, "Though he was in the form of God, he did not deem equality with God something to be grasped at. Rather, he emptied himself and took the form of a slave, being born in the likeness of men" (Phil 2:6-7).

It was this self-emptying of Jesus that led St. Francis to embrace a life of such intense poverty to which all of us, his sons and daughters, must be faithful.

Poverty is our life. It is both inward and social. Being poor means emptying ourselves and loving those who slap us in the face.[121] It means not appropriating to ourselves either our will or the talents God has given us,[122] or any task or ministry.[123] Giving ourselves wholly to obedience[124] not keeping any goods to ourselves but giving everything over to the Lord to whom all belongs.[125]

**Article 17** says: "Let them remember that we are to have nothing of this world except food and clothing." Our poverty therefore must be expressed visibly in dress,[126] housing, means of transport[127] the refusal of money and property[128] for Article 17 also says: "They shall be profoundly suspicious of money." Our poverty is also expressed in our work as a means of subsistence[129] and by our nearness to poor people.[130] This is why the concluding paragraph of Art. 17 says: "Let them rejoice when

---

[121] Adm XIV:4; FA:ED I, 134.
[122] Adm II:3-4; FA:ED I, 129.
[123] ER XIV:4; FA:ED I, 73.
[124] Adm III:3-6; FA:ED I, 130.
[125] Adm VII; XI:4; XIX:1-2; FA:ED I, 132, 133, 135; ER XVII:17; FA:ED I, 76.
[126] ER II:14; FA:ED I, 65; LRII:14-16; FA:ED I, 101; Test 16; FA:ED I, 125.
[127] ER XV:1-2; FA:ED I, 73; LR III:12; FA:ED I, 102.
[128] ER VIII:3; FA:ED I, 69-70; LR IV:1-3; FA:ED I, 102.
[129] ER VII:1-15; FA:ED I, 68-69; LR V; FA:ED I, 102-103; Test 20-22; FA:ED I, 125.
[130] ER IX:1-16; FA:ED I, 70-71.

they live among the outcast and despised, among the poor and the weak, the sick and the lepers and those who beg in the streets."

Besides the above-mentioned poor, we also have those who suffer from loneliness and isolation, incapacity to cope with life, loss of meaning and purpose in life, loss of hope, helplessness and boredom. All these forms of misery, which are often hidden behind masks of material wealth and well-being, also need our help.

We must especially examine our means of subsistence and our lodging to see if it would not be fitting to insert ourselves in today's economic structures through a salaried job (intellectual or manual) and by living in rented quarters; such an option will influence the number of brothers and sisters possible in a fraternity and will affect our lodging, our clothing and our whole style of life. It will bring us closer to the working classes of society and help us avoid big institutions and bureaucracies which make us established and are seen as signs of power.

As far as money is concerned, the use of which is explicitly forbidden by the rule, we must open our eyes to the obvious fact that its value and significance have completely changed today. As a consequence, an absolute refusal of its use is no longer possible. On the other hand, we are to reject all forms of capitalism and are to live in such a way that our future is not guaranteed. Poverty is insecurity with a total dependence on God who is total richness and totally self-sufficient. The surplus from our salaries can be turned over to the service of the most poor.

In this perspective it would be helpful to reconsider our apostolates. Rather than having our own apostolates, organizing them, maintaining them, propagating or defending them, it would be better if the competent brothers or sisters place themselves at the service of existing structures in the Church or in society excepting only those which are manifestations of wealth and power, to work in them without any collective desire to dominate.

Poverty for Franciscans is not merely a virtue, it is a whole way of life. We should understand this poverty in all its Gospel dimensions. It is the basic attitude of man to receive salvation. It is made up of the awareness of sin and of man's powerlessness, of an absolute trust in God alone, and in His merciful and free love. Poverty, humility and the spirit of childhood are the names the Gospel gives to this attitude. We attribute to ourselves only our own limitations and our sins. This is the interior dimension of poverty which is above all an openness to the richness of God and a trust in His salvation. It is our vocation to bear witness to this two-fold dimension of poverty in the Church and the world today, namely our total dependence on God and our complete detachment from created things.

Whatever its exterior expression – and we know this depends on the time, the setting and the concrete situation – it must be perceptible to the men and women of today.

Poverty as our way of life affects every aspect of our life. It affects our prayer life because before God we are His poor needy children not even able to utter His Name without the help of His Holy Spirit. It affects our spirit of joy so inherent to our Franciscan vocation.

Humility excludes all material or spiritual power, all forms of domination, all will to power. As a community and as individuals we present ourselves as servants whom no one need fear because we seek to serve and not to dominate or impose ourselves on others even for spiritual purposes. Humility requires of us a spirit of childhood, lowliness, simplicity, even a certain naïvete before people and events.

Lowly and subject to all, Francis says in his first Rule, we must be servants, brothers and friends.[131] This is only possible if there is sincerity in our hearts with no pretense, no prestige or power.

**Article 18** enjoins us to live as pilgrims, as travelers and strangers in this world. This, I am sure, is easy for us to understand as most of us here are strangers in this place.

> *"Travel light,*
> *Less luggage,*
> *More Comfort."*

This, says our Text in Article 18, is the summit of the most exalted poverty which makes us heirs and kings of the kingdom of Heaven. It makes us poor in earthly goods but raises us high in virtue and acceptable in the eyes of Almighty God.

Holding fast to this most exalted poverty for the sake of our Lord Jesus Christ, may we never long for anything else under heaven.

---

[131]ER VII:2-3; FA:ED I, 68; Test 19; FA:ED I, 125.

## CHAPTER VI
## OF FRATERNAL LIFE

### SR. MARIE-BENOÎT LUCBERNET, S.S.F.A.

*When God gave me some brothers...*

For Francis, fraternal life is the groundwork on which the whole of Franciscan life is woven.

Poverty, minority, conversion are fundamental values; they are lived within this background of fraternity.

Every chapter of the project bears the mark of it:

—the bond of communion between the brothers and sisters and all the members of the Franciscan family is stressed in article 3,

—training includes an initiation to fraternal life,

—charity produces an increase in universal love,

—the outcome of work provides for everybody's needs.

We could find further examples.

Poverty leaves us free from attachment to a position, to power, material goods, and thus enables us to love.

The title of Chapter 6: "Of Fraternal Life" is aimed at bringing out a certain quality of relationship within and outside the group, with every man, with the whole universe and the whole creation.

### I. ARTICLE 19 TRIES TO EXPRESS THE REASON OF FRATERNAL LIFE

A. Fraternity, God's gift

  1. Fraternal love has its roots in Jesus Christ who became himself our brother, "He, the eldest of many."

> "He has given us the example, revealing to us that every man is a brother: 'In so far as you did this to one of the least of these brothers of mine, you did it to me.'"

> "For the love of God," assembled in the very name of that love, wanting to live for and bear witness to that love:

> "The brothers and sisters should love one another," wanting to keep and put into practice the Lord's commandment: "love one another as I have loved you," and "by this love you

have for one another, everyone will know that you are my disciples."

This fraternal love is not to remain in the intellectual sphere or in the mind only, but it must be actualized in deeds. Francis enjoined us: "All the Friars should preach by their example."

2. Fraternal love is a consequence of our choice of absolute poverty. This is creating an interdependence between all the members of the fraternity.

Everyone may, in all trust and liberty, express their desires, each being solicitous about others and giving them what they need.

"They must prove their love by deeds."

"The friars should have no hesitation about telling one another what they need, so that they can provide for one another."

This mutual help is also an expression of minority.

This type of relationship is not confined within the circle of the fraternity, nor even of the congregation, or even best, of the Franciscan family, but it is only a stepping-stone to enable us to open ourselves without delusion to universal love creating a claim on our human relationship.

B. The sick brothers and sisters are looked after with particular care; here lies the test of the quality of our fraternal relationship.

Fraternal love does not depend on efficiency, profit – is he productive or not, does he render service – the brother is loved for himself, the sister is loved for herself, simply because he or she is loved by God, because he is God's gift, God's present.

"They are blessed who love their brethren as much when they are sick and cannot repay them, as when they are well and can repay them." This free love takes the form of a beatitude for Francis, who was very solicitous about his sick brothers.

C. The Kingdom groups us, fraternity spurs us on seeking the will of God, submitting ourselves to it, sticking to it in all and for all and giving thanks unceasingly.

No matter what happens to them, they should give thanks to the Creator. They should accept willingly the condition in which they find themselves, being in sickness or in health.

This text does not concern the sick only, but all the brothers and all the sisters, in whatever circumstances and state they may be. What matters is to wish to do the will of God and to give thanks.

**II. ARTICLE 20: HOW TO DEAL WITH TRANSGRESSIONS IN FRATERNAL LIFE.** If fraternal life is a gift from God, it is also a deeply human reality.

A. This form of life is exacting and is not always easy: weaknesses, faults may happen, offences towards other brothers or sisters through words or actions.

The depth and truth of fraternal love reveals itself in fraternal forgiveness.

"If disharmony arises among them because of something said or done, they should ask forgiveness of one another at once with humility, before they offer their gift of prayer to the Lord."

The question is not to find out who is right or wrong, but to ask humbly forgiveness of one another, before turning to our God and our Father.

B. In the same way, a brother or a sister may transgress the form of life they have professed: they should neither be put to shame nor reproached, but forgiveness should be shown towards them as it is asked in the *Letter to a Minister*:

"And if you have done this, I wish to know in this way if you love the Lord and me, His servant and yours: that there is not any brother in the world who has sinned – however much he could have sinned – who, after he has looked into your eyes, would ever depart without your mercy. And if he were not looking for mercy, you would ask him if he wants mercy."[132]

It is such behavior that we wanted to recall and formulate here:

"And if he would sin a thousand times before your eyes, love him more than me so that you may draw him to the Lord; and always be merciful with brothers such as these. And you may an-

---

[132]LtMin 9-10; FA:ED I, 97.

nounce this to the guardians, when you can, that, for your part, you are resolved to act in this way."[133]

C. The fraternity is not a community made up of pure, perfect people, where only the weak, the black sheep would fall....

Everyone, in their turn, needs to be supported by others. We help one another to live what we have promised, carrying each other's burdens.

If we acknowledge our weakness, there is no more reason for trouble and anger on account of anyone's sin.

We should not lose our peace on account of anyone's sin, "no matter what kind of sin has been committed, if the religious person is upset or angry, he is only drawing blame upon himself." Who are who to judge others? Only God can judge.

"That servant of God who does not become angry or disturbed at anyone lives correctly without anything of his own."[134]

Our purpose in this chapter was to express these attitudes of Francis, putting the stress on persevering in peace.

"Everyone must be very careful not to be angry or vexed on account of anyone's sin, because anger and vexation hinder love in themselves and in others."

Fraternal life cannot exist without mercy and forgiveness, which brings the brother back into the fraternity and constantly, builds it.

---

[133]LtMin 11-12; FA:ED I, 97-98.
[134]Adm XI:3; FA:ED I, 133.

# Chapter VII
## The Obedience of Love

### Sr. Maria Honoria Montalvo, F.M.I.

Your presence in this extraordinary Assembly, in the Franciscan Year, is the cause of a great joy for the heart of the whole Church: and that presence in the name of 200,000 members of the Franciscan Third Order Regular is also God's manifestation to the present day's world which is in such need of discovering God's presence in its life, its history and its evolution, in listening to God's voice, the Holy Spirit. It also has to come back to this life of obedience, "…I will not boast about myself unless it is about my weakness…" (2 Cor 12:5); in the light of the Church teaching and of our brothers' needs, to live the mystery of Jesus Christ's saving obedience is the summit of poverty and humility and takes up a crucial place in the project of Franciscan life.

The most perfect way of a "life in penance" is, undoubtedly, a life according to the evangelical counsels which involves a total self-renunciation so as to love for God alone, in a permanent "no" to ourselves, in a constant endeavor to follow on our Lord Jesus Christ's footsteps, so that the "yes" said to God would condition and lead the whole life to an always greater resemblance to Christ, the Son of God, made man.

Christ's obedience to his Father constitutes the heart of the mystery of Redemption. Christ, obedient to the Father until death for us all, has destroyed man's sin at its root, once for all, "…for our Lord Jesus Christ gave His life that He would not lose the obedience of His most holy Father,"[135] thus, putting right the disorder caused by our disobedience. Only thanks to Christ's death by obedience, a new communion between God and man was possible, for "by one man's obedience many will be made righteous." Thanks to Christ's Cross, the Church is assembled as a community of sons obeying to God: "…according to the foreknowledge of God the Father, consecrated by the Spirit to a life of obedience to Jesus Christ and purification with his blood. Favor and peace be yours in abundance" (1 Pt 1:2). Whoever rejects obedience to God is not willing to serve his brothers. Francis says it over and over again: "If the brothers, wherever they may be, cannot observe this life, let them have recourse to their minister as soon as they can, making this known to him. Let the minister, on his part endeavor to provide for them, as he would wish to be provided for him were he in a similar position. Let no one be called

---

[135]LtOrd 46; FA:ED I, 120.

'prior,' but let everyone in general be called a lesser brother."[136] "I did not come to be served, but to serve, says the Lord."[137]

To be a minister and a servant means to do as the others want and acknowledge them as lords. The Christian is not only a man obedient to God, but also the servant of his brothers for the edification of the Church, according to the example of Christ's obedience.

No servant is greater than his master; no messenger is greater than the man who sent him. Only those who remain truly obedient will be "blessed by the Lord"[138] as "servants of God" who enjoy already the liberty that all will attain at the end of times.

Our Franciscan obedience, in the Church, makes us live with Christ his own obedience to his Father, submitting ourselves to the will of a minister. Because "each" member of Christ's Body – the Church – must care for the others, so that if one part is hurt, all parts are hurt with it and if one part is given special honor, all parts enjoy it (1 Cor 12:26), so obedience will bring to all the members of the Church strength and blessings, salvation and sanctification. It is why Francis rightly says: "For this is loving obedience because it pleases God and neighbor."[139]

Consequently, it takes into account the second aspect of religious obedience: the service of the brothers after Christ's example. "Likewise, let all the brothers not have power or control in this instance, especially among themselves...."[140] In the same spirit, Saint Clare exhorts her sisters in her Rule: "Let them be always eager, however, to preserve among themselves the unity of mutual love which is the bond of perfection."[141]

So obedience is transformed into strength to build up the Kingdom and to bring peace, which had been destroyed by sin but given back to us, through the Redemption as Christ's peace. Thus, we take part in the building up of the Church, through obedience to God and to our neighbor, through union of hearts in charity and of spirits in truth, obeying today to Christ's voice and order, as Francis did: "Go then, and rebuild it for me."[142] He prepared himself to obey and gave himself completely to the fulfillment of this command (2 Cor 10:18).

Like Francis, with all our heart, let us beseech God to give us the strength to obey and let us say to Him: "Most Holy and Glorious God, enlighten the darkness of my heart and give me a true faith, a certain

---

[136]ER VI:1-3; FA:ED I, 68.
[137]Adm IV:1-3; FA:ED I, 130.
[138]ER V:17; FA:ED I, 68.
[139]Adm III:6; FA:ED I, 130.
[140]ER V:9; FA:ED I, 67.
[141]FlCl 10:7; CA:ED, 123.
[142]L3C V:3; FA:ED II, 76.

hope and perfect charity; sense and knowledge Lord, that I may carry out your holy and true command."[143]

---

[143]PrCr; FA:ED I, 40.

## CHAPTER VIII
### DE VITA APOSTOLICA

### SR. MARGARET CARNEY, O.S.F.

It is a human tendency to regard anything that is last in a series as being least in importance. As I introduce my presentation on the last chapter of our Rule text, I am most eager to assure you that such is not the case with this chapter. The Work Group made a conscious choice to place our description of our ministry last in the text. The sequence of the preceding chapters provides a description of the foundation of our Gospel call: our Franciscan identity, our rootedness in prayer, our internal relationships and our attitude towards ministry. The life, which is thus fashioned, must of necessity flow outward to others in our ministry. By giving a description of our interior lives and the life of fraternity beforehand, we set the stage for understanding the link between contemplation and action that should characterize our apostolic desire to be peacemakers.

This eighth chapter, then, is a culmination of all that precedes it. This chapter describes the quality of mission, of service which should flow from the inner dynamism of the Spirit of the Lord calling us to fraternity, humility, prayer and fidelity to the Church.

I will now try to share the thought that supports the choices we made in creating these articles. I will be especially anxious to show how the passages from the writings of Francis enlighten us when read in their full context. Thus, I will often refer to passages from his writings that are not explicitly incorporated here, but which provide the context for the ones, which do appear in our three articles on the Apostolic Life.

### ARTICLE 25

In the first sentence of this article we find the Great Commandment – the cornerstone for our apostolic spirituality. Francis quoted this commandment in both of his letters to the penitents of his day.[144] The New Testament passages referred to in the text of Francis's *Letters* are worth considering. In the 22nd chapter of Mathew's Gospel, Jesus is being tested by the Pharisees and Sadducees. When they try to trap him with a question about the most important commandments, it is this Great Commandment, which he offers. Then in Chapter 23 he continues to address them with a warning against hypocrisy. He concludes his criticism of his questioners by asserting: "…they do not practice what they preach" (Mt 23:3). He also exhorts his listeners at this point to see that the greatest among us must be the servant of the others (Mt 23:11-12).

---

[144] 1LtF 1:1; FA:ED I, 41; 2LtF 18; FA:ED I, 46.

Francis, too, calls for actions that correspond to our words, our ideals. In the *First Letter to the Faithful*, he urges: "…and we give birth to Him through a holy activity which must shine as an example before others.[145] Again in the *Second Letter to the Faithful*, he relates "fruits worthy of penance" to love of neighbor.[146] It is also interesting to note that he recalls the image of the Good Shepherd who gives his life for his sheep.[147] So, in choosing this text as the first sentence of Article 25, we are reminded of this powerful teaching in which Francis links the command that we be converted to God and to service to our neighbor in imitation of the Good Shepherd.

The second sentence is taken from the *Letter to the Order*, verses 8-9.[148] It is helpful to consider this citation in context. If we look at the section of the letter from which it is taken[149] we see that this section describes the missionary spirit that Francis wishes for his brothers. Here are the elements that he describes:

—we must listen to the voice of God's Son calling us,

—we must keep his commands wholeheartedly,

—we extol God in our works (this is the reason for our mission – to convince the world of God's power),

—we must be patient and disciplined and obedient,

—the Father disciplines us as sons being led to faith's perfection (Heb 3:13).

There is a reference in this section to a passage from Tobit 13:4-6 in which we are called to turn to the Lord so that He will turn to us and have mercy upon us. The mission then depends upon conversion to the Father and a single-hearted absorption with his will, and his glory.

So in the first article of this chapter we see that love for others depends upon our love for God and that we are further called to go into the world with a special mission to glorify God by our words and our deeds.

In the second article of the chapter we find the specification of that mandate.

---

[145]1LtF 1:10; FA:ED I, 42.
[146]2LtF 25-26; FA:ED I, 47.
[147]1LtF 1:13; FA:ED I, 42.
[148]LtOrd 8-9; FA:ED I, 117.
[149]LtOrd 5-11; FA:ED I, 116-117.

## ARTICLE 26

In reflecting upon the best way to speak of our mission in the world, we felt that it was of great importance to place clearly before ourselves the central characteristics of our apostolic lives, not the specific forms and works that our ministry has assumed in the many centuries and cultures in which our congregations have been situated.

While Francis, in describing the mission of the friars in the Rules of 1221 and 1223, places great emphasis on the specific task of preaching, a constant thread through his writings and Rule is the call to move others to the love of God by peaceful and humble conduct.

We are also aware of the fact that an important historical development within our tradition was the growth of works of charity and mercy undertaken by our Congregations from the 13th century to the present. The diversification of these works of mercy undertaken by Franciscans of our Order in every century and across the globe attests to the urging of the Spirit calling us to new expressions of the charismatic grace of our founder, Francis. Francis, however, did not live to see this flowering forth of the lives of the congregations of the Third Order. Thus, no single text of his own writings clearly encompasses the spirit we wish to preserve and extend in the Rule. Therefore, we selected a passage from one of the biographies that we believe best summarizes the spirit that is essential to our apostolates no matter what form they take. This beautiful passage from the *Legend of the Three Companions* calls for an integration of personal presence and spirituality with external deeds. It also demands that we always strive to reach others in a way that leads them to interior wholeness and healing. In an era of escalating violence of every description, we have yet to truly experience the full power of this passage as a criterion for discerning our apostolic effectiveness.

In the third sentence of this article, we find three actions proposed: to heal, to bind up, to reclaim. This triple description of our mission evokes the image of Christ as the one who came to heal the sick, to tend to those who were without hope, to gather the lost sheep of the house of Israel. Likewise, it evokes our images of Francis as he cared for the lepers and the sick cautioned against harsh judgments against the weak clergy, the rich, and called those in danger of falling away from the true faith to penance. Finally, it calls forth for us a procession of images of which we can be trustworthy heirs – the long line of good works done for the sick, the ignorant, the needy of every sort for whom our brothers and sisters have spent their lives through the centuries of our Order's history, whether in education, nursing, pastoral care, missionary work.

The fourth and fifth sentences of this article are taken from the *Rule of 1221*, Chapter 16.[150] We know that this part of the Rule of Francis had a great impact upon the Church since it institutionalizes the concept of missionary work for a religious order. If we study this entire chapter of the first Rule, we find within it the following elements:

—the friars are sent as lambs among wolves,

—the discernment of the mission by the friar and superior,

—two forms of witness: 1) peaceful Christian conduct and 2) proclamation of the word leading to conversions,

—because of being given over to Christ, we face every enemy with confidence,

—call to martyrdom described in compilation of New Testament texts.

In making a choice of texts for this article we quite deliberately chose two sentences that clearly indicate that the task of making peace will, perhaps, demand of us that we suffer from the "principalities and powers" of this world and that we may have to suffer death for the sake of justice.

We did not make this decision easily. With great care and sensitivity we wondered about the implications of our choice. We realized that while Francis often speaks of peaceful conduct, he does not use language or concepts that sound equal to our contemporary language and ideas of social justice. However, when we reflected upon the manner in which Francis related to people and events in his society, we found that he did, in fact, work and speak in such a way that he recognized problems of inequality and injustice and found ways often creative, always inspired, to bring about harmony among people vowed to enmity.

We considered the fact that enemies "visible and invisible" which surround us today are indeed powerful and that we are more and more called to experience our powerlessness from the world's standpoint so that we must rely upon the Spirit of the Lord. It is this same Spirit to whom Francis appeals in Chapter 17 of the *First Rule* to breathe forth a spirit of humility, patience and simplicity in our works.[151]

We considered the fact that when Francis worked on his rule he was responding to the request of the Church, of the pope, for laborers in the mission field. We realized that the Church is calling us today to see that our ministries must take into account the situation of our world in light of the Gospel. Since the close of the Council, in particular, papal and episcopal documents have introduced a new world of thought and

---

[150]ER XVI; FA:ED I, 74-75.
[151]ER XVII; FA:ED I, 75-76.

speech – a new demand for our ministry. Consider a few sentences from the document of the Synod of 1971.

"Listening to the cry of those who suffer violence and are oppressed by unjust structures, and hearing the appeal of a world that by its perversity contradicts the plan of its Creator, we have shared our awareness of the church's vocation to be present in the heart of the world by proclaiming the Good News to the poor, freedom to the oppressed, and joy to the afflicted…. Action on behalf of justice and participation in the transformation of the world fully appears to us as a constitutive dimension of the preaching of the Gospel, or in other words, of the Church's mission for the redemption of the human race and its liberation from every oppressive situation."

We concluded that Francis would today do what he did in the 13th century: he would take into account the needs and the call of the Church and fashion the ministry of the Order accordingly, and for that reason we determined to make this call to witness to justice in the world central to the text concerning our apostolic lives. We did so conscious of the fact that we take an ancient tradition of works of mercy and peace-making and blend them into a single call to aid in the creation of a new world order by our proclamation of the Gospel and our service to our neighbors. It is a new – or renewed – way of envisioning our mission. We offer it conscious of the fact that once again the Church is numbering its martyrs anew; that our brothers and sisters in many lands face death for the sake of the Gospel. Their courage and their shedding of blood calls out to us not to be fainthearted or ambiguous in our response. Their heroic witness gives us the courage to believe that this demand of Francis, that we be prepared to face death for the sake of the Lord, may be today a grace for the Order and the Church, in spite of our fears.

## Article 27

This article is composed of texts from Chapter 17 of the Rule of 1221.[152] This is the chapter that describes the attitudes needed by the preacher on his missionary travels. It especially warns against pride and vainglory. It proposes another layer of meaning for poverty since it demands that the apostolic person does not cling to the results of the work accomplished, and not work for personal pride and satisfaction.

This text also seemed appropriate since it mentions some of the ways in which the follower of Francis may fulfill the apostolic call and shows the variety in the Order which includes both contemplative and more actively ministerial congregations. In the first article of this Rule, we affirm that we will live in poverty and follow the life and example of St.

---

[152] ER XVII; FA:ED I, 75-76.

Francis. In this last article, poverty is again expressed in the humility and simplicity that refers all good to God. Our tasks of prayer, working, serving others are not personal riches or talents that we may appropriate to ourselves. By our constant thankfulness, we witness to this very important aspect of our Third Order apostolic spirituality.

## Conclusion

The tradition of our Order regarding apostolic life is a rich heritage. We have tried to express it in these texts in a way that grounds our works, in a profound biblical spirit of contemplative dependence upon the power of goodness of God. We have tried to unite our hopes with the hope of the Church that the salvation of Christ's death can come to all only if justice and peace are offered to all as the ground of human life and hope. We have tried to place before ourselves the necessity of realizing our own poverty in the face of the world's needs and the truth that even the power to proclaim Jesus as Lord comes through the working of the Holy Spirit within us.

# THE 1982 RULE TEXT

# 4

## THE 1982 RULE TEXT

### A WORD OF EXPLANATION

We present in the following pages the final text of the Rule of the Third Order Regular, as canonically approved by Pope John Paul II on December 8, 1982. On the left is the original Latin text with the biblical references and, in footnotes, the references to Franciscan early sources, mainly the writings of Francis and Clare. On the right is a new English translation with, in footnotes, the variances with the 1982 translation[1] (R82) and the 1997 translation[2] (R97).

---

[1] *The Rule and Life of the Brothers and Sisters of the Third Order Regular of St. Francis and Commentary*, M. Carney and T. Horgan, eds. (Pittsburgh: Franciscan Federation, 1982).

[2] *The Rule and Life of the Brothers and Sisters of the Third Order Regular of St. Francis and Commentary*, M. Carney, †T. Horgan and J-F. Godet-Calogeras (Washington: Franciscan Federation, 1997).

## Regula et Vita Fratrum et Sororum
## Tertii Ordinis Sancti Francisci

Ioannes Paulus Papa II ad perpetuam rei memoriam.
Franciscanum vitae propositum nostra quidem aetate, haud secus ac superiore tempore, complures viros et mulieres evangelicam sitientes perfectionem Regnumque Dei appetentes sine intermissione allicit. Ad sancti Francisci Assisiensis exemplar adhaerescentes sodales Tertii Ordinis Regularis sectari ipsum contendum Iesum Christum, dum fraterno vivunt in consortio, evangelica consiglia oboedientiae, paupertatis, castitatis votis publicis observanda suscipiunt et in varii gencris operositatem apostolicam incumbunt. Quo perfectius suae vitae propositum exsequantur, adsidue orationis usum frequentant, germanam inter se excolunt caritatem atque vera utuntur paenitentia et abnegatione christiana.

Cum autem hae singulae franciscalis vitae propositi partes ac rationes luculenter in "Regula et vita fratrum et sororum Tertii Ordinis Regularis sancti Francisci" comprehendantur cumque prorsus ita descriptae conveniant vero franciscali instituto, Nos pro apostolicae potestatis Nostrae plenitudine statuimus, edicimus, decernimus ut hoec Regula propriam habeat vim momentumque ad genuinae franciscalis vitae sensum fratribus et sororibus explanandum, usquequaque videlicet perpensis lis omnibus quae de hac re iam suo tempore edixerant predecessores nostri Leo Decimus et Pius Undecimus Constitutionibus Apostolicis "Inter cetera" et "Rerum condicio."

Quoniam novimus quanta diligentia curaque hae "Regula et vita" cursum renovatae accommodationis perfecerit quamque feliciter ad optatam consensionis metam pervenerit communibus ex disceptationibus et inquisitionibus, votis et elucubrationibus, idcirco fore certi confidimus ut propositos fructus effectusque renovationis adfatim in posterum consequatur tempus.

Haec autem voluntatis Nostrae significatio praecipimus ut firma usque sit virtutemque exserat suam tam nunc quam posthac, contrariis quibuslibet rebus minime obsistentibus.

Datum Romae, apud Sanctum Petrum, sub anulo Piscatoris, die VIII mensis decembris, anno Domini MCMLXXXII, Pontificatus Nostri quinto.

## RULE AND LIFE OF THE BROTHERS AND SISTERS
## OF THE THIRD ORDER REGULAR

JOHN PAUL POPE II AS A PERPETUAL MEMORIAL

Much as in past centuries, the Franciscan proposal of life even in our times continually draws many men and women desirous of evangelical perfection and thirsting for the reign of God. Inspired by the example of saint Francis of Assisi, the members of the Third Order Regular set forth to follow Jesus Christ by living in fraternal communion, professing the observance of the evangelical counsels of obedience, poverty and chastity in public vows, and by giving themselves to innumerable expressions of apostolic activity. To actualize in the best way possible their chosen way of life, they dedicate themselves unreservedly to prayer, strive to grow in fraternal love, live true penance and cultivate Christian self-denial.

Since these very elements and motives for living the Franciscan proposal are clearly present in the "Rule and Life and the Brothers and Sisters of the Third Order Regular of Saint Francis" and since they are clearly in accord with the genuine Franciscan spirit, we, in the fullness of our apostolic authority, determine, declare and order that the present Rule have the force and importance to illustrate to the brothers and sisters this authentic meaning of the Franciscan life, while bearing in mind that our predecessors Leo X and Pius XI, with the Apostolic Constitutions *Inter cetera* and *Rerum conditio* presented on this matter in their own times.

Since we know how diligently and assiduously this "Rule and Life" has traveled its path of *aggiornamento* and how fortuitously it arrived at the desired convergence of different points of view through collegial discussion and consultation, proposals and studied amendments, for this reason with well-founded hope, we trust that the longed for fruits of renewal will be brought to full realization.

We decide, moreover, that this our decision have force from this moment on and be effectively binding both in the present and in the future, everything to the contrary notwithstanding.

Given at Rome, at Saint Peter's under the ring of the Fisherman, on the 8th day of December, 1982, the fifth year of Our pontificate.

## Regula et Vita Fratrum et Sororum Tertii Ordinis Regularis Sancti Francisci

### Verba sancti Francisci sectatoribus suis dicta[1]

Omnes qui Dominum diligunt ex toto corde, ex tota anima et mente, ex tota virtute (Mk 12:30) et diligunt proximos suos sicut se ipsos (Mt 22:39), et odio habent corpora eorum cum vitiis et peccatis, et recipiunt corpus et sanguinem Domini nostri Iesu Christi, et faciunt fructus dignos poenitentiae: O quam beati et benedicti sunt illi et illae, dum talia faciunt et in talibus perseverant, qui requiescet super eos spiritus Domini (Is 11:2) et faciet apud eos habitaculum et mansionem (Jn 14:23), et sunt filii patris caelestis (Mt 5:45), cuis opera faciunt, et sunt sponsi, fratres et matres Domini nostri Iesu Christi (Mt 12:50).

Sponsi sumus, quando Spiritu Sancto coniungitur fidelis anima Domino nostro Iesu Christo. Fratres ei sumus, quando facimus voluntatem patris qui in caelis est (Mt 12:50); matres, quando portamus eum in corde et corpore nostro (1 Cor 6:20) per divinum amorem et puram et sinceram conscientiam; parturimus eum per sanctam operationem, quae lucere debet aliis in exemplum (Mt 5:16).

---

[1]1LtF 1 (Volterra Document); FA:ED I, 41..

# RULE AND LIFE OF THE BROTHERS AND SISTERS OF THE THIRD ORDER REGULAR OF SAINT FRANCIS

## WORDS OF ST. FRANCIS TO HIS FOLLOWERS[1]

All who love God[2] with their whole heart, with their whole soul and mind, and with their whole[3] strength, and love their neighbor as themselves, and who despise their tendency to vice and sin,[4] receive the Body and Blood of our Lord Jesus Christ and bring forth from within themselves fruits worthy of true penance: How happy and blessed are these men and women when they do these things, and persevere in doing them because the Spirit of the Lord will rest upon them and God[5] will make a[6] home and dwelling place with them. They are the children of the heavenly[7] Father whose works they do. They are the spouses, brothers and sisters,[8] and mothers of our Lord Jesus Christ.

We are spouses[9] when the faithful soul is united by the Holy Spirit with our Lord Jesus Christ. We are for him[10] brothers and sisters[11] when we do the will of the[12] Father who is in heaven. We are mothers when we bear Him in our hearts and bodies with divine love and with pure and sincere consciences, and when[13] we give birth to Him through our holy actions[14] which must shine in example to others.[15]

---

[1]R82: *Epistola ad fideles: Recensio prior* 1, 1 to 190 [sic]; R97 *Letter to the Faithful* I 1:1-19.

[2]R82: "the Lord."

[3]R82, R97: omit "whole."

[4]R82, R97: "the tendency in their humanity to sin."

[5]R82: "the Lord."

[6]R82, R97: "his."

[7]R97: omits "heavenly."

[8]R82: omits "and sisters."

[9]R82, R97: "his spouses."

[10]R82: omits "for him"; R97: "his" instead of "for him."

[11]R82: omits "and sisters."

[12]R97: omits "the."

[13]R82: omits "when."

[14]R82, R97: "a holy life."

[15]R82, R97: "…which should enlighten others because of our example."

O quam gloriosum est, sanctum et magnum in caelis habere patrem! O quam sanctum, paraclitum, pulchrum et admirabilem talem habere sponsum! O quam sanctum et quam dilectum, beneplacitum, humilem, pacificum, dulcem, amabilem et super omnia desiderabilem habere talem fratrem et talem filium: Dominum nostrum Iesum Christum, qui posuit animam pro ovibus suis (Jn 10:15) et oravit patri dicens: Pater sancte, serva eos in nomine tuo (Jn 17:11), quos dedisti mihi in mundo; tui erant et mihi dedisti eos (Jn 17:6). Et verba quae mihi dedisti, dedi eis, et ipsi acceperunt et crediderunt vere, quia a te exivi et cognoverunt, quia tu me misisti (Jn 17:8). Rogo pro eis et non pro mundo (Jn 17:9). Benedic et sanctifica (Jn 17:17) et pro eis sanctifico me ipsum (Jn 17:19). Non pro eis rogo tantum, sed et pro eis qui credituri sunt per verbum illorum in me (Jn 17:20), ut sint sanctificati in unum (Jn 17:23) sicut et nos (Jn 17:11). Et volo, pater, ut ubi ego sum et illi sint mecum, ut videant claritatem meam (Jn 17:24) in regno tuo (Mt 20:21). Amen.

## I. In Nomine Domini! Incipit Regula et Vita Fratrum et Sororum Tertii Ordinis Regularis Sancti Francisci

1. Forma vitae fratrum et sororum Tertii Ordinis Regularis sancti Francisci haec est: Domini nostri Iesu Christi sanctum Evangelium observare, vivendo in obedientia, in paupertate et in castitate.[2] Sequentes Iesum Christum exemplo sancti Francisci[3] tenentur plura et maiora facere observantes praecepta et consilia Domini nostri Iesu Christi et debent semetipsos abnegare (Mt 16:24) sicut unusquisque promisit Deo.[4]

---

[2]LR I:1; ER I:1; FA:ED I, 100, 63-64; Fl.Cl I:2: CA:ED 109.
[3]FLCl VI:1: CA:ED 117.
[4]2LtF 36-40; FA:ED I, 48..

How glorious it is, how holy and great, to have a Father in heaven! How holy, consoling, beautiful and wonderful it is to have such a Spouse! How holy and how loving, pleasing, humble, peaceful, sweet, lovable and over all things desirable[16] it is to have such a Brother and such a[17] Son, our Lord Jesus Christ[18] who gave up His life for His sheep and prayed to the Father,[19] saying: Holy Father, keep in your name those whom You gave Me in the world; they are Yours and You gave them to Me. And the words[20] which You gave Me I gave to them, and they accepted[21] and truly believed that I came from You.[22] And they know that You have sent Me.[23] I pray for them and not for the world. Bless them and sanctify them. I sanctify Myself for their sakes. I do not pray only for these but also for those who, through their word, will believe in Me, may they be holy in oneness as We are Father,[24] I want[25] that where I am they too may be with Me so[26] that they may see My glory in Your reign.[27] Amen.[28]

## I. IN THE NAME OF THE LORD! HERE BEGINS THE RULE AND LIFE OF THE BROTHERS AND SISTERS OF THE THIRD ORDER REGULAR OF SAINT FRANCIS[29]

1. The form of life of the Brothers and Sisters of the Third Order Regular of Saint Francis[30] is this: to observe the Holy Gospel of our Lord Jesus Christ, living in obedience, in poverty and in chastity. Following Jesus Christ at the example of Saint Francis,[31] they are held to do

---

[16]R97: "...desirable over all things...."

[17]R97: omits "such a."

[18]R82: "How glorious it is to have so holy and great a Father in Heaven; and to have such a beautiful and admirable Souse, the Holy Paraclete; and to have a Brother and Son, so holy, beloved, blessed, humble, peaceful, sweet, lovable and desirable over all things...."

[19]R97: "God."

[20]R82, R97: "word."

[21]R82, R97: "accepted it."

[22]R82, R97: "...that it came forth from You."

[23]R82, R97: "...and they have accepted that you sent me."

[24]R97, "God."

[25]R82, R97: "wish."

[26]R82, R97: "...maybe and..."

[27]R82, R97: "kingdom."

[28]R82, R97: omits Amen.

[29]R82: Instead of *In the Name of the Lord! Here begins the Rule and Life of the Brothers and Sisters of the Third Order Regular of St. Francis* the Rule reads Chapter 1: Our Identity; R97: adds Chapter 1 Our Identity.

[30]R82: omitted "of the Third Order Regular Rule of St. Francis."

[31]R97: "Blessed."

2. Fratres et sorores istius Ordinis cum universis qui Domino Deo intra sanctam Ecclesiam catholicam et apostolicam servire volunt in vera fide et poenitentia perseverent.[5] Hanc conversionem evangelicam vivere volunt in spiritu orationis et paupertatis et humilitatis. Et abstineant ab omni malo et perseverent usque in finem in bono[6] quia ipse Filius Dei venturus est in gloria et dicet omnibus qui eum cognoverunt et adoraverunt et ei servierunt in poenitentia: Venite, benedicti Patris mei, percipite regnum quod vobis paratum est ab origine mundi (Mt 25:34).[7]

3. Fratres et sorores promittunt obedientiam et reverentiam Papae et Ecclesiae catholicae. Eodem spiritu his qui ad servitium fraternitatis instituti sunt obediant.[8] Et ubicumque sunt et in quocumque loco se invenerint, spiritualiter et diligenter debeant se revidere et honorare ad invicem.[9] Et unitatem et communionem cum omnibus familiae franciscanae membris foveant.

---

[5]ER XXIII:7; FA:ED I, 83-84.
[6]ER XXI:9; FA:ED I, 78.
[7]ER XXIII:4; FA:ED I, 82.
[8]LR I:2-3; FLCl I:3-5; FA:ED I, 100; CA:ED, 109.
[9]ER VII:15; LR VI:7-8; FA:ED I, 69, 103.

more and greater things in observing[32] the precepts and counsels of our Lord Jesus Christ. They must deny[33] themselves as each has promised God.[34]

2. With all in the holy Catholic and apostolic Church who want to serve God,[35] the brothers and sisters of this Order are to persevere in true faith and penance. They want[36] to live this evangelical conversion of life in a spirit of prayer, of poverty, and of humility. Let[37] them abstain from all evil and persevere to the end in doing good because God's Son[38] Himself will come again in glory and will say to all who acknowledged, adored and served him in penance:[39] Come, blessed of My Father, receive the reign[40] that has been prepared for you from the beginning of the world.

3. The brothers and sisters[41] promise obedience and reverence to the Pope and the Catholic Church.[42] In this same spirit they are to obey those who have been placed in the service of the fraternity.[43] And wherever they are, or in whatever situation they are in, they should spiritually and diligently show respect and honor[44] to one another. They should also foster unity and communion with all the members of the Franciscan family.

---

[32]R82, R97: "let them recognize that they are called to make greater efforts in their observance of…"

[33]R82, R97: "Let them deny…"

[34]R82: "…each has promised the Lord."

[35]R82: "…who wish to serve the Lord."

[36]R82, R97: "They wish…"

[37]R82, R97: "Therefore, let…"

[38]R82: "…God the Son…"

[39]R82, R97: "…acknowledge, adore and serve him in sincere repentance…."

[40]R82, R97: "…take possession of the kingdom…."

[41]R82: "The sisters and brothers…"

[42]R82: "…and the Holy Catholic Church."

[43]R82: "…those called to be ministers and servants of their own fraternity." R 97: as R82 except "community" instead of "fraternity."

[44]R82, R97: "…they should diligently and fervently show reverence and honor…."

## II. DE VITA ISTA ACCIPIENDA

4. Illi qui Domino inspirante veniunt ad nos volentes hanc vitam accipere benigne recipiantur. Et opportuno tempore ministris praesentabuntur quibus potestas est in fraternitatem admittendi.[10]

5. Ministri certiores fiant aspirantes vere fidei catholicae adhaerere sacramentisque ecclesiasticis. Si illi idonei sint, vitae fraternitatis initientur. Et omnia ad hanc vitam evangelicam pertinentia eis diligenter exponantur, praesertim haec verba Domini: Si vis perfectus esse, vade et vende omnia quae habes, et da pauperibus (Mt 19:21; Lk 18:22) et habebis thesaurum in caelo, et veni, sequere me. Et si quis vult post me venire, abneget semetipsum et tollat crucem suam et sequatur me (Mt 16:24).[11]

6. Sic Domino ducente incipiant vitam poenitentiae scientes quod omnes continuo convertendi sumus. Conversionem et consecrationem ad vitam evangelicam significantes vilibus vestibus induantur et simpliciter conversentur.[12]

7. Finito vero tempore probationis recipiantur ad obedientiam promittentes vitam istam semper et regulam observare.[13] Et omni cura et sollicitudine postposita satagant, quocumque modo melius possunt, servire, amare, honorare et adorare Dominum Deum mundo corde et pura mente.[14]

---

[10]Test 1; ER II:1-3; LR II:1; FLCl II:1; FA:ED I, 124, 64, 100; .CA:ED, 110
[11]LR II:2-6; FLCl II:2-4; ER I:1-3; FA:ED I, 100; CA:ED, 110; FA:ED I, 64.
[12]ER II:14; FA:ED I, 65.
[13]LR II:11; FLCl II:8.; FA:ED I, 101; CA:ED, 110.
[14]ER XXII:26; Adm XVI; FA:ED I, 79-80, 134.

II.[45] ACCEPTANCE INTO THIS LIFE

4. Those who through the Lord's[46] inspiration come to us wanting[47] to accept this way of life are to be received kindly. At the appropriate time, they will[48] be presented to the ministers who hold power in the fraternity.[49]

5. The ministers shall ascertain that the aspirants truly adhere to the Catholic faith and the Church's sacramental life. If the aspirants are found fitting,[50] they are to be initiated into the life of the fraternity.[51] Let everything pertaining to this Gospel way of life be diligently[52] explained to them, especially these words of the Lord: If you want to be perfect, go and sell all your possessions and give to the poor. You will have treasure in heaven. Then come, follow Me. And if anyone wants to come after Me, one must deny oneself, take up one's cross and follow Me.[53]

6. Led by God,[54] let them begin a life of penance, conscious that all of us must be continuously[55] converted. As a sign of their conversion and consecration to Gospel life, they are to clothe themselves plainly and to live in simplicity.

7. When their initial formation is completed, they are to be received into obedience promising to observe this life and rule always. Let them put aside all preoccupations and worries.[56] Let them only be concerned to serve, love, honor, and adore God,[57] as best they can, with a single heart and a pure mind.[58]

---

[45]R82, R97: Chapter II.

[46]R97: "God's."

[47]R82: "…come to us desiring…"

[48]R82, R97: "…they are to…"

[49]R82: "…ministers of the fraternity who hold responsibility to admit them." R97: as R82 except "community" instead of "fraternity."

[50]R82: "If they are found to have a vocation…"

[51]R97: "community."

[52]R82, R97: omits "diligently."

[53]R82: And "if anyone wishes to follow me, let him deny himself, take up his cross, and follow me." R97: "as is."

[54]R82: "Led by the Lord…"

[55]R82, R97: adds "and totally."

[56]R82 R97: "…all attachment as well as every care and worry."

[57]R82: "…adore and honor the Lord God."

[58]R82: "…with singleheartedness and purity of intention."

8. Semper in seipsis faciant habitaculum et mansionem ipsi qui est Dominus Deus omnipotens, Pater et Filius et Spiritus sanctus,[15] ita ut in amorem universalem cum cordibus indivisis crescant, sese continuo convertentes ad Deum et proximum (Jn 14:23).

## III. De spiritu orationis

9. Ubique, omni loco, omni hora et omni tempore fratres et sorores credant veraciter et humiliter et in corde teneant et ament, honorent, adorent, serviant, laudent, benedicant et glorificent altissimum et summum Deum aeternum Patrem et Filium et Spiritum sanctum.[16] Et adorent eum puro corde, quoniam oportet semper orare et non deficere (Lk 18:11); nam Pater tales quaerit adoratores.[17] Eodem spiritu officium divinum in unione cum universali Ecclesia celebrent. Illi et illae quos Dominus ad vitam contemplationis (Mk 6:31) vocavit cum laetitia quotidie renovata suam dedicationem Deo manifestent et amorem celebrent quem Pater pro mundo habet qui nos creavit, redemit et sua sola misericordia salvabit.[18]

---

[15]ER XXII:27; 1LtF I:5-10; 2LtF 48-53; FA:ED I, 80, 42, 48-49.
[16]ER XXIII:11: FA:ED I, 85-86.
[17]ER XXII:29-30; FA:ED I, 80.
[18]ER XXIII:8; FA:ED I, 84-85.

8. Within themselves, let them always make a home and dwelling place for the one who is Lord[59] God almighty,[60] Father and Son and Holy Spirit so that, with undivided hearts, they may grow[61] in universal love by continually turning to God and to neighbor.

## III. SPIRIT OF PRAYER[62]

9. Everywhere and in all places, at all times and in all seasons[63] the brothers and sisters are to have a true and humble faith. From the depths of their inner life let them love, honor, adore, serve, praise, bless and glorify the[64] most high and sovereign[65] God, eternal[66] Father and Son and Holy Spirit. With all that they are, let them adore God[67] because we should pray always and not lose heart: this is what God[68] desires. In this same spirit let them also celebrate the Liturgy of the Hours in union with the universal[69] Church. Those whom[70] the Lord has called to the life of contemplation, with a daily renewed joy should manifest their[71] dedication to God[72] and celebrate the love that God has[73] for the world,[74] when God created us, redeemed us, and will save us by mercy alone.[75]

---

[59]R82: "for the Lord."

[60]R82, R97: "…a dwelling place and home for the Lord God almighty…"

[61]R82, R97 uses the word "increase."

[62]R82: Chapter III: The Spirit of Prayer.

[63]R82, R97: "Everywhere and in each place, and in every season and each day…"

[64]R82, R97: "…glorify our…"

[65]R82: "…and eternal…"

[66]R82: "…who is…"

[67]R82: "…let them adore Him…"

[68]R82: "…what the Father…"

[69]R82, R97: "…with the whole…"

[70]R82, R97: "The sisters and brothers whom…"

[71]R82, R97: adds the word "special."

[72]R97: omits "to God."

[73]R82: "…celebrate the Father's love…"

[74]R 97: "the divine love for the world…"

[75]R82: "It was He who created and redeemed us, and by His mercy alone shall save us." R97: "It was God…"

10. Dominum regem caeli et terrae (Mt 11:25) fratres et sorores laudent cum universis creaturis eius et gratias ei agant quod per sanctam voluntatem suam et per unicum Filium suum cum Spiritu sancto creavit omnia spiritualia et corporalia et nos ad imaginem suam et simimilitudinem.[19]

11. Sancto Evangelio se totaliter conformantes fratres et sorores in mente considerent et servent verba Domini nostri Iesu Christi qui est verbum Patris, et verba Spiritus sancti quae spiritus et vita sunt (Jn 6:63).[20]

12. Participent sacrificium Domini nostri Iesu Christi et recipiant Corpus et Sanguinem eius cum magna humilitate et veneratione, recordantes quod Dominus dicit: Qui manducat carnem meam et bibit sanguinem meum habet vitam aeternam (Jn 6:54).[21] Exhibeant omnem reverentiam et omnem honorem, quantumcumque poterint, sanctissimo Corpori et Sanguini Domini nostri Iesu Christi ac sacratissimis nominibus et verbis scriptis eius in quo quae in caelis et quae in terris sunt pacificata sunt et reconciliata omnipotenti Deo (Col 1:20).[22]

13. Et in omnibus suis offensis fratres et sorores non tardant interius punire per contritionem et exterius per confessionem et faciant fructus dignos poenitentiae.[23] Debent etiam ieiunare, sed studeant semper esse simplices et humiles.[24] Nihil ergo aliquid aliud desiderent nisi Salvatorem nostrum qui se ipsum per proprium sanguinem suum sacrificium et hostiam in ara crucis obtulit pro peccatis nostris, relinquens nobis exemplum ut sequamur vestigia eius.[25]

---

[19] ER XXIII:1; CtC 3; FA:ED I, 81-82, 113.
[20] 2LtF 3; FA:ED I, 45.
[21] ER XX:5; FA:ED I, 78.
[22] LtOrd 12-13; 1LtF 1; Test 12; FA:ED I, 117, 74, 125.
[23] Adm XXIII:3; 2LtF 25; FA:ED I, 136, 47.
[24] Adm XIX:2; 2LtF 45; FA:ED I, 135, 48.
[25] ER XXIII:9; 2LtF 11-14; FA:ED I, 85, 46.

10. With all creation[76] the brothers and sisters should praise God[77] Ruler of heaven and earth, and give thanks because, by the holy will and through the only Son with the Holy Spirit, God created all things spiritual and material, and created us in God's[78] image and likeness.[79]

11. Since the brothers and sisters[80] are to be totally conformed to the Holy[81] Gospel, they should reflect upon[82] and keep in their mind[83] the words of our Lord Jesus Christ Who is the word of the Father,[84] as well as the words of the Holy Spirit which are spirit and life.

12. Let them participate in the sacrifice of our Lord Jesus Christ and receive His Body and Blood with great humility and veneration[85] remembering the words of the Lord: Whoever[86] eats My flesh and drinks My blood has eternal life. Moreover, they are to show the greatest possible reverence and honor for the most sacred name, written words and most holy Body and Blood of our Lord Jesus Christ, through whom all things in heaven and on earth have been brought to peace and reconciliation with Almighty God.

13. Whenever they commit sin the brothers and sisters, without delay, are to do penance interiorly by sincere sorrow and exteriorly by confession.[87] They should also do worthy deeds that manifest their repentance they should fast but[88] always strive to be simple and humble.[89] They should desire nothing else but our Savior, who offered Himself in His own Blood as a sacrifice and victim[90] on the altar of the Cross for our sins, giving us example so that we might follow in His footsteps.

---

[76]R97: "creatures."

[77]R97: "the."

[78]R97: "the divine."

[79]R82: "The brothers and sisters are to praise the Lord, the king of heaven and earth, with all his creatures and to give him thanks because, by his own holy will and through his only Son with the Holy Spirit, He has created all things spiritual and material and made us in his own image and likeness."

[80]R82, R97: "Since the sisters and brothers…"

[81]R82, R97: omits the word "Holy."

[82]R82: omits the word "upon."

[83]R82, R97: uses the word "hearts."

[84]R97: "God."

[85]R82, R97: uses the word "reverence."

[86]R82: uses the word "He."

[87]R82, R97: "…by confessing their sins to a priest."

[88]R82, R97: "…and always …"

[89]R82: adds "especially before God."

[90]R82, R97: omits "and victim."

**IV. De vita in castitate propter regnum caelorum**

14. Attendant fratres et sorores in quanta excellentia posuerit eos Dominus Deus, quia creavit et formavit eos ad imaginem dilecti Filii sui secundum corpus et similitudinem secundum spiritum (Col 1:16).[26] Per Christum et in Christo creati, istam formam vitae elegerunt, quae in verbis et exemplis Redemptoris nostri fundata est.

15. Castitatem propter regnum caelorum (Mt 19:12) profitentes, solliciti sunt quae Domini sunt (1 Cor 7:32) et nihil aliud habent facere, nisi sequi voluntatem Domini et placere sibi.[27] Et omnia ita faciant ut caritas erga Deum et universos homines ex operibus eluceat.

16. Meminerint se per eximium gratiae donum vocatos esse ad manifestandum in vita sua illud mirabile Ecclesiae mysterium, quo divino sponso Christo coniuncta est (Eph 5:23-26).

17. Prae oculis habeant imprimis exemplar beatissimae Virginis Mariae, Matris Dei et Domini nostri Iesu Christi. Hoc faciant secundum mandatum beati Francisci, qui sanctam Mariam maxime veneratus est, Dominam et Reginam, quae virgo ecclesia facta est.[28] Et recordentur, quod immaculata Virgo Maria seipsam dixit ancillam Domini cuius exemplum sequantur (Lk 1:38).

---

[26]Adm V:1; FA:ED I, 131.
[27]ER XXII:9; FA:ED I, 79.
[28]SalBVM 1; FA:ED I, 163.

## IV. LIFE IN CHASTITY FOR THE SAKE OF THE REIGN OF GOD[91]

14. Let the brothers and sisters[92] keep in mind how great a dignity God[93] has given them because God[94] created them and formed them in the image of the[95] beloved Son according to the flesh and in God's[96] own likeness according to the Spirit. Since they are created through Christ and in Christ, they have chosen this form of life which is founded on the words and example[97] of our Redeemer.

15. Professing chastity for the sake of the reign of God,[98] they are to care for the things of the Lord and they seek nothing else[99] except to follow the will of God[100] and to please God.[101] In all of their works charity toward[102] God and all people should shine forth.

16. They are to remember that they have been called by a special gift of grace to manifest in their lives that wonderful mystery by which the Church is joined to Christ her divine[103] spouse.

17. Let them keep[104] the example of the most Blessed Virgin Mary, the Mother of God and our Lord Jesus Christ, ever before their eyes. Let them do this according to the mandate[105] of Blessed[106] Francis who held Holy Mary, Lady and Queen, in highest veneration, since she is the virgin made church. Let them also remember that the Immaculate Virgin Mary whose example they are to follow called herself the handmaid of the Lord.

---

[91]R82: Chapter IV: The Life of Chastity for the Sake of the Kingdom.
[92]R97: "sisters and brothers."
[93]R82: "...the Lord God..."
[94]R82: "...because He..."
[95]R82: "...image of His..."
[96]R82: "...and in His..."
[97]R82, R97: "...and deeds..."
[98]R82, R97: "...sake of the kingdom of heaven..."
[99]R82: "...they have nothing else to do..."
[100]R82: "...the Lord..."
[101]R82: "...to please Him."
[102]R82, R97: "...the love of..."
[103]R82, R97: omits the word "divine."
[104]R82, R97: "Let the brothers and sisters..."
[105]R82, R97: "...according to the exhortation..."
[106]R82: "...of Blessed ..."

## V. De modo serviendi et laborandi

18. Sicut pauperes fratres et sorores, quibus gratiam dedit Dominus serviendi vel laborandi, serviant et laborent fideliter et devote, ita quod, excluso otio animae inimico, sanctae orationis et devotionis spiritum non extinguant, cui debent cetera temporalia deservire.[29]

19. De mercede vero laboris pro se suisque fratribus et sororibus corporis necessaria recipiant et hoc humiliter sicut decet servos Dei et paupertatis sanctissimae sectatores.[30] Et omnia quae supersint pauperibus studeant erogare. Et numquam debent desiderare esse super alios, sed magis debent esse servi et subditi omni humanae creaturae propter Deum (1 Pt 2:13).[31]

20. Fratres et sorores sint mites, pacifici et modesti, mansueti et humiles, honeste loquentes omnibus sicut decet. Et ubicumque sunt vel vadunt per mundum, non litigent neque contendant verbis, nec alios iudicent, sed ostendant se gaudentes in Domino (Phil 4:4) et hilares et convenienter gratiosos.[32] Et salutationem dicant: Dominus det tibi pacem.[33]

---

[29]LR V:1-2; FLCl VII:1-2; FA:ED I, 102; CA:ED, 119.
[30]ER II:4; IX:8; FA:ED I, 64, 71.
[31]2LtF 47;FA:ED I, 48.
[32]LR II:17; III:10; ER VII:16; FA:ED I, 101, 102, 69.
[33]Test 23; FA:ED I, 126.

**V. Way**[107] **to serve and work**

18. As poor people, the brothers and sisters to whom God has given the grace of serving or working should serve and work faithfully and devoutly so that, while avoiding idleness, the enemy of the soul, they should not extinguish the spirit of holy prayer and devotion, that all material goods must serve.[108]

19. In exchange for their work,[109] they may accept anything necessary for their own material[110] needs and for that of their brothers and sisters.[111] Let them accept it humbly as is expected of those who are servants of God and followers[112] of the most holy poverty. Whatever they may have over and above their needs, they are to give to the poor. And let them never want to be over others. Instead they must[113] be servants and subjects to every human creature for God's sake.[114]

20. Let the brothers and sisters be mild, peaceful and unassuming, gentle and humble, speaking honestly to all in accord with their vocation.[115] Wherever they are, or wherever they go throughout the world they should not be quarrelsome, contentious, or judgmental towards others. Rather, it should be obvious that they are joyful, good-humored, and happy in the Lord, as they ought to be. And in greeting others, let them say, the Lord[116] give you peace.

---

[107]R82, R97: Chapter V. The…

[108]R82: "As poor people, the brothers and sisters to whom the Lord has given the grace of serving or working with their hands, should do so faithfully and conscientiously. Let them avoid that idleness which is the enemy of the soul. But they should not be so busy that the spirit of holy prayer and devotion, which all earthly goods should foster, is extinguished." R97: "As poor people, the sisters and brothers to whom God has given the grace of serving or working should serve and work faithfully and devoutly. Let them avoid that idleness which is the enemy of the soul. They should not be so busy, however, that they would extinguish the spirit of holy prayer and devotion, which all earthly goods should serve."

[109]R82, R97: "…for their service or work…"

[110]R82: "…their own temporal…"

[111]R82: "…sisters or brothers."

[112]R82: "…and seekers…"

[113]R82, R97: "…they should…"

[114]R82: "…the Lord's sake."

[115]R82: "Let the sisters and brothers be gentle, peaceful and unassuming, mild and humble, speaking respectfully to all in accord with their vocation." R97: same as R82 except "brothers and sisters."

[116]R97: "God."

## VI. De vita in paupertate

21. Omnes fratres et sorores studeant sequi humilitatem et paupertatem Domini nostri Iesu Christi qui, cum dives esset super omnia (2 Cor 8:9), voluit ipse in mundo cum beatissima Virgine matre sua eligere paupertatem et semetipsum exinanivit (Phil 2:7).[34] Et recordentur quod nihil aliud oportet nos habere de toto mundo nisi, sicut dicit apostolus, habentes alimenta et quibus tegamur, his contenti sumus (1 Tm 6:8).[35] Et caveant multum a pecunia.[36] Et debent gaudere, quando conversantur inter viles et despectas personas, inter pauperes et debilis et infirmos et leprosos et iuxta viam mendicantes.[37]

22. Qui vere pauperes sunt spiritu, exemplum Domini sequentes nihil sibi appropriant nec alicui defendunt, sed tanquam peregrini et advenae (1 Pt 2:1) in hoc saeculo vivunt. Haec est illa celsiduto altissimae paupertatis quae nos heredes et reges regni caelorum instituit, pauperes rebus fecit, virtutibus sublimavit (Jas 2:5). Haec sit portio nostra quae perducit in terram viventium (Ps 141:6). Cui totaliter inhaerentes nihil aliud pro nomine Domini nostri Iesu Christi in perpetuum sub caelo habere velimus (Mt 10:27-29).[38]

---

[34]ER IX:1; 2LtF 5; FLCl VI:3; FA:ED I, 70, 46; CA:ED, 118.

[35]LR VI:3-4; FA:ED I, 103.

[36]ER IX:1; LR VI:3-4; ER VIII:11; FA:ED I, 70, 103, 70.

[37]ER IX:2; FA:ED I, 70.

[38]LR VI:1-2, 4-6; ER VII:13; Adm XIV; FLCl 8:1-2; FA:ED I, 103, 69, 133-34; CA:ED, 119.

## VI. LIFE IN POVERTY[117]

21. Let all the brothers and sisters[118] zealously follow the humility and poverty[119] of our Lord Jesus Christ. Though rich beyond measure, with the most blessed Virgin, His mother, He wanted to choose poverty in this world and he emptied Himself.[120] Let them remember that of the whole world we shall have nothing but as the Apostle says, having[121] something to eat and something to wear, with these we are content.[122] Let them particularly beware of money. And let them be happy to live among the outcast and despised, among the poor, the weak, the sick, the lepers and those who beg on the street.[123]

22. The truly poor in spirit, following the example of the Lord, neither appropriate nor defend anything as their own, but live in this world as pilgrims and strangers.[124] So excellent is this most high poverty that it made us heirs and rulers of the reign of God.[125] It made us materially poor, but rich in virtue. Let this poverty alone be our portion because it leads to the land of the living. Clinging completely to it let us, for the sake of our Lord Jesus Christ, never want anything else under heaven.

---

[117]R82, R97: Chapter VI: The Life of Poverty.

[118]R22: R97 "…the sisters and brothers…"

[119]R82, R97: "poverty and humility."

[120]R82: "Though rich beyond measure, He emptied Himself for our sake and with the holy virgin, His mother, Mary, He chose poverty in this world." R97: as R82 except "with the most Blessed Virgin."

[121]R97: "have."

[122]R82, 97: "Let them be mindful that they should have only those goods of this world which, as the Apostle says, "Provide enough food and sufficient clothing; with these we are content."

[123]R82: "…the unwanted, the oppressed, and the destitute."

[124]R82, 97: "The truly poor in spirit, following the example of the Lord, live in this world as pilgrims and strangers. They neither appropriate nor defend anything as their own."

[125]R82, 97: "…of the kingdom of heaven."

## VII. De vita fraterna

23. Propter amorem Dei fratres et sorores diligant se ad invicem, sicut dicit Dominis: hoc est praeceptum meum ut diligatis invicem sicut dilexi vos (Jn 15:12). Et ostendant ex operibus dilectionem quam habent ad invicem (Jn 12:18; 1 Jn 3:18).[39] Et secure manifestet unus alteri necessitatem suam, ut sibi necessaria inveniat et ministret.[40] Beati sunt, qui tantum diligerent alterum, quando est infirmus, quod non potest eis satisfacere, quantum quando est sanus, qui potest eis satisfacere. Et de omnibus, quae ipsis accidunt, referant gratias Creatori,[41] et quales vult eos Dominus[42] tales se esse desiderent sive sanos sive infirmos.

24. Si contingeret inter eos verbo vel signo occasionem turbationis aliquando suboriri, statim (Mt 5:24), antequam offerat munus orationis suae coram Domino (Mt 18:35), unus alteri humiliter veniam petat. Si quis graviter neglexerit forman vitae quam professus est, admoneatur a ministro vel ab aliis qui eius culpam cognoverint. Et illi non faciant ei verecundiam neque detractionem, sed magnam misericordiam habeant circa ipsum.[43] Sed omnes attente cavere debent ne irascantur et conturbentur propter peccatum alicuius, quia ira et conturbatio in se et in aliis impediunt caritatem.[44]

---

[39]ER XI:5-6; TestCl 18; FA:ED I, 72; CA:ED, 61.
[40]ER IX:10; FA:ED I, 70.
[41]ER X:3; FA:ED I, 71.
[42]Adm XXIV: FA:ED I, 136.
[43]LtMin 15: FA:ED I, 98.
[44]LR VII:3; FLCl 9:3-4; FA:ED I, 104; CA:ED, 121.

## VII. FRATERNAL LIFE[126]

23. Because God loves us, the brothers and sisters should love each other, for the Lord says, "This is my precept,[127] that you love one another as I have loved you." Let them manifest their love for each other in deeds. With confidence let them make known their needs to one another so that each can find and offer to the other that which is necessary.[128] Blessed are those who love the others when they are sick and unable to serve, as much as when they are healthy and of service to them.[129] Whether in sickness or in health, they should only want what God wishes for them. For all that happens to them let them give thanks to our Creator.

24. If discord caused by word or deed should occur among them, they should immediately and humbly ask forgiveness of one another even before offering their gift of prayer before God.[130] If anyone seriously neglected[131] the form of life all professed, the minister, or others who may know of it, are to admonish that person. Those giving the admonition should neither embarrass nor speak evil of the other, but show great mercy.[132] Let all be carefully attentive not to become angry or disturbed[133] because of another's sin. For anger and disturbance impede charity[134] in themselves and in others.[135]

---

[126]R82, R97: Chapter VII: Fraternal Love.

[127]R82, R97: uses the word "commandment."

[128]R82: "Also whenever they meet each other, they should show that they are members of the same family. Let them make known their needs to one another."

[129]R82: "Blessed are they who love another who is sick and seemingly useless, as much as when that brother or sister is well and of service to them."

[130]R82: "…before the Lord."

[131]R82, R97: "And if anyone seriously neglects…"

[132]R82, R97: "…great kindness."

[133]R97: "disturbed."

[134]R97: "love."

[135]R82: "Let all be careful of self righteousness, which causes anger and annoyance because of another's sin. These in oneself or in another hinder living lovingly."

## VIII. De obedientia caritativa

25. Fratres et sorores, exemplo Domini Iesu qui posuit voluntatem suam in voluntate Patris,[45] recordentur quod propter Deum abnegaverunt proprias voluntates.[46] In omnibus capitulis quae faciunt primum quaerant regnum Dei et iustitiam eius (Mt 6:33) et sese exhortentur ut possint regulam quam promiserunt melius observare et fideliter sequi vestigia Domini nostri Iesu Christi.[47] Non habeant potestatem vel dominationem maxime inter se.[48] Per caritatem spiritus (Gal 5:13) voluntarie serviant et obediant invicem. Et haec est vera et sancta obedientia Domini nostri Iesu Christi.[49]

26. Unum tenantur semper habere ministrum et servum fraternitatis[50] et ei teneantur firmiter obedire in omnibus quae promiserunt Domino observare et non sunt contraria animae et isti regulae.[51]

27. Illi qui sunt ministri et servi aliorum eos visitent et humiliter et caritative moneant et confortent eos.[52] Et ubicumque sunt fratres et sorores qui scirent et cognoscerent se non posse regulam spiritualiter observare, ad suos ministros debeant et possint recurrere. Ministri vero caritative et benigne eos recipiant et tantam familiaritatem habeant circa ipsos ut dicere possint eis et facere sicut domini servis suis: nam ita debet esse quod ministri sint servi omnium.[53]

---

[45]2LtF 10; FA:ED I, 46.
[46]LR X:2; FLCl 10:2; FA:ED I, 105; CA:ED, 122.
[47]ER XVIII:1; Test 34; FA:ED I, 76, 127.
[48]ER V:9; FA:ED I, 67.
[49]ER V:9, 14-15; FA:ED I, 67-68.
[50]LR VIII:1; FA:ED I, 104.
[51]LR X:3; FLCl 10:2; FA:ED I, 105; CA:ED, 122.
[52]ER IV:2; FLCl 10:1; FA:ED I, 66; CA:ED, 122.
[53]LR X:4-6; FLCl 10:3; TestCl 19; FA:ED I, 105; CA:ED, 122, 61.

## VIII. OBEDIENCE IN LOVE[136]

25. Following the example of the Lord Jesus[137] who made his own will one with the Father's, the brothers and sisters[138] should remember that, for God, they have given up[139] their own wills. Therefore, in every Chapter[140] they have let them seek first God's reign and God's justice,[141] and exhort one another to better observe with greater dedication the rule they have professed and to follow faithfully in the footprints of our Lord Jesus Christ.[142] Let them neither dominate nor seek power especially[143] over one another, but let them willingly serve and obey one another[144] with the charity[145] which comes from the spirit.[146] This is the true and holy obedience of our Lord Jesus Christ.

26. They are always to have one of their number as minister and servant of the fraternity[147] whom they are strictly obliged to obey in all that they have promised God[148] to observe, and which is not contrary to conscience and[149] this rule.

27. Those who are ministers and servants of the others should visit, admonish and encourage them with humility and charity.[150] Should there be brothers or sisters anywhere who know and acknowledge that they cannot observe the Rule according to its spirit, it is their right and duty to have recourse to their ministers. The ministers are to receive them with charity and kindness they should make them feel so comfortable[151] that the brothers and sisters can speak and act towards them just as an employer would with a worker. This is how it should be because[152] the ministers are to be servants of all.

---

[136]R82, R97: Chapter VIII. The Obedience of Love.

[137]R82, R97: "…Our Lord Jesus Christ…"

[138]R82, R97: "…the sisters and brothers…"

[139]R82: "…they should give up…"

[140]R82: "…in every kind of Chapter…"

[141]R82, R97: "…the kingdom of God and its justice…"

[142]R82: "…and exhort one another to observe this rule which all have professed more exactly, as well as how they might more faithfully follow in the footprints of Our Lord Jesus Christ."

[143]R82, R97: omits the word "especially."

[144]R82: "…obey each other…"

[145]R82: "…that genuine love…" R97: "mutual love."

[146]R82: "…from each one's heart."

[147]R97: "community."

[148]R82: "…the Lord…"

[149]R82, R97: "…conscience or…"

[150]R82, R97: "…and love."

[151]R82, R97: "the ministers are to receive them with such love, kindness, and sympathy…"

[152]R82: omits the word "because."

28. Et nullus sibi appropriet aliquod ministerium; sed statuto tempore ipse libenter munus suum dimittat.[54]

## IX. De vita apostolica

29. Fratres et sorores Dominum diligant ex toto corde, ex tota anima et mente, ex tota virtute et diligant proximos suos sicut se ipsos (Mt 22:39; Mk 12:30). Et exaltent Dominum in operibus suis (Tb 13:6) quoniam ideo misit eos in universo mundo ut verbo et opere dent testimonium voci eius et faciant scire omnes quoniam non est omnipotens praeter eum (Tb 13:4).[55]

30. Sicut pacem annuntiant voce, sic in cordibus suis et amplius habeant. Nullus per eos provocetur ad iram vel scandalum, sed omnes per mansuetudinem eorum ad pacem, benignitatem et concordiam provocentur.[56] Nam fratres et sorores ad hoc vocati sunt ut vulneratos curent, alligent confractos et erroneos revocent. Et ubicumque sunt recordentur quod dederunt se et reliquerunt corpora sua Domino Iesu Christo. Et pro eius amore debent se exponere inimicis tam visibilibus quam invisibilibus, quia dicit Dominus: Beati qui persecutionem patiuntur propter iustitiam, quoniam ipsorum est regnum caelorum (Mt 5:10).[57]

---

[54] ER XVII:4; FA:ED I, 75 .
[55] 1LtF 1:1; LtOrd 8-9; FA:ED I, 41, 117.
[56] L3C XIV: 58; FA:ED II, 101-02.
[57] ER XVI:10-12; FA:ED I, 74.

28. No one is to appropriate any office or ministry whatsoever;[153] rather each should willingly relinquish it when the time comes.

## IX.[154] APOSTOLIC LIFE

29. The brothers and sisters are to love God[155] with their whole heart, their whole soul and mind and with all their strength, and to love their neighbor as themselves. Let them glorify God[156] in all they do. Sent into the whole world by God, they should give witness by word and work to God's voice and make known to all that only God is all-powerful.[157]

30. As they announce peace with their lips, let them be careful to have it even more within their own hearts. No one should be roused to anger[158] or insult on their account; rather, all should be moved to peace, kindness[159] and harmony[160] because of their gentleness. The sisters and brothers are called to heal the wounded, to bind up those who are bruised, and to reclaim the erring. Wherever they are, they should recall that they have given themselves up completely and handed themselves over totally to the[161] Lord Jesus Christ. Therefore, they should be prepared to expose themselves to every enemy, visible and invisible, for love of the Lord because He says:[162] Blessed are they who suffer persecution for the sake of justice, theirs is the reign of God.[163]

---

[153]R82, R97: "…whatsoever as if it were a personal right…"

[154]R82, R97: Chapter IX.

[155]R82: "…love the Lord…"

[156]R82: "…glorify the Lord…"

[157]R82: "For He has sent them into the world so that they might give witness by word and work to His voice and to make known to all that the Lord alone is God." R97: "Sent into the whole world they should give witness by word and work to God's voice and make known to all that only God is all powerful."

[158]R82, R97: uses the word "wrath."

[159]R82, R97: uses the word "goodwill."

[160]R82, R97: uses the word "mercy."

[161]R82, R97: "…to Our…"

[162]R82: "…for the love of Him for the Lord says…"

[163]R82, R97: "…theirs is the kingdom of heaven."

31. In caritate quae Deus est (1 Jn 4:16) omnes fratres et sorores, sive orantes sive servientes sive laborantes, studeant se humiliare in omnibus, non gloriari nec in se gaudere nec interius se exaltare de bonis verbis et operibus, immo de nullo bono quod Deus facit vel dicit et operatur in eis aliquando et per ipsos. In omni loco et in omnibus adiunctis agnoscant omnia bona essa Domini Dei altissimi et dominatoris omnium rerum[58]; et ipsi gratias referant a quo bona cuncta procedunt.[59]

### Exhortatio et benedictio

32. Attendant omnes fratres et sorores quod super omnia desiderare debent habere spiritum Domini et sanctam eius operationem.[60] Et semper subditi sanctae Ecclesiae stabiles in fide catholica paupertatem et humilitatem et sanctum Evangelium Domini nostri Iesu Christi quod firmiter promiserunt observent.[61]

Et quicumque haec observaverit in caelo repleatur benedictione altissimi Patris et in terra repleatur benedictione dilecti Filii sui cum sanctissimo Spiritu Paraclito et omnibus virtutibus caelorum et omnibus sanctis. Et ego frater Franciscus parvulus vester servus, quantumcumque possum, confirmo vobis intus et foris istam sanctissimam benedictionem.[62]

---

[58]ER XVII:5-6; FA:ED I, 75.
[59]ER XVII:17; FA:ED I, 76.
[60]LR X:8; FLCl 10:7; FA:ED I, 105; CA:ED, 123.
[61]LR XII:4; FLCl 12:11; FA:ED I, 106; CA:ED, 125.
[62]Test 40-41; FA:ED I, 127.

31. In the charity which God is[164] all the brothers and sisters, whether they are praying or serving or working, should strive to be humble in everything.[165] They should not, because of good words, works, and even anything good that God does, speaks and works in and through them, seek glory or rejoice or exult interiorly.[166] Rather, in every place and circumstance, let them acknowledge that all good belongs to the most high Lord God[167] and Ruler of all things. Let them always give thanks to the one from Whom all good proceeds.[168]

EXHORTATION AND BLESSING

32. Let all the brothers and sisters be mindful above all things that they must desire to have the Spirit of God at work within them.[169] Always subject to the Holy Church[170] and established in the Catholic faith, let them observe[171] the poverty and humility and the holy Gospel of our Lord Jesus Christ which they have firmly promised.[172]

Whoever will observe these things shall be filled with the blessings of the most high Father in heaven, and on earth with the blessing of the[173] beloved Son, with the most[174] Holy Spirit, the Paraclete[175] and with all virtues of heaven[176] and with all the saints.

And I, little Brother Francis, your servant,[177] in so far as I am able, confirm to you within and without this most holy blessing.

---

[164]R97: "In the love which is God."

[165]R82: "In that love which is God all the brothers and sisters, whether they are engaged in prayer, or in announcing the Word of God, or in serving or doing manual labor should strive to be humble in everything."

[166]R82: "They should not seek glory, or be self-satisfied, or interiorly proud because of a good work or word God does or speaks in or through them."

[167]R82: omits the word "God."

[168]R82: "...to Him from whom we receive all good."

[169]R82, R97: "Let the sisters and brothers always be mindful that they should desire one thing alone, namely, the Spirit of God at work within them."

[170]R82: "...obedient to the church..."

[171]R82, R97: "let them live according to the..."

[172]R82, 97: "...solemnly promised to observe."

[173]R82: "...of His..."

[174]R82: omits the word "most."

[175]R82, R97: omits the word "Paraclete."

[176]R82, R97: omits "of heaven."

[177]R82, 97: "And I, Brother Francis, your little one and servant...."

# FIRST GENERATION
# COMMENTARIES

# 5

There is a "genre" of Franciscan literature typically referred to as Commentaries on the Rule. From the earliest generations, the friars and sisters who wanted to establish their fidelity to the original intentions of Francis and Clare, did so very often by writing or searching out expositions of the Rule that would guide them to right action and pure intentions. From an early point in the work on the various drafts of the Rule text, those who had to report, explain and guide the consultation found themselves creating commentaries of their own. Sometimes these took the form of lectures, written essays, reports to federations, etc. However, anyone intimately connected with the work of getting the text approved had to find ways to share the material and its meaning with a broad audience. It was these early experiences that alerted Work Group, CFI and BFI members to the importance of providing a path for interpretation once the text was approved.

There is no monopoly on who may create a commentary. However, when cultural groups that are still evolving towards international leadership roles start to inculturate this text and its values, new commentaries will arise. New generations will have new knowledge of Franciscan sources to bring to the table. New world and ecclesial concerns will influence the emphases on one or another value.

For those who must transmit the history of this text, we provide early commentaries. The criteria for selection was simple: the members of the BFI (Raffaele Pazzelli), CFI (Roberta Cusack) and Work Group (Margaret Carney, Thaddeus Horgan, Jean François Godet-Calogeras) were the primary "witnesses" of the text's meaning. Their ability to convey fundamental insight places their work in a privileged position historically. With the passage of time, these first commentaries will be seen as dated and culturally conditioned. They will, however, still constitute the earliest strata of interpretation. These are included in this Source Book to provide future teachers with that foundational material.

# Margaret Carney, O.S.F. and †Thaddeus Horgan, S.A.

## THE RULE AND LIFE OF THE BROTHERS AND SISTERS OF THE THIRD ORDER REGULAR OF ST. FRANCIS AND COMMENTARY

## FRANCISCAN FEDERATION, 1982

### THE BEGINNING OF THE RULE AND LIFE OF THE BROTHERS AND SISTERS OF THE THIRD ORDER REGULAR OF ST. FRANCIS

Since the fifteenth century the name of our Order, the largest in the Catholic Church with more than 116,000 members in more than four hundred congregations and institutes, has been the Third Order Regular of St. Francis.

Even though the canonically approved title dates to the fifteenth century, the designation of "Third Order" can be traced to the earliest biographies of Francis. Francis's early chroniclers eagerly relate the wisdom that prompted him to point out three distinct patterns of Gospel life. Inspired by God and influenced by the circumstances of his time, Francis was capable of expanding his *forma vitae* to allow for different emphases given to fundamental Gospel values in different styles of Gospel living.

Francis combined zeal for preaching the saving word of the Gospel with an inclusive vision that left room for every person of good will to share his inspiration concerning the mystery of salvation. The fruit of this flexibility and zeal can be seen today in the multiplicity of congregations that have made their home in the Third Order Regular.

The distinctions that exist among the Three Franciscan Orders are not distinctions implying difference in status but differences of emphases in the spirituality and mission of each Order. Together we comprise one worldwide family, inspired by the Gospel spirit of Francis and Clare of Assisi.

### WORDS OF SAINT FRANCIS TO HIS FOLLOWERS[1]

The origin of the ancient Third Order was in the penitential movement that pre-dated St. Francis by six hundred years. Members of this movement committed themselves to a life of continual conversion to Gospel ideals by a program of public and private acts of prayer and penance.

---

[1]1LtF 1-19; FA:ED I, 41-42.

Some secluded themselves in hermitages while others remained in secular occupations or associated themselves with a specific church or monastic house. Francis himself expressed his early experience at conversion by adopting these practices.

When his first followers were asked for an explanation of identity, they called themselves the "penitents of Assisi." When the Pope approved the Rule of the Friars Minor in 1209, Francis and his followers ceased being penitents canonically. Francis and the friars did, however, continue to minister to and influence the penitents of their day. When these medieval *conversi* (converted ones) asked for specific spiritual direction from Francis, he offered guidelines. These became the foundation of the third form of Franciscan Gospel life, the Third Order. Citations from the sources on this point include: 1C XV:37; AP 19; 1LtF and 2LtF; LM 4:6-7; L3C VIII:27, X:36, and 37; LPer 34; and ER XXIII:7. The earliest (circa 1215) authenticated writings of St. Francis for the penitents is technically called the *First Version of the Letter to the Faithful*.

The prologue to this Rule text is the first part of that *Letter*. It was chosen to remind us that our origins go directly back to Francis himself and to enable us to reflect often on his specific words to the penitents who wished to follow Christ after his example.

The Third Order Regular began to be formed within the lifetime of St. Francis. Franciscan lay penitents began living in community, professing vows – the canonical definition of religious – and performing works of charity. Many of our particular founders and foundresses wanted to "follow Christ after the example of St. Francis" and can rightly be called latter-day penitents who wished to incarnate one of several aspects of Franciscan Gospel life. Many, too, were lay Franciscans before becoming religious. The Secular Franciscan Order stems from the same roots as our Third Order Regular. The Rule approved by Paul VI for the Secular Franciscan Order (SFO) also has this *Letter* as its prologue. Thus, its placement within our revised Rule further serves to express our common origin and affinity with our secular Franciscan brothers and sisters.

## Chapter I: Our identity

At the outset (and throughout) it should be noted that this is a spiritual document containing values, attitudes and principles necessary for a way of life. The opening words of the text, *Forma vitae* (the "form," or "style of life") do not mean regulations (which belong in Constitutions or directories), but a clear, brief, and fundamental statement of principles projected by Francis to his followers about our way of living "according to the Gospel."

Using the Church's criteria *Lumen Gentium* 45 and *Perfectae Caritatis* 2 for discerning anew the basic values of a particular order,[2] those responsible for developing this text formed it around four values: penance, (biblical *metanoia*), contemplative prayer, poverty, and minority (humility). Other values associated with our Order: simplicity, joy, works of mercy and the pursuit of peace through justice, are all manifestations of these fundamental values. Fraternity/community is regarded not as a value, but as the social reality of committed relationships in which we live out our Gospel witness.

The text is largely in the words of Francis as the citations indicate.[3] The Rule of 1221 and the first part of the Testament provide a foundation for the sequence of ideas. We are Franciscans following Francis's style of Gospel life. We are Franciscans who claim to follow the Gospel spirit of Francis as he first shared it with the townspeople of Assisi. The specific charism of our Third Order is continuous conversion.

## Article 1
In summary Article 1 states:

a. This is a spiritual document about our

b. Identity and life which is centered in

c. Observing the Gospel. It notes that we are

d. Franciscan, followers of Francis's third form of Gospel living,

as well as

e. Religious who profess the Church's

f. Canonical vows.

## Article 2
Characteristic of Franciscan Third Order Regular spirituality is its emphasis that turning to God and being conformed to Christ is never accomplished once for all. These are ongoing religious experiences. To be faithful to the Gospel, as Francis's experience shows, we have to do

---

[2]Austin Flannery, ed. "Lumen Gentium," *Vatican II: The Counciliar and Post Conciliar Documents* (Collegeville: The Liturgical Press, 1975), 406; "Perfectae Caritatis," 612-613.

[3]Complementary citations from the writings of St. Clare are added in italics.

penance always.[4] This *second* article notes the centrality of *metanoia* in our Order's spirituality. It is the root value of our tradition and flowers forth in poverty, minority and contemplation. *This article, therefore, is the charism statement of the Third Order Regular.*

Francis's own words are used to explain *metanoia*, or biblical penance. Unfortunately, today many misunderstand even Francis's use of *in vera fide et poenitentia, in true faith and in penance.* Since this is so, Francis' words from both the Rules of 1221 and 1223 are employed. According to Francis, *metanoia/poenitentia* as a style of Gospel life has three basic elements:[5]

> *a. To acknowledge God* – in creation, in the word of Scripture, in the manifest goodness of God, and especially in the words, life, deeds, and teachings of the Lord Jesus Christ. This is what persevering in true faith means. To persevere further implies:

> *b. To adore God* – concretely with one's whole life by living prayerfully, in a childlike way, with purity of heart, in poverty and in loving obedience which impels the true Gospel person, and

> *c. To serve God* – in one's neighbor by service in charity and "action on behalf of justice" in the promotion of peace (Mt 25:34).

From this rootedness in "evangelical conversion" the fruits of contemplation, poverty and minority grow. The remainder of this Rule becomes an exposition of this dynamic convergence in the life of the Franciscan penitent.

## ARTICLE 3

Article 3 begins by expanding that part of Article 2 that concerns *vera fide*. The Church is the guardian and teacher of the truth of Revelation. In this light, fidelity to the Church becomes one of the ways to "persevere in true faith." Specifically, this article refers to fidelity to the leaders of the Church: the pope and the bishops. We are to be of service by living our Gospel life as a witness within the Church, as well as by announcing "penance and peace" to all. This article calls us to a deep unity within the universal Church, our local churches, and especially within our own communities or fraternities which should be microcosms of the Church itself. We are called to be turned totally to God and to manifest this by living the Gospel intensely after the example of St. Francis.

The place where we are to do this primarily is within our own fraternity/community. Like the Church, our congregations need structure

---

[4]Test 1-26; FA:ED I, 124-126.
[5]ER XXIII; FA:ED I, 81-86.

and leadership. Obedience to our ministers becomes another sign of this fidelity. Of equal importance is our reverence for each other. Since we are all spiritual daughters and sons, we actively promote harmony with all branches of our vast Franciscan family.

**Summary Note:** In Article 1, the phrase "living in obedience" comes first because this expressed the new style of religious life that Francis envisioned. Entrance into religious life was no longer entrance into a monastery, but reception into the common bond of obedience to shared beliefs and inspiration by all members. Obedience is to faith, to Christ, to the Gospel, to the Church, to the minister, to one another. This obedience is never arbitrary, however, but mediated through the Church, the Rule and our constitutions. This comes up again in Article 7. Today we rightly object to a solely canonical notion of obedience obeying legitimate commands, which fail to understand the all-embracing nature of obedience in the thought of Francis. His notion is much larger than the limited, sometimes legalistic notion of the vow. This again points to the necessity of reading this text as a spiritual document, that is as maximal, rather than as a legal or minimalistic text.

## Chapter II: Acceptance into this life

### Article 4

This chapter considers formation and the ongoing process of *metanoia*. It should be noted that all four fundamental values (conversion, prayer, poverty and minority) of our Franciscan Life will now begin to appear in each chapter. Each chapter may refer to specific values, but because Gospel life is one, all four constitute the fabric of the Rule text in each of its parts. Although this chapter obviously deals with formation, a closer look reveals that the understanding of formation is of a process that extends throughout life. Such an integrated concept of formation has been the subject of much study and encouragement in recent years.

In Francis's and Clare's own experience, conversion was the result of God's inspiration (Art. 4). Therefore, according to them, an aspirant wishing to follow this Gospel way of life must be inspired by the Spirit. *Metanoia* is manifested in our tradition of Franciscanism by living the Gospel literally after the example of St. Francis and St. Clare through poverty (Art. 5), humble service (Art. 7), and prayerfulness (Art. 8). And this commitment and consecration is a life-long process and experience (Art. 6).

## Article 5

More specifically, Articles 4, 5, and 6 reflect Francis's initial conversion experience as much as they reflect his instruction about formation. For Francis, it is essential that one be convinced that his or her call is from God. This implies discernment carried out through dialogue between the individual and representatives of the community. The minister is to ascertain that the one called is "truly Catholic" and genuinely faithful to the Church. The candidate is to be initiated into the life of the community/fraternity. This statement is the text's first explicit reference to the essentially formative character of Franciscan living and ongoing conversion. As Francis and Clare experienced and reflected in their Testaments, the textbook of our religious formation is the Gospel. The Gospel is explained to candidates, especially those parts that express radical and complete self-giving to God. For Clare and Francis divesting self of all that could hinder total conversion is requisite for the journey in Christ's footprints.

## Article 6

This article is among the most direct in the Rule Text. It is addressed to the novice. "Let them begin...." It is addressed to all: "Let them begin...." The continuous life of penance is always begun anew. It is our ongoing religious commitment. That is why the word "consecration" is used in the second sentence. With Francis, everything must be concrete, not ideal. Therefore, our surrender to God is manifested by giving possessions to God's poor people (Art. 5). If one begins and pursues a life of evangelical conversion, then the simplicity of Christ's life should characterize the Franciscan's total living, beginning with the very clothes on one's back. Conversion to God implies being counter-cultural. To be such is not merely a matter of clothing but of one's entire lifestyle.

The wording for this article was carefully discussed in view of the issue of religious habit. The general admonition to "clothe themselves plainly" was selected because this article must be flexible enough to apply to men's and women's communities; groups of contemplatives or ministerial life; communities of widely varying histories and customs, and communities working where the political situation renders the wearing of a habit impossible. Nevertheless, the tradition of the Order to always manifest a penitential life by dressing in a way that is counter-cultural is preserved.

## Article 7

This article refers to life profession and the attitudes Francis says are necessary once one has begun a life of penance. The expression "to be received into obedience" has special meaning. It means profession into a type of religious life that is not monastic. Instead of commitment to stability of place, one is bound to a familial relationship with others equally committed to total conversion and the observance of the holy Gospel. The living link for all in the fraternity/community is the minister whom all are to obey and who is to encourage the others to do "...all they have promised the Lord to observe..." (Art. 26). Mutual responsibility for our Gospel living and for one another is a principle found in Clare and Francis's writings.

The fundamental attitudes and evangelical values of poverty and minority (second sentence) are presented by Francis as characteristics that we should develop in our ongoing observance of "this life and Rule." They will be treated in subsequent chapters. Directed by obedience and freed of attachment by poverty, we are thrust towards a chaste union with the person of Christ. This summation of vowed consecration leads to the final article of the chapter.

## ARTICLE 8

Our turning to God is to be so complete that nothing less than union with God in Christ through the Spirit is to be our life's objective. The article likewise indicates that being filled with God's life and love is to be continually manifested by love for neighbor. Doing the works of mercy – the "fruits befitting our repentance," as Francis would say – has been the constant tradition of the congregations and institutes of our Order.

**Summary Note:** Article 5's second sentence is a translation of the sense of the phrase *si illi idonei sint.*[6] In Article 7 *finito vero tempore probationis*[7] likewise is translated in the sense intended for today. The last line's *mundo corde et pura mente* is also translated according to the intended sense. It could be translated literally, but this and similar phrases are frequently found in this text. To avoid repetition and to be more specific in English, other words than the literal translations are used.

## CHAPTER III: THE SPIRIT OF PRAYER

From the exhortation to make ourselves a dwelling place for the Trinity, we move to this third chapter that summarizes key elements of prayer in the Franciscan tradition. We know that neither Clare nor Francis offered a complicated prayer method. They call their followers to prayer with a decidedly contemplative dimension – to be present to God who is

---

[6]Literally translated "if they are suitable."
[7]Literally translated "the time of probation truly having been completed."

present to all creatures is prayer. They require that our prayer be Trinitarian. Our prayer is always addressed to God in the Son by the power of the Spirit.[8] Our prayer is to be Incarnational. We become alive to God's deeds in the greatest gift of God, the Incarnation, in which God becomes one with us in the Son. The purpose of all Franciscan Prayer, then, is to give God ceaseless praise and thanksgiving for all God has done and does in creation and in our re-creation in Christ.

## ARTICLE 9

Prayer is a way of life for us – all the time and everywhere. We should be so filled with God that adoration flows from the depth of our inner life (*puro corde*) with joy and thanksgiving. We should want nothing else (*et non deficere*) because our God wills to be one with us. This is the holiness to which we are called. Our every day should thus be sanctified. In Francis's time, this sanctification of the day was given clear expression in the Divine Office. This is still the Church's understanding of the Liturgy of the Hours. We pray with the Son in his Mystical Body celebrating God's gift of salvation throughout the day. Today, as the "General Instruction," for the Liturgy of the Hours notes, it is also the intercessory prayer for the Church and the world. It becomes for us both a turning to God and to our neighbor. For Francis, praying the Office is also a sign of fidelity to the Church's tradition of daily praise and intercession.

The second paragraph of this article addresses the many congregations within our Order of specifically contemplative life. All of us are called to contemplative prayer, but we are strengthened and enriched by the brothers and sisters who embrace the life of intercession and adoration in an exclusive way. Their lives within our Third Order Regular family witness to the diversity supported by our common charism.

## ARTICLE 10

The motivation for our life of ceaseless prayer is described. Francis's love for creation and his insight into its meaning is central. Notice that we praise "with" all creatures. The created world is the expression of God's goodness and the theater of God's redemptive love for us. Because we are made in God's image, it is possible for us to seek union with God as we do God's will. Thus, the Franciscan does not flee the world in order to "escape" to God, but seeks immersion in its sacramental reality.

---

[8]Francis's dictated paraphrase of the "Our Father."

## ARTICLE 11

In Celano's *First Life*, we see Francis given over to "persistent meditation" and "penetrating consideration" of the Scriptures.[9] Like Francis, we seek "spirit and life" in the words of the Gospel.

## ARTICLE 12

Francis calls for "humility and reverence" as dispositions for receiving the Eucharist. After the Fourth Lateran Council, Francis and the friars played a crucial role in helping to reform Eucharistic theology and devotion. As we study this text, we remember that our understanding of "humility and reverence" is deepened to include the renewed meaning of the communitarian dimensions of the Eucharist given by the Council of our day, Vatican II. "Participation" then, becomes the by-word of renewed and reformed Eucharistic theology and practice among us.

This article cites two other traits – often translated into specific "devotions" – associated with Franciscans and, indeed, with every reform movement in the Western Church. These are reverence for the holy and saving name of Jesus and respect for the sacred character of the words of the Gospels. For Francis, such respect is a sign of conversion and our readiness to put God's word into effect. Jesus continues his saving work (the meaning of his messianic titles) through the power of his presence in the Gospels and the Eucharist.

## ARTICLE 13

Here we find the second meaning of *poenitentia* in the writings of Francis; that is, contrition (Art. 2). The article portrays the reality of human weakness and our need for help in making our way to God. We must embody the life of grace in practical ways.

Repentance is both interior and exterior and is marked by authenticity when it produces deeds befitting true contrition. Fasting is one of those deeds.

Fasting can be regarded in both the literal and symbolic senses. It is a way to make ourselves literally experience in our bodies the need for God. It is God-oriented, a means to express conversion. Symbolically, fasting means to free ourselves from whatever clutters up our lives. This is why simplicity is mentioned here and followed by minority (humility), which will be considered more fully in the next chapter.

The words "especially before God" are intended to draw us to the famous statement of Admonition 19: "What one is before God, that one is

---

[9]1C XXX:84; FA:ED I, 254-255.

and no more."[10] We may fool others, but never God. Our penitence must be honest, without affectation.

The article closes by inviting us to contemplate the Paschal Mystery. Through Christ we have access to God despite our sinfulness. The height of Franciscan contemplation is this transformation into Jesus Christ "who chose to be crucified because of the excess of his love"[11] for us.

## CHAPTER IV: THE LIFE OF CHASTITY FOR THE SAKE OF THE KINGDOM

### ARTICLE 14

Drawing upon the insight expressed in Article 10 – namely, that the material universe is good – the call to a life of chastity is described as a preferential love for Christ. This love does not negate the potential of human development. Rather the whole of a man or woman's life is gathered into this consecration of the person's innermost self to the Lord.

This article situates chastity in the overall context of Gospel living and roots it in the wonder Francis experienced when contemplating women and men in God's plan for creation and redemption.

### ARTICLE 15

This article specifies the preceding one by relating attitudes Francis had regarding chastity for the sake of the Kingdom. This gift is intimately related to poverty that frees us by protecting the growth of the Word within our lives from the choking thorns and rocks of temporal cares. This chastity is not a privatized aspect of religious vocation, but empowers us to witness to God's primacy in practical visible ways, especially charity towards our neighbor.

### ARTICLE 16

Here we find an exhortation reflecting the passages in the *Letters to the Faithful* in which Francis compares the love of the disciple to the love of a spouse. Such nuptial imagery has a venerable tradition that includes Scripture, the early Church Fathers and the mystics – including Francis, Clare, Bonaventure and numerous other Franciscan saints. This is a powerful image, which invites us to confidently expect the grace of deep personal union with our God.

---

[10]Adm XIX:2, FA:ED I, 135.
[11]LMj 13:3; FA:ED II, 632.

ARTICLE 17

Mary is *par excellence*, the Spouse of the Holy Spirit and the Mother of the Church. In her *Magnificat* we find summarized all of the longing hope of the *anawim*, God's poor little ones, whose hope rested solely upon God's power to satisfy, deliver, and console them. For that reason we look to Mary as the exemplar of reliance upon the God's power and loving concern for others' needs.

CHAPTER V: THE WAY TO SERVE AND WORK

There are three historic reasons why minority, the subject of this chapter, developed into a principal characteristic for the Order of Friars Minor. They were: the clericalization of the Order; Francis's inspiration based on Gospel reflection; and the socio-political situation of Assisi in the saint's day. Francis wanted his brothers and sisters always to be *minores* in contrast to the *majores* (the wealthy and powerful) of his day. He wanted them to be like Christ, humble and truly submissive to all. And he wished his friars to be servants of the Word rather than set apart as a clerical class or hierarchical monastic community.

If minority can be historically verified as a central feature of the life of the Friars Minor, in what sense is it appropriate as a value fundamental to the life of the Third Order Regular? While we share the meaning of this value with the Friars Minor, we find added meaning in our tradition. Intrinsic to the life of penance are the works of mercy. Our turning to God is only authentic, as the Johannine literature in Scripture points out, when it is manifested by love for neighbor (1 John 4:20). The life of conversion is ongoing because it is growing adherence to the God of love. The experience of *metanoia*, therefore, projects one into the ongoing and daily reality of God's little ones, the marginal, the helpless and the unwanted. Like St. Francis who concretely expressed his experience of conversion by embracing a leper, by caring for the poor, by attending the sick and suffering, and by calling God's people to peace, so, too, have congregations in the Third Order Regular continually committed themselves to the works of charity. Congregations founded during the past two centuries particularly have had the works of charity as their apostolic purpose. This is the context in which Third Order congregations have come to appreciate minority.

The words of Jesus in Matthew 25:31-46 explain minority's importance. It is the least who are the object of the Lord's loving concern. Jesus identifies himself with the "least" (Mt 25:40). Minority means to conform oneself, through a life of penance, to Christ who is the servant of God sent into the world, the place of our redemption. It is the "holy ground" where we live God's redeeming will with our brothers and sisters. Minority means cherishing life as sisters and brothers, bringing good news to the poor, proclaiming freedom to captives, giving sight to the blind, setting the down-trodden free and announcing God's year of favor (Lk 4: 17-19). *Metanoia* and Jesus' announcement of the nearness of the Kingdom (Mk 1:15) are inextricably linked because childlikeness, minority, is the on thing necessary for entrance into the Kingdom (Mt 18:13; Mk 10:16; Lk 18:17; Jn 3). An aspect of Francis's insight into the Gospel was that all the other qualities of Gospel life are counsels. "Littleness" is an absolute requirement for the Kingdom (Mt 19:14). The adult experience of this "littleness," or "childlikeness," before God is the joyful awareness that one is the subject of the pure love and favor of God. Is this anything other than the basic awareness and attitude needed throughout life for total and continuous conversion?

This chapter considers those attitudes Francis projects, since reception "into obedience" (Art. 1 and 7) brings us into a form of life, which, unlike monasticism, is at once immersed in the world and yet stands against it. Francis is concerned that we commit ourselves to actual identity with the *minores*, the poor and powerless. In his day, they had to work and had to serve the *majores*. That explains the language of the three articles of this Chapter. But more importantly, the constant tradition of our Order and the continuing current teaching of the Church call us to this posture. As Third Order Franciscans we are called to live as brothers and sisters with all people, especially with the poor, the marginalized and those who are without voice in our world.

### ARTICLE 18 AND ARTICLE 19

In Article 13, we gazed upon the poor crucified Christ. In Article 17, we looked to Mary, the lowly servant who is lifted up by God. With such models before our eyes we seek to enter into the meaning of minority for our lives.

If we walk in Christ's footsteps, we will be actually poor: *sicut pauperes*. As all poor people must, we work and serve as God gives the talent, but we do not work ourselves to death. ("Let them avoid that idleness...") This was stated so as to indicate that there is a legitimate form of "idleness," that which allows for leisure and contemplation. Francis' balanced view of the relationship between prayer and work is spelled out in view of our contemporary tendency to "workaholism" and the "heresy of good works."

Let us summarize several aspects of work that Francis offers and which these articles try to encompass:

a. Work is a way we identify with the poor;

b. We willingly do manual labor;

c. By our works, we give good example;

d. We work to provide for each other, our ministries, and ourselves;

e. Whatever we have beyond our needs we give to other people;

f. We work to avoid idleness;

g. We never work in ways that snuff out prayerfulness;

h. We do not work to accumulate wealth.

Finally, since we want to have the mind of Christ (Phil 2:5-12), our self-perception is one of servanthood. Francis concretized the ideal into an attitude. We should not seek to be "over" others by domination or manipulation. Rather, he urges us to be filled with peace to announce it "by word and example"[12] and to do so joyfully.

### Article 20
This is the positive aspect of the final point made in Article 19. When we enter into association with people for any reason, we seek to exhibit qualities proclaimed by Christ in the Beatitudes. Because of our respectful attitude, Francis warns that we should not judge others even if they appear untouched by the Gospel.[13] They are touched, however, by our witness to joyfulness in God. This alone makes our peaceable greeting credible (Article 30).

### Translation notes
The sense of *laborandi* in Article 18 is "manual labor." *Laboris* in Article 19 is intended to mean any form of work or service. In Article 20 the sense of *sicut decet* is "in accord with their vocation," literally it means, "as becomes them."

### Chapter VI: The life of poverty

This chapter considers the value of evangelical poverty as Francis and Clare taught it and the attitudes that would manifest a person's assimilation of this "treasure." To turn to God continuously means to put on Christ, to walk in Christ's footprints. That we can do so is the good news. For Clare and Francis the word of this Good News could only be made flesh in the same way in which the Eternal Word became flesh – by

---

[12]Adm VII:4; FA:ED I, 132.
[13]LR II:17; FA:ED I, 101.

choosing poverty and life among the poor. Evangelical poverty has both personal and social dimensions. They translate their personal surrender to Jesus into an insistence upon material poverty in order to mirror faithfully the One who has nowhere to lay his head.

As an attitude of heart, poverty is the admission of our powerlessness to save ourselves and the acknowledgment in faith that God wills our salvation. It is absolutely necessary to the life of conversion. God is totally good and sent Jesus, the Incarnate Word, among us to hand back all humanity, all creation in fact, to a loving God. To recognize God's "all good" self-sufficiency and our creaturely need for God is the basis in faith for evangelical poverty. Francis would have us live this acknowledgement and never appropriate what is properly God's.[14] We own only our limitations and our sinfulness.[15] Positively, evangelical poverty calls us to be totally open only to the divine riches.

Evangelical poverty, or poverty of spirit, equally means actual material poverty. As such, poverty becomes the condition that best preserves us in the state of total dependence on God. Material poverty is the sign of our uncluttered and converted selves. It further associates us with those who have always been closest to the Lord, the helpless poor to whom the good news is proclaimed. For Francis and Clare all these aspects of poverty constitute "Evangelical poverty."

## ARTICLE 21

In the *Rule of 1221* and in his *Testament,* Francis gives us the reason why poverty is so central to our way of life. He does not define poverty. He simply and clearly points to Christ and says, "He is evangelical poverty," Christ is our way to God. And he chose humility (minority) as the way for humanity to be turned anew to God. Jesus emptied himself and became poor for our salvation (*kenosis*). We choose the poverty of Christ to receive salvation. This self-emptying is the process involved in Franciscan poverty. It implies total dependence on Providence. This poverty is safeguarded by identification with the poor. In the Third Order Regular tradition, this has most often been expressed by "deeds befitting our conversion," or doing the works of mercy.

Mary is mentioned in this article deliberately because it is in the context of Christ's saving activity that Franciscan Marian devotion is centered. The words "Crib and Cross" capture the essence of this devotion.[16]

The phrase about money expressed Francis's thought on the danger of the destructive force of greed. Money was not to be touched because

---

[14]Adm II:1-5; FA:ED I, 129.

[15]Adm V:1-8; FA:ED I, 131.

[16]SalBVM; FA:ED I, 163; OfP 1 Antiphon; FA:ED I, 141.

of its misuse in thirteenth century commerce. For us the danger is not in physically handling money, which has become available to all classes, but in the acquisitive and competitive spirit it breeds. This is the sense of the phrase *et caveant multum a pecunia*. In his writing on work, Francis admonishes that no one work to accumulate wealth for the same reason.

## Article 22

In this article Clare's and Francis's ideal of poverty is presented without risking the needless difficulties created when poverty is equated with rejection of any form of ownership. Canonical reality today is that as religious in simple vows, we do retain the right to own goods. Our concern, therefore, should be to foster freedom from attachment and proprietary instincts that cause us to live and act like the wealthy. The Gospel call to detachment is radical for Francis and Clare and embraces spiritual and intellectual as well as material goods. In Article 20, for instance, this highest form of poverty is advocated: be nonjudgmental! Judgment belongs to God. Christ in his humanity and humility did not judge us, but redeemed us. With that as the criterion, the wedding of evangelical poverty to our own personalities, shown in our attitudes toward persons, circumstances and things can be called nothing less than maximal. God's Providence, in this light, takes on a much deeper significance than mere provision or protection alone. Such was the radical poverty of Christ – the poverty Clare and Francis hold out to us.

## Chapter VII: Love of brothers and sisters

Before commenting on the content of this chapter, it is important to acknowledge that the translation and interpretation of this chapter and all of the articles that use the term *fraternitas* pose a very difficult problem for those of us who must translate the official Latin text into English. In the meetings in Germany, Belgium and Rome, attention was given to the problems that would be created for English speaking members of the Order who desire the use of inclusive language in our documents. Two facts emerged in the discussion on this difficulty. First, while the major European languages allow for translations of the terms that were not offensive to those participating in the dialogue on the Order, there is, as yet, no clear consensus about how to translate the term that speaks of a very important Franciscan value – fraternity. We acknowledge that more discussion is needed among the English-speaking members in view of the sensitivity we want to foster regarding the importance of non-sexist language. Until such dialogue can lead us to new horizons, however, we judge that, at this time, we should use in our translation the word literally and present to our membership the explanation of religious significance that the idea of fraternity held for Francis and Clare, as it was developed in the composition of their Rules.

The significance of the word fraternity in the vocabulary of Clare and Francis is found in their insights that Jesus became brother to all of us in the Incarnation. Thus fraternity is a special descriptive word indicating a *relational commitment* rooted in our relationship to this elder Brother of ours. Since we are received into the obedience of this relationship, we are not bound to place (e.g., monastery). By the inspiration and power of the Spirit, our Gospel life means being ever open to a deeper relationship with God in Christ in whose footsteps we walk. Our loving service to each other and all creatures manifest this relationship. Our conversion, prayer, poverty and minority are enfleshed in the fraternity/community where we experience our God giving us the power to love one another. We are talking about something more than a communal structure, school of discipline, or team approach to ministry. We are talking about a life lived in constant consciousness of the equality of our relationships rooted in our relationship to our Brother, Jesus Christ.

## ARTICLE 23

What is the basis of our life together? God's love. This love incarnate is Jesus Christ. Following his example, we want to love our brothers and sisters by deeds. This love further must be made concrete, because we have chosen a literal living of the Gospel that makes us interdependent and servants to all.

Francis urges concrete expression of mutual trust. The sick and handicapped will experience love that values their human dignity over and above functional productivity. With the compassion for the sick that characterizes many of his writings, Francis challenges our standards of mutuality. The sick, in their turn, are admonished to search for God's will in the midst of suffering and to exemplify reliance upon God's care.

This article clearly shows Francis's realism. All is not ideal in our lives together. When relationships are weakened, we must repair them according to evangelical norms. This article notes the need for personal and shared responsibility for life together. The minister cannot be the sole agent of reconciliation. In addition to our call to be messengers of peace, we are warned of the corruptive force of pride and competitiveness. Righteousness undermines both poverty of spirit and love and so must be avoided.

## ARTICLE 24

Here we consider our failures of being sisters and brothers to one another. If someone causes offense, our concrete attitude should be: mutual forgiveness without accusation. We belong to one family; we originate in a single impulse of divine love.

### Chapter VIII: The obedience of love

The Gospel of John provides us with a profound portrait of the obedience Jesus renders to his Abba/Father. Francis and Clare embraced this mysterious and powerful call to walk in the pathways of Jesus. The only way to be turned to God is in, with, and through Christ, the Way. The underlying attitude necessary for genuine conversion, then, is obedience, the obedience of Christ (Art. 2). As consecrated followers of Clare and Francis's project of Gospel conversion, we live as Christ did in poverty, minority and community/fraternity. And as we have consistently seen, they bring this ideal down to earth. The framework of evangelical obedience is the brotherhood or sisterhood. This is why this chapter is positioned here. Francis's form of life is characterized by obedience as much as by poverty because it is based on *metanoia,* the inspiration of the Lord given to each member to live the Gospel completely.[17] To emphasize this, Francis's term for obedience is used in the title: *Obedientia caritativa,* the obedience of love.[18] Its motive is that "God so loved the world..." (Jn 3:1-3; 4:7-21). It is both love for God and mutual love among ourselves.

It is also helpful to note that this chapter is not a description of the practice of the vow of obedience in the canonical or constitutional sense. Rather, it is an unfolding of Gospel obedience in fraternity/community from which the vowed commitment takes its ecclesial vitality.

### Article 25

Franciscan obedience is self-emptying, therefore, its intrinsic relationship to poverty. As Christ did, we seek to conform our wills to the God who sends us. Francis projects this obedience to ministers and members alike. The will of God is our salvation. "For God" then, we conform our wills to the divine plan for humanity's redemption (Chapter 4). This involves witness and ministry for the sake of true justice. We are called to be credible signs of salvation (witness) as well as instruments of God's reconciliation (mission). Chapters, whether general, regional or local, are explicit structures intended to enable us to renew repeatedly our living and ministry. Notice again, the emphasis on shared responsibility. With such emphasis, the chapter is described as the first vehicle for rendering obedience. The third sentence stresses the poverty of obedience.

---

[17] LR X:1-12; FA:ED I, 105.

[18] Adm III:6; FA:ED I, 130.

Domination and manipulation represent willful possessiveness. There is no place for this in Franciscan life. Mutual service is what characterizes the obedience of Jesus.

## ARTICLE 26 AND 27

These two articles should be taken as a unit. They concern the minister of the community/fraternity who has authority with reference to what all have promised the Lord. While the "limits" of obedience are defined (it is guided by the Rule and conscience), Franciscan tradition clearly affirms the role of the minister whose personal authority is meant to be of service to unity, reconciliation, and fidelity within the fraternity/community. Therefore, the minister is not to exercise authority as the powerful of the world do. This service is to be offered with humility, love, and kindness. In fact, the "servant-spirit" of the ministers should be evident to all especially those who seek help in being faithful to what they have professed.

## ARTICLE 28

Here the relationship of poverty to obedience is translated into an admonition to all. No one is to appropriate or possess any office, ministry, assignment, or service. Presented here is the unmistakable call to continuous conversion present in all roles of authority in the Order.

## TRANSLATION NOTE

In the second sentence of Article 27, note that *spiritualiter observare* does not mean, "spiritually observe," but "observe according to its spirit."

## CHAPTER IX: APOSTOLIC LIFE

The sequence of the preceding chapters is based upon the plan Francis developed in the *Rule of 1221*. These chapters describe the foundation of our call, our special Franciscan identity, our rootedness in prayer, our internal relationships and our attitude of service. The poverty and obedience of Jesus invite us to single-hearted consecration to His love. The life thus fashioned will, of necessity, flow outward to others. By describing our interior lives and the life we live together in fraternity/community beforehand, we can now better understand the link between contemplation and action that should characterize our evangelical call to be peacemakers.

Since *metanoia* is our basic charism, its relationship to apostolic action should be seen as the cornerstone of our Franciscan evangelical spirituality. Turning to our neighbor presumes our turning to God. Francis understands the activity of service as an extension of prayer. The citation here of the Great Commandment relates this to his early directives to the penitents in the opening passage of both *Letters to the Faithful*.[19] We are called to go into the world (Chapter V) to give witness, first by our lives and then by our work, to the saving power and presence of God in this world. This ninth chapter then, is a culmination of all that precedes it.

## ARTICLE 29

The opening sentence of this chapter re-echoes the magnificent theme that originates in the Book of Deuteronomy, the Shema, the "Great Commandment." Jesus affirms this commandment as the cornerstone of human response to God's revelation of covenanted love. Francis seized upon this insistence of the Lord and made this passage the opening mandate in his directives to the first members of our Order. In the *First Letter to the Faithful* he writes, "... and we give birth to Him through a holy life which should enlighten others because of our example."[20] Again in the *Second Letter to the Faithful*, he relates, "worthy fruits of penance" to love of neighbor.[21] Note that as Francis urges us to be grateful of our profound union with the Lord in the Spirit, he recalls the image of the Good Shepherd who gives his life for his sheep.[22] In this way, Francis links *metanoia* and service to neighbor.

The citation from the *Letter to the Order* comes from a description of the missionary spirit that Francis wants to inculcate in his followers. He desires the following commitments:

a. We must listen to the voice of God's Son calling us;
b. We must keep God's commands wholeheartedly;
c. We are to extol God in our words;(This is the reason for our mission: to convince the world of God's goodness.)
d. We are to be patient, disciplined, and obedient.

As God's children we are disciplined so that we will achieve faith's perfection (Heb 3:13). Francis's use of the passage from Tobias (4:16) in which we are called to turn to God, so that we will receive mercy, emphasizes again that conversion to the divine will is the foundation of all mission.

---

[19] 1LtF 1:1; FA:ED I, 41; 2LtF 18; FA:ED I, 46.
[20] 1LtF 1:10; FA:ED I, 42.
[21] 2LtF 26-27; FA:ED I, 47.
[22] 1LtF 1:13; FA:ED I, 42.

## ARTICLE 30

In his *Rule of 1221*, Francis describes the mission of the brothers in terms of preaching peace and penance. Those of his followers who were not clerics and who formed local penitential communities translated this call to be peacemakers by serving others through spiritual and corporal works of mercy. This service was especially significant in the extension to social outcasts or those whose needs were not met by existing social and ecclesiastical structures. This is the origin of our tradition of congregational apostolic works. In a striking departure from the method of using only the writings of Francis as source material, this article includes a citation from one of the early biographies, the *Legend of the Three Companions*.[23] This lovely passage captures the essential spirit of reconciliation and evangelization that should characterize the diverse ministries we specify in our constitutions.

The section from the *Rule of 1221* also has particular significance as used here. The decision by Francis to include as part of the Rule the call of missionary preaching had enormous impact upon the Church of his time. In the sixteenth chapter of this Rule he offers a program for the apostolate:

a. The brothers are sent as lambs among the wolves;
b. The discernment for a mission is to be done both by the brother and the minister;
c. Two forms of witness are offered:
   1. Peaceful Christian conduct;
   2. Announcing the Word;
d. Because we are given over to Christ, we face every enemy with confidence.

Our prayer and our ministry are modeled on Christ's poverty and obedience (Phil 2:5-11) that led him to surrender himself to death on the Cross. For this reason, Francis enjoins us to follow Christ in struggling against the "principalities and powers" of this world even though that struggle may lead to actual martyrdom.

Modern pontiffs, synods, and episcopal documents prod us to embrace participation in the transformation of the world as a fundamental element of our preaching of the Gospel. Thus, our new Rule combines a seven-century tradition of works of mercy and charity with the biblical imperative, heard anew in our day, to proclaim the Good News to the poor and oppressed. As Francis responded to the call of Lateran Council IV to the renewal of Church life and mission, we try to envision and renew our evangelical calling in harmony with the contemporary Church.

---

[23] L3C XIV:58; FA:ED II, 101-02.

This ecclesial energy is evident in both Episcopal pronouncements and plans as well as numerous initiatives among Church members who seek the common good in the name of Christ.

## Article 31

Our service is rooted in a humility marked by gratitude and total dependence upon the loving compassion of God. In the depth of our poverty, we know that we are "unprofitable servants" no matter how much we accomplish externally and that all glory belongs to God, who is all our good.[24]

### Exhortation and blessing

The Exhortation consists of two parts. First is a summation of the Rule in which the "last" word parallels the "first." We hear Francis saying, "Brothers and Sister, let us begin to serve God."[25] Secondly, Francis offers a central insight into the ongoing character of the charism of our Order. The death of Francis was not the death of his inspiration or his charism. This is kept alive in us, and in the Church, by the operation of the Holy Spirit.

And finally, if we are faithful to this charism that is guarded by poverty and humility, we will be blessed. The blessing from the Testament closes the text and provides a link to the Rule of 1927 and thus to the past Rules of our Order upon which this one was built and whose authentic spirit it hopes to preserve and renew.

Pax et bonum!

---

[24]Adm II, V, VI, VII, XIV; FA:ED I, 129-34; 2LtF; FA:ED I, 45-51.
[25]1C VI:103; FA:ED I, 272-73.

# Raffaele Pazzelli, T.O.R.

## COMMENTARY OF THE RULE AND LIFE OF THE BROTHERS AND SISTERS OF THE THIRD ORDER REGULAR OF SAINT FRANCIS

### PADUA, 1983

#### TRANSLATED FROM THE ITALIAN BY NANCY CELASCHI, O.S.F.

## INTRODUCTION

### 1. NATURE OF THE DOCUMENT

This Rule is an inspirational document. In the Church's constant tradition and experience, contrary to common opinion, a rule is not a set of laws but rather a complex of attitudes by which one lives the Gospel. Living the Gospel besides being the duty of every Christian is the public and solemn commitment of every religious. And, as there are various ways and characteristics of living the Gospel, it follows that there are diverse rules. A particular way or characteristic of living the Gospel constitutes a distinct spirituality. Thus we easily see the direct correlation between rule and spirituality. Correlation, but not identification.

As there are not many spiritualities in the history of the consecrated life, or religious life, there are not very many rules. In fact, there have not been many rules in the history of the Church: up until the time of Francis there were mainly only three: those of St. Basil, St. Augustine and St. Benedict. It is already an exception that there are three Rules in the Franciscan Order, one for each of the three Orders he established. It would be inconceivable for the Third Order Regular to have more than one Rule.

A rule, on the other hand, does not have to contain the entire spirituality of a religious order which follows it. (Thus, for example, we see that today more than one hundred fifty religious orders and congregations follow the Rule of St. Augustine; these do not have a common origin, purpose and spirituality.) The spirituality, however, should be expressed well in the constitutions which are different for each religious order or congregation.

A rule, therefore, is different than the constitutions. These also, in certain aspects, are inspirational documents, but they must first of all completely express the particular charism of a certain congregation.

This Rule, which is intended for the large Third Order Regular family, both male and female (the approximately four hundred congregations which compose it) should, therefore, represent and express the basic unity of this Franciscan family, while the constitutions which are proper to each of the congregations represents their plurality and pluralism.

In summary, we can therefore affirm that this Rule:

a. is a spiritual document which presents a characteristic way of living the Gospel: a way of living prayer, fraternity, the apostolic life, etc.;

b. presents the principal basic and common attitudes and behavior of the entire Franciscan family of the Third Order Regular;

c. contains a common storehouse that is at the basis of our unity. Here we find the fundamental values of the Franciscan family: poverty, minority, penance-conversion, and the contemplative life values woven into the fabric of the fraternity and lived in simplicity and joy;

d. it was written for men's and women's congregations, both of active and contemplative life.

### 2. CHARACTERISTICS

a. Essentially this Rule contains and presents St. Francis's Gospel project as described in his Testament (Test 14-23). This was his way of living the Gospel.

b. It is written almost exclusively with the words of St. Francis. Thus the transitory nature of language is avoided; otherwise, language which would be modern today could be outdated in a few years' time. Therefore it is a classic text, in line with Franciscan thought and tradition; a text which could and should be translated and explained in modern language, that is language which is up to date, and should be interpreted for the life of every particular today to come.

c. It will be a source of ongoing formation because it is a tool which requires of each generation a knowledge and a deep appreciation of the Franciscan texts.

d. This Rule presents the Franciscan religious life in conformity with the Church's teaching in its latest form, as expressed in the documents of the Second Vatican Council.

e. This text can also be considered as a renewal of the Rule of Pius XI of 1927. In fact, it contains all the fundamental values found in that one, plus the spiritual values developed in the various initial documents spoken of in the introduction, that is, the basic text (the French text) which emphasized poverty and minority; the Madrid Statement, which emphasized penance-conversion; the Dutch text, which emphasized peace-making; and the decision at Grottaferrata to include the contemplative life.

The congregations can and should preserve their own identity. In no way does this Rule impede them. As we have already observed, it is up to the individual congregations to express their particular charism in their own constitutions. The congregations which had already written their constitutions in accordance with the documents mentioned above will find no contradiction reconciling them with this text, because it also contains the values expressed in those documents.

### 3. TITLE

This title, even if it is not exactly identical with any of those that preceded it, preserves the two essential elements of the two Rules given previously and exclusively to this form of life. The two Rules are that of Leo X of 1521 and that of Pius XI of 1927. The two elements are:

a. This Order has always included brothers and sisters, and there was always one Rule for both;

b. The two former Rules both contain the expression Third Order and the concept of Regular, even though the concept may be expressed in a different way.

The name Third Order has been one of the most common and constant terms since the time of the Rule of Nicholas IV (1289). Recently, with the new Rule approved by Pope Paul VI (June 24, 1978) the Third Order Secular has assumed the title of the Secular Franciscan Order. Based also on this decision, the Work Group at Brussels recommended using the name of Regular Order of St. Francis for the Rule. The General Assembly, however, for reasons of clarity and the fact that a large number of the congregations preferred the traditional Third Order Regular, decided to keep that title.

### 4. PROLOGUE

This Prologue is the first part of the *Recensio prior* (first draft) of St. Francis's *Letter to the Faithful*.[1] The text, discovered by Paul Sabatier in codex 225 of the Guarnacci Library in Volterra, Italy and published by him in 1900, contains, according to the thinking of the experts, an exhortation written by the saint to penitents who followed his spiritual guidance, that is to the members of the movement which later became known as the Third Order of St. Francis. The document, with all probability written during the first years of his itinerant preaching, contains

---

[1] 1LtF; FA:ED I, 41-44.

only a few essential ideas, those which form the base of his more developed teaching as it contained in the longer form of the *Letter to the Faithful*.[2]

In it Francis first of all gives a clear indication of what penance means and involves. In fact, in the first few lines five elements are listed:

1. love of God;

2. love of neighbor;

3. opposing the sinful tendencies of fallen human nature;

4. have recourse to the sacraments, especially the Eucharist;

5. in all things yield the fruits of the conversion which has taken place.

These are the things that penitents should do. St. Francis emphasizes that the result of such conduct and perseverance in it will be the achievement of the ultimate happiness which people desire: How happy and blessed are these men and women when they do these things, and persevere in doing them, because such things will cause the soul of the penitent to be inserted into the life of God's Trinitarian life: because the Spirit of the Lord will rest upon them and the Lord will make His home and dwelling place with them. They are the children of the heavenly Father whose works they do. They are the spouses, brothers and mothers of Our Lord Jesus Christ.

For Francis, this is living in penance; this is its essential nature.

It has been pointed out that in no other writings of St. Francis do we reach such heights of spirituality nor is the insertion of the soul into the Trinitarian life expressed so precisely or in such lofty terms.

Therefore, the General Assembly in Rome decided to place this document as the Prologue of the New Rule, following the example of the Secular Franciscan Order, with which the Third Order Regular shares a common origin and the honor of having received such a noble exhortation directly from St. Francis.

COMMENTARY

This commentary on the Rule is intended to be simple and able to be understood by everyone. For each article two things will be indicated: the contents and attitudes; thus it will indicate schematically first, what the article is considered to contain and then what our attitudes should be in regard to these contents. Almost always, there will be brief considerations at the end.

---

[2]2LtF; FA:ED I, 45-51.

CHAPTER ONE

The title of the chapter, with its expression Rule and Life (which sounds strange to us) is a medieval formula indicating that this is a definition of the identity of the brothers and sisters of the Third Order Regular of St. Francis. Rule and Life does not mean a set of rules for our life, but rather an explanation of the values, behavior and principles which should constitute our life, or which will become our life. Thus it is also another way of saying that we are facing a spiritual document which does not put an emphasis on practical norms, but on the attitudes which must affect our behavior.

> The form of life of the Brothers and Sisters is this: to observe the Holy Gospel of Our Lord Jesus Christ, living in obedience, in poverty and in chastity. Following Jesus Christ after the example of St. Francis, let them recognize that they are called to make greater efforts in their observance of the precepts and counsels of Our Lord Jesus Christ. Let them deny themselves as each has promised the Lord.

*Contents:*

a. We are Franciscans; therefore St. Francis's classic formula is repeated: The form of life is this, etc.

b. We live the vowed life as true religious.

*Attitudes:*

What will our attitudes be when we consider who and what we are? They are the same attitudes of Francis, which we seek to preserve and maintain namely:

a. Observe the Gospel. Francis was eminently the man of the Gospel. We are therefore invited to become imbued with the dynamism of these Gospel values and behaviors which St. Francis's life, example and writings propose to us. In all this there is no beginning or ending limit. It is a penetration which can barely pierce the skin or can strike at the depths of one's heart, leading to the true repetition of Francis's attitudes and behavior in all aspects of life.

b. Living in obedience, in poverty and in chastity, that is, observing in a special way the precepts and counsels of Our Lord Jesus Christ, according to the Church's interpretation for religious. We are not speaking only of the evangelical counsels, that is the vows, but of all the teachings, directives, and even internal and external attitudes which the Lord wants from His closest followers: those who make this following of Christ the declared intention of their life. This is indicated in the words "they are called to make greater efforts," and corresponds to the Church's current teaching,[3] according to which the religious life is the Christian life lived intensely.

## Article 2

This article is the charismatic declaration of the Third Order Regular; thus it indicates the specific nature of this Order. It is living evangelical conversion (penance-*metanoia*) as St. Francis taught us; a continuous conversion to God, lived in a spirit of prayer (including the contemplative life), Gospel poverty and humility. Thus the article establishes a relational order among the four elements or fundamental values which permeate this Rule.

In the second part of the article three dynamic aspects of living in penance are given; at the same time they are both practices and motivating principles for further activity:

a. Knowing the Lord. This is eternal life: that they know you, the only true God, and Jesus Christ, whom you have sent (Jn 17:3);

b. Adoring the Lord. This is the effect of knowing him and, in its turn, it is the principal dynamic for those who follow it, that is, through

c. Serving the Lord. This means living for him, giving him glory, spreading his Kingdom, but also bringing all this about through service, the love of one's brothers and sisters. Indeed, whoever does not love the brother or sister he sees, cannot love the God whom he does not see (I Jn 4:20).

It should be noted that the Gospel words mentioned in this article, "Come, blessed of my Father ..." are addressed to those who practice the works of mercy; in fact, the Gospel. The passage continues: "For I was hungry and you gave me food, I was thirsty and you gave me drink, a stranger and you welcomed me, naked and you clothed me, ill and you cared for me, in prison and you visited me" (Mt 25:36-36). The active works of charity are, together with continuous conversion, the main characteristics of this Order.

*Attitudes:*
a. A living faith;

b. Continuous conversion;

c. Avoiding evil and, most of all, doing good.

---

[3]*Perfectae Caritatis*, 1.

## Article 3

The article emphasizes two realities:

 a. We belong to the Catholic Church. This is no small matter, and we cannot forget following Francis's example which involves:
 1. Total adherence to Catholic doctrine, expressed in the phrase obedience and reverence to the Pope and the holy Catholic Church;
 2. Therefore, fidelity to the Church.
 b. We belong to the extended Franciscan family. This demands:
 1. Fidelity to one's own congregation;
 2. A sense of belonging, unity and communion, with the members of the other Franciscan families.

*Attitudes:*

 a. Concerning the Church:
 1. Obedience and reverence to the Pope;
 2. Obedience and reverence to the other members of the hierarchy, therefore, to one's bishop;
 b. Concerning the Franciscan Family:
 1. Obedience and reverence to the superiors of one's own congregation;
 2. Spirit of Union, fraternity and particularly good relations with the other Franciscan families and their members.

## Chapter Two: Acceptance into this life

The second chapter describes the various stages of formation and emphasizes the corresponding Gospel attitudes required in both the candidate and the community which accepts them in regard to this formation, both initial and ongoing.

Beginning with this chapter, the four values which the C.F.I. and the responses of the congregations indicated were essential in this Rule (poverty, minority, penance-conversion and contemplation) begin to emerge as the plot which runs through the whole document.

## Article 4

Those who through the Lord's inspiration come to us desiring to accept this way of life are to be received kindly. At the appropriate time they are to be presented to the ministers of the fraternity who hold responsibility to admit them.

*Contents:*
Who is the candidate?

a. One who is moved and inspired by the Lord;

b. One who desires this kind of life;

c. One who has been presented to the minister who has the authority of admitting him or her. Nothing is specified here because the details on this point will be indicated in the constitutions and specific statues of each congregation. The first two points, however, emphasize the essential requirements of every vocation.

*Attitudes:*

a. Openness, response, acceptance of the divine inspiration;

b. Examination of one's will and capacity to respond adequately to the inspiration for this particular type of life.

This article also emphasizes that formation is a dialogical process in which both the candidate and the community have their own responsibilities.

### Article 5
*Contents:*

a. The responsibility of the minister (the superior entrusted with that task) to examine the candidate and determine his or her adherence to the Catholic faith and the Church's sacramental life;

b. Initiation into the life of the fraternity which, for Francis, is first of all accepting the entire Gospel, which is the text book for all Franciscans, and especially the phrases he cites.

*Attitudes:*

a. Discernment of the candidate on the part of the community/fraternity through the action of the minister;

b. A sense of responsibility in communicating and helping the candidate understand the Gospel and the Gospel sense of a vocation to the Franciscan life.

The biblical citations included are fundamental for Francis. Therefore, they are included in their entirety, as Francis did in the *Regula non bullata*.

## ARTICLE 6

*Contents:*

The beginning of religious life in this Order. Its characteristics are:

a. It will be a life of conversion to God;

b. Conversion is an interior movement; however, there should be a corresponding external sign which tells others that the person is dedicated and consecrated to that type of life.

*Attitudes:*

a. The desire to dedicate oneself to a life of conversion and consecration to God according to the Gospel;

b. The desire to manifest this dedication externally as well.

The expression "conversion to God" is the kernel of the entire penitential spirituality which should and must be treated in the particular instructional documents. It should also be noted that penance-conversion (Gospel *metanoia*) is presented in this Rule as the basic characteristic of this Order.

## ARTICLE 7

This article refers to perpetual profession. The second part concerns the attitudes necessary for living what has been professed.

*Contents:*

a. Profess (be received into obedience) to live this form of religious life forever;

b. This essentially consists in serving, loving, honoring and adoring the Lord totally and exclusively (with singleheartedness and purity of intention), with no other attachment or worry.

*Attitude:*

Be disposed to:

a. Promise to live this type of life forever;

b. To the exclusion of all other concerns.

## ARTICLE 8

*Content:*

It is ongoing formation which will be:

a. Conversion to God. The phrasing of this article is nothing other than an accurate, although different, definition of continuous conversion;

b. Conversion to one's neighbor, that is, in growing in love of God, love of neighbor will be manifested, as the Lord commanded.

*Attitudes:*

a. Dedication to a contemplative life;

b. Dedication to a life of external, active charity.

The terminology of this article insists once again, as the preceding one, but with different expressions (with undivided hearts, they may increase in universal love) on the exclusive dedication to the love of God and love of neighbor which is a result of loving God.

## Chapter Three: The spirit of prayer

Proceeding logically from article 8, the Rule calls our attention to the life of prayer, which will be the main way of tending continually to God, i.e. conversion.

This chapter is a brief summary of what prayer is in the Franciscan tradition. For Francis prayer is Trinitarian and Christocentric: it is characterized by the contemplative qualities of praise and thanksgiving. We continually praise God for what he is and for what He had done and does in creation and in the re-creation in Christ. We become part of God's life through his greatest work, the Incarnation, in which God became one with us through the power of the Holy Spirit. Francis's Christocentricity, and ours, is based on faith and on our life of prayer.

The articles of the chapter emphasize the various aspects and diverse forms of Franciscan prayer.

## Article 9
*Content:*
Adoration

Prayer is a way of life for every Franciscan: everywhere and in each place. We should therefore be so filled with God that praising him with joy (with all that they are) should be a necessity of our life. We should want nothing else (and not lose heart), because the Father wants to be united with us. This is the holiness to which we are called. Everyone of our days should be sanctified in this way.

For Francis, the sanctification of the day found a clear expression in the divine office which was recited at various hours. This is also the Church's intention in the concept of the Liturgy of the Hours. We pray to the Father, together with the Son, in His mystical Body which celebrates God's gift, salvation, throughout the whole day. Today the Liturgy of the Hours, as the Church teaches, is also an intercessory prayer for the Church and the world. For Francis the recitation of the Hours is also a sign of fidelity to the Church.

The second part of the article was added specifically for those communities of the contemplative life which follow the Third Order Regular Rule and therefore live continuous conversion to God in the most excellent and exclusive form. Since these consecrated persons are a vital part of the Order, the rest of the congregations want to participate in their renewed joy in continuously celebrating the Father's love for the world.

## ARTICLE 10
*Contents:*

a. Prayer of praise;

b. Spirit of thanksgiving.

Praise and thanksgiving are the main attitudes in the field of prayer, and they are also characteristically Franciscan. Therefore, we must be particularly attentive that our prayer, both individual and common, should maintain this characteristic.

We must be more and more convinced that the main purpose of prayer is to draw us closer, to unite us to God. When this happens, God himself will see to it that we receive those graces and favors which in His love He knows are convenient or useful to us on our journey to Him.

This article reminds us that, having been created in God's image and likeness, if we allow that image and likeness to work naturally, or better supernaturally, in us, it will be easy, (or natural) to seek and find union with God.

We should also note that we are invited to praise God with all His creatures to recall the sense of brotherhood with all of creation which Francis expressed so nobly and poetically in his *Canticle of the Creatures*.

## ARTICLE 11
*Contents:*

a. Meditation on the Word of God, especially the Gospel;

b. Putting the Word of God into practice.

*Attitude:*
Conformity to Christ, after the example of St. Francis.

Here Francis's attitudes in front of the Word of God are emphasized; this would require a lengthy explanation. There are, however, two essential points:

1. Francis considered the Word of God which he read or heard as addressed to him. After hearing or reading it, he acted *in conformity* with it, because it was in that Word he saw the message which the Lord sent him for that particular moment. We need only recall some of his basic decisions which were made precisely after hearing the Word: the Gospel opened three times in the church of St. Nicholas (now the crypt underneath the Post Office in Assisi), and listening to the passage on the mission of the apostles in Santa Maria degli Angeli.[4]

2. For him the word of Scripture is spirit and life. Francis repeats this expression several times. It is enough to recall the conclusion of the *Letter to the Faithful*, in both the first and second versions about the fragrant words of Our Lord: they should accept them with kindness and a divine love and since they are spirit and life, they should preserve them together with their holy manner of working even to the end.[5]

## Article 12
*Contents:*

a. Participation in the Lord's sacrifice;

b. Reception of the Eucharist;

c. Respect for the Eucharist and everything concerning it;

d. Eucharistic adoration.

*Attitudes:*

a. Conviction that in the Eucharist we are brought to peace and are reconciled; therefore, convinced of its necessity;

b. Humility and reverence, especially in receiving it;

c. Practical respect, also in externals, for the Eucharist, that is, the proper care for everything concerning it (sacred vessels, linens, altars, etc.).

Historically, these are Francis's attitudes.

---

[4]LMj III:1-3; FA:ED II, 542-44.
[5]1LtF 2:19-21; FA:ED I, 44.

We should note that today, in humility and reverence we must also include the renewed understanding of the community dimension of the Eucharist given us by Vatican II.

In the words "they are to show the greatest possible reverence and honor for the most holy Body and Blood of our Lord Jesus Christ" we must expressly include also Eucharistic adoration, perpetual or periodic, concerning which many of our congregations have particular traditions, traditions which the new Rule is not intended to suppress.

It should also be recalled that, after the Fourth Lateran Council in 1215, Francis and his friars were among the principal promoters of the new Eucharistic devotion and theology.

## ARTICLE 13
*Contents:*

a. Interior penance for sins;

b. Recourse to the Sacrament of Reconciliation;

c. Fasting as a fruit of penance;

d. Accepting the cross.

*Attitudes:*

These are the attitudes which, in Franciscan spirituality, should accompany the important elements contained in this article:

a. First of all, we should insist on the *internalization* of the conversion, which means contrition for our failings;

b. Repentance is both interior and external. Ordinarily the Church demands recourse to the Sacrament of Reconciliation for the full remission of sins. We must accept this, and have recourse to it, in a spirit of humility.

c. Fasting here indicates and includes the external mortifications which should be understood in a Franciscan sense: they have value if they are the means and aid for interior conversion, for tending towards God. Truly seeking to be humble and simple is always preeminent.

d. The second part of the article invites us to contemplate the paschal mystery. Through Christ who offered Himself to the Father as a sacrifice and victim, we have access to God despite our sinfulness. The highest point of Franciscan contemplation is our transformation into Him who, out of an excess of charity, wanted to be crucified.[6]

---

[6] LMj 13:3; FA:ED II, 632.

## CHAPTER FOUR: THE LIFE IN CHASTITY FOR THE SAKE OF THE KINGDOM

The international organizations charged with the composition of this Rule, especially the Work Group that met in Brussels, were convinced, at least the majority of them, that it was not necessary to present a specific chapter on chastity. According to them, Francis's thought on it already influenced the entire text and was particularly evident in articles 7, 8 and 26, especially expressed in the concept to serve, love, adore the Lord God with singleheartedness and purity of intention, pervaded by the exclusive disposition by which one dedicates his or her own self to the love and service of God. Following a discussion of alternative proposals, the General Assembly in Rome (1982) accepted this point of view.

The Congregation for Religious and for Secular Institutes, however, was not of the same opinion; therefore, the B.F.I. later presented this chapter which was then accepted as an integral part of the Rule.

It logically follows the topic of prayer which already emphasizes our union with God. In fact, chastity's goal is to emphasize and perfect that union.

### ARTICLE 14
*Contents:*

    a. Invitation to consider our dignity;

    b. The meaning of our choice.

*Attitudes:*

    a. Sense of gratitude for such a dignity;

    b. The awareness of the motives for our choice.

These words taken from the Admonitions represent Francis's theological intuition which will later be developed in Franciscan Christological doctrine.

The Redeemer's life, example and invitation are at the base of our positive response in favor of this form of life.

### ARTICLE 15
*Contents:*

    a. The significance of chastity for the sake of the Kingdom;

    b. Concern for the things of the Lord;

    c. These motives should be manifested in daily life.

*Attitudes:*

a. Correspondence in the lofty spirit of the contents;

b. Awareness that charity will also be manifested externally through chastity.

The scriptural demands help us to understand the deepest meaning of the Gospel phrase "for the sake of the Kingdom." It informs us that this is not a *final* expression, but a *causal* one; that is, we do not dedicate ourselves to a life of chastity in order to be freer and more available to build the Kingdom of God, but because of its superabundant presence in us. Thus, in each religious Christ's existential experience is repeated; He was so taken by and absorbed with the urgency and presence of the Kingdom that He could not do anything other than dedicate Himself totally to its fulfillment. The presence of God's sovereignty and majesty does not leave room for other loves or concerns.

## ARTICLE 16
*Content:*
We represent that wonderful mystery of the Church, which is the union of Christ with His spouse, the faithful gathered together.

*Attitude:*
We are imbued with his reality.

Here the Rule makes its own the biblical theme of the spiritual union of Christ and the Church, an idea that already is already prefigured in the Old Testament, in the marriage of Yahweh and the people of Israel.

Religious, by their vow of chastity, with which they renounce marriage, reflect this complete dedication to the one Lord which, in its turn, is the reflection of the spiritual marriage which unites the Church with her one and only love, Christ the Lord.

This is not a way for living isolated or separated, or apathetic about society, but a way which is generous and munificent and, there should be no need to mention it, based exclusively on faith.

## ARTICLE 17
*Contents:*

a. The Blessed Virgin is the ideal example;

b. In imitation of St. Francis.

*Attitudes:*
a. Venerate Mary, Lady and Queen, virgin made church;

b. Imitate her, especially in her self-definition as the handmaid of the Lord.

It should be the concern of every Franciscan to deepen his or her knowledge of the particularities of Francis's devotion to Our Lady in his upbringing in the Christian culture and in special love for St. Mary of the Angels. The example of such a father is theological reason for our devotion to Mary.

### CHAPTER FIVE: THE WAY TO SERVE AND WORK

A Franciscan spiritual document, such as this, must be faithful to Francis's evangelical project, clearly specifying the attitudes which we must adopt concerning the two realities of *being in the world* and *being identified with the People of God*. Our reception into the community (by our profession) admits us into a form of life which, different than monasticism, is at the same time immersed in the world (since the greater majority of our congregations are *active*), and yet contrary to the world's values (because we are *religious*). Therefore, it is very important to understand the special context for Francis's directives concerning the use of time, service of our neighbor and work. For Francis, conversion means a two-fold self-giving: giving one's self to God, and giving of one's self to our neighbor (Art. 8). Like Christ in the Gospel and like Francis in his society after his conversion, we do not identify with the *maiores*, that is, with the rich and powerful who are served, but rather with the *minores*, that is, with the lowly people of every category, and with those who serve. We are *the servants of salvation* through our witness and ministry.

### ARTICLE 18
*Contents:*

a. Obligation to work, because like Christ, we are poor;

b. Work should not be an impediment to the life of the spirit.

*Attitudes:*

a. Fidelity and devotion in this obligation;

b. Take the time we should dedicate to God.

We must really consider the section which says that, having avoided idleness, they should not be so busy that the spirit of prayer and devotion is extinguished. Work lies between idleness and prayer, and we must avoid either extreme. The article is expressed in such a way as to indicate that there must also be time for non-work, in the strict sense of the word, time for legitimate recreation; and time for prayer, contemplation, the perfection of the spirit. Conscious of the spirit of activism which even affects religious communities, the article is meant to recall the Franciscan vision of balance between prayer and action: action permeated by prayer and prayer enriched by action constitute but one movement and moment.

ARTICLE **19**
*Contents:*

a. The legitimacy of the just recompense for work, to be used for life's necessities and the works of the congregation;

b. The obligation of giving the excess to the poor.

*Attitudes:*

a. Even in this legitimacy, it is necessary to recall humility and poverty;

b. To feel like servants and subjects; humility and joy.

Perhaps it would be useful to mention the aspects and qualities which can make work good and meritorious (positive aspects) and those which make it harmful or less advantageous (negative aspects), which can be found in the writings of St. Francis. It is clear that we must choose and make the former grow in us and avoid the latter.

*Positive Aspects*

1. Work seen as a way of identifying with the poor who have to work in order to live;

2. Readiness to do even manual labor;

3. By working we give good example;

4. We work in order to provide for ourselves, for our brothers or sisters who are no longer able to work, and for the works of our ministry;

5. What we have over and above these needs should go to the poor.

*Negative Aspects*

1. Work done to accumulate wealth;

2. Work which impedes our prayer life;

3. Work done only to avoid idleness, but with no other purpose.

Taking into consideration also that by working one can achieve a prestigious position, the article reminds us that our Franciscan understanding of work should be especially that of service; therefore, we should in no way seek to be over others, or to control or manipulate them.

ARTICLE 20
*Attitudes:*

a. Humility, which is concretized in being gentle, peaceful and unassuming; mild and humble, speaking honestly;

b. Avoid arguments, disputes and negative judgments about others;

c. Cultivate Franciscan joy: be joyful, good-humored;

d. Be messengers of peace.

This article spells out the aspects or positive attitudes which must flow from the last exhortation of the preceding article: they should be servants and subjects to every human creature for the Lord's sake. When we enter into relationship with other persons, whatever our motive, we must act with the qualities Christ proclaimed in the Beatitudes which are paraphrased to some extent in this article. Francis admonishes us especially not to judge others, even if they seem to be far from the Gospel norm.

Being messengers of peace has a long tradition in the history of the penitents. The hermits-penitents also used to leave their remote places in order to make peace among cities or factions within a city. This characteristic should be practiced in different ways today, by trying to bring reconciliation to those who are separated from the Church or the sacraments, and becoming involved in ecumenical work. We must announce peace by work and example, and do so joyfully.

CHAPTER SIX: THE LIFE OF POVERTY

The chapter is intended to show the value of evangelical poverty as it was understood, experienced and taught by Francis and the attitudes deriving from it. Strictly speaking, the chapter does not concern the vow of poverty; here, as in other places, the Rule merely intends to present an inspirational and evangelical basis which can serve for further reflection and legislation. However, the legislation should be found in the constitution which, as we have observed several times, is proper to each congregation.

## ARTICLE 21
*Contents:*

    a. The reason for this life in poverty: the example of Christ and Mary;

    b. Some practical norms:

        1. Be content with what is necessary.

        2. Beware of money.

        3. Prefer the poor, the weak, the unwanted.

*Attitudes:*

    a. Total dependence on divine Providence;

    b. Intimately feel a part of the poor.

In his *Testament* and elsewhere, Francis gives us the reason why poverty is so central to his call. He does not give a definition of poverty nor tell us what it implies; he looks at the Christ of the Gospels and says "This is evangelical poverty." Christ is the center of our life. He chose poverty as He chose humility. He emptied himself (*kenosis*) for love of us. For Francis, Christ is our only way to go to the Father, and his was a journey in poverty. This Franciscan poverty also signifies total dependence on Divine Providence. Poverty is safeguarded by our identification with the poor and made concrete by our service among the poor, service which has always been expressed in our tradition as the works of mercy.

Mary is mentioned here by Francis himself, associated with Christ's poverty and humility, and with His salvific action.

The additional phrase about money expresses Francis's thinking about the danger of the destructive power of avarice. Money was not to be touched because of the bad use people made of it, especially in business in the thirteenth century. For us the danger is not in handling money, which is even a common thing among the poor, but in the acquisitive and competitive spirit which it produces.

## ARTICLE 22

*Content:*
How do we live this life? Appropriating nothing.

*Attitudes:*

    a. Live as pilgrims and strangers;

    b. Being co-heirs of the kingdom of heaven with the poor and being concerned to be rich in virtue.

In this article Francis's ideal of poverty is presented without risking the needless difficulties created when poverty is equated with rejection of any form of ownership. Canonical reality today is that as religious in simple vows, we do retain the right to own goods. Our concern, therefore, should be to foster freedom from attachment and proprietary instincts that cause us to live and act like the wealthy. The Gospel call to detachment is radical for Francis, and embraces spiritual and intellectual as well as material goods. In Article 20, for instance, this highest form of poverty is advocated: be non-judgmental. Judgment belongs to God. Christ in His humanity and humility did not judge us, but redeemed us. With that as the criteria, the wedding of evangelical poverty to our own personalities, shown in our attitudes toward persons, circumstances and things can be called nothing less than maximal. God's Providence, in this light, takes on a much deeper significance than mere provision or protection alone. Such is the radical poverty of Christ, the poverty Francis holds out to us.

## CHAPTER SEVEN: FRATERNAL LOVE

On this important element of religious life lived in community, the Rule proposes the fundamental values of the Gospel and, at the same time, a few particular directives. The first article describes the spiritual bases for such fraternal relations and the second indicates some safeguards or remedies when those relations are threatened or have been broken.

### ARTICLE 23

*Content:*
The reason for fraternal love: because the Lord loves us and wants us to love one another.

*Attitudes:*

    a. Conquering love, demonstrated in deeds;

    b. Disinterested love; therefore, love for one's sick brothers or sisters;

    c. Spirit of thanksgiving to the Lord and acceptance of life's various circumstances (sickness, failure, etc.).

Evangelical poverty, freely chosen, places us in a situation of interdependence with one another. Precisely because we are poor, we need one another. This fraternal love, which is translated into attention for others in need, finds its basis in Christ who is the brother of each of us; we love one another as our Brother has loved us and loves us.

Part of our poverty consists in making our needs known to our brother or sister, asking alms of them.

Truly fraternal love is not affected by a person's productivity, nor by the productivity of your brother or sister.

For Francis the test of this openness is precisely how much love one has for the brother or sister who is sick.

## ARTICLE 24

*Contents:*

The necessity of asking and granting pardon in case of faults against charity;

a. The necessity of admonition in case of failings against the Rule;

b. The necessity of avoiding anger or resentment in those cases.

*Attitudes:*

a. Pardon and gentleness;

b. Perseverance in peace.

From these suggestions we see all of Francis's human realism. He understood that not everything in our fraternal living is ideal, that it is not always as it should be. When fraternal relationships are weakened or threatened, we must repair them according to the Gospel norms. Here we see the need for personal and shared responsibility; that is, not only of the superior, but of all the members of the fraternity, for their community life. The minister cannot be the sole agent of reconciliation and pardon.

Given that, in concrete cases, feeling that one is right can endanger poverty of spirit, and therefore, charity, the article does not point out who should take the initiative. It will be the one who has learned more completely the Gospel and Franciscan meaning of charity.

## CHAPTER EIGHT: THE OBEDIENCE OF LOVE

Without a doubt, our theological motive for obedience is Christ. He who is our way to return to God, to tend towards God describes Himself, especially in St. John's Gospel, as obedient to the Father. This attitude, so necessary for genuine conversion, is the exercise of our obedience, in imitation of that of Christ.

Francis makes this theology very concrete: for him the way of Gospel obedience is fraternity and in fraternity. For this very reason this chapter comes immediately after the one on life in fraternity.

In order to highlight the particular meaning that Francis gives to obedience, the title *the obedience of love* has been used; this means obeying out of love. Franciscan obedience finds its motive in John's teaching: God so loved, and the sign of God's love is love for one another in fraternity.

From this we see clearly that on this topic also the Rule, more than just the vow, treats the value of obedience, from which we must derive the proper attitudes.

### Article 25
*Contents:*

a. The reason for obedience: the Father's will following the example of Christ;

b. Nature and purpose of chapters (community gatherings);

c. Appreciating obedience.

*Attitudes:*

a. Seeking the kingdom of God and its justice;

b. Eliminating the spirit of power and dominion;

c. Mutual obedience.

Franciscan obedience is self-emptying or self-stripping: hence its intrinsic relationship with poverty. As Christ did, we seek to conform our will to that of the Father who sent Him and inspires us. Francis wanted this obedience in everyone, in the ministers as well as in the members of the fraternity.

We must be credible signs of salvation at the same time that we must be instruments of reconciliation. This allows and demands our witness and on behalf of his plan for the redemption of humanity.

Fraternal gatherings in chapter are the practical structures which help us renew and reform the witness and this ministry.

The last part of the article emphasizes the poverty of obedience which must be present in the members of the fraternity as well as in the minister. Domination and manipulation represent a desire for possession; in the Franciscan life there is no room for this. It is mutual service which better characterizes Christ's obedience.

## ARTICLE 26
*Contents:*

a. The necessity of the minister;

b. Obedience to the minister.

*Attitude:*
Spirit of obedience, which is not separated from shared responsibility.

## ARTICLE 27
*Contents:*

a. The minister's duties: visit, admonish, exhort;

b. Recourse to the minister in case of difficulty in observing the Rule (not private decisions, but rather with the minister);

c. The minister's appropriate behavior in such circumstances.

*Attitudes:*

a. Confidence on the part of the brothers and sisters;

b. Spirit of charity on the part of the minister.

Articles 26 and 27 should be considered together. They concern the minister of the fraternity who has authority in regard to all that the brothers and sisters have promised the Lord to observe. While the limits of obedience are defined by the Rule and conscience, Franciscan tradition emphasizes the role of the minister who is the center and fulcrum of unity, reconciliation and fidelity. At the same time the minister must not exercise his or her authority in the way that the world's powerful people do. The minister's service should be offered with humility, love and kindness. The servant-like spirit of the minister should be evident to all, and especially to those who seek in him or her help in being faithful to what they have promised.

N.B. The Latin *spiritualiter observare* in No. 27 has been translated as *observe according to its spirit* (the spirit of the Rule), and not literally as "spiritually observe."

**ARTICLE 28**
*Content:*
Ministries and services

*Attitude:*
Not appropriating ministries and services

The relationship which should exist between poverty and obedience is translated here in a concrete admonition for everyone. Precisely because we are poor, no one should appropriate an office, ministry, responsibility, or service. No one is indispensable. We must not allow the subtle and corrosive effects of power to creep into the Franciscan spirit.

**CHAPTER NINE: APOSTOLIC LIFE**

This topic is considered in the last chapter because it logically concludes the succession of elements of the Evangelical project of Francis which form the outline of this Rule: the vocation to evangelical conversion; initiation to this life, prayer, mutual service and life in fraternity. Like Francis, we must help others know the Father's universal love, and there you have our ministry and apostolate. We must, however, also emphasize some particularities of our Order in this field, those which concern the union of contemplation and action, and our tradition of being messengers of peace and people dedicated to the works of mercy, which is the second basic aspect of our life of continuous conversion.

**ARTICLE 29**
*Contents:*

　　a. Love of God, love of neighbor;

　　b. In the Order, the coexistence of the contemplative and active life

*Attitudes:*

　　a. Be pervaded by the love of God and neighbor;

　　b. It is the Lord who sends us to give witness to his love by word and work.

The intimate relationship between conversion and apostolic activity is the cornerstone of our Franciscan Spirituality. Our turning to our neighbor presupposes our turning to God, and is a reflection of it. Francis characterizes the activity of his apostolate as an extension of prayer, and most of all as a practical sign of the love of God and neighbor which he recalls on the highest level in his directives to the Penitents.[7]

We are called to bear witness in the world to God's redemptive power and presence first with our lives and then with our activities. The evangelical life and the proclamation of the Gospel must be almost like the same thing. Thus in our Order we see the fusion of the active and contemplative life which is emphasized in Article 9.

## Article 30
*Contents:*

   a. Messengers of peace;

   b. Life of active charity;

   c. Another emphasis on chastity;

   d. Ready to give witness.

*Attitudes:*

   a. Grow in the spirit of peace that is, in meekness, goodness, harmony;

   b. Love of neighbor in active charity, that is in the forms traditional to the congregation; the possibility of new forms;

   c. Always be ready to give witness.

The diverse charitable and apostolic activities of our congregations today can all be summed up in the phrase "to announce peace." While, in fact, it was our tradition to describe our ministry in terms of the corporal works of mercy or active charity, this new vision is in conformity with the new call of the Church, to see the results of every service in justice and peace terms. (We need only recall the words of Pope Paul VI: "If you want peace, work for justice.") This vision is applied just as well to the prayer life of the contemplative communities as to the activity of the apostolic ones. As has already been mentioned (cf. article 20, above), being messengers of peace can assume new forms today.

As for all that regards our apostolic charitable activity, that is our works of active charity, we can generally affirm, in every congregation, a high degree of fidelity to the original or traditional forms. It is necessary to emphasize and to open our hearts to this view that, while this fidelity is a good thing, it is not essential for remaining faithful to the spirit of charity which influenced our founders or foundresses. Whatever new local

---

[7]1LtF 1; FA:ED I, 41-42.

or environmental circumstances show is necessary or fitting, it is more than licit to begin forms which are more in conformity with the needs of contemporary society, with the expression of our Christian love and in the Franciscan tradition.

(We should note that the phrase from the *Legend of the Three Companions* "... the brothers and sisters have been called to heal the wounded, etc.," was the only intentional exception to the decision to use only the writings of St. Francis in drafting this Rule, because it embraces and magnificently describes all of the categories of the works of mercy to which, by our common tradition, the various parts of this Order have dedicated themselves.)

Our prayer and our ministry are based on that of Christ, whose poverty and obedience led Him to give Himself completely, even unto death on the cross. Likewise we, working in various fields to announce peace, must be ready to face every kind of enemy, for love of the Kingdom of God.

### ARTICLE 31
*Contents:*

a. Constant humility;

b. Gratitude to God.

*Attitudes:*

a. Preserve humility in all things (talents and work);

b. Acknowledge that the Lord alone is the source of all good, and thank Him for it.

Our service and ministry must be rooted in humility, which is accompanied by feelings of gratitude to God and dependence on His pleasure. In the depths of our poverty we know that we are useless servants; therefore we should be grateful for the good words and works that God says and does through us at times, and we should proclaim that all the glory belongs to Him, from Whom all good things come.

### EXHORTATION AND BLESSING

### ARTICLE 32
*Contents:*

a. Preserve the spirit of the Lord;

b. Work according to what you have promised.

*Attitude:*
Continually remember and live the main virtues of our
evangelical conversion

This concluding article is a very brief synthesis of the essentials of this Rule. We could say that these last words echo the first, as they also echo Francis's final exhortation to his sons: "Brothers, let us begin!"

The Franciscan charism was not sealed shut with the death of Francis: it has a continuity, that is, it has the power to stimulate words and works in us as we continue to live in the words and works of our Father.

If we are faithful to this charism, we shall be blessed.

The blessing, taken from the Testament, closes this text, as it closed the Rule of 1927, and therefore represents a further link of continuity between this Rule and those that preceded it in the long story of the Third Order Regular of St. Francis.

*Pax et Bonum!*

# Jean François Godet

## Rule and Life of the Brothers and Sisters of the Third Order Regular of St. Francis: Presentation and Commentary

## *Analecta TOR,* XVIII:139 (1985): 11-21.

### Presentation

### I. Nature of the Text

Francis of Assisi was a true and passionate disciple of Jesus Christ. All his life he wanted to walk following his Lord. Few Christians have been so open and attentive to the presence of Jesus Christ in their lives. Radical faithfulness to the Gospel was for Francis a continuous experience. This is the very essence of the Franciscan charism.

The Second Vatican Council within the great movement of evangelical renaissance which it proposed to the Church of Christ, asked religious to return to the inspiration of their founders. Those who want to live in the manner of Francis of Assisi heard the appeal and returned to the Little Poor Man and to the evangelical form of life that was his.

Many congregations of the Third Order Regular, looking at the Rule of 1927, discovered that this Rule was confined by the language and mentality of the time when it was drafted. It no longer seemed capable of defining our identity or our common values in an inspirational manner. It was not in accord with the Church's new directives and it did not propose our evangelical life in a biblical manner nor in a style that clearly reflects the spirit of our founder. It was not, therefore, surprising, that many soon thought about a renewal of our Rule as well as a renewal of our evangelical form of life.

This new awareness gave birth to a profound research about the inspiration of Francis of Assisi and the common elaboration of a new text. This new text would be faithful to this inspiration of Francis and, at the same time, to the historical expression of this inspiration in the Congregations of the Third Order Regular which today exist all over the world. The text of the renewed Rule was accepted by a vote of the superiors general, both masculine and feminine, convened at the International Franciscan Assembly at Rome, March 1-10, 1982. His Holiness, Pope John Paul II confirmed it by the Brief, *Franciscan vitae propositum.*

Francis wished that those who would live like him be authentic evangelical men and women. What springs from man's heart does make him what he is, says the Lord (Mt 15:10-20). Inspired by the Lord, Francis proposes to us who want to live like him, fundamental evangelical values and attitudes so that we may be true disciples of Jesus Christ and radically follow in his footsteps. After we have really assimilated and made these fundamental values and attitudes ours, we will live the Gospel in a Franciscan way. The intention of the Rule is unique: to express Francis's vision of our form of life. This is a life of total and continuous conversion to God and neighbor through the fundamental values and attitudes which Francis considers necessary for radical evangelical life. We are invited to grasp these values, to test their dynamism and to really be, within the pale of the Church, men and women who live the Gospel of our Lord Jesus Christ.

Wishing to express the form of evangelical life translated into action by Francis, the new text of the Rule aims, therefore, in its most profound sense, to be an inspirational text. In no way does it intend to give regulations or laws. For that purpose each congregation has its own constitution that must take into account the particular charism of the respective founders, canon law, cultural circumstances, particular customs and the Rule itself. By reference to the Rule, the constitutions apply the values, attitudes and principles embodied in it to a particular congregation.

There is not a sole and unique way to live the Gospel. The multiplicity of religious families within the Church proves this. Francis, inspired himself by the Lord and influenced by the circumstances of his time, has given birth to three orders, all of them showing the same fundamental charism. The three orders are characterized by the special stress put on the values that Francis proposes in order to live the Gospel radically and by the styles of evangelical life derived from them. Nevertheless, we are only one family sprung from the same brother.

The Third Order Regular is comprised of more than four hundred congregations. Some are apostolic; others are devoted to contemplation; still others are both apostolic and contemplative. The majority are feminine, but a certain number are masculine. All of these congregations share one unique Rule, and each has its own character. Often located in particular cultures and reflective of them, they are nevertheless one Order because they have common Franciscan values presented in a unique Rule.

In order to propose Francis's form of evangelical life with more exactitude to all in the Third Order Regular, the Rule utilizes his own writings. To utilize Francis's own words means to utilize the Spirit's words which inspired him to express his gifts. Francis's words seize again his experience of the evangelical values and attitudes that the Lord gave him to live. In this sense Francis's words have a very special importance for us. Furthermore, the text is not linked to the language of a given epoch but remains a source of reflection for our whole life and for this text, we must know the sources and Franciscan history. Just as we need to study Holy Scripture constantly, we must constantly study our Rule. That will help us to profit more from our heritage. For the first time in its history, the Rule of the Third Order Regular has been written with Francis's own words. For this reason; this text cannot be simply a document, but it must be an inspiration to live, to share and to pass on.

## II. FOUR FUNDAMENTAL VALUES

The study of Francis's writings and of the history of the Third Order Regular allow us to say that four values can be considered fundamental for the Franciscan Life in our Order. They are conversion, contemplation, poverty and minority. These values are the content of our Rule; they make of it the spiritual document that it is. They represent a common treasure, the basis our unity.

These fundamental values are far from being independent from one another. On the contrary, they support and penetrate each other in order to inspire all the concrete attitudes of our Franciscan evangelical life. They are not exclusive either. Simplicity, joy, charity, mercy, justice all are embraced by our fundamental values. What about fraternity? We do not call it a fundamental value because it is the value present everywhere upon which the whole Franciscan building is constructed.

## III. FRANCIS'S EVANGELICAL PROJECT

Inspired by God, Francis conceived with his brothers a project of evangelical life, which he put into writing. From his Rule – in the wording of 1221 as well as the definitive text of 1223 – and also from his Testament, it stands out that the great lines of his evangelical project were quite simple. Identity of this life, entry and formation, prayer, work and service, life in poverty, fraternal life in obedience, testimony and mission: this is the general plan followed by Francis and reproduced in our Rule.

## COMMENTARY

### PROLOGUE: WORDS DIRECTED BY FRANCIS TO HIS DISCIPLES

The prologue of the Rule is integrally the first part of Francis's letter to the brothers and sisters of Penitence, the words of the first *Letter to the Faithful*. As such, this text reminds us that the Third Order of St. Francis, secular as well as regular, has its first origin in the Order of Penitence. That is why we find it also as the prologue to the Rule of the Secular Franciscan Order. Through the centuries many founders and foundresses of congregations of the Third Order Regular were secular Franciscans before establishing their congregations. The insistence on conversion in our way of living the Gospel is a central point shared by the brothers and sisters of the Secular Franciscan Order as well as those of the Third Order Regular.

## CHAPTER ONE: IN THE NAME OF THE LORD! THIS IS THE RULE AND LIFE OF THE BROTHERS AND SISTERS OF THE THIRD ORDER REGULAR OF ST. FRANCIS.

The title of the first chapter, beginning with the words of Francis's traditional usage, "In the name of the Lord" (a phrase often found in his writings) says clearly that the text which follows is a spiritual document indicating values, attitudes and principles necessary to a certain life-style.

Article 1 reminds us of this at the outset by making use of the words "form of life." This first chapter summarizes the entire Rule and defines specifically what we are in the Church. This article says that we are religious of the Third Order Regular of Saint Francis who seek to live according to the Gospel as brothers and sisters. The word "order" is to be understood in its ancient meaning. It indicates a group of persons that is well defined and situated within a greater ensemble. Each Order has its own internal structure. The Third Order Regular is composed of juridically independent congregations, sharing the same kind of evangelical life. Our Order is designated as "regular" because we lead a religious life in community, profess a rule (*regula*) and take the three canonical vows. It is named "third" because it is the third order founded by Saint Francis, following the Friars Minor and the Poor Clares.

Article 2 emphasizes that penance, understood in its true and profound sense of conversion, is in the center of the spirituality of our Order. Converting ourselves to God and conforming ourselves to the Christ of the Gospel are never acts complete once and for all, but permanent religious experiences. Doing penance or converting ourselves, according to the expression of Francis himself, means three things. We recognize (acknowledge) the Lord in the creation, in the Scriptures, in all things, but especially in the words, the life, the action and teachings of our Lord Jesus Christ. We worship (adore) the Lord in the totality of our lives, living in prayer, minority, poverty, purity of heart and loving obedience following the example of Jesus Christ. We serve the Lord in our neighbor by practicing the commandment of love and engaging ourselves on behalf of justice and peace.

Article 3 begins by a restatement of the second article's opening: As Franciscan brothers and sisters we situate ourselves in the bosom of the Church which guards and transmits the revealed Truth. Our fidelity will express itself by our obedience and deference towards authority of the Church, to the pope and bishops who are in charge of guiding the people of God. And since our Order is, like the Church, in need of structures and guides, we will have the same attitude towards our ministers. More-over, we are invited to a genuine fraternity, not only in the universal and local Church, in our congregations and fraternities, but also with all those men and women who share with us the spiritual heritage of Francis of Assisi. The quality of our brotherly love will be the testimony of the authenticity of our evangelical life.

CHAPTER TWO: ACCEPTANCE INTO THIS LIFE

It is clear that this chapter treats of formation, but a close look at the text reveals that the processes of formation are those of continuing conversion, which must be present all through our lives. We are never finished with the task of ongoing conversion and conversion to the Gospel leads us to poverty, to humble service and the spirit of prayer.

Article 4 and 5 reflect simultaneously Francis's initial experience of conversion and his instructions concerning formation. For Francis it is essential that the person who comes to share our life take this step under the "inspiration of the Lord". The members of the fraternity shall receive the person with kindness and shall help the candidate to discern the source of decision. Is this a call from God? The fraternity, in the person of the ministers, has obligations to itself and to the candidates. The minister must make sure that the candidate is really catholic and authentically faithful to the Church. If such is the case in actions as well as in words, the candidate is initiated into the life of the fraternity, a fraternity which is always itself in formation. The Gospel is explained carefully, especially those radical demands Jesus makes of those who want to follow him: distribution of their possessions among the poor and self-renunciation.

Article 6 appeals to all the members of the fraternity. Our life of conversion is a perpetual beginning; the engagement is dynamic and permanent. This will be manifest in our manner of dressing and our way of life. All of this will be simple and without affectation, thus signifying that it is God whom we seek.

Article 7 relates to perpetual profession and the attitudes Francis declares necessary when one has begun a life of penance. The expression "being received into obedience" signifies that one pledges oneself to live the bond of fraternal relations with others who are also pledged to total conversion and observance of the holy Gospel.

Article 8 develops the conclusion of the preceding article and concretizes it. We must become the house of God. The object of our life is nothing less than union with Christ through the Spirit. This presence of God in us, purifying and unifying our heart, will itself work continuously through love for our neighbor. Putting charity and mercy to work has always been an important characteristic of the history of our congregations and our fraternities. In the Franciscan tradition turning to God always includes turning to our neighbor.

## CHAPTER THREE: THE SPIRIT OF PRAYER

If our life is turned towards God in the imitation of Jesus Christ, then it is evident that prayer is a fundamental value constitutive of our form of life. It is necessary to pray without intermission says the Lord. Prayer is more than a measure of time, more than gestures and words. It is the real respiration of the children of God whether they are standing or lying down, working or reposing. This is exactly how Francis understood it.

Article 9 says in Francis's words that we must constantly – at all times and everywhere – guard our hearts in God and adore him. It is in this same spirit that the brothers and sisters shall celebrate the liturgy of the hours, the praise in the rhythm of time, in union with the whole Church. And the brothers and sisters, pledged to a contemplative life shall, by their joyful existence manifest that God loves us and saves us constantly.

Our prayer is above all a praise of God "with all the creatures." Francis well understood how much they tell us about the Creator, ourselves being the summit of creation made as we are in God's image and the Son's likeness. Article 10 reminds us of this invitation to praise and thanksgiving.

As Francis's life demonstrates, full conformity to the Gospel is only possible through the mediation on the Word of our Lord Jesus Christ in the Holy Scriptures and all the events by which the Holy Spirit speaks to us today. We must not only meditate; we must observe and incarnate. That is the tenor of Article 11.

Article 12 speaks of the Eucharist. The Eucharist is the gesture Jesus left to his disciples as a memorial of him. This is why the brothers and sisters receive the Body and the Blood of the Savior. It is thus that they will receive his life and partake of his sacrifice. If Jesus has given his life for universal peace and reconciliation, our participation in his sacrifice engages us to give our life for our brothers and sisters in our turn.

Life conversion, reconciliation also has to be constantly renewed because of our imperfections. The brothers and sisters, Article 13 tells us, shall celebrate reconciliation through the sacrament of Penance and yield fruits worthy of penance, simplicity and humility. Because it is the Lord who saves, it is He whom we must desire, his footsteps we must follow.

CHAPTER FOUR: THE LIFE OF CHASTITY FOR THE SAKE OF THE KINGDOM

Created in the image and likeness of Christ, the brothers and sisters wish to live following his example (Article 14).

We also want to answer his appeal by professing chastity in celibacy for the Kingdom of Heaven manifesting in everything the love that animates us (Article 15) and the mysterious union of Christ and his Church (Article 16). We should always remind ourselves of the example of the most perfect "handmaid of the Lord" holy Mary, Mother of the Lord, the Virgin who became the Church (Article 17).

CHAPTER FIVE: THE WAY TO SERVE AND WORK

After giving up everything in order to be poor and follow Christ who lived as a poor man, the brothers and sisters must work for their sustenance so as not to burden others. That was Francis's experience. As he repeats in his Testament before his death, work was an important reality for him throughout his life. But Francis had acquired an evangelical vision of work. He did nothing without taking into consideration the thing that was to be done and the way in which to do it. In his following of Christ he had discovered the whole, the true dimension of that human reality which is work. If for the brothers and sisters, work is a consequence of their choice to live as poor people, it is also a grace of the Lord. For that reason they must work with fidelity and devotion. As a man of concrete practicality Francis reminds us also that work as an activity can also be a service. It can be an unpaid activity for persons who cannot pay or from whom we do not want remuneration. It can also mean work compensated by wages. For Francis, service and work require the same mentality and the same commitment. It is true that service and work allow us to be rid of destructive idleness; it is not good for a human being to be without productive activity. Service and work, however, must nourish and develop the "spirit of holy prayer and devotion" treated of in Chapter Three. Service and work are also occasions of adoration, praise of God while they are equally opportunities to make fruitful the gifts we have received from the Lord. This is the whole intent of Article 18.

By their work the brothers and sisters provide their livelihood. However, they will be content with the "necessary," without seeking to capitalize, to increase wealth. The condition for entering the fraternity – distribution of one's goods to the poor – continues as an obligation throughout life. To follow Christ we must repeat the same gesture each time material goods recur as an obstruction in our path. Furthermore, while poor in earthly goods, the brothers and sisters shall also be poor in power. They refuse domination and choose, for God's sake, to be submissive to everybody, to be servants and minors, smaller than all others (Article 19).

Work brings the brothers and sisters into relation with people. It is the simple and daily reality by which they are sent into the world among people. As servants and minors, the brothers and sisters will be a leaven of fraternity by their meekness and amiability, their refusal to judge and their joyfulness. Everywhere they shall be bearers and artisans of peace (Article 20).

## CHAPTER SIX: THE LIFE OF POVERTY

For Francis the choice of living in poverty does not originate in abstract reflection, be it religious or social. For him poverty is a Lady whom he chooses for his companion. This same Lady was chosen as companion by the Lord. For this reason the brothers and sisters choose a humble and poor life after the example of Jesus and Mary, his mother. This choice has three concrete expressions: being content with what is necessary; strongly distrusting money as a vehicle of false values and injustice and division among peoples; living joyfully among the poor of this world (Article 21).

Article 22 shows that poverty expresses the choice of the brothers and sisters to depend wholly upon God as the only necessary good. At the same time, poverty chosen and lived in imitation of Jesus Christ allows them the liberty of establishing new human relations. By refusing to enter into rivalry for power and possessions, by living as "pilgrims and strangers," the brothers and sisters offer communion and solidarity to all and, as Francis says, an occasion for practicing goodness.

## CHAPTER SEVEN: FRATERNAL LOVE

Fraternal life is for Francis the weft over which the entire life in the imitation of Christ is woven. It marks all the elements of his evangelical project beginning even with our "names": brothers, sisters. This chapter accentuates this quality of fraternal relation inside and outside of our congregations.

Brotherly and sisterly love has its roots in Jesus Christ who made himself our brother and asks us to love one another as he has loved us. Our familial love will be the love of action. The radical poverty of the brothers and sisters will embody this incarnated love, challenging them to interdependence and mutual service. Our neighbor's necessity is the occasion of service and love. This love is gratuitous corresponding to the image of God's love. This will be seen to the especially true in the case of illness. Whatever may happen, nothing must impede the brothers and sisters from rendering thanks to God and trying to correspond with his will (Article 23).

As Article 23 describes the contents of a life among brothers, among sisters, so Article 24 speaks of the obstacles and shortcomings of this life. Following the example of God's merciful attitude towards us, the shortcomings of our shared life can be transformed into a superabundance of mutuality. If the situation is one of personal offense, our attitude should be one of reciprocal forgiveness, a willingness to cancel our account of the wrongs inflicted. If the situation is that of shortcomings in our form of life, we should not resort to humiliation and reproach. Admonition should be offered with pardon and mercy and all offer to rebuild the broken way together. The brothers and sisters will always be on guard against getting angry or troubled for that impedes charity.

## CHAPTER EIGHT: THE OBEDIENCE OF LOVE

Francis chose to live in obedience because of Jesus Christ. It is the life of Christ that provides the content of this obedience. In his love of the Father, Jesus united his own will with that of the Father. That is why the brothers and sisters, living in the same love, have renounced self-centeredness so as to "seek together the Kingdom of God and his justice." Since we wish to obey God, we obey each other by listening, encouraging and serving one another lovingly with no one trying to dominate (Article 25).

Each community shall always have one of its members serve as minister and servant, looking after the life of the community. In order to better observe what they have promised the Lord, the brothers and sisters actively obey their ministers, always guarding themselves against anything that would be contrary to the soul and to our Rule (Article 26).

The service of the ministers takes place in visiting, admonishing (humbly and lovingly) and encouraging the others. They are accessible to a degree that allows the brothers and sisters to have recourse to them without fear (Article 27). All service is entrusted for a time because it is always necessary to be on guard against appropriating anything, even a service (Article 28).

## CHAPTER NINE: APOSTOLIC LIFE

The entire life in the imitation of Christ bears a missionary, apostolic dimension: The disciples are sent to give testimony. This ninth and last chapter of the Rule is its culmination and is supported by everything that went before.

Article 29 reminds us that all of our activity is inseparable from contemplation. Love of God comes first and it is He who sends us to the world to manifest his glory by our acts.

The brothers and sisters have a mission of peace and justice. They shall work at reconciliation and peace, in themselves and around themselves. Like Christ into whose keeping they have surrendered themselves, they will bring by deeds mercy to the wounded, the bruised the lost ones fearlessly risking even their lives (Article 30).

In our testifying, whatever we may do, we are to be especially on guard against pride and vainglory. Nothing of what we do, neither our prayer, nor our work, nor our service to others belongs to us. Everything comes from God. The brothers and sisters return all to him in thanksgiving (Article 31).

## EXHORTATION AND BENEDICTION

In the end Francis reminds us that we must desire to be animated by the Spirit of the Lord. Therefore let us live poor and humble lives, following our Lord Jesus within the pale of the Church (Article 32).

All those brothers and sisters who live in this manner will be blessed by God. The Franciscan can confirm this from experience. This life leads to God in peace and happiness.

## Jean François Godet-Calogeras

## COMMENTARY ON THE RULE AND LIFE OF THE BROTHERS AND SISTERS OF THE THIRD ORDER REGULAR OF SAINT FRANCIS

### UNPUBLISHED, 1991

### INTRODUCTION

#### 1. NATURE OF THE TEXT

Francis of Assisi was a faithful and passionate disciple of Jesus Christ. All his life he wanted to follow in the footsteps of his Lord. Few Christians have been as open and attentive to the presence of Christ in their life. Radical fidelity to the gospel was for Francis an ongoing experience. This is the essence of the Franciscan charism.

Since the Second Vatican Council in the great movement of the rebirth of the Gospel that it proposed to the Church of Jesus Christ, nearly thirty years have passed in which religious men and women have been asked to return to the inspiration of their founders and foundresses to rediscover the source of their founding. Those who wish to live in the manner of Francis of Assisi have heard the call and returned to the Little Poor One and to the evangelical form of life that was his.

Many congregations of the Third Order Regular gave their point of view regarding the Rule promulgated in 1927, noticing that this Rule showed signs of its own times in which it was composed and that it seemed incapable of defining our identity or our common values in an inspirational manner. It was not in agreement with the new directives of the Church and did not portray our evangelical life in a biblical way or in a way that clearly reflected the spirit of our founder. It is not surprising, then, that they thought about a renewal of the Rule and of our evangelical form of life.

This idea gave birth to profound research on the spirit of Saint Francis of Assisi and the communal writing of a new text, faithful at the same time to the inspiration of Francis and to the historical expressions of this inspiration in the Third Order Regular that exist today throughout the world. The new Rule was voted on by the general superiors of men's and women's communities gathered at the Franciscan International Assembly in Rome from March 1-10, 1982. His Holiness, Pope John Paul II, approved it on December 8, 1982, by the letter *Franciscanum vitae propositum*.

Francis desired that the men and women who would live as he did, would be authentic evangelical men and women. That which proceeds from their hearts is that which makes them who they are, said the Lord (Mt 15:10-20). Inspired by the Lord, Francis shows us, who desire to live like him, the evangelical values and fundamental attitudes that we should have as true disciples of Christ if we are to follow in his footsteps. So we will have to truly assimilate and make our own these fundamental attitudes and values to live the Gospel in a Franciscan way. The intention of the Rule is unique, to explain the vision of Francis about our form of life. This is a life of total conversion to God and neighbor through literal observance of the Gospel. This is why the text gives us the fundamental values and attitudes that Francis tells us are necessary to live a radical Gospel life. We are invited to hold on to these values and to explore their dynamism and to be truly within the Church and the world, men and women who live the Gospel of our Lord, Jesus Christ.

Wanting to explain this Gospel form of life that God inspired Francis to follow and put into practice by Francis and the brothers and sisters who joined him, the new text of the Rule intends above all, in the most profound and the strongest meaning of the word, to be an inspirational text, a text that inspires life and gives life a spirit. The new Rule of the Third Order Regular of Saint Francis does not pretend to give regulations or laws. Each congregation has its own constitution that should take into account canon law, the particular charism of their respective founders and foundresses, cultural circumstances, particular customs and the Rule. In reference to the Rule, the constitutions apply the values, attitudes and principles contained in this Rule to a particular congregation.

There is not only one way to live Gospel. The multiplicity of religious families in the Church shows this. Francis himself, inspired by the Lord and influenced by the circumstances of his time has given birth to three Orders, but all three express the same charism. The three orders are characterized by a particular emphasis placed on certain values that Francis proposed for living the Gospel radically, and by evangelical life styles that are derived from them. However we are a single family, coming from the same brother.

The Third Order Regular brings together more than 400 congregations. Some are apostolic, others are contemplative, and still others are apostolic and contemplative. The majority among them are women's communities, but some are also men's communities. All of these congregations share one Rule, and each brings its own character. Often reflecting a particular place and culture they are, however, an Order because they have common Franciscan values presented in a unique Rule.

In order to more faithfully propose the Gospel form of life of Francis to all those who are part of the Third Order Regular, the Rule uses his own writings. To use the very words of Francis is to use the words that the Spirit inspired him in order to express his gifts. The words of Francis recapture his experience of the evangelical values and the attitudes that the Lord gave him to live. In this sense, the words of Francis have for us a very special importance. Moreover, they make the text of the Rule a text that is not linked to a given time, but a text that remains a source of reflection for all our life and a source of ongoing formation.

In order to fully appreciate the contents of the text it is necessary for us to know the Franciscan sources and the Franciscan history. As it is necessary for us to continually study the Holy Scripture, so we have to also constantly study our Rule. This will help us to take greater advantage of our heritage. For the first time in history, the Rule of the Third Order Regular has been written with the words of Francis. Because of this, the text cannot be a simple document, but an inspiration to live, to share and to pass on.

## 2. Four Fundamental Values

The study of the writings of Francis and those of the history of the Third Order Regular tells us that four values can be considered fundamental for Franciscan life in our order. These are *conversion, contemplation, poverty* and *minority*. These values are the content of the Rule. They make the document the spiritual one that it is. They represent a common treasure that is the basis of our unity.

These fundamental values are far from being independent from each other. On the contrary, they are linked and intertwined to inspire all the concrete attitudes of our Franciscan evangelical life.

Neither are they exclusive: simplicity, joy, charity, mercy, for example, are values which comprise our four fundamental values.

Regarding *fraternity*, one shall not call it a fundamental value, for it is *the* value that is present everywhere and on which the entire Franciscan edifice is built.

## 3. The Gospel Plan of Francis

Inspired by God, Francis and his brothers designed a plan of Gospel living that he put into writing. From his Rule – the *Early Rule* as well the *Later Rule* – and from his *Testament*, it appears that the main lines of this evangelical project were quite simple.

> Identity of this life: ER I; LR I; Test 14
> Entrance and formation: ER II; LR II; Test 16-17
> Prayer: ER III; LR III; Test 18
> Work and service: ER VII; LR V; Test 19-21
> Life in poverty: ER VIII, IX; LR IV, VI; Test 22

Fraternal life and obedience: ER V, 1X; LR VI:7-9, 10; Test 27-33
Witness and mission: ER XIV-XVI; LR III:10-14, XII:1-2; Test 23

Such is the general plan followed by Francis that our Rule reproduces.

## COMMENTARY

### PROLOGUE: WORDS OF SAINT FRANCIS TO HIS DISCIPLES

All who love God with their whole heart, with their whole soul and mind, and with their whole strength, and love their neighbor as themselves, and who despise their tendency to vice and sin, receive the Body and Blood of our Lord Jesus Christ and bring forth from within themselves fruits worthy of true penance;

How happy and blessed are these men and women when they do these things, and persevere in doing them because the Spirit of the Lord will rest upon them and God will make a home and dwelling place with them. They are the children of the heavenly Father whose works they do. They are the spouses, brothers and sisters, and mothers of our Lord Jesus Christ.

We are spouses when the faithful soul is united by the Holy Spirit with our Lord Jesus Christ. We are for him brothers and sisters when we do the will of the Father who is in heaven. We are mothers when we bear him in our hearts and bodies with divine love and with pure and sincere consciences, and when we give birth to him through our holy actions which must shine in example to others.

How glorious it is, how holy and great, to have a Father in heaven! How holy, consoling, beautiful and wonderful it is to have such a Spouse! How holy and how loving, pleasing, humble, peaceful, sweet, lovable and over all things desirable it is to have such a Brother and such a Son, our Lord Jesus Christ who gave up his life for his sheep and prayed to the Father, saying: Holy Father, keep in your name those whom You gave me in the world; they are Yours and You gave them to me. And the words which you gave me I gave to them, and they accepted and truly believed that I came from You. And they know that You have sent me. I pray for them and not for the world. Bless them and sanctify them. I sanctify myself for their sakes. I do not pray only for these but also for those who, through their word, will believe in Me, may they be holy in oneness as We are Father, I want that where I am they too may be with Me so that they may see My glory in Your reign. Amen.

The prologue of the Rule is integrally the first part of the exhortation to the brothers and sisters of penance, which is taken from Francis's *Letter to the Faithful*. As such, this text reminds us that the Third Order of Saint Francis, Secular as well as Regular, finds its origin first of all in the order of penance. This is why we also find it as the prologue to the Rule of the Secular Franciscan Order. Many of the founders and foundresses of congregations of the Third Order Regular were secular Franciscans before founding their congregation. The importance of conversion in our way of living the Gospel is a central point shared by the brothers and sisters of the Secular Franciscans and of the Third Order Regular.

The fundamental elements of the Franciscan Gospel life are brought together here:

Conversion, radical change of life through penance – This is a reorientation toward God according to the Gospel;

To have the Spirit of the Lord and its holy operation – This is to act and behave in such a way as to show that we are inspired by that Spirit;

To become home, the dwelling place of God;

To become son and daughter of the Father, doing his works;

To become spouse, brother, sister and mother of Jesus sharing the same breath, the same spirit, doing as Jesus the will of the Father, and giving birth to Jesus through exemplary works.

One such life is happy and blessed. God created us for happiness and for happiness without limits and without end in union with Him.

## Chapter 1: In the Name of the Lord! Here begins the Rule and Life of the Brothers and Sisters of the Third Order Regular of Saint Francis.

1. The form of life of the Brothers and Sisters of the Third Order Regular of Saint Francis is this: to observe the Holy Gospel of our Lord Jesus Christ, living in obedience, in poverty and in chastity. Following Jesus Christ at the example of Saint Francis, they are held to do more and greater things in observing the precepts and counsels of our Lord Jesus Christ. They must deny themselves as each has promised God.

2. With all in the holy Catholic and apostolic Church who want to serve God, the brothers and sisters of this Order are to persevere in true faith and penance. They want to live this evangelical conversion of life in a spirit of prayer, of poverty, and of humility. Let them abstain from all evil and persevere to the end in doing good because

God's Son Himself will come again in glory and will say to all who acknowledged, adored and served him in penance: Come, blessed of my Father, receive the reign that has been prepared for you from the beginning of the world.

3. The brothers and sisters promise obedience and reverence to the Pope and the Catholic Church. In this same spirit they are to obey those who have been placed in the service of the fraternity. And wherever they are, or in whatever situation they are in, they should spiritually and diligently show respect and honor to one another. They should also foster unity and communion with all the members of the Franciscan family.

The first chapter describes the nature, identity and the way of life of the Third Order Regular within the Church and within the Franciscan Movement.

The title, beginning with the words *In the name of the Lord*, according to traditional medieval usage is seen often in the writings of Francis and says clearly that the text that follows is a spiritual document, a document that indicates values, attitudes and necessary principles for a certain way of life. The beginning of article 1 confirms it in using the words "form of life." This first chapter summarizes the whole Rule and specifically defines what we are in the Church.

*Article 1* says that we are religious of the Third Order Regular of Saint Francis who want to live according to the holy Gospel as brothers and sisters.

We are called *brothers and sisters*. These words belong to a current language, even a familiar language. They are words that the whole world uses and of which the entire world instinctively knows the meaning. And these are the words that have been chosen by Francis and by Clare to designate those who joined them. They could have used other qualifying words: companions, confreres or colleagues. Rather, they chose the words "brothers and sisters" for their distinct content. To be brother or sister is not a title, but a quality of relationship. Brother and sister are words that designate a type of relationship between human beings. We are not brother or sister if we are all alone. It is necessary to be in relationship with others in order to be able to develop a fraternal relationship. We are never brother or sister once and for all. On the contrary, each encounter brings a new challenge. We will be brother or sister in the measure that we develop fraternal bonds.

The word "Order" is to be taken in its ancient meaning: It refers to a well-defined group of persons, situated in a larger group, like the Church or the society. In the Middle Ages, the whole society was "in orders," that is to say divided into categories, or recognized classes. And each individual has a social existence to the degree that he or she is situated in an order. To exist and to be recognized, it is necessary to belong to an established order: the order of clerics, monks, knights, physicians, lawyers, workers, etc. Each order has its own internal structure, conditions for belonging, exterior signs and activities.

The Church has kept this ancient organization of orders just as certain professions such as soldiers, physicians, and lawyers for example. Religious orders and priestly orders are clearly defined and situated within the Church. The Third Order Regular of Saint Francis is made up of juridically independent congregations who share the same Gospel way of life. Our Order is *Regular* because we live a religious life in community, professing a rule and the three canonical vows. This distinguishes us from a secular order that is made up of persons living in the world. Our Order is called *Third* because it is the third order begun with St. Francis after the Friars Minor and the Poor Sisters.

But beyond all the differences that exist among the different Franciscan orders, the most important is the project that they have in common: *to observe the Holy Gospel of Our Lord Jesus Christ.* This principle is the basis on which a form of life is built. "The Most High Himself revealed to me that I should live according to the form of the Holy Gospel," said Francis in his Testament.[1] To observe the Gospel, to follow in the footsteps of Our Lord, Jesus Christ, this is what defines the Franciscan family, whatever the Order. These words are found at the beginning of all documents explaining the form of Franciscan life: the Rule of the Friars Minor,[2] the Form of Life of the Poor Sisters[3] and the *Letter to the Faithful.*[4]

*Article 2* begins by highlighting that the brothers and sisters of the Third Order Regular are situated within the Catholic (that is to say universal) and apostolic (that is to say missionary) Church, to serve the Lord God with others. Belonging to the Church will be developed in the next article. This article demonstrates that penance, understood in its true and profound sense of conversion, radical change (in Greek: *metanoia*) is at the center of the spirituality of our Order: to convert oneself to God and to conform to the Christ of the Gospel are never actions done once and for all, but ongoing religious experiences. To do penance or to convert oneself, according to the words of Francis himself, is to be always turned toward God, and to recognize the Lord in Creation, in the Holy Scriptures, in all things and in particular in the words, life, deeds and teachings of the Lord Jesus; to adore the Lord in the totality of our life in

---

[1] Test 14; FA:ED I, 125.
[2] ER Prol:2; LR I:1; FA:ED I, 63, 100.
[3] FLCl 1:1; CA:ED, 109.
[4] 2LtF; FA:ED I, 45-51.

living in prayer, minority and poverty, purity of heart and loving obedience in the example of Jesus Christ; to serve the Lord in our neighbor, practicing the commandment of love and working for justice and peace. Penance according to the Gospel is not a question of individual practices of mortification; it is not a question of hurting oneself or making sacrifices, but of living. Penance is a matter of love: It is by love that we can enter the Reign of God (Mt 25:31-46).[5]

*Article 3* begins by reiterating what was said in the beginning of article 2: As Franciscans we are part of the Church which holds and teaches revealed truth. Belonging to the Church has always been considered essential for Francis: to live the Gospel of Jesus Christ, he wants to belong to the Church of Jesus Christ. From his Testament, as from two editions of the Rule, it is clear that Francis wanted to be obedient to the Church. The Latin *oboedire* means to be an attentive listener.

Our fidelity expresses itself by our obedience and our respect toward the authorities of the Church, the pope and the bishops who have the responsibility to guide the people of God. And we have the same attitude toward our ministers of our congregations, who like the Church, need structure and guidance. Moreover, we are invited into a true fraternity, not only within the Church, both universal and local, in our congregations and fraternities, but also with all who share with us the spiritual heritage of Francis of Assisi. The quality of our fraternal love will be the witness of the authenticity of our evangelical life.

CHAPTER 2: THOSE WHO WISH TO SHARE IN THIS LIFE

4. Those who through the Lord's inspiration come to us wanting to accept this way of life are to be received kindly. At the appropriate time, they will be presented to the ministers who hold power in the fraternity.

5. The ministers shall ascertain that the aspirants truly adhere to the Catholic faith and the Church's sacramental life. If the aspirants are found fitting, they are to be initiated into the life of the fraternity. Let everything pertaining to this Gospel way of life be diligently explained to them, especially these words of the Lord: "If you want to be perfect, go and sell all your possessions and give to the poor. You will have treasure in heaven. Then come, follow me. And if anyone wants to come after me, one must deny oneself, take up one's cross and follow me."

---

[5]ER XXIII:4; FA:ED I, 82..

6. Led by God, let them begin a life of penance, conscious that all of us must be continuously converted. As a sign of their conversion and consecration to Gospel life, they are to clothe themselves plainly and to live in simplicity.

7. When their initial formation is completed, they are to be received into obedience promising to observe this life and Rule always. Let them put aside all preoccupations and worries.

Let them only be concerned to serve, love, honor, and adore God, as best they can, with a single heart and a pure mind.

8. Within themselves, let them always make a home and dwelling place for the one who is Lord God almighty, Father and Son and Holy Spirit so that, with undivided hearts, they may grow in universal love by continually turning to God and to neighbor.

It is clear that this chapter deals with formation. But looking closer at the text, it appears that the process of formation is never ended. Initial formation becomes ongoing formation; for it is a question of a life of permanent conversion. Not only is one never finished converting oneself, but also conversion to the Gospel leads us to poverty and humble service, and to the spirit of prayer.

*Articles 4 and 5* reflect at the same time the experience of the initial conversion of Francis and his instructions concerning formation.

For Francis it is most important that the one, who comes to us desiring to share our life, does so and makes this step *under the inspiration of the Lord.* It is God who takes the initiative. It is God who breathes life into a person.[6] The members of the fraternity will receive the person with kindness and help them to discern the origins of their desire and if they are truly responding to a call from God.

The fraternity in the person of its ministers has particular obligations toward itself and toward the candidate. The minister should ascertain that the person called is really Catholic and authentically *faithful to the Church.* If that is the case in deeds as well as words, the candidate will be initiated into the life of the fraternity, which is and will always be formative. The Gospel will be taught with care; in particular, all of the *radical teachings of Jesus* for those who want to follow in his footsteps: giving of all one's goods to the poor and renouncing oneself. In order to enter into life according to the Gospel, the only condition is to not be encumbered by anything, not by possessions, nor properties, and not even by oneself. Life in the footsteps of Jesus demands a vacuum, an emptiness that God can fill with what a human being really needs. Those who have nothing except following Jesus need nothing else except their own good will.

---

[6]Test 1, 4, 6, 14, 23-39; ER II:1; LR II:1, XII:1; FA:ED I, 124-127, 64, 100, 106.

Those who have something should leave it – in principle, giving to the poor. All share the same treasure: following in the footsteps of Jesus.

*Article 6* is addressed to all the members of the fraternity and not only to novices. Our life of conversion is a perpetual beginning; our commitment is dynamic and permanent. It is in everyday life, in the manner that we dress and in our way of life, that our choice, our commitment will be manifested: the clothes that one wears, the type of home where one lives, the type of food one eats, how welcoming one is, how one is in other's homes, how one travels, and all the trivial matters of everyday life are signs of the Spirit living in us. "One judges a tree by its fruits," says Jesus (Mt 12:33). The brothers and sisters will take to heart to show that they have chosen to be centered on God, to be turned toward God, to have God as a point of reference in all things. Not wanting to worry about anything else, they will show exteriorly what they are interiorly, they will show by the way they dress and their behavior, both personal and communal, the simplicity of their lives.

*Article 7* deals with perpetual profession and the attitudes that Francis says are necessary when one has begun a life of penance. The initial phase of formation completed – initiation at the same time practical and theoretical, there is a commitment. But the traditional expression in the Franciscan family for expressing this commitment, this profession is *to be received into obedience.*

This expression goes back to the centuries when the first religious communities appeared. It stresses the engagement in a group of human beings. Franciscan life is not defined by an individual commitment or by a material structure (a place or a building), but by the quality of interpersonal relationships. Those who commit themselves permanently to the Franciscan life are received in a community of brothers or sisters, who promise to listen attentively to each other, to obey each other. One commits oneself to live in a fraternal relationship with others who are equally committed to total conversion and the observance of the holy Gospel. The fraternal community allows one to leave behind worries and cares, and to turn together toward God.

*Article 8* develops the end of the preceding article and concretizes it. We should become a dwelling place for God, a place where God lives: the objective of our life is nothing less than union with God in Christ through the Spirit. This presence of God in us purifies and unifies our heart, so that we can grow. Our love will become universal and be continually manifested in the love of neighbor. Placing love and mercy in deeds has always been an important characteristic in the history of our congregations and fraternities. In the Franciscan tradition, as in all of Christian tradition, to turn toward God is at the same time to turn toward one's neighbor. The attitude of Francis reflects what we find in the letters of the great apostles, James and John: we cannot love God, whom we do not see, if we do not love our neighbor whom we see. God and neighbor are inseparable.

CHAPTER 3: THE SPIRIT OF PRAYER

9. Everywhere and in all places, at all times and in all seasons the brothers and sisters are to have a true and humble faith. From the depths of their inner life let them love, honor, adore, serve, praise, bless and glorify the most high and sovereign God, eternal Father and Son and Holy Spirit. With all that they are, let them adore God because we should pray always and not lose heart: this is what God desires. In this same spirit let them also celebrate the Liturgy of the Hours in union with the universal Church.

Those whom the Lord has called to the life of contemplation, with a daily renewed joy should manifest their dedication to God and celebrate the love that God has for the world. God created us, redeemed us, and will save us by mercy alone.

10. With all creation the brothers and sisters should praise God Ruler of heaven and earth, and give thanks because, by the holy will and through the only Son with the Holy Spirit, God created all things spiritual and material, and created us in God's image and likeness.

11. Since the brothers and sisters are to be totally conformed to the Holy Gospel, they should reflect upon and keep in their mind the words of our Lord Jesus Christ who is the word of the Father, as well as the words of the Holy Spirit which are spirit and life.

12. Let them participate in the sacrifice of our Lord Jesus Christ and receive his Body and Blood with great humility and veneration remembering the words of the Lord: "Whoever eats my flesh and drinks my blood has eternal life." Moreover, they are to show the greatest possible reverence and honor for the most sacred name, written words and most holy Body and Blood of our Lord Jesus Christ, through whom all things in heaven and on earth have been brought to peace and reconciliation with Almighty God.

13. Whenever they commit sin the brothers and sisters, without delay, are to do penance interiorly by sincere sorrow and exteriorly by confession. They should also do worthy deeds that manifest their repentance they should fast but always strive to be simple and humble. They should desire nothing else but our Savior, who offered himself in His

own Blood as a sacrifice and victim on the altar of the Cross for our sins, giving us example so that we might follow in his footsteps.

If our life is turned toward God in the following of Jesus Christ, it is surely obvious that prayer is a fundamental, constituent value, of our form of life. We must pray always, says the Lord. Prayer is more than a measure of time, more than deeds or words. Prayer is the true breath of the children of God whether they are awake or asleep, at work or at rest.

It is just the way Francis perceived prayer. Thomas of Celano wrote, "when praying, he was no longer a man at prayer, but prayer made man."[7]

*Article 9* tells us in the words of Francis himself that we must always, in all times, in all places keep our hearts in God and adore him. Prayer is above all a way of being, a state: to have one's heart in God, with him to know oneself in God's presence, always and everywhere. This changes life.

It is in this spirit that the brothers and sisters shall celebrate the Liturgy of the Hours, those praises following the rhythm of the time in union with the whole Church. The brothers and sisters vowed to the contemplative life shall show by their joyous life that God loves us and saves us unceasingly.

Franciscan prayer is above all a praise of God with all His creatures. Francis had understood so well how much Creation speaks of the Creator, that the summit of creation is the human being, man and woman made in the image and likeness of the beloved Son of God: "Consider O human being, in what great excellence the Lord God has placed you. God has created you and formed you to the image of God's beloved Son according to the body, and in God's likeness according to the spirit," wrote Francis at the beginning of Admonition 5.[8]

*Article 10* of our Rule reminds us of this invitation to praise and thanksgiving. As Francis showed throughout his entire life, full conformity to the Gospel is only possible through meditation on the words of our Lord Jesus Christ who is *the Word* of the Father and of the entire Holy Scriptures and even of all the events in which the Spirit has not ceased to speak from age to age and who continues to speak to us today. And it is not only a question of meditating, but also of keeping faithfully. Such is the content of *Article 11*. The word, if it comes from God, gives spirit, breath and life, in a dynamic movement.

---

[7]2C LXI:95; FA:ED II, 310.

[8]Adm V:1; FA:ED I, 131.

*Article 12* speaks of the Eucharist. The Eucharist is the gesture Jesus left to his disciples in memory of himself: bread and wine shared, as a sign of a life given out of love, that of Jesus first, and then ours. This is why the brothers and sisters shall receive the Body and Blood of the Lord. In doing so they will receive His life and will be transformed by Him. Since Jesus Christ has given his life for universal peace and reconciliation, our participation in his sacrifice engages us to give our life for our brothers and sisters.

Like conversion, *reconciliation* is continual and constantly needed because of our sins and failures. The brothers and sisters, says *Article 13*, will celebrate reconciliation through the sacrament of Penance and by worthy works of penance. To celebrate means to rejoice that something exists. Reconciliation must have already taken place before it can be celebrated in the sacrament. And if there is reconciliation, it will bear fruit, and one will see that something has changed. For there cannot be reconciliation without conversion, without change.

*Fasting* understood within the Gospel perspective is also a fruit of penance as long as one stays simple and humble, that is to say the opposite of being complicated and proud. There is a negative concept about fasting: fasting as privation or abstinence. The Franciscan and evangelical concept of fasting is positive. It is a way to nourish one's body so that it be turned toward God like the heart. In other words, fasting is the "prayer of the body." It is less a question of depriving oneself or abstaining than of choosing one's food according to the type of life that one wants to live. Responding to a question of Agnes of Prague about fasting, Clare cites Francis and explains the practices of the San Damiano community, but she insists on humility: "Our flesh is not made of bronze, and our strength is not made of rock."[9] It is not a question of aiming for austerity, but of living well and in good health in order to bring honor to the Lord. Fasting is really a spiritual diet: To give the body what it needs to glorify one's Creator, to choose the necessary food so that the body be like the spirit that animates it, turned toward the Lord. For it is him that we should desire, it is his footsteps that we must follow with all our being.

---

[9]3 LAg 38; CA:ED, 53.

CHAPTER 4: THE LIFE OF CHASTITY FOR THE KINGDOM OF HEAVEN

14. Let the brothers and sisters keep in mind how great a dignity God has given them because God created them and formed them in the image of the beloved Son according to the flesh and in God's own likeness according to the Spirit. Since they are created through Christ and in Christ, they have chosen this form of life which is founded on the words and example of our Redeemer.

15. Professing chastity for the sake of the reign of God, they are to care for the things of the Lord and they seek nothing else except to follow the will of God and to please God. In all of their works charity toward God and all people should shine forth.

16. They are to remember that they have been called by a special gift of grace to manifest in their lives that wonderful mystery by which the Church is joined to Christ her divine spouse.

17. Let them keep the example of the most Blessed Virgin Mary, the Mother of God and our Lord Jesus Christ, ever before their eyes. Let them do this according to the mandate of Blessed Francis who held Holy Mary, Lady and Queen, in highest veneration, since she is the virgin made church. Let them also remember that the Immaculate Virgin Mary whose example they are to follow called herself the handmaid of the Lord.

Francis was very conscious of the dignity of the human person, created in the image and likeness of God (Gn 1:26), created by Christ and for him (Col 1:16). Verse 1 of Admonition V cited earlier clearly attests to this. One who has perceived the image of God in oneself has been transformed by this vision. Clare also in her correspondence with Agnes of Prague marveled at the splendor of the human being, image of God, in Jesus and in herself: "Place your spirit in the mirror of eternity [Christ], place your soul in the splendor of God's glory, place your heart in the figure of the divine substance, and be entirely transformed through contemplation into the image of his divinity."[10] Those who embrace the Franciscan way of life founded on the Gospel want to grow into the image of God who is in them (*Article 14*).

They also wish to respond to God's call in professing *chastity for the Kingdom of heaven*, showing in their daily life, the love that animates them (*Article 15*). As religious the brothers and sisters of the Third Order Regular are celibate. That is to say not married. But, chastity is much more than that and concerns as well other Christian men and women who are married: because for whoever wants to live the Gospel, celibacy

---

[10]3 LAg 12-13; CA:ED, 51.

and marriage are matters of chastity. As in fasting, there is a negative perception about chastity – what one abstains from, that is what one is not permitted to do, and a positive vision according to which chastity is the behavior that suits, that corresponds to the form of life that one has chosen.

In his writings, Francis does not define chastity. He names it in the beginning of the Rule[11] along with obedience and poverty, because this triad defines a form of religious of life. (Obedience, poverty and chastity will become later on in canon law the focus of the religious vows.) Francis also asks that our body be chaste to receive Christ[12] and that the words of those who preach be chaste.[13] What does Francis mean by "chaste"? Although he was unlettered, he has a just understanding of the word. We find it in the *Canticle of Brother Sun* or of the Creatures: "Praise be to you, my Lord, through Sister Water, which is useful and humble and precious and chaste."[14] The water of which Francis sings is of course pure water, water as it should be. This water is chaste, that is to say that it is flowing and transparent, it is not murky, we can see through it. A chaste human being is one who is not "murky," a human being who, on the contrary, is transparent. That human being allows the light to pass through him, and we can see in him the image of the Creator.

Chastity is not only individual. It also has a communitarian dimension. The brothers and sisters by their form of life, constitute units of the Church. And the Church is the spouse of Christ (Eph 5:23-26). This mystery should be manifested by the Church, that is to say by the lives of those who compose it (*Article 16*).

On the way to chastity and to transparency to God, the brothers and sisters have an excellent example, particularly dear to Francis: Mary, the Mother of Jesus, who is called "the servant of the Lord". Throughout her life, Mary carried Jesus, brought him to the world, helped him to grow, while listening to him, trying to understand him, and following him up to his infamous death on the cross. Mother of Jesus, Mary was without a doubt also his first disciple, the model of the believers. The brothers and sisters should always keep in mind the example of the most perfect servant of the Lord, Holy Mary, the mother of the Lord and, according to the words of Francis in his salutation to the Blessed Virgin Mary, "virgin made church"[15] (*Article 17*).

---

[11]ER I:1; LR I:1; FA:ED I, 63, 100.
[12]2LtF 14; FA:ED I, 46.
[13]LR IX:3; FA:ED I, 105.
[14]CtC 7; FA:ED I, 114.
[15]SalBVM 1; FA:ED I, 163.

CHAPTER 5: THE MANNER OF SERVING AND WORKING

18. As poor people, the brothers and sisters to whom God has given the grace of serving or working should serve and work faithfully and devoutly so that avoiding idleness that is the enemy of the soul, they shall not extinguish the spirit of holy prayer and devotion, that all the other material goods must serve.

19. In exchange for their work, they may accept anything necessary for their own material needs and for that of their brothers and sisters. Let them accept it humbly as is expected of those who are servants of God and followers of the most holy poverty. Whatever they may have over and above their needs, they are to give to the poor. And let them never want to be over others. Instead they must be servants and subjects to every human creature for God's sake.

20. Let the brothers and sisters be mild, peaceful and unassuming, gentle and humble, speaking honestly to all in accord with their vocation. Wherever they are, or wherever they go throughout the world they should not be quarrelsome, contentious, or judgmental towards others. Rather, it should be obvious that they are joyful, good-humored, and happy in the Lord, as they ought to be. And in greeting others, let them say, the Lord give you peace.

The brothers and sisters have abandoned everything in order to follow as poor people Christ who lived on this earth as a poor person. But this does not at all mean that they are waiting without doing anything, hoping that everything would fall from the sky. They want to acquire what is necessary for living by working and so not be in charge of others. This was the very experience of Francis. As he repeated it again with force before his death in his Testament, work was for him an important reality during his whole life of following Christ: "And I worked with my hands, and I want to work and I wholeheartedly want that all the other brothers work on something honest. Those who do not know should learn, not out of greedy desire to receive a compensation for their work, but for the example and to rid themselves of idleness."[16]

But Francis had acquired an evangelical vision of work. No matter what he did or how he did it, in following Christ, he discovered the real issue, the true dimensions of the human reality that is work.

If work is a consequence of their choice of living poorly, it is also for the brothers and sisters a *grace of the Lord*: "The brothers to whom the Lord has given the grace of working, shall work faithfully and devotedly,

---

[16]Test 20-21; FA:ED I, 125.

and in such a way that they avoid idleness, the enemy of the soul, but should not extinguish the spirit of holy prayer and devotion, that all other temporal things should serve."[17] Work understood as grace, this means that it contributes to the goodness and happiness of the person. This is why it requires *fidelity and devotion*, a certain duration and commitment. Then, work in the Franciscan way is neither a pastime nor slipshod work. The first Franciscans were appreciated for the quality of their work and the trust that people could place in them.

Always a concrete human being, Francis reminds us also that the activity of work can be a service – that is, unpaid service to people who cannot pay or whom one does not charge – or a work remunerated by a salary. For Francis, service and work demand the same conception, the same commitment. The model is, as in other places, the Master, Jesus: whatever one does, whatever the activity, one must be in the midst of others as someone who serves (Lk 22:27). Moreover, if the service and the work allow one to eliminate destructive idleness – for it is not good for a human being to stay inactive, they should above all nourish and develop the *spirit of holy prayer and devotion* which was the subject of chapter 3: Service and work are equally and occasion of adoration, of praise to God, while at the same time they develop and make fruitful the talents that we have received from God. This is the entire content of *Article 18.*

It is by their work that the brothers and sisters provide for their needs. However, they should be content always with what is *necessary*, and never want to accumulate. The condition for entering into fraternity – to give all one's goods to the poor – remains valid for all of life: to follow Christ, to stay available, we will repeat the same act each time that the goods come back to encumber, to burden our way. Moreover, besides being poor in material wealth, the brothers and sisters also want to be poor in power: they refuse to dominate and choose, because of God and the example of Jesus, to be under, that is to say, placed beneath all, to be *servants* and *minor*, lesser than all (*Article 19*).

Work puts the brothers and sisters in relation to people. It is a simple, everyday reality by which they are sent into the world in the midst of people. It is within this ordinary, daily relationship that evangelization happens, the announcement of the Good News: God is with us, God loves us; it is to love and be loved that is important, for that is true happiness. That is why in being servants and minors, the brothers and sisters will be leaven of fraternity by their gentleness, their kindness, their refusal to judge, and their joy. Everywhere they will be forces of *justice* and artisans of *peace* (*Article 20*). Not the peace that is the absence of war, but

---

[17]LR V:1-2; FA:ED I, 102.

the peace of God, the peace that reigns when all beings and all things are according to the plan of creation, a plan that is the fruit of love. The last chapter of the rule will insist again on this work of peace, which is the true mission of the Franciscan Family.

## CHAPTER 6: THE LIFE IN POVERTY

21. Let all the brothers and sisters zealously follow the humility and poverty of our Lord Jesus Christ. Though rich beyond measure with the most blessed Virgin, his mother, he wanted to choose poverty in this world and he emptied himself. Let them remember that of the whole world we shall have nothing but as the Apostle says, having something to eat and something to wear, with these we are content. Let them particularly beware of money. And let them be happy to live among the outcast and despised, among the poor, the weak, the sick, the lepers and those who beg on the street.

22. The truly poor in spirit, following the example of the Lord, neither appropriate nor defend anything as their own live in this world as pilgrims and strangers. So excellent is this most high poverty that it made us heirs and rulers of the reign of God. It made us materially poor, but rich in virtue. Let this poverty alone be our portion because it leads to the land of the living. Clinging completely to it let us, for the sake of our Lord Jesus Christ, never want anything else under heaven.

For Francis, to live in poverty does not come from an abstract reflection, whether religious or social. For him, poverty is a lady whom he chooses as a companion, because she was the one chosen by his Lord. It is a matter of the heart. It is always love that takes the first step.

Hence the brothers and sisters will live *humble and poor* in the example of Jesus and Mary, his mother. Evangelical Franciscan poverty is not an idea and is much less an ideology. It is a concrete way of using material goods and of cultivating relationships between people, relationships inspired by the Spirit of the Lord, and not by the spirit of the world. In following Jesus, to be poor is first of all a question of spirit – of breath, not of intellect, but it is as well a social and economic behavior that manifests this spirit: to be content with the necessary; to strongly beware of money, false value and source of injustice and division between people; to live joyfully among the poor whom the society despises, but who are so dear to God's heart (*Article 21*).

*Article 22* shows how much poverty expresses the choice of the brothers and sisters to *totally depend on God*, the only good and the only necessary. There is a radical refusal to follow false values and to fall into the lust for appropriation and domination, that are only illusions for one's own security. Evangelical poverty makes one free. At the same time, this poverty, chosen for the love of Jesus, and lived in following his footsteps, allows us to develop freely new human relationships. Because they refuse to enter into the struggle for power and property, because they live as *pilgrims and strangers* everywhere in this world, the brothers and sisters can offer humankind what everyone so ardently desires in the depth of their being: *fraternity*, and, as Francis liked to repeat, opportunities to practice *goodness*. Evangelical poverty frees the energies of goodness and of love that God has placed in human beings, made in God's image.

CHAPTER 7: FRATERNAL LIFE

23. Because God loves us, the brothers and sisters should love each other, for the Lord says, This is my precept, that you love one another as I have loved you. Let them manifest their love for each other in deeds. With confidence let them make known their needs to one another so that each can find and offer to the other that which is necessary. Blessed are those who love the others when they are sick and unable to serve, as much as when they are healthy and of service to them. Whether in sickness or in health, they should only want what God wishes for them. For all that happens to them let them give thanks to our Creator.

24. If discord caused by word or deed should occur among them, they should immediately and humbly ask forgiveness of one another even before offering their gift of prayer before God. If anyone seriously neglected the form of life all professed, the minister, or others who may know of it, are to admonish that person. Those giving the admonition should neither embarrass nor speak evil of the other, but show great mercy. Let all be carefully attentive not to become angry or disturbed because of another's sin. For anger and disturbance impede charity in themselves and in others.

For Francis, fraternal life is the canvas on which all of life is woven in following Christ. All of the elements of his evangelical form of life are marked by this, beginning with our name, brothers and sisters, a name that, as was mentioned earlier in the commentary on chapter 1, is not an acquired title, but a quality of interpersonal relationship to strive for always. The goal of this chapter is to place in the forefront this quality of fraternal relationship, both inside of and outside of our congregations.

*Article 23* describes the contents of fraternal life. Fraternal love has its roots in Jesus Christ. It is he, the Son of God, Master and Lord, Who has become the brother par excellence, our brother, and has asked us to love one another as he has loved us (Jn 13:13-14; 14:34-35). Consequently, our fraternal love is love shown in deeds. If it were limited to a declaration of intention or to beautiful words, it would be nothing. "Faith without works is dead in itself" (Jas 2:17).

In the practice of fraternal love the role of radical poverty of the brothers and sisters is important: Poverty according to the Gospel elicits interdependence and mutual service. The need of our neighbor, whatever its nature, invites us to serve and to love. This love is free, in the form of the love of God. This shows itself to be true in particular when one is sick. It is when things are not going well, when there are difficulties that one can see exactly where one is. Trials reveal more than successes.[18] Whatever happens, nothing should discourage the brothers and sisters from giving thanks to God and from seeking to do his will.

*Article 24* speaks of the problems, the conflicts and the sins against fraternal love. This article reminds us that evangelical life is not for perfect beings, and that it will happen that at times it does not work. There is nothing abnormal about that. Jesus himself said that he came for the sick and the sinners (Mt 9:12-13; Mk 2:17; Lk 5:31-32). With the example of God's merciful attitude toward humankind, the difficulties, the conflicts and the sins of fraternal life, instead of destroying the fraternity, can transform it into greater fraternity.

In the case of a personal offense, the attitude shall be one of mutual forgiveness without trying to count the faults and the wrongs that have been done. In the case of sin against our form of life, one shall not crush the brother or the sister with shame or reproach. It will be right to admonish the brother or the sister, certainly, but it will be particularly important to offer forgiveness and mercy in order to resume the journey together.

In any case, the brothers and sisters shall avoid becoming angry and upset. When one becomes angry or upset, one becomes possessed by the problem, or even the evil committed, and one becomes incapable of speaking or acting inspired by love. Anger and agitation impede charity. Francis and Clare had noticed it both in and around themselves.[19]

## CHAPTER 8: THE OBEDIENCE IN LOVE

25. Following the example of the Lord Jesus who made his own will one with the Father's, the brothers and sisters should remember that, for God, they have given up their own wills. Therefore, in every Chap-

---

[18]Adm XIII:2; FA:ED I, 133.
[19]LR VII:3; FA:ED I, 104; FLCl 9:5; CA:ED, 121.

ter they have let them seek first God's reign and God's justice, and exhort one another to better observe with greater dedication the rule they have professed and to follow faithfully in the footprints of our Lord Jesus Christ. Let them neither dominate nor seek power especially over one another, but let them willingly serve and obey one another with the charity which comes from the spirit. This is the true and holy obedience of our Lord Jesus Christ.

26. They are always to have one of their number as minister and servant of the fraternity whom they are strictly obliged to obey in all that they have promised God to observe, and which is not contrary to conscience and this rule.

27. Those who are ministers and servants of the others should visit, admonish and encourage them with humility and charity. Should there be brothers or sisters anywhere who know and acknowledge that they cannot observe the rule according to its spirit, it is their right and duty to have recourse to their ministers. The ministers are to receive them with charity and kindness they should make them feel so comfortable that the brothers and sisters can speak and act towards them just as an employer would with a worker. This is how it should be because the ministers are to be servants of all.

28. No one is to appropriate any office or ministry whatsoever; rather each should willingly relinquish it when the time comes.

It is because of Jesus Christ that Francis chose to live in obedience. It is also the life of Christ that gives the context of this obedience.

*Obedience* and to *obey* are words that unfortunately are very badly misunderstood. In many cases, for many people, to obey means to carry out an order. It is often said that one who is obedient always does what he or she is told to do. If such is the usual understanding of these words, we are far from the Gospel reality and the meaning they have in Jesus' words and in in the New Testament.

To obey comes from the Latin *oboedire*, a word that comes from \**ob-audire* that means to turn toward in order to listen. In his love for the Father, Jesus is constantly attentive to what the Father says; because of this he has placed his will in the will of his Father.[20] That is why one can say of Jesus that he was obedient until death, and death on a cross (Phil 2:8). It is not because God had commanded him to die on the cross. Such a commandment would not correspond at all to the all-loving God and Father that Jesus reveals. But Jesus was so much listening, obedient to the Father that he could not be separated from him, not even by a

---

[20]2LtF 10; FA:ED I, 46.

horrible death on the cross. The obedience of Jesus was perfect. Nothing and nobody could take precedence over the loving relationship that united the Father and the Son. The Father loves the Son, and the Son loves the Father and wants to do what pleases Him. That is the joy, the happiness and the life of the Son, to do the will of the Father, the source of love.

Such is the obedience of Jesus and such is the model of Franciscan obedience. The writings of Francis speak about it again and again; often Francis invokes it: "through obedience." One of his admonitions explains in a very clear and concrete way his understanding of obedience:

> The Lord says in the Gospel: Whoever has not renounced all that he possesses cannot be my disciple (Lk 14:33), and, Whoever wants to save his soul will lose it (Lk 9:24). He abandoned all that he possesses and loses his body,[21] the man who offers himself completely in obedience into the hands of his prelate.[22] And whatever he does and says, which he knows not to be against the will of that prelate, provided that what he is doing is good, this is true obedience. And if from time to time the subject sees better and more useful things for his soul than those that the prelate prescribes, he shall voluntarily sacrifice his will to God and strive to accomplish through action those of the prelate. Such is the obedience of love because it satisfies God and neighbor. But if the prelate asked something of the subject that is against his soul, although he should not obey, however, he should not leave. And if because of this he endures the persecution from others, he should love them more because of God. For, he who endures persecution rather than wanting to be separated from his brothers truly lives in perfect obedience because he lays down his soul for his brothers.[23]

We find in this text attitudes inspired by authentic obedience, "perfect," in the likeness of Jesus: renouncing one's own will; being attentive; listening to one who is "before, in front of us," one who is placed at our head; deciding voluntarily to do what pleases the other, provided that it is not against the health of our soul, for something bad cannot be the will of God and cannot be a matter of obedience.[24] If we must disagree, however, let it not be a cause of separation. This point is found in the sentence: "Such is the obedience of love because it satisfies God and the neighbor." Perfect obedience is an obedience of love.

This is why the brothers and sisters, in the same love, have given up being self-centered to *seek together the reign of God and God's justice.* And

---

[21]That is, his own will.
[22]That is, the one who is placed at the head.
[23]Adm III:1-9; FA:ED I, 130.
[24]2LtF 41; FA:ED I, 48.

as they obey God, they mutually obey one another, listen to, encourage and serve one another with love, and nobody seeks to dominate the others (*Article 25*).

Because the body needs a head, as Christ is the head of the body, which is the Church (Col 1:18), each community will always have one of its members who is a minister and servant, overseeing the life of the fraternity and its members. It is not a question of having power over others, but of serving: "The leaders of nations keep them under their power and the important ones under their domination. It should not be like this among you. On the contrary, if someone wants to be important among you, he must be the servant, and if someone wants to be first among you, he must be your slave," says Jesus (Mt 20:25-27). Francis takes up these two words, *minister et servus*, minister and servant, servant and slave. In the example of Jesus, the one who is placed at the head is at the service of the body.

And the brothers and sisters, so that they can be faithful and better observe all that they have promised the Lord, shall actively obey their ministers, always minding what would be against the soul and our rule (*Article 26*).

The *service of the ministers* of the fraternity will be to visit, to admonish with humility and love, and to encourage. The ministers will be accessible so that the brothers and sisters would not be afraid to come to them: there should be no fear among members of the same family (*Article 27*).

*All service is given for a time*, for one should be careful not to appropriate anything, even a service. And a service should not impede life, either because it weighs too much and too long on the shoulders of the servant, or because one has identified oneself with a service (*Article 28*).

### CHAPTER 9: APOSTOLIC LIFE

29. The brothers and sisters are to love God with their whole heart, their whole soul and mind and with all their strength, and to love their neighbor as themselves. Let them glorify God in all they do. Sent into the whole world by God, they should give witness by word and work to God's voice and make known to all that only God is all-powerful.

30. As they announce peace with their lips, let them be careful to have it even more within their own hearts. No one should be roused to anger or insult on their account; rather, all should be moved to peace, kindness and harmony because of their gentleness. The sisters and brothers are called to heal the wounded, to bind up those who are bruised, and to reclaim the erring. Wherever they are, they should recall that

they have given themselves up completely and handed themselves over totally to the Lord Jesus Christ. Therefore, they should be prepared to expose themselves to every enemy, visible and invisible, for love of the Lord because He says: Blessed are they who suffer persecution for the sake of justice, theirs is the reign of God.

31. In the charity which God is all the brothers and sisters, whether they are praying or serving or working, should strive to be humble in everything. They should not, because of good words and works even anything good that God does, speaks and makes in and through them, seek glory or rejoice or exult interiorly. Rather, in every place and circumstance, let them acknowledge that all good belongs to the most high Lord God and Ruler of all things. Let them always give thanks to the one from Whom all good proceeds.

All life in following Christ has within itself a missionary and apostolic dimension: disciples are sent to give witness. This ninth and last chapter of the rule is the culminating point, highlighting all that precedes it.

*Article 29* recalls that our action is inseparable from our contemplation. Franciscan life is a life according to the Gospel. All our life, we remain disciples of Christ, in apprenticeship. In the school of Christ, it is therefore necessary for us to constantly contemplate and to act in order to learn. To look at Christ and to then act, following his example. The love of God is first and it is God who sends us into the world to show his glory by our deeds.

The brothers and sisters have a *mission of peace and justice*. All of Francis's life shows that: peace in Assisi, peace in Gubbio, peace in Arezzo, peace with the Muslims. Francis was an artisan of peace, that is to say that he worked for peace. However, as was said earlier about *Article 20*, not for just any peace, but for peace that reigns when all is according to the plan of the Creator. When God reigns, then creation is at peace. War – or absence of peace – is found where God is not reigning, where creation has not conformed to the plan of the Creator. Francis worked to bring God's peace by working for God's justice.

This is the task that is always entrusted to the brothers and the sisters. They have to work unceasingly for *reconciliation* and for *peace* within and around themselves and thus they have to work for the reign of God. Like Christ to whom they have given up everything, they show *mercy* in deeds toward all who are wounded, bruised or lost, without fear, not even for their own life. As God has for creation an infinite tenderness, the brothers and sisters shall have the womb of a mother for all those whom the society has damaged (*Article 30*).

However, in our witness, whatever we do, we shall particularly keep watch against pride and vainglory. Let us never forget that nothing that we do, neither our prayer nor our work, nor our service to others belongs to us. The only things that we can claim are our vices and our sins.[25] But all good comes from God who alone is good.[26] Thus, the brothers and sisters shall return to God what belongs to God, and be thankful for God's goodness (*Article 31*).

### Exhortation and Blessing

32. Let all the brothers and sisters be mindful above all things that they must desire to have the Spirit of God at work within them. Always subject to the holy Church and established in the Catholic faith, let them observe the poverty and humility and the holy Gospel of our Lord Jesus Christ which they have firmly promised.

Whoever will observe these things shall be filled with the blessings of the most high Father in heaven, and on earth with the blessing of the beloved Son, with the most Holy Spirit, the Paraclete and with all virtues of heaven and with all the saints.

And I, little Brother Francis, your servant, in so far as I am able, confirm to you within and without this most holy blessing.

We end this rule (*Article 32*) with Francis's own words[27] which remind us of the essentials of our form of life, that above all we should desire to be animated by the Spirit of the Lord Jesus. For this, we shall be poor and humble within Christ's Church. God will bless all those who live like this. Francis is able, from his own experience, to confirm this: this life leads to God in peace, happiness and fullness.

---

[25]ER XVII:7; FA:ED I, 75.
[26]ER XVII:18; FA:ED I, 76.
[27]LR X:8; FA:ED I, 105; FLCl 10:9; CA:ED, 123.

# Roberta Cusack, O.S.F.

## Commentary of the Rule and Life of the Brothers and Sisters of the Third Order Regular of Saint Francis

### Unpublished, 1982-2002-2006

My personal interest in the need for a "new" TOR Rule began in 1968. As a member of my congregation's International General Chapter in Muenster, Germany, I became acquainted with the renowned Franciscan scholar, Fr. Kajetan Esser, O.F.M., who directed the gathering. At that particular Chapter we were beginning to speak of re-writing our General Constitutions, following the mandates of Vatican Council II. I suggested to the Chapter Body the need to do something about the Third Order Regular Rule of 1927 before we started talking about a new Constitution. The formators in the States, of which I was one, found the TOR Rule of 1927 irrelevant as it did not speak well for St. Francis's charism and our modern needs. With that, I thought Fr. Kajetan would pronounce me anathema immediately. Little did I dream that this man was the greatly respected Gamaliel guru of the Order. And neither did I know that he had just completed a new commentary on the 1927 Rule that he autographed and gave to each of us.

However, prior to his death in July 1978, Fr. Kajetan Esser had copies of some of the drafts of the proposed rules on his desk and was in agreement with the need to renew the text of 1927, as he expressed in a letter to me.

I also recall a wonderful story told by Fr. Roland Faley, T.O.R., and Fr. Thaddeus Horgan, S.A., about their experience as colleagues in Rome. They went to the Congregation for Religious with the same suggestion of a need for a new TOR Rule. They were told that only saints write rules and that they should go home and live our 1927 Rule. Undaunted by that news, we all carried on under the inspiration of the Spirit of Jesus.

In the Third Order Regular tradition we acknowledge our shared charism as a life-long process of "conversion." This excites us toward being deeply and forever concerned with a yearning for God and an invitation for God to turn us around, to shape and form our lives according to God's Word in us. All of God's people are called to this conversion process. Some of us have simple or small conversion experiences, while others – like Clare and Francis of Assisi – knew more dramatic and radical challenges. But we must change and we must grow. We of the Third Order Regular tradition recognize this as our most special gift to be lived out as "modern day penitents of Assisi." We view this as an emerging call to develop and grow in an ever more free, fresh, creative, and imaginative Christian life-style. Then we, too, may be branded with that same foolishness which typified a Paul, a Clare, a Francis, and each of our founding Sisters and Brothers.

It is with a sacred blend of both joy and sadness that I recall the work of our Third Order Regular, International Franciscan Commission (CFI), and the Rule Task Force begun in the late 1970s. I participated and experienced the privilege and the challenge of that great job as an elected member of the International Commission of nine Sisters and Brothers, representing the various language speaking groups throughout the world. I believe this was one of the most dramatic conversion experiences of my Franciscan life up to that point. Little did I dream of what would follow. I do recall an American group challenging me in Assisi outside of the Assembly hall in 1979. Some of the American Major Superiors shared that they thought our being together was of no value and unworkable, and they felt like going back home to the U.S.A. But Sr. Patrice Kerin, O.S.F., President of the Franciscan Federation, challenged me: "Roberta, if you do not take up this task, don't be coming around to our Sisters preaching conversion and the other values." At this I felt like a little lamb being led to the slaughter – such was the overwhelming experience of standing alone at those first international meetings. This begins my memories of the fourth revision of our TOR Rule after nearly 800 years of our history!

The impediments in progressing toward a unified international understanding of our historical foundation were indeed monumental. However, God's Spirit most powerfully worked toward the conversion of each of our hearts. All of us I'm sure, members of the BFI, the CFI, and Work Group, as well as people from each country active in research toward the development of the new Rule, clung to our own convictions. Ultimately each of us had to let go of some of our deep-seated dreams and often narrow opinions and ideas. I recall the French called their document the "Martyr Text" in having to let it go. A lot of dying happened in our Franciscan hearts as we stretched on spirited tip-toe and with widely expanded hearts in the attempt to permit God's Holy Wisdom to act upon the challenge at hand, blessing our TOR tradition with new spirit and life. Our desire for a unified revision of the Rule kept us going and together as a group, in spite of the multitude of cultural differences and understandings of our TOR historical origins and experiences.

Volumes could be spoken and written on our work as it unfolded. But it suffices to look at the end results – that of an extremely spirited Franciscan Rule! My heartfelt thanks to Margaret Carney, O.S.F. and Thaddeus Horgan, S.A. for blindly consenting to become members the Work Group. I am immensely grateful to our Good God and to all who gave so generously of themselves, whether by prayer or engaged in the formal process, or as members of working committees in the various TOR religious communities throughout the world. However, somewhere along the line I feel a more in-depth account of the real courageous story of the process would be beneficial, a twentieth century *Fioretti* if you will. This type of story-telling might serve to enkindle a freeing of the fire in the hearts of future generations of Franciscans.

In past years I've had the privilege and challenging opportunity of directing our English-Speaking Pilgrim Center in Assisi, as well as processing, with many Sisters and Brothers, through their renewal, retreats, and chapters. What claims my attention presently is not so much my personal excitement over our "New" Rule. Rather it is the realization that many members of our TOR family do not know our Rule or have no interest in it, and perhaps are neither energized nor desire to live according to its spirit and life. So many have told me they have not looked at the Rule text since the days of Roots and Wings Programs or similar workshops or retreats. Unfortunately some of our Brothers and Sisters have received none or very limited input on the TOR Rule. Therefore, it is unlikely that the Rule has deeply touched their daily lived experience, nor are they able to own it. This jolting realization has urged me, together with a nudge from some of our Franciscan family, to write a renewed heartfelt statement. I realize I am only one TOR Franciscan who also needs daily growth in the challenge of our Rule. Like almost everything else, even commentaries come and go and need to be continually adapted and revised for our cultures and changing times. John Lozano once said, "Myths and rituals remain alive to the extent to which they are open to reinterpretation." We Franciscans have the blest fortune of celebrating with so many stories and rituals.

Our final meeting held in Rome's *Domus Pacis*, in March1982, gathered 192 TOR General Ministers International or their delegates. There were 260 participants from thirty-seven countries on five continents. During the Papal Audience, John Paul II focused his address on Francis's *Siena Testament*. In the Testament, Francis summarizes what he believed needed to be our major concern:

—Love, respect for and fidelity to the Order, our particular religious Institute, our communities, one another;
—Love and respect holy "lady poverty";
—Love and be faithful to the Church.[1]

The TOR Assembly with a vote of 188/2 overwhelmingly approved our TOR Rule.

---

[1] 2MP 5:87; FA:ED III, 333.

Cardinal Pironio greeted us with the wish that this Rule be a "new stimulus" for a life of renewed generosity in our Franciscan religious living. Pope John Paul II confirmed this document of our new *Rule and Life* on December 8, 1982, authorizing the promulgation with the letter *Franciscanum Vitae Propositum*, "The Franciscan Form of Life." The official text is in Latin, but each country has the responsibility of translating it for their appropriate language group. I routinely ask myself how and to what extent this basic text focuses the Gospel for me and is enhancing my Franciscan journey.

Experience has taught me that much of the great enthusiasm of our early wise outlines, wonderful seminars, workshops, workbooks and retreats, "Roots and Wings" programs – all great attempts to teach and study, absorb, live and love the Rule – might have become tarnished through the years. We cannot permit this to happen. What a pity if we fail to hand on the profound and practical richness of our Rule.

St. Francis calls the Rule our *Book of Life, the hope of salvation*, the marrow of the Gospel, the way of perfection, the key to Paradise, *the pact of an eternal covenant*.[2] "So we do possess the prophetic message as something altogether reliable. Keep your attention closely fixed on it, as you would on a lamp shining in a dark place until the first streaks of dawn appear and the Morning Star rises in your hearts" (2 Pt 1:19). Regarding the Rule, Francis added, "that we should die with it."[3]

Now, years later, I need to question whether this "new" Rule text continues to energize my coming and going, my community, the Order, the Church, the Universe. Thomas of Celano tells us, in the same passage referred to above that Francis left a wonderful blessing to those who would be zealous about our Franciscan Rule. I pray we will ever hunger for another portion of that blessing at this time as new generations of TOR Franciscans come as gifts to the movement, and we are now viewing life frequently fractured through the lens of terrorism and as a world gone mad with extreme violence.

That being said, I need to add that what really preserves the charism is not the documents but the Holy Spirit in the heart of each member. Our entire Franciscan tradition speaks to this. Everywhere we go we touch and leave our spiritual DNA. What do we TOR penitents want to leave on this earth today? How powerful is that? It is as powerful as the Risen Lord who sends us forth with His Spirit.

---

[2] 2C CLVII:208; FA:ED II, 380.
[3] 2C CLVII:208; FA:ED II, 380.

## WORDS OF ST. FRANCIS TO HIS FOLLOWERS (VOLTERRA DOCUMENT 1: 1-19)

Experts feel this was an exhortation written by St. Francis to the penitents who followed his spiritual guidance, who later became identified as the Third Order of St. Francis. In it Francis gives an indication of what living as or being penitent means and involves.

In this, the first chapter of the first edition of his *Letter to the Faithful* (also called the Volterra Letter after the Library where it was located, and *recensior prior*, meaning first edition), St. Francis speaks as one with authority, with the spirit of prophecy, as he addresses us "in the Name of the Lord." *In nomine Domini.*[4] In the opening phrase Francis alludes to the great Jewish prayer formula, the Shema, "Hear, O Israel, the Lord is our God, the Lord alone! Therefore, you shall love the Lord, your God, with all your heart, and with all your soul, and with all your strength… drill, speak, bind and write, …" (Dt 6:4-9). These are the basic principles of the whole Mosaic Law called The Great Commandment. Francis must have been moved by this holistic mandate, as it is repeated in his writings. Hints of this same text are found in articles 9 and 29 of the TOR Rule. The mercy we receive is indeed the love of our God in living our life as modern day penitents of Assisi!

True freedom comes from the indwelling of Christ Jesus' Spirit as we strive to live this with sincerity and truth. Paul writes, "May Christ dwell in your hearts through faith, and may charity be the root and foundation of your life" (Eph 3:17). This is fulfilled as we enter the great awesome relationship with our God – as children, spouses, parents, sisters and brothers of our Lord Jesus Christ. This union then is evidenced in our desire to know, do and ever be in the will of our God, consciously, lovingly, and sincerely bearing the God-self in our very bodies, minds, spirits and emotions. This incarnational living is a graced example. Our challenge, like Paul's, is to be the holy exchange of that permanent presence of Christ among all people, through the power of the Holy Spirit. What a sacred trust we have been given as special agents of the Spirit! Our relationship to the Triune God is expressed and emphasized in three paragraphs in this Prologue.

Francis, then, continues to encourage us with his effective repetition, a flair for the dramatic and ecstatic style of movement. As he gains momentum in the dance of expressing God's love and presence, Francis simply cannot say enough in praise of our good God. Within this framework, Francis quite naturally quotes Jesus' High Priestly prayer for us, his intimate ones, sister and brother penitents (Jn 17). Just as Jesus

---

[4]K. Esser, *Opuscula Sancti Patris Francisci Assisiensis* (Grottaferrata: Collegium S. Bonaventurae, 1978).

yearns for our love, presence and union forever so, too, these texts are most important to Francis and to us as his followers.

Unfortunately, Chapter 2 of this same *Letter to the Faithful* is omitted in the Third Order Regular Rule.[5] It is contained in the Secular Franciscan Order Rule. Regrettably omitted, because in this conversion process we are ever so human, and in many ways we all offend each day. However, with sincere daily-renewed efforts we have Jesus' solemn word that in the new age of fullness, we are going to shine in splendor forever (Mt 19:20).

## I. In Nomine Domini!

As we journey through the text, we find it corresponds to the life of Francis, as reflected in the many source references of the Early Documents.

**Article 1** – Expresses that we are followers of Christ after the example of Saints Francis and Clare of Assisi. It tells us how to be Franciscan and how to live out our Gospel call more faithfully.[6] All of these texts share how Francis himself practiced what he preached with confidence, and in ever so many of the sources we are told he was greatly concerned with giving us good example. Are we concerned about giving good example for the building up of the Church?

The word "observe" or some form of it is used in our text about twelve times in the English translation. A Carmelite priest was once present for one of our Rule workshops. He became very excited about this *observare*. He explained to us that it meant much more than our common understanding of doing something or keeping a law or paying attention. In medieval usage, "observe" implies deeply entering into and identifying radically with the Gospel way of life. After the call "to make greater efforts," I'm inclined to add "daily." I believe that without this consistent daily discipline we all too easily and quickly move away from that determined goal of uncluttering our lives from the complex to the simple through the daily struggles so unique to each of us.

**Article 2** – This is our long-debated charism statement, for which the rest of the Rule is merely an exposition of the necessary dynamic process entailed in conversion. Fr. Raphael Pazzelli, T.O.R., calls it a "charismatic" statement of the TOR family. We are hopefully moving

---

[5] 1LtF 2:1-22; FA:ED I, 43-44.

[6] L3C XIII:54; FA:ED II, 99; LMj, 12:8; FA:ED II, 626-27; 1C XV:36-37; FA:ED I, 214-17.

from the complex to the simple, from the "bitterness to the sweet." This is very counter-cultural.

Coming to know who the true God is in our daily lives is never a simple matter. Hence, turning to God responsibly through our call to evangelical conversion is a magnificent grace gift! The desire, so very essential for continual living of our penitential vocation, comes through the spirit of contemplation, conversion, simplicity, and littleness as God's creatures.[7] These four fundamental or basic values discovered in every Franciscan Rule of the four Orders are to be lived out in the context of fraternal life in a spirit of joy. They are God's gracious gifts to us as we make greater efforts daily to avoid evil and persevere in knowing, doing and, indeed, in becoming God's will. These four values actually appear in every chapter of our TOR Rule and are hopefully found in each chapter of our individual Franciscan lives.

With this persistent effort to know, to worship and to serve our God in sincere repentance, we do hope with great expectation to be met by Christ Jesus at that magnificent homecoming. Then we will be greeted by a heartfelt loving embrace and welcomed to the grand fullness of God's loving union (Mt 25:34). We note in Article 6 how our charism is spelled out more directly.

The second part of this article calls to mind the three aspects of living penance:

> —Knowing the Lord in Jesus Christ – "for this is Eternal Life" (Jn. 17: 3);
> —Adoring the Lord as the result of knowing him;
> —Serving the Lord as we live for Him and the building up of the Kingdom.

**Article 3** – Speaks of our fidelity to the Church, the Pontiff, and our Bishops, our Franciscan family and most especially to our unique Institutes in reverence and obedience[8] (Siena Testament). This fidelity enables our perseverance.

This is not always easy in an age of conflicting views on areas of *vera fides*. "Infallible" statements, differing styles of authority among the hierarchy, diocesan and congregational structures, and critical contemporary issues often bring us to division and, at times, to the cutting edge, not unlike the experiences of Clare and Francis at the birth of the Movement. Daily testing of the Spirit in one's heart is imperative. Francis's and especially Clare's words and behavior tell us it is sometimes neces-

---

[7]L3C X: 37-38; FA:ED II, 90.
[8]2MP 5:87; FA:ED III, 333.

sary in conscience to gracefully and respectfully disagree with authority figures.[9] It might be comforting to realize that like each of us, these authority persons, too, will one day pass away.

Fostering unity and communion with all members of our vast Franciscan family is for us another expression of holy poverty. We are each so small in this tremendous family of Franciscans – we do need each other. In the process of coming to the truths of our history, it might be tempting to judge each other and play God. It matters little who came first, our age, where our saints were born, which community is the largest, who is doing the greatest ministry, who might be attracting the most candidates, or has accumulated or disinherited the largest portion. The question is, am I passionately yearning to be faithful to the Spirit of Jesus adorning my heart? Do I truly seek to be reverent toward all and forever try to develop the spirit of union with our entire Franciscan family?

## II. Acceptance into this Life

**Article 4** – Entering into relationships and living this unique life-style follows the initial Franciscan conversion experience as it did for Clare and Francis and our founding persons, and as is greatly emphasized in the Prologue to our Rule.[10] God's initiative, inspiration and a deep heartfelt desire to live the Franciscan way are a necessity for this lifetime process.[11]

French Archbishop Jacques de Vitry left letters describing the life style of the early Franciscan community. His observations are very worthwhile reading regarding the foundation of the Order.[12]

In *The Remembrance of the Desire of a Soul*, Thomas of Celano tells us that the Order is for all, rich and poor, learned and unlearned.[13] Francis is emphatic in insisting that the Holy Spirit is the General Minister/Servant. However, the servant of each Institute, ever in consultation with the members, bears the responsibility of admitting those whom God sends to us. But all members are to receive and welcome newcomers with heartfelt gratitude as God's gifts to the Order. How has our interest, encouragement, outreach and communication been to possible candidates?

---

[9]2LAg 17; CA:ED, 48.
[10]1LtF; FA:ED I, 41-44.
[11]1C XIII:32-33; FA:ED I, 210-23.
[12]"Writings of Jacques de Vitry"; FA:ED I, 579-80.
[13]2C CXLV:193; FA:ED II, 371.

**Article 5** – Tells us the Minister, or her/his delegate, integration mentor or formator, is responsible for introducing the candidate into our way of life. These must determine the candidate's understanding and desire to live the true faith, *vera fides*. During another TOR Rule program attended by a Minorite friar and his novices, the director shared his excitement over this phrase, *vera fides*. He told us he once had a friar supposedly all prepared to make solemn vows who somehow expressed he did not believe in the Sacred Presence in the Eucharist. How important discernment is at every stage of one's development. If after holy discernment one is believed to have a vocation, one is admitted into the Franciscan family. It is important to remind ourselves that we must be ready to face the same challenging requirements in our own living as we expect of our new members.

As noted in Article 4, Thomas of Celano shares a powerful expression of Francis's heart and, we hope, of each of our hearts in response to God's call. As a priest explained the Gospel to Francis and his early followers, Francis responded, "This is what I want," he said, "this is what I seek, this is what I desire with all my heart."[14] Yet, I blush when I realize how much clutter I have accumulated in spirit and in fact since the first fervor of my response to God's call so many long years ago.

For Clare and Francis, the Gospel was the only formation text. In his Testament, Francis tells us there was no one to show him what to do when God gave him brothers. God made it clear that we must live the Gospel.[15] *Metanoia* is to discover the living of the Gospel. As God calls us daily to become our very best selves, God likewise certainly sustains us. Like the medieval pilgrims we too must ever be eager to dispose ourselves, take up our particular burdens of life and follow our Lord Jesus. Most assuredly the process of conversion takes daily time and patience, and our generous God gives each of us exactly what is needed as we make our way. Related to this, Bonaventure tells us of St. Francis: "Through the merits of the Mother of Mercy, he conceived and brought to birth the spirit of the Gospel truth."[16] Hopefully, we will be granted the same. What a powerful role model we have in our simple little founder.

**Article 6** – This article with its directness is addressed to the novice in each of us. It does spell out our charism. Responsibly turning to God through evangelical conversion of life is a forever lifetime journey in our process of *metanoia*. Francis's first biographers, Celano and Bonaventure, have left us

---

[14]1C IX:21-22; FA:ED I, 201-02.
[15]Test 14; FA;ED I, 125.
[16]LMj 3:1; FA:ED II, 542.

marvelous stories relating how Francis himself was always urged to make greater efforts in love, particularly as he faced newer struggles.[17]

The *sign* of our conversion and consecration to the Gospel continues to be a point of tension for some, particularly on the international level. Clearly this sign cannot be legislated, and we must respectfully accept what is deemed proper for each culture and in each religious institute. Some congregations have never worn a habit. Gospel persons are not defined solely by their clothing but also behavior. This was the intent of Francis.[18] Francis changed from "flesh to spirit" and from "bitterness to sweetness" in attitude and behavior. We most convincingly show ourselves to be Beatitude people in the manner by which we greet and treat one another in our concrete experiences. This is what constitutes counter-cultural living. So there must be some sense of separation from the affluent society … in style, in place of dwelling, cars, etc.

According to the scripture scholar, Fr. Roger Karban, Mark 8:27-35 closes the passage by having Jesus remind his followers of the *first way* of dying with him: "Those who wish to come after Me must deny themselves, take up their cross and follow Me" (Mk 8:34). Scripture scholars believe it wouldn't have made sense until after his own crucifixion for the historical Jesus to use the word "cross" in this context. So he probably told his followers to carry their *Tau.*

Tau is the last letter of the Hebrew alphabet – a "T." Pious Jews used it to show they were totally open to Yahweh's will. More than 1,000 years later, Francis used it in the same way as the penitents in the early church. In our culture we say someone did something from A to Z. Hebrews said from Aleph to Tau, or simply, to the Tau. Carrying your Tau means the same as expressed in Deutero-Isaiah, to listen for and respond to God speaking in your life. It's easy to understand, after Jesus' death and resurrection, how Christians converted the Tau into a cross. Mark believed the first step in dying with Jesus revolved around a willingness to imitate Jesus' determination to accept God's will as his own. Only by losing one's life on that level would one eventually save one's life. According to James it's the sort of "work" which gives life to faith (Jas 2:14-18).

**Article 7** – Completing formal formation invites one to make perpetual profession and to live forever (*observare*) the vowed life by which we are received into the obedience of relationships in the Franciscan family. We publicly say our vows to God to live this form of life forever, but within the context of a particular Franciscan religious institute. Putting aside

---

[17]LMj 14:1; FA:ED II, 640. 1C VI:103; FA:ED I, 272-73.
[18]2C VI: 10-11; FA:ED I, 249-50.

all attachment, care, worry and anxiety are perhaps the greatest form of non-appropriation for many of us.

Every member of community bears the mutual responsibility of developing the fundamental Gospel attitudes. In our extremely complex and global era it is certainly difficult to focus totally on "serving, loving, adoring and honoring" our good God "with singleness of heart" as Francis suggests. Fidelity to the vow of celibate chastity has never been easy, and today it seems to be a monumental task. The *Legend of the Three Companions* has a wonderful pericope describing this eagerness in the lives of our early Friars.[19]

**Article 8** – This article emphasizes that our entire life's objective is to quest passionately after that celibate chaste union with our God. To make of one's heart a fit "dwelling place" for the Triune God is the perpetual goal toward which we hunger in our daily conversion process to become free spirits … love me, be true and we'll make a "dwelling place." This implies dedication to a contemplative life as well as dedication to a life of external and active charity. This article echoes the second paragraph of the Rule's Prologue.[20] Thomas of Celano and Bonaventure expand well on what it took to discover and establish this "dwelling place" in the early birth of the movement (Jn 14:23).[21]

It is never an easy question, but it is essential to daily ask ourselves what the Gospel calls us to in terms of the anointing received by our vowed consecration. What an awesome gift to realize God's desire to make a "dwelling place" within our hearts. May we burn with that same ardor of charity so alive in Clare and Francis.

### III. SPIRIT OF PRAYER

**Article 9** – Prayer was a value very dear to Francis and Clare. Our prayer is to be present to God as a life-style in our way of life, everywhere and at all times. Again we have overtones of the great Jewish prayer formula, the Shema (Dt 6:4-9).[22] It is a primary way of turning continually to God in the conversion process. This article again blends the active and contemplative life.

---

[19]L3C XI: 45; FA:ED II, 94-95.

[20]1LtF 2-3; FA:ED I, 41.

[21]1C XV: 38; FA:ED I, 217; LMj 4:1-3; FA:ED II, 550-51.

[22]*Rule and Life of the Brothers and Sisters of the Third Order Regular of St. Francis: 25th Anniversary Edition*, J-F. Godet-Calogeras, trans. (Washington: Franciscan Federation, 2007), 3, 14. From now on: *Rule and Life*.

In his *Letter to Anthony*, Francis instructs us clearly as to the significance of prayer ... that we are to let nothing disturb or interfere with the spirit of prayer and devotion.[23] The *Later Admonition and Exhortation* describes the primary ingredients of the depth of our inner life.[24] Prayer for Francis was getting lost in love. Love and adore and worship in Spirit and in truth. Pray and praise day and night. He lived before *devotio moderna* and before terms like meditation and contemplation came into existence. For Francis, prayer is eminently simple and is only being present to the Lord whether it is at the Liturgy of the Hours, Eucharist, meditation, private prayers or daily tasks.

In our liturgical prayer we show our fidelity to the Church and our sincere desire to make holy the day, each day, carrying everyone in our hearts, those we like and those we seem not to like, because we must love all, even our "lepers." in Christ.

The second part of this article focuses on those TOR Congregations who profess contemplative prayer as their special aim—that loving companionship with God. However, this second paragraph certainly applies to every Franciscan person. Hopefully we do strive to experience a daily-renewed joy by our praises and in showing special dedication to God and in celebrating God's love for and with all of creation. For Francis, love of God was most surely directed toward creation. He was beside himself at the thought of any aspect of the Incarnation. We marvel at the Creator's great mercy and compassion in restoring all things in Christ. In Bonaventure's *Itinerarium* he describes the ultimate expected goal of the Franciscan pilgrim's journey in God's mercy as "mystical union with ecstatic unction and burning affections."[25] I believe this is what moved Saints Clare and Francis and how they most experienced God's love; hence their continual desire for a compassionate heart. I pray for continual re-creation. St Bonaventure describes very frequently in his *Major Legend* how St. Francis grew in this same way, and we all desire this same profound contemplative experience both on very good days and on difficult ones alike, turning always to the "Mercy Seat" who is Christ Jesus.

**Article 10** – Calls us to praise God with all of creation and indeed with the entire universe as we seek immersion in this world's sacramental reality and there find God's reflection. Being made to God's own image and likeness, as icons, we realize it is therefore possible and expected that we passionately strive to be in God's will each day. We ourselves want

---

[23]LtAnt 1-2; FA:ED I, 107.

[24]2LtF 19-21; FA:ED I, 46-47.

[25]*Bonaventure: The Soul's Journey Into God; The Tree of Life; The Life of St. Francis*, E. Cousins, trans. (New York: Paulist Press, 1978), 110-16.

to become those images, the icons of the Lord as Clare instructs us to "gaze, consider, contemplate, and imitate."[26]

**Article 11** – Calls us to remember that it is God's living Word in our lives that conforms us to Christ. How important it is to keep that Word crisp and fresh and alive and involved in our concrete life experience as it is truly addressed to us. Like Clare and Francis, we are ever seeking the spirit and life of God's Word in our hearts as well as putting that Sacred Word into practice. We remind ourselves of Francis and the first brothers hearing the Word of God in the Church of St. Nicholas and Our Lady of the Angels in 1205.[27]

**Article 12** – Participation needs to be a key word of our theology and practice of the Sacraments. Clare and Francis lived at a time of great Eucharistic reform. Francis writes of this in Admonition I.[28] This article deals with respect for the Eucharist, adoration of the Blessed Sacrament, and the power of the Holy Name of Jesus. Gradually we will surely come to realize our need in this regard and have the holy wisdom to participate freely of these lavish gifts. The dispositions of humility and reverence must accompany our sacramental and devotional life. Francis and the early community were among the primary movers of the new Eucharistic theology and devotion after the Fourth Lateran Council in 1215. Francis puts us on the alert against popular heresies.

**Article 13** – Tells us we must literally and symbolically make "greater efforts" at sincere reconciliation, frequenting the sacrament of penance that is a very powerful grace, and by other means as an ongoing practice. I believe good spirited discernment and creativity are necessary in order to arrive at a healthy balance in our deeds of repentance, especially regarding fasting. Our goal must always be purification and transformation of the heart. We ought daily to beg for an appreciation of the cross and for the time and energy from which flows the living of the mystery of the cross in our lives. My hope is that the Franciscan family might take steps in celebrating the Sacrament of Penance with meaningful creativity. Fr. Raphael Pazzelli, T.O.R., tells us that the highest point of our Franciscan contemplation aims at our transformation. We have the means to become Him who out of love willed to be one of us even unto being crucified.[29]

---

[26]2LAg 19-20; CA:ED, 49.

[27]LMj 3:1; FA:ED II, 542. The importance of the Word of God can also be found in 1C XXX:84; FA:ED I, 254-55 and LMj 11:1; FA:ED II, 612.

[28]Adm I; FA:ED I, 128-29.

[29]LMj 13:3; FA:ED II, 632; 1C IXX: 54; 1C XV:40; FA:ED I, 228-29; 219.

**IV. LIFE IN CHASTITY FOR THE SAKE OF THE REIGN OF GOD**

Finally, when it came time to discuss celibate chastity in the General Assembly we were led by Fr. Luis Cuesta, T.C., a member of the BFI. Fr. Cuesta with his little mischievous smile said, "My Sisters and Brothers, I was once Novice Master and am now General Superior for many years. I thought I knew all about the vow of celibate chastity. However, now I'm not so sure as I try to write something for 200,000 Franciscan men and women."

Also, this was the surprise chapter in our Rule. It was not included in our text approved and blessed at the final meeting of the Assembly of Major Superiors at Rome in 1982. Between the time of that meeting and the time the text was presented to Sacred Congregation for Religious Institutes and approved, a very intentional statement was inserted. It is a good statement but was never specifically treated in any previous Franciscan Rule. Perhaps today it is more significant and needed. The charism of our vow of celibate love is a tremendous gift holding immense power and positive healing energy. This vow is evident in articles 7, 8 and 29.

**Article 14** – Calls us to appreciate and remember how truly great we are in radiating God's creative love, and this brings us to proper reverence for self and all of creation. We are reminded of our preferential option for the special love of Christ Jesus. God Incarnate by His deeds and words gives us the context of our vow of love. In this we radically choose Jesus as Number One, Lord of our Lives!

**Article 15** – I am reminded of the primacy of the Reign of God in considering my vow of love in this article. I am ever amused at Francis's statement that "they have nothing else to do except to follow the will of God and to please God."[30] I am tempted to respond: "If you only knew, Francis, of the obstacles in our twenty-first century!" However the focus of God's love must be like nothing else in comparison, for we must never look backwards. The challenge of the last sentence of this article is that we are to radiate God's love toward all at all times! What a goal for our Franciscan hearts! This is like the call to religious to be the "splendid manifestation of God's presence" as we are encouraged in *Perfectae Caritatis*. All God asks is that we daily attempt to live this.

Thomas of Celano tells us that the will of God was always Francis's highest philosophy and he took every means to discover that holy will.[31]

---

[30]ER XX:9; FA:ED I, 79.
[31]1C II:91; FA:ED I, 261-62; LMj 12:1-2; FA:ED II, 622-24.

Francis's prayer before the San Damiano Crucifix and the closing prayer of his *Letter to the Entire Order* are powerful reminders of our founder's attitude of eagerness and enthusiasm toward God's will. Other key source documents state that this was a constant concern in the founder's heart that we be free to build the Kingdom of God within us.

**Article 16** – Exhorts us to remember that our lives are to bear witness to the wonderful mystery of the union of the Church to Christ her Spouse. Our vow of celibate chastity reflects the dedication and spiritual marriage that unites us with our only love, Christ Jesus. In the first letter of St. Clare to St. Agnes of Prague, she expresses so clearly what this intimacy with the Lord Jesus is about, drawing on the nuptial imagery of Scripture and our initial Franciscan story.[32] A wonderful reflection is found in Paul's letter to the Ephesians: "May Christ find a dwelling place in our hearts through faith" (Eph 3:14-17).

**Article 17** – Here we are to remember the role model we have in the Order's Poor Lady, Queen, Mary the Mother of God. Our Franciscan Mariology is strong. Genuine devotion to Mary is a great gift and she offers wonderful and inspiring insight to enhance our experience of a fruitful chaste life. Yes, we do venerate our Lady as "Virgin made Church" as Francis, describes her in his *Salutation to the Virgin*, and so we strive to imitate her as the Order's "Poor Lady."[33]

### V. THE WAY TO SERVE AND WORK

**Article 18** – I believe it is good to read this article in the context of the clericalism in the Church as well as the class divisions at Francis's time which was not too unlike our own experience in many respects, given the power and abuse experienced in the hierarchical and societal structures.[34] Francis offers a Gospel message to counteract that social-political situation. Clearly, we are to bear ourselves as one of the "poor people" who responsibly work for our living, willing to serve any need.[35] However, we are never to be so busy that the spirit of prayer and devotion suffers. Holy leisure is also a great need.[36]

---

[32]1LAg; CA:ED, 43-46.

[33]SalBVM; FA:ED I, 163. Additional references are made in ER IX:5; FA:ED I, 70; Adm I:14-17; FA:ED I, 129; 2C LI:83; FA:ED II, 302; 2C CLI:199-200; FA:ED II, 374-75; LMj 9:3; FA:ED II, 598-99.

[34]A. Fortini, *Francis of Assisi* (New York: Crossroads Publications, 1981), 252-61.

[35]2MP 3:75; FA:ED III, 322.

[36]*Rule and Life*, III:7-9. Supportive materials are found in ER XXII-XXIII and LtAnt; FA:ED I, 78-86; 107.

**Article 19** – We are expected to humbly receive whatever we need in exchange for our service. And if we accumulate over and above we are to give this to the needy. Today this calls for prudent and spirited discernment as we must provide for our health and aging needs in a society which all too often neglects these. We must responsibly plan so as not to be a burden on others, yet trusting in God's care for us. In all of our activities, whether simple tasks or in highly professional responsibilities, our attitude and behavior must remain that of a simple joyful servant for Christ Jesus' sake. How greatly this style is needed in our bureaucratic society where there are so many people hurting from gross injustices while others accumulate in what appears to be a greedy capitalistic life-style. Identification with the needy people and learning from them is a remarkable blessing for our Franciscan way of life. Sr. Mary Luke Tobin, S.L., has told us to "Go out on the limb because that's where the Fruit is." So how can I/we ever get to the global vision in order to come to the cutting edge of society?[37]

**Article 20** – Expresses how we are to behave as followers of Christ Jesus and our gentle loving founder. To be genuinely joyful, good-humored and happy in the Lord, and greeting all with peace and blessing, is indeed counter-cultural. It demands deep trust in God, but often brings forth a negative response just as it did in Francis's culture. The world of today needs this joy, peace, and blessing in our terrible blunder of declared war on terrorism. Aren't most of our American society living in fear while arrogantly proclaiming our great power, our bigness, our wealth, our speed, our being the best...especially with our pre-emptive strikes and collateral damage? How do I radiate the gifts of the Holy Spirit when announcing peace by word and example?[38]

### VI. Life in Poverty

Poverty for Franciscans is not simply a virtue, but it is a whole way of life. In India they have a motto as shared by Sr. Ignatia Gomez, a member of the Work Group: "Travel light + Less Luggage = More Comfort." However, when we have nothing left but God, then for the first time we become aware that our God is enough!

Fr. Thaddeus Horgan, S.A., often defined poverty as "simply knowing our need for God." How truly blesssed we are in knowing our need for

---

[37]1C IV:8; FA:ED I, 188-89. Complementary material is found in L3C VII:21-22; FA:ED II, 81-82.

[38]L3C VIII:26; FA:ED II, 84-85; supportive material is found in LMj 3:2: FA:ED II, 543; 1C XV:41; FA:ED I, 219-20.

God. Truly the Reign of God is ours! As we own and admit to this powerlessness to save and care for ourselves, we more totally open ourselves to receive the riches of our God. This chapter, too, is *not* about a vow but rather it gives us an inspirational and gospel basis for our reflections.

**Article 21** – Calls to memory the poverty and humility of our Lord Jesus Christ. We safeguard our poverty today by our identification with the great number of Christ's poor in our cities. As Timothy calls us, we should be content with enough food and sufficient clothing (1 Tm 6:8). Many of us of the TOR tradition do not know extreme poverty or suffer material want. Identification with the poor by simple living is perhaps where the great invitation to conversion calls us today, and indeed it is where one might experience a fresh transformation in spirit. We voluntarily vow to live this. The underprivileged have a great deal to teach us as, hopefully, we learn from them in the holy exchange.[39] Francis and his formative experiences were with the poor and lepers. We try to live poorly because of Christ Jesus and His Mother. They truly were the embodiment of *evangelical poverty*.[40]

**Article 22** – In trying to live as "pilgrims and strangers," communities often know the burden and the security of having corporate wealth by which we are able to serve others. Most important is that we do minister as servants and avoid any haughty attitudes and behaviors that suggest power and wealth or lording it over others. Francis never mentions poverty, and the TOR tradition of poverty is different from that of the Friars Minor. We do have and own property. Ours is in making our living simply which means not acting like haughty owners, while making our goods available to the poor. There is not the emphasis of leaving all things material. We are to live "most high poverty" only with the spirit and attitude of *sine proprio* of the First Order. This "most high poverty" is Francis's own term. It was not accepted at first by the General Assembly because it held the idea of going about barefoot and in smelly ragged habits. Whereas it is really to reflect the attitude of the beatitudes. Somehow it is necessary for us to be sufficiently stripped in order to be enabled to completely trust and have confidence in Almighty God while letting go of all else.[41] In the sixth verse of the *Salutation of the Virtues* Francis tells us "whoever has one virtue and does not offend against others, possesses all of the virtues."[42]

---

[39]Fortini, *Francis of Assisi*, 28.

[40]ScEx 44; FA:ED I, 544. Additional references are also found in 2C XXV:55; FA:ED II, 284-85; 2MP 12-18; FA:ED III, 265-69.

[41]1C XV: 39; FA:ED I, 218; 1C XVI:42; FA:ED I, 220-21.

[42]SalV 6; FA:ED I, 164.

Especially in our living situation we must ever strive to dispossess our-selves of any form of greed. This greed destroys every genuine form of community on all levels. We certainly include here the various forms of poverty – being non-judgmental, having a healthy healing attitude toward all, letting go of little and big hurts, resentment and cynicism. There is no end to what the human heart might give up.

## VII. Fraternal Life

Originally we translated this chapter as "fraternal life." However, there was such a problem with the English translation that this was eventually changed to community. This lacks something of the depth of meaning we have from the word *fraternitas*. Theologically, we understand *fraternitas* to mean Christ is the center of community around whom the rest of us gather. He is *the* brother of us all. The term *fraternitas* translates in the duality in other languages meaning both male and female. Even though our translation of the word into community is lacking, it is much more acceptable than fraternity until we come up with a better solution to the language difficulty. The primary point of reference is not us but Jesus!

**Article 23** – tells us that it is God's love that is the basis of all of our loves, and our love is but a reflection of God's love. Special love should be given toward members of the Franciscan family, as we are truly of the same spiritual ancestral heritage, regardless of any issues that might continue to be divisive among us. Particularly when we attempt to "make our needs known with confidence," we are expressing a great deal of trust. Much care must be taken never to betray that trust. We do need one another. Clare and Francis placed emphasis on love and care for the sick members. Certainly there must be shared responsibility for creating community in our smaller Institutes as well as in our large international Franciscan family. Much of our experience and appreciation of community life has been based on a monastic model, because this is how we grew up in our religious institutes. However, Francis stresses not so much place and conditions as on relationships.[43]

**Article 24** – A very deep level of honesty and humility is needed to humbly acknowledge our faults and weaknesses and immediately ask forgiveness when we have failed. This is truly counter-cultural and particularly difficult for most Americans. This exchange of mutual

---

[43]L3C XI:41; FA:ED II, 92-93; 2MP 5:90, FA:ED III, 337-38; *The Canticle of Exhortation to Clare and her Sisters*, CA:ED, 393-94.

trust and compassion is but a reflection of God's constant attitude toward each of us. Our Franciscan obedience binds us not to a place or to a particular ministry but to each and every relationship rooted in Christ Jesus.[44]

The honest and sacred exchange of fraternal correction is often uncomfortable for most of us to give or to receive. But it is the responsibility of every member to share the process. It seems those Sisters and Brothers more closely bonded in friendship are called to live this more readily and radically in their relationship with a hurting sister or brother. True love demands and commands this. We cannot place the responsibility only onto the ministers. I believe the real test of maturity and sincere honest motivation is obvious in the manner of giving and receiving correction. It is healthy to ask ourselves daily how we are trying to live life more lovingly. Who models this for me? And what kind of an example am I offering to my sisters and brothers? We all have a great responsibility in this regard. Fr. Raphael Pazzelli, T.O.R., suggests the initiative should be taken by the one who has learned more completely the Gospel and Francis's meaning of charity. We might here ask ourselves, "How often do I pretend ignorance in this regard?" Rather, may we go forth and produce lovely fruits always!

## VIII. OBEDIENCE OF LOVE

We recall it took much explanation at the General Assembly on the Rule text to focus on Jesus' obedience as that of pure and total love. This chapter title is not to imply that our obedience will ever be simple or easy, but it tells us we must look to Jesus who did what he did out of passionate love. This chapter, too, is *not* about the vow of obedience but rather it offers an inspirational and scriptural basis.

The meaning of *relationships* is integral to understanding the obedience of Francis. In the *Salutation of the Virtues*, "lady love," holy love is partnered with holy obedience, and the two really do express something essential in Francis's vision.

**Article 25** – This chapter speaks to the new form of life which Clare and Francis envisioned. As "Sister Death" approached, Francis seemed to return to an even greater sense and desire for this need in a new form to "begin again." We are to remember that we're obeying for the love of God. We enter into a common bond of obedience where we share beliefs and inspiration by faith in Christ, the Church, community and

---

[44]1C XIV:34-35; FA:ED I, 213-14; 2C CXV: 155; FA:ED II, 347.

our General Minister; where we come to experience and grow in the obedience of love. Christ Jesus left us a radical example expressed in Paul's great kenotic passage, "Your attitude must be that of Christ Jesus Who emptied Himself..." (Phil 2: 5-11). This is what moved Francis to want to do likewise, *propter Jesus Christus*. So the Creator's love was foundational for Francis, with the obedience of Jesus as his underlying attitude.[45]

Sincere and honest Franciscan chapters, in their various creative forms, are essential to enable ongoing revitalization and to observe meaningful obedience. They should contain practical structures that help us renew and reform our obedience. I believe it was the genius of St. Francis to create such opportunities for an ever-renewed enthusiasm and the urgency of living our commitment on a deeper level. I believe local and general chapters are a great means of creating and remaining honest as in our exchange with members who perhaps know us the best.

In this article we are again called to exhort and admonish one another and to willingly serve and obey each other. This always calls for self-emptying. The emphasis is ever on responsible obedience.

**Article 26** – (Articles 26 and 27 are best seen as a unit.) We are challenged to develop and live as servant in attitude and behavior in the deepest sense of our vocation. However, the minister of the community represents the official living connection between the Institute and the outside world and the Church in every legal capacity. Wisdom particularly demands ongoing discernment and attentive listening obedience on the part of all who are called to the servanthood task just as it does for each and every member.[46]

**Article 27** – The servants or ministers must fulfill their duties of admonishing, visiting, exhorting, encouraging and giving good example to each member with a heartfelt attitude of *sine proprio*. "...the Brothers and Sisters should be glad to serve and obey one another in a Spirit of charity."[47] They are never to exercise their authority as the powerful of the world. St. Francis clearly teaches us the community leadership must remember that they are merely workers, i.e., employees, in the service of the community according to Francis's ideals "...and Jesus began to wash his disciples feet" (Jn 13). Therefore, it is most important that they very convincingly model the spirit of servant, especially toward those sisters

---

[45]SalV 3; FA:ED I, 164; L3C XIV:57-60; FA:ED I, 100-03; LMj 6:5; FA:ED II, 572-73.
[46]1C XII: 29-31; FA:ED I, 207-10.
[47]ER V:1-17; FA:ED I, 67-68.

and brothers who seek their help in being faithful to what they have promised.[48]

Some of the major superiors felt we had made a mistake in the text by placing the superior in the role of "employee" while the community was in the situation of "employer." This is another of Francis's radical demands of us in our penitential journey. It's really from St Francis![49] As Chesterton tells us, "Francis sees the world upside down." To be a minister or servant means to be obedient to those we serve. This speaks of being counter-cultural.

**Article 28** – In this article we are reminded that we are all very dispensable, and should be willing to change positions. Hopefully no one will desire to hold on to his or her authority roles.[50] In many primary sources we see St. Francis in the role as founder and visionary of the Order who experiences the need to resign for a variety of reasons.[51]

It seems to me that with the brief terms of office this article is a bit easier to accept and practice. However, there are individuals and communities where the change from any authority role does not come easy. I feel it is unfortunate for any quality community to believe no other person is capable of serving well in leadership office by God's grace.

## IX. Apostolic Life

This chapter makes the connection between *metanoia* and ministry, and between contemplation and action. It is the summation of all that has been said in the Rule.

**Article 29** – May we ever love our God, praise our God, and imitate Jesus in our charitable service to the poor. This chapter begins with the greatest command, the attitude of the Hebrew Shema Dt 6:4-9, TOR Prologue, and Art 9. It describes how Francis spells out the missionary spirit he wants us to have and which is such a vital part of our Franciscan consecrated life, which we all need to hear repeatedly. We do want to glorify God in all we do by our works of mercy.[52]

---

[48]2C CXXXIX: 184-86; FA:ED II, 364-66; 2MP 4:80; FA:ED, vol. 3, 324-26.

[49]LR X:1-12; FA:ED I, 105.

[50]Adm III and IV; FA:ED I, 130.

[51]2C CIV:143; 2C CXI: 151; FA:ED II, 340, 344-45; LMj 6:4; FA:ED II, 571; 2MP 3:64; FA:ED III, 307-08.

[52]LMj 12:7; FA:ED II, 625-26.

# CONTEMPORARY COMMENTARIES

# 6

## CONTEMPORARY COMMENTARIES

The passage of more than two and a half decades, when viewed against the eight centuries of Franciscan history, is a negligible period of time. Or is it? We look back eagerly to learn what the first generations of friars thought of their obligations when questions Francis could not have imagined disturbed their peace and shadowed their practice. With this historical knowledge to guide us, we see the importance of giving careful attention to the first manifestations of development in our understanding of this text. How does the passage of time create a new lens by which to view the meanings of words, to promote new interpretation and to demand revision of first assumptions?

Some immediate examples come to mind. When translating the passage from the *Early Rule* IX:2 in actual lectures or classes, we had a tendency to "explain away" the use of the term *leper*. After all, speakers argued, leprosy was a thing of the past, so we gave the listener the easy pathway out of the dilemma and used such equivalents as "the marginalized," the "abandoned," or the *anawim*. Then came the explosion of AIDS. Suddenly the actual and symbolic value of the place of the leper in the early Franciscan discovery of the Gospel mandates took on new power. Within a very short time an initial commentator's temptation towards political correctness was vanquished. Instead, the recognition of the power of the story of the leper as the agent of Francis's conversion for our time and ourselves grew steadily.

The role of inclusive language in the translations used in the U.S.A. has been a topic of continual dialogue. Difficulties posed by adhering closely to the language of Francis and Clare were frequently brought forward by large number of North American members. In response, a new translation of the text was developed in 1996-97 by Godet-Calogeras and Carney at the request of the Franciscan Federation of the U.S.A.

Continued research into the dating and intentions behind what are now called the *Earlier Exhortation* and the *Later Admonition and Ex-*

*hortation* necessitate constant re-thinking by teachers of the Rule text. When it was approved the study of what was then designated as the *Letter to All the Faithful* was in its infancy. Much has been done to deepen our understanding of both texts' origins, audience and dates of birth.

Here, then, are four new essays on the fundamental values of the *Rule and Life*. They are bridges between the very first decades of commentary and teaching and the work to be done by each new generation to fulfill its stewardship of the charism.

# Roland J. Faley, T.O.R.

## RECAPTURING A VISION: CONVERSION

A quarter century has passed since the revised Rule of the Third Order Regular of St. Francis was approved and promulgated by Pope John Paul II. Over the course of these twenty-five years, many of the people involved in the work of revision have died. Fewer still are those who participated in that process from the beginning. As one of those few still with us, I welcome the opportunity to reflect on the Rule Project which, despite its modest and feeble beginnings, resulted in a true religious landmark.

The Second Vatican Council remains a starting point for this effort. In underscoring the importance of religious life in the Church, the Council called religious to a renewal in spirit and in structure to bring religious life into a contemporary setting. This call of the Council received a welcome and enthusiastic endorsement from the Church's religious. The Franciscan Third Order Regular was no exception.

It should be noted that the Third Order Regular has a very special meaning as applied to a very specific Order within the Franciscan family known as the TOR. But it has also come to include a diverse development of the Franciscan spirit through the centuries. The greater number of Franciscan institutes that have been founded over the last several centuries are part of the Tertiary tradition and follow the TOR Rule of Life.

The *Rule of Life* is the basic document in the life of any religious institute. If it was written by the founder himself or herself, it remains unchanged and stands as a fundamental statement of the founder's purpose, as is the case with the Dominicans, the Franciscan Friars Minor, and the Benedictines. When such was not the case, a rule could be subject to revisions and adaptations through the centuries. Such was the case with the Franciscan Third Order Regular.

When the Council called religious institutes to structural renewal, it looked principally to the constitutions or practical *norma* by which the life of the institute is regulated. The original Third Order Regular accomplished this in the general chapter of 1969; the renewed constitutions were approved in the early 1970s.

While this work of renewed constitutions was generally well received throughout the Order, it evidenced, at the same time, a notable and unfortunate *lacuna*. For Franciscan tertiaries the fundamental document, or *Rule of Life*, dating from 1927 was sadly out of date and lacked an authentic expression of the Order's spirit. More important than the constitutions was the need for a meticulous revision of the Rule. But such would require a special permission of the Holy See and the willingness of the many TOR congregations within the church, all of whom would be affected by a revision of the Rule.

Since the revision of the Rule was seen to be of paramount importance, the machinery was quickly set in motion. Thaddeus Horgan of the Society of the Atonement and myself spearheaded the work within our own religious order. We were both stationed in Rome at the time and were thus offered a unique opportunity to collaborate.

Our initial work culminated in what became known as the Madrid Document, which was approved at a congress of the male Tertiary religious held in Madrid, Spain in 1974.[1] It was an early attempt at charism rediscovery. But it was in the wake of Madrid that we realized that any revision of the Rule would have to be a broad-based collaborative effort of men and women religious. There was a fairly universal agreement on the inadequacy of the Rule of 1927, but the problem lay in finding the way to engage the many Tertiary congregations.

An opening was discovered when we learned that the desire for a new Rule had led some areas of the world to begin the work of a provisional text, much as we had done at Madrid. The foremost among these efforts was that of the French-speaking tertiaries that had already produced a provisional text. We established contact with the French Federation in the interests of opening the door to collaboration. Through the French we were brought into contact with a German initiative as well. Rather than authoring competing documents, we were interested in drawing on the best of all efforts to develop one text that would then be satisfactory to all.[2]

We soon found out that this was to be no easy task. Each group worked out of a set of preconceptions in which there were both convergences and divergences. The joint meetings of the latter part of the 1970s at times led to impasses that were not easily resolved. But the desire of all participants was to arrive at a single unified text. The climactic moment came in 1982 when an International Franciscan Congress was held in Rome to review and refine the proposed Rule. The Congress marked an incredible moment in the history of Franciscan life, with the final approval of the new Rule, promulgated officially by John Paul II on December 8, 1982.

What is the distinctive mark or charism of Franciscan Tertiary life? The answer is to be found in the earliest designation of the Order: The Order of Penance of Francis of Assisi. The Order of penitents in the

---

[1] P. McMullen, "Fourth Franciscan Tertiary Inter-Obediential Congress," *Analecta Tertii Ordinis Regularis Sancti Francisci* XIII:123 (1974): 141.

[2] For information on the development of the Third Order Rule including the French and German Rule see P. McMullen, "The Development of the New T.O.R. Rule," *Analecta Tertii Ordinis Regularis Sancti Francisci* XIX:143 (1987): 365-410.

church did not begin with Francis; it actually predated him by centuries. Initially instituted for sinners who were publicly alienated from the church and were seeking restoration, it eventually welcomed those who wished to enter upon a life of penitence, even though they were guilty of no serious public sins. This Order of Penance had its highs and its lows through the centuries, but received a renewed impetus in the middle ages, especially through the efforts of Francis who saw it as an avenue of holiness for people living outside the confines of the traditional religious life.

But of what did this penitential life consist? To a considerable extent the term "penance" had come to be identified with acts of mortification and self-denial. It was the external forms of penance such as fasting, abstinence, and self-denial that were in the forefront, and not the biblical notion of a basic change of life. One of the major contributions of the Madrid Document was a return to this biblical notion of penance as conversion of life, with the hope that this would be highlighted in any revision of the Rule.[3]

It was felt that any revision of the Rule had to see penance as a central value. This was seen primarily in the sense of a "turning around" in life. The Greek verb *metanoein* rendered the Hebrew *shub* that in its most concrete sense meant a "turning around" on the road. This meaning carries over into the New Testament's call to conversion of life, which signified a change of direction in life or the Pauline assertion of setting aside the "old person" and walking now in a newness of life.[4]

The French proposed Rule text listed four fundamental values of Franciscan Tertiary life: conversion (penance), prayer, poverty and humility. In an earlier text these were seen to have equal value. However, studies of the Tertiary or penitential movement showed that such was not the case. All the values listed had great value but conversion was the overarching value. The other three had to be seen in the light of penance, which remains always the dominant value. This was explained and voted on by the entire assembly. This is very clear in the all-important article two of the Rule wherein conversion of life is highlighted and the other three values are seen as specifications of the way conversion is lived. The main thrust of the Rule is summarized in Article Six. "Led by God, let them begin a life of penance, conscious that all of us must be continuously

---

[3]For information on the Madrid Document see *The Statement of Understanding of Franciscan Penitential Life: Issued by the IV Franciscan TOR Penitential Congress*, R.M. Delaney and T. Horgan, eds. (Madrid, Spain, 1974).

[4]For a development of this concept see R. Faley, "Biblical Considerations of Metanoia," *Analecta Tertii Ordinis Regularis Sancti Francisci* XIII:123 (1974): 13-33.

converted."[5] This identity of the basic charism of the Tertiary movement can be said to have been rediscovered in the revised Rule. This was very evident to the present writer who remembers well a chapter of his own order earlier in the latter part of the twentieth century wherein there was a consideration of the Order's official title: "The Third Order Regular of St. Francis of Penance." A well-intentioned chapter father found that title much too long and unwieldy and made the proposal of the "of Penance" be dropped. Such would have meant the elimination of the Order's charism from its title.

## LIVING THE CHARISM

The key to living this Gospel way of life is summarized for us in the *recensio prior* or early edition of Francis's *Letter to the Faithful*, which good scholarship holds was written for the early penitents. Although prone to sin, the life of the penitent is centered on the Body and Blood of Christ and thus brings forth from within his or herself fruits worthy of true penance. We are the "spouses, brothers, and mothers of the Lord. Spouses when united by the Spirit with Christ; brothers when we do the will of the Father; mothers when we bear him in our hearts and give birth to him through a holy life...."[6]

In the troubled and in many ways unbelieving world in which we live, various ways suggest themselves as to how this charism of conversion may find expression. There is, first of all, a ministry to the unchurched and disaffected. So far has much of Europe drifted from its spiritual moorings and so de-Christianized has it become that any effort to insert a reference to the Christian faith as part of its legacy was rejected in drawing up a new European constitution. Countless baptized persons have a disconnect with the church throughout their lives. This is a fertile field for ministry on the part of Franciscan penitents. There are new and imaginative programs today that are geared to re-engage the faith life of those who have become separated from the church.

Much of what will and can be done depends on the number of possible personnel. Today we are living with diminishing numbers in western countries that impedes the adoption of new ministries. But the possibilities are almost limitless in terms of what might be undertaken. With the charism of penance and reconciliation, the times suggest many possibilities.

---

[5]*Rule and Life of the Brothers and Sisters of the Third Order Regular of St. Francis: 25th Anniversary Edition*, J-F. Godet-Calogeras, trans. (Washington: Franciscan Federation, 2007), 15.

[6]2LtF 51-53; FA:ED I, 49.

## CENTERS OF SPIRITUAL LIFE

A Spiritual Life center offers many possibilities for ministries connected with the charism of reconciliation. Retreats and days of reflection that highlight overcoming alienation from God with the re-emergence of a vital faith life flow easily from such a venue. Retreats geared especially toward alienated groups find a natural setting in such a center. Spiritual problems connected with divorce, gender identity, drug or alcoholic addiction needs to be addressed in very specific terms, but they often fall under the category of spiritual alienation. There are, in addition, those people who have simply wandered from their faith. In many instances they are not antagonistic just very much "at sea." Programs offered by religious Penitents are a natural fit for these people, who are all too numerous in our times.

There are also those persons who are interested in knowing more about Catholicism and may be moving toward it for the first time. Very often prospective converts carry the weight of difficult problems and serious issues that have never been addressed. A Spiritual Life center which is specifically geared toward reconciliation can be of inestimable value in this regard. What is important for Tertiary religious who undertake such ministries is to keep a clear focus on reconciling ministries. To return to generic ministries certainly is a help to souls but it clearly dulls the penitential charism.

A prison ministry offers distinct possibilities for Tertiary religious. Personal experience has shown this writer that prisoners are people who wallow in a well of rejection and isolation. Many show a desire for new beginnings and the cultivation of a spiritual life. Incarcerated people are far from public view but should not be overlooked. These people often believe that their return to God and the church will be long and tortuous. The Franciscan message of "peace and goodness" frequently receives a welcome reception.

## AN AIDS MINISTRY

The Third Order Regular has a fledgling vice province in South Africa. They are in the process of planning a ministry for people afflicted with HIV/AIDS. South Africa is one of the countries that has been most devastated by this widespread disease, and there are many of the poorest who are in dire need of care and assistance. The most recent assembly of the friars in South Africa saw this ministry as most compelling and voted to begin the process of undertaking a new apostolate. It is a step such as this which not only brings hope to people's lives; it also energizes the religious community as well.

What remains true in this entire discussion is the importance of selecting ministries that are clearly linked with the basic charism. To opt

for ministries solely because of diocesan need or other factors will undoubtedly render a service but the distinctive charism of the Order will
also be lost.

## THE SECULAR FRANCISCAN ORDER

Worthy of note in this time of recapturing a vision is the fact that the
original Franciscan Order of Penance is historically rooted in what is
today known as the Secular Franciscan Order. Initially a lay movement
which, has been noted, preceded Francis by centuries, the Order embraced
people of all walks of life who were experiencing a newfound conversion
of life. These were principally people who lived a domestic life while
following the *Rule of Life* for Franciscan penitents. In the course of time,
groups of these lay penitents joined forces in living a community life and
pursuing a particular ministry. Eventually they became recognized as an
expression of active religious life in the Church and today are an integral
part of the Third Order Regular.

This proved to be a time of historic proportions, especially for women
religious. Through much of the Middle Ages, expressions of religious
life for women were restricted to cloistered or enclosed life. Women religious of the active life had not yet appeared in the Church's life. The
Penitents, however, never lost their active ministry, even though they
lived in community.

Out of this development was born the Third Order Regular as distinguished from the seculars. They were eventually recognized as religious in the church but who were the heirs of the Franciscan penitential
movement. This is but to say that the Franciscan tertiary religious find
their origins in the original penitential movement. Even though the lay
dimensions of the Secular Franciscans today has its own Rule of Life, the
fact remains that the TOR and the SFO spring from the same soil and an
identical guiding spirit.

Such being the case, an alliance in ministry is a natural consequence
of this common origin. The promotion of the Secular Franciscan Order
should be an integral part of the Tertiary religious life. In many parts
of the world, Secular Franciscanism is in need of a true revitalization.
It must be made relevant to the life of the young and not be left solely
to those who after many years of service have now reached their senior
years.

Today, team efforts bring religious and laity together in ministry. For the
tertiaries such should be seen as a very logical step. Ministry to the poor
and the alienated, the imprisoned and the addicted, as well as other forms
of outreach are able to find common ground among Secular and Regular
Franciscan tertiaries. To join hands, to the extent possible, in the apostolic
life is another way for the penitential charism to be given fuller play.

## POVERTY

Nothing has caused more discord and division within the Franciscan family. The "most high poverty," *altissima paupertas* of the Friars Minor led not only to prolonged and heated discussion but even division within the Order. But it should be noted the Lady Poverty never attained such an exalted position in the Tertiary tradition. The reason is clear enough. The first Penitents were people living in their homes with normal financial responsibilities. They earned money and used it for themselves and the broader community.

Their life style was simple and ostentation was assiduously avoided. In the earliest rules of life we learn of the monthly distribution of excess funds for the needs of the poor. There is every reason to believe that this use of money extended to the time of community life among the Tertiaries. Eventually what has now become the traditional understanding of poverty became the norm for all religious, and the original concept was lost. Some tertiaries have returned to the idea of the common fund, monies collected monthly and dedicated to a needy cause.

This is a type of poverty that touches the life of each community member. While a modest and simple life style remains normative for all tertiaries, as is emphasized in the Rule's chapter on poverty, there is the added feature of everybody's contribution to the needs of others, which makes poverty a much more relevant feature of religious consecration.

There is a certain poverty of life that is part of religious consecration. In the Order of Penance it is part of that interior liberation which puts Christ as the center of life. But it is not in itself the driving force of the Franciscan Penitent's life in God. This is clear from a history and study of the Order's growth and development. Authenticity requires that this spirit be recaptured today.

## AN ETHIC OF NON-VIOLENCE

Jesus preached an ethic of non-violence, which is eminently clear in reading the New Testament. In the face of hostility the Christian is advised to adopt a posture of love and forgiveness. That this was a keynote feature of Francis's life is unquestionable. His constant salutation of "Peace and Good" was more than a pious greeting. Conflict resolution was at the heart of his intervention in any troubled situation.

Instead of participating in the crusades, Francis traveled by boat to dialogue with the Muslim Sultan and was accorded genuine respect. It is not surprising, therefore, to learn from the early Rule of the Penitents that they did not bear arms. There is no evidence that Francis was a vocal critic of the Church-sponsored crusades, but it was certainly not his preferred response. Nor is there any indication that the Penitents were prevailed upon to participate.

Unfortunately, today we live in an atmosphere of violence. Senseless violence and killing are part of the life in our major cities. Governments resort to war even when there is no direct provocation. Iraq is a prime example. It was a war undertaken preemptively allegedly to rid the world of a ruthless dictator. But it proved to be a war that unleashed suppressed enmities within a country and led to the dreadful loss of thousands of Iraqis and several thousand United States troops.

Voices that argue for peace are more necessary today than at any point in history. Military force may at times be necessary but only after every possible avenue of diplomacy has been exhausted when facing a serious threat. The penitential tradition has a long and favorable history in this regard. Its presence should not be lost today.

### The Sacrament of Reconciliation

Most people involved in pastoral ministry in the Church today would readily admit that the sacrament of Reconciliation does not enjoy a widespread appreciation. It is still within the realm of living memory that weekends within a parish saw many hours given over to the administration of this sacrament. Today it has fallen into widespread disuse. Part of this is due to the fact that for many people it was never a pleasant experience. Others fail to see its necessity, arguing that sin can be forgiven through a private and personal approach to God. Some people are simply indifferent to the issue.

Reconciliation stands at the very heart of the penitential tradition. Tertiaries can and should be among its foremost promoters, through preaching, through parish missions, and especially through the education of the young. Reconciliation can be shown to be experienced as a very peaceful and joy-filled experience. It serves as a mirror reflecting our soul and shared with another person whereby we can better see ourselves and open ourselves more readily to the infusion of God's love.

The ways in which this can be done are varied. The point is that it should be seen as a key feature of those who live by a charism of reconciliation and who seek to share it with others.

Admittedly we are only at the beginning of the realization of a recaptured charism. This writer has proposed a number of ways in which the charism can be brought to life in the church today. There are certainly other ways than those highlighted here. But the fact remains that the future requires some visioning if the charism is not to remain a "dead letter." The relevance of a penitential or converted life and ministry is perhaps more relevant today than at any time. Those whose efforts worked to recapture that vision are now prepared to hand the torch to a new generation. The penitents of the Franciscan Third Order have more than enough ways to bring their basic spirit to life.

# Suzanne M. Kush, C.S.S.F.

## THE CONTEMPLATIVE-ACTIVE STANCE OF FRANCISCAN PRAYER

In my early years as a Franciscan woman, my understanding of contemplation had a monastic tone, evoking a connotation of withdrawal from the world for the purpose of introspection. While being involved in active ministry the day was structured around the schedule for liturgical and personal prayer. Personal prayer was a very private experience with a vertical orientation between God and self. Furthermore, formators were encouraging us to have a balance between the contemplative and active world. The word balance was interpreted as both worlds receiving equal time since these were viewed as separate worlds. This created a real tension as ministerial expectations increased.

This understanding and practice began to change for me shortly after the approval of the revised Third Order Regular Rule. I remember attending a presentation given by Margaret Carney, O.S.F. for Third Order Franciscans. The explanation of the TOR Rule and what it meant to be a Franciscan woman began to provide some clarity and began to ease inner tension. The presentation resonated with what I felt deep within. Becoming acquainted with the Franciscan literary tradition found in the *Omnibus of Sources* and reflecting on the new Third Order Regular Rule continued the ongoing process of change. As my awareness was heightened, insights were also found in the most unexpected places. Reading a short story entitled "Chin Lin" by Edward Hays provided an understanding of living contemplatively. A waitress at a Chinese restaurant, Chin Lin, began her day in meditation. Everyone recognized that Chin Lin was not an ordinary waitress by her manner of serving the patrons and her attention in selecting an appropriate fortune cookie for each patron at the end of the meal.[1] Chin Lin was attentive to the restaurant guests because the inner eye of her heart was opened each morning in contemplation. Some might say that this is just a nice tale. However, the narrative illustrates what it means to live contemplatively. It was these experiences that provided the framework to probe more deeply the meaning of this term. While much can be written on Franciscan contemplation, I will attempt to articulate the unfolding of my understanding of living contemplatively.

The Franciscan value of contemplation was of particular importance to me since the documents of the congregation of which I am a member describe the community as being contemplative-active. In our desire to

---

[1]Edward Hays, "Chin Lin," *Twelve and One Half Keys* (Leavenworth: Forest of Peace Publishing, 1981), 19-22.

obtain some clarity, the words contemplative-active took on an entirely new meaning. The hyphen made all the difference! The lens through which I began to understand the meaning of the Gospel life changed by focusing on the interrelationship between the significance of the times when Jesus went off to pray and the times he ministered to the people. The emphasis was not only on the fact that Jesus or Francis went off to pray but also that mercy was shown to the people. The contemplative-active stance was a part of the rhythm of their lives. It was comforting to realize that this way of living was not easily understood by Francis and his early companions. This struggle was captured in the writings of Francis's earlier biographers. Celano writes that "St. Francis did not put his trust in his own efforts, but with holy prayer coming before any decision, he chose not to live for himself alone.... For he knew that he was sent for this: to win for God souls...."[2] Francis discerned his need for time for prayer and time for love of neighbor. Thus, Francis espoused the vertical dimension and added the horizontal, that is, relationship, with his brothers and sisters. The Volterra Document, included in the introduction to the Third Order Regular Rule, clearly articulates this relationship. "All who love God with their whole heart, with their whole soul and mind, and with their whole strength and love their neighbor as themselves...."[3] Francis, through his example of prayer, elucidates the meaning of "neighbor." His immediate love of neighbor was extended to the *minores* and the untitled of Assisi. As Francis continued his faith journey the concept of neighbor extended beyond Assisi to Egypt and the Sultan Malek al-Kamil. This is of particular importance today in the Twenty-first Century. Technology has altered the concept of neighbor by eliminating borders to include all of the cosmos.

Although Francis does not provide a clearly defined *method* of prayer he does illustrate an *attitude* of prayer. Francis's understanding of con-templation was twofold. Francis in solitude was embraced by the uncon-ditional love of God and recognized God's presence in his life. In turn, this gift that Francis received was shaped by his life and relationship with others. Contemplation leads to a deeply intentional way of living. The word "intentional" suggests living with an awareness of not only what is apparent but also what is a reality on a much deeper level, one that is both cognitively and affectively experienced. This way of living suggests a removing of obstacles that prevent our seeing and experiencing the beauty and truth that the mystery of life holds. Being in relationship – being sister and brother – unfolds one of the mysteries of life through

---

[2] 1C XIV:35; FA:ED I, 214.

[3] Jean François Godet-Calogeras, trans. *The Rule and Life of the Brothers and Sisters of the Third Order Regular of St. Francis, 1982-2007 25th Anniversary Edition* (Washington, DC, Valley Press, Inc, 2007), 3.

contemplation. While Francis in the *Later Rule* wrote: "Wherever the brothers may be sent and meet one another, let them show that they are members of the same family."[4] This is accentuated today by the ever-increasing connectedness provided by technology. Contemplating this connectedness reveals the richness of our diversity, the commonness of our humanity and relatedness as sister and brother. This is possible only in letting go of prejudices and differences. It means seeing with the heart of God.

Another way of stating this is that through an awareness of God's presence in the myriad of ways that God speaks to us through all of creation, God empowers us to see that which is ordinary in an extraordinary way. A personal experience comes to mind. A number of years ago I accompanied visitors on a boat ride to the base of Niagara Falls. The thought of the boat negotiating the swirling waters of the Niagara River and the power of Niagara Falls filled me with much anxiety and fear. However, as the boat approached the magnificent Falls those feelings dissipated into feelings of gratitude and praise.

Reflecting on this experience provides an understanding that the prayers of Francis are filled with thanksgiving and praise. The words "let us bless," "give praise," "glory," "blessing" are found throughout his writings. *The Office of the Passion* provides an example: "Let us bless the Lord God living and true! Let us always render Him praise, glory, honor, blessing and every good. Amen. Amen."[5] Gratitude is an active response of an individual to the love of God and neighbor that we receive and experience. It is also a self-transcendent attitude recognizing God's freely given gift calling one to move beyond oneself, and the obstacles which holds one bound and by allowing oneself to be transformed. Therefore, a grateful life calls one to live intentionally, moving beyond our obstacles and opening one to experience God's goodness.

Contemplative moments can take place in the quiet of a solitary space or within a crowd. Vacationing with my sister and brother-in-law at the Grand Canyon provided a profound contemplative moment. Admiring the beauty at the South Rim, I found myself moving away from the many tourists. The silence of the canyon was almost deafening. Brief, powerful moments of contemplation can occur during the ordinariness of daily activity. The ability to recognize changes and inner movements that take place within the solitude of one's being is to live contemplatively. One is moved, aware of inner stirrings amidst the stress and the multitasking we are so often involved in. At times this can be challenging. It is at such times that withdrawing and being replenished with God's love is impor-

---

[4] LR VI:7; FA:ED I, 103.
[5] OfP; FA:ED I, 141.

tant, for we come to realize we cannot do it alone. Through this journey I have come to appreciate the wisdom of our founding mothers introducing monthly days of reflection and annual retreat. However, hermitage *moments* can afford us time throughout the day, and at ministry, recalling God's presence in the persons and events that we encounter.

Francis emphasized the need for continuous prayer as reflected in the *Later Admonition and Exhortation* "...And day and night let us direct praises and prayers to Him ... for we should pray always and not become weary." This suggests to us that contemplation is not necessarily reserved for a particular place or a particular stance. Where we are, and whomever we are with, are sacred.[6] Francis suggests to us that contemplative living is attainable for those open to being transformed by God's mercy.

Gratitude, awareness of God in the midst of activity, and the desire to pray always is possible when there is an intimacy with God. This relationship provides the foundation of living the evangelical life. The relationship of the contemplative-active life as espoused by Francis is reflected in *The Rule for Hermitages*. Reference is made in this text to Martha and Mary. This well-known pericope often focuses on "...Mary has chosen the better portion..." (Lk 10:42) and is interpreted in the monastic sense of solitude over service. However, Francis in *The Rule for Hermitages* provides a different perspective. Francis writes, "Let the two who are mothers keep the life of Martha and the two sons the life of Mary."[7] "Hermitage is a time to rest through both prayer and sleep. Rest for the body and rest for the spirit."[8] It is a time for restoring and renewing. When one has been renewed then one serves those who served. *The Rule for Hermitages* concludes with "the sons, however, shall periodically assume the role of the mothers, taking turns as they have mutually decided."[9] This speaks of mutuality and relationship. *The Rule for Hermitages* suggests that the friars integrate contemplation and service. Further reflection on *The Rule for Hermitages* suggests that the primary service to others is to preach the Gospel. Contemplating or praying with the Word fills the individual with God so that one can speak from the fullness of God's love. An individual filled with God's love is also able to meet the needs of one's neighbor in compassion and mercy. The guidance that is received in prayer assisted Francis in responding to the

---

[6]Michael Blastic, "Prayer in the Writings of Francis of Assisi and the Early Brothers," *Franciscans at Prayer* ed. Timothy Johnson (Leiden: Brill Hotei Publishing, 2007), 14.

[7]RH 2; FA:ED I, 61.

[8]Jean François Godet-Calogeras, "*Illi Qui Volunt Religiose Stare In Eremis*: Eremitical Practice in the Life of the Early Franciscans," *Franciscans at Prayer* ed. Timothy Johnson (Leiden: Brill Hotei Publishing, 2007), 327.

[9]RH 10; FA:ED I, 62.

realities of daily living. Thus, Francis's service was not only preaching the Word of God but also challenging the social, political and economic status quo of Assisi.

Another vertical experience of contemplation are those that are practiced in a communal setting. Shared reflection on the Scriptures, the writings of Francis and Clare or foundresses provides a depth of gratitude to the myriad of ways that God speaks to us. This communal sharing with sisters and brothers allows us to live more deeply. It is in the sharing of God-moments with one another, with those with whom we share the journey that we are called to see a new light and are challenged to greater fidelity. The fraternal life lived in communion with those God has given us is reminiscent of Francis and the brothers in which they reported "the good things which the merciful Lord was doing for them, and if they had been somewhat negligent and ungrateful, they humbly ask and carefully accept correction...."[10] Sharing prayer with those that we journey with creates a "we" rather than an "I" that could separate us from "the Other." Contemplating in this manner calls us to conversion, to surrendering one's assumptions and biases, and to come to a new way of understanding and loving.

Francis and Clare of Assisi clearly witnessed living for others in a contemplative-active stance as expressed by Jacques de Vitry: "...During the day they go into the cities and villages giving themselves over to the active life in order to gain others; at night, however, they return to their hermitage or solitary places to devote themselves to contemplation...."[11]

In the original commentary on the Third Order Rule written by Margaret Carney and Thaddeus Horgan, the contemplative dimension is defined as being "present to God who is present to all creatures in prayer."[12] To be present to God evokes within me the awareness that God is the focus of my life; God breaks into our human reality. One such experience occurred during the Advent Season a few years ago while visiting a Mexican mission. While I rode in a pick up truck in a very rural area, a mother and her four-year-old son were walking the five miles to town. In order to make room for them in the very small cab, we sat Juan Carlos on my lap. As we began the ride to town this four-year-old's face began to change, his tired look was transformed to pure delight and wonder. He saw his familiar surroundings in a new way. Juan Carlos' short stature only allowed him to see the dirt road. However, at a new height he saw elements of his surroundings that he had never been able to see. This was

[10]IC XII:30; FA:ED I, 209.

[11]"Writings of Jacques de Vitry"; FA:ED I, 579.

[12]Margaret Carney and Thaddeus Horgan, *The Rule and Life of the Brothers and Sisters of the Third Order Regular of St. Francis and Commentary* (Washington, DC: Franciscan Federation, 1997), 45.

a contemplative moment. Since this experience took place during the Advent Season, I came to realize that this was an Incarnational moment – Jesus' presence breaking into daily life in a very unexpected way.

We do not need to go to far-away places for this to happen. It simply requires us to see with the heart the many ways God's presence is made known to us in the Word, Eucharist and in daily living.

In summary, Franciscan contemplation is rooted in the here and now. It is dynamic, ever-evolving. Living contemplatively challenges us to open our eyes to all of life about us, not only in a sensate manner but also with the eye of the heart. Living contemplatively is transformative, for we are called to live a life centered in Christ by walking in the footprints of Christ. Living contemplatively is a call to be truly human, the person that we were truly created to be, in God's love and in sharing that love with others. Thus, through living a contemplative-active life we not only share God's Word but also the Spirit of the Word.

# Ann Bremmer, O.S.F.

## POVERTY: "I'M GOD; YOU'RE NOT"

Living the Rule over the past 25 years has taught me so much about myself, the love of God, and how I am called to live in communion with others. This essay traces the journey of how the Rule has fashioned my understanding of poverty and how it has influenced my life. I begin with my initial impressions of poverty based on the Rule of 1927 and then share stories of how my lived experience of poverty was shaped by the new Rule. This is followed by my attempt at integrating this into a theological understanding of how I am called to live Gospel poverty and ends with some reflections on how to live the Rule with authenticity.

### REFLECTIONS ON POVERTY PRE-APPROVAL OF THE RULE

These are a few recollections on poverty during my initial formation.

• I don't recall taking a lot of time studying the actual Rule of 1927 since we knew a new Rule was about to be birthed. Perhaps my memory and that of my novice director may be very different! I do remember endless walks with my directress as we talked about poverty, chastity and obedience – what the "vows" meant to me and how I thought I would be able to live them. I also remember her saying that I would "grow" into them.

• I also remember struggling with the term "poverty." I could not quite reconcile how we "took a vow of poverty" as if it were a "good." At that time, my thinking was more literal. I knew I would never be socio-economically poor. But I could understand poverty as the call to live simply. I also remember innocently thinking – "this will be easy" since I am one of thirteen children and grew up living relatively simply.

• Once on a visit home, I was engaged in a conversation with one of my brother's friends. He was criticizing my decision to enter religious life. He said something like: You will take a vow of poverty, but your family will live it by financially supporting you throughout your life. It had never occurred to me that my choice would be a burden to my family. I remember making a decision then to prove by brother's friend wrong.

• I remember not being able to articulate within myself what makes Franciscan poverty different from any of the other sisters with whom I was attending intercommunity novitiate classes. Although it bothered me somewhat, I never verbalized it.

• One time I remember talking to a second year novice about something I was considering doing/buying. I can't remember any of the details except her response to me, "Ask! Ask for whatever you want. The worst they can say is 'no.'" I knew inside myself that was not the "right" answer in light of everything else we were studying about Francis.

• One of the greatest influences was an article we read on poverty written by Wayne Hellmann. The focus of the article was on our innate poverty and original sin. In the article Wayne wrote about our fundamental poverty – we are creature, not creator and our sin comes from trying to be something we are not. Creature not Creator – I knew that this was significant; and I naïvely thought – oh, I don't think I will make that mistake. How wrong I was!

In 1982 the Sacred Congregation for Religious and Secular Institutes gave approval of the *Rule and Life of the Brothers and Sisters of the Third Order Regular of St. Francis.* There were many celebrations and Franciscan Third Order congregations across the world embraced the new Rule. I was a temporary professed sister. Animated discussions on the new Rule followed and I attended the gatherings of "Roots and Wings" where the Rule was taught. In my enthusiasm, I read the Rule and reread it, hoping to live it faithfully. I began to think about the implication of trying to embrace poverty as a value not just as a vow. At times it was confusing to me, I would think: how can I embrace the gift of life and yet be detached, isn't embracing and being detached a contradiction? At other times the values that permeate the Rule were not clear to me – I could not distinguish one from another. Poverty, obedience, love, humility all seemed interchangeable. I'd find myself asking: "Is this poverty or humility?" And then, at one point I just let go. I took the wisdom of my novice director to heart: I "would grow to understand."

### "IN TELLING THE STORY, THE MEANING WILL UNFOLD"
As I began writing stories, some of them seemed so simplistic, unworthy of telling, and yet, I had to write them out because this was my journey. Like playing the game Sudoku – you don't start with complex puzzles, you learn by doing the easy ones first. So, I share the stories.

When I entered the community, I wanted to be a missionary. And although it was not the foreign missions, as temporary professed sisters we went to New Mexico to work with a member of the community on an Indian reservation. Water was precious. It was brought into the Center in barrels and it had a sulfuric smell. We used the same dishwater for breakfast, lunch and dinner. At first I had a hard time drinking the water because of the smell, but I thought – this is what these people have and

I am here "as a pilgrim," I need to take what is offered and not ask for something else for the TOR Rule states: "…with these we are content."[1]

Implications of poverty started to "show up" in different ways. After having had an experience of "mission" in New Mexico, I asked to further explore opportunities for a foreign mission experience. When I came to discuss my findings with a Council member, she asked me to consider attending a meeting regarding missions in the United States based on a directive that resulted from a General Chapter. I remember thinking, "I'll attend, but I am going to …" Yet, while at the meeting, I listened. I listened to what the Chapter directive was, and entered into the process of discernment in order to decide the next step. There was prayer time during that meeting and I found myself writing a list of pros and cons about going. Although I had my heart set on going to a foreign mission and I had already decided that I was not going to volunteer to work with this project, to my utter surprise, I volunteered to be one of the sisters going to start our mission in Texas. Why? My personal desire weighed less than the community's discernment. Although I was only there for two years, the whole experience was profound; I still am in contact with many of the people. I had to "let go" of what I wanted and, in return, I was graced in so many ways!

By the early 1990s I was in my early 30s, I was vocation director busy about many things. I was affirmed by my community in my abilities and often heard, "Annie, if you can't bring in vocations, nobody can." As time went on, I started to subliminally take on that "messiah complex" of "if you can't bring in vocations, nobody can." I was often working when my peer/sisters were off and I began to struggle with making sense as to why I was doing what I was doing. Life outside of religious life seemed to hold more for me. I took a leave of absence as I tried to find what God wanted of me, for me. I went to a woman for spiritual direction and she had me pray over the parable of the prodigal son. It hit me like a lead balloon – I had the attitude of the older brother. I was bemoaning all that I was "doing for God" and not receiving anything in return. Somewhere along the line, I had identified myself with my work and misunderstood my relationship with God.[2] I realized that I had appropriated all my work as my own and in that appropriation lost the sense of my relationship, my dependency on God. I found that in a subtle way I had been trying to be

---

[1] *Rule and Life of the Brothers and Sisters of the Third Order Regular of St. Francis: 25th Anniversary Edition*, J-F. Godet-Calogeras, trans. (Washington: Franciscan Federation, 2007), Art. 21, 11. From now on: *Rule and Life*.

[2] Adm XIX: "Blessed is that servant who does not consider himself any better when he is praised by people that when he is considered worthless, simple, and looked down upon, for what a person is before God, that he is and no more"; FA:ED I, 135.

"Creator" and not "creature." In my awareness I asked God what I should do. I knew that religious life was what really held fullness of life for me, but I was afraid of what people, and sisters, in particular, would say if I asked to come back. I had to humble myself and ask. As difficult as that time was, it was also very blessed. I was free to choose Franciscan religious life again. And, the response I had anticipated was proven wrong. My sisters welcomed me home; some shared their own struggles. It was as if I met some of my sisters for the first time. I knew that if I gave myself to my community, I had to embrace fraternity. It dawned on me that I had taken on the mentality that I had joined "to do for community." I finally began to understand that fraternity would be one of my greatest blessings and also call the most out of me.

In subsequent years, I became an administrator in our congregation's health care system. This brought all kinds of new challenges as I lived the Rule. I found myself in a professional position that demanded attention to and involvement with finances, budgets, negotiations, political agendas, "ego's," prestige, power and privilege. Time became a very precious commodity. I had to take time each day to find the means to work in "that world" without getting sucked into the values that often adorn the position I held. Taking a stance for those in need, I often found myself "alone" with the knowledge and decision I had to make – which was poverty for me.

It was during this time that one of our Community Ministers thought it would be good if each of us had a cassette tape of the Rule. During my tenure at the hospital, I would often play that tape, drawing on the inspiration of our Rule hoping that if I listened to it long enough, like gazing upon the mirror of the cross,[3] I would live the wisdom held within.

By the early 2000s, the decision to sell the health system was made. The sale was transacted through Orphan's Court, and I was asked to stay on to see the process completed. The main facility was closed in order to convert it into a children's hospital. The whole experience was riddled with "letting go": from lacking the words to say to people as they said "good-bye," to being blamed for the closure, to walking the halls by myself at midnight as I met the "new owners" and handing over the keys, or watching buildings being torn down while I worked literally a few feet away from the demolition. On one occasion, as I watched a tractor plunk out pieces of metal rods from rubble, I remember hearing God say to me, "What is important will be plucked out of the rubble – like that wire. The spirit, love and devotion for which patients were cared for by so many will live in the halls that will be built for children." I remember the peace I experienced in letting go.

---

[3]4LAg 23; CA:ED, 56.

Over and again I would remind myself of a story I once heard:

A spiritual director was guiding a sister on retreat for a week. She began by asking, "What is it that you desire to receive during the retreat?" The woman responded, "I just want to know who is God and who am I." So the spiritual director gave her some Scripture passages and off the sister went. Each day the director would begin by asking the sister what she discovered; and each day the sister responded gloomily that she did not hear or discover anything. This went on for most of the week. Finally on the last day, the sister responded, "I kept asking God, 'Who are You and who am I? Who are You and who am I? And finally I heard God say, "I'm God and you're not!"

In a delightful way, I would hear God remind me: "I'm God, you're not, Annie." Though difficult to hear at times, I found an inner freedom and was able to attend to what needed to be done.

The poverty I embraced gave me the strength and the joy I needed during those days. I did not let "the closing," with all the work that had to be done, hold me back from living. Inspired by our vocation director, I was invited to start a house of discernment. The whole experience was an incredible journey. The house we moved into needed a lot of "fixing up." Four of us sisters worked every weekend, Friday through Sunday, for the month of July and part of August to get the place ready. I was astonished that they were willing to give so much of their time to this project! And, the women with whom I lived in the discernment house taught me so much. One example stands out among many.

It was the end of our first year. Three of us, two young women, and I had formed a community of faith, support and trust over the year. We were planning a dinner with a prayer service to end the year. Both of them had made decisions about what they wanted to do next with their lives and were moving out. Two weeks before the planned celebration, a young woman of 19 moved into the house. She needed a place to stay while she volunteered at the Thomas Merton Center for the summer. She was not able to join us for the prayer service. In the service we did a ritual of reconciliation. A pan filled with sand was held by one of us while another wrote a symbol of her sinfulness: behaviors and attitudes that fractured our relationships during the year. The one holding the pan would then shake the pan till the symbol disappeared as a sign of forgiveness. The ritual in itself was a powerful experience of mercy and love.

Two days later, the pan still sat in our prayer room. We had come in to pray evening prayer when the young woman asked about its significance. We explained to her what we had done. Then one of the women who had gone through the ritual turned to me and asked, "Did you understand my symbol, my sinful tendency?" I had. She then asked me to tell her about what I thought it meant. Her openness was astounding.

In turn, I asked her about my symbol with its significance. Again a profound sharing took place. Finally, the young woman who observed our sharing began to share about her sinful tendencies and what she really desired. I was profoundly struck by the grace God invited each of us to experience. In our openness to the other, the risk of being vulnerable, our lives were greatly blessed.

The years surrounding the "hospital" are filled with stories and layers of letting go; yet I still find myself at times, holding on. The invitation to take seriously the gift of our Rule permeated my life with the fundamental values of minority, poverty, contemplation and obedience, of my human frailty and dependence on God.

More recently, my poverty is oriented toward two things: "time" and "dependency." I work full-time for Franciscan Pilgrimage Programs while running a foundation for my congregation. I live in a mentoring house with three other professed sisters and three women in formation. A good portion of my time is spent in Europe. I say that my poverty is my time – meaning I am so blessed to live with such good women! I miss our fraternal life when I am away – our prayer, our faith sharing, the service we do together with the poor, our "family nights," and the genuine interest in each other's families. And yet, when I am home, there is work to be done! And, I want to share the gift of my education, so I find myself saying "yes" to "outside" engagements.

The second aspect is "dependency." As a leader of Franciscan pilgrimages, I need to be well prepared to "break open" the history as well as some of the theological and spiritual dimensions of a sanctuary for those on the pilgrimage. And, I have to "let go" of my control so that God is able to do what God wants to do in each person. Some times that is hard to do. I want to control factors that I have no control over. Though I am aware of the tension I have with both my time and my dependency on God, those are also the very things I find delight in letting go of, so that God can take over. It truly is an exploration into God's extravagant love!

## Education Reflected Upon

*I have dealt with great things that I do not understand; things too wonderful for me, which I cannot know. I had heard of you by word of mouth, but now my eye has seen you* (Job 42: 1-3).

In 2003, I was given permission to study at St. Bonaventure University in the School for Franciscan Studies. This was sheer gift. I often felt like the disciples sharing about their encounter of the Risen Lord on their way to Emmaus – my "heart burned" as I studied and reflected upon the gift of our Franciscan tradition.

To try to express all that informs my present understanding of how I am invited to live following in the footprints of Jesus as inspired by our Rule would be nearly impossible. However, I do offer these few reflections that have helped me continue to plumb the wisdom that poverty has to offer. Francis himself sets the stage by reflecting on his own conversion experience. In 1226, at the end of his life, Francis writes his *Testament* – his last message to his brothers reiterating all that was important to him. He says:

> The Lord gave me, Brother Francis, thus to begin doing penance in this way: for when I was in sin, it seemed too bitter for me to see lepers. And the Lord Himself led me among them and I showed mercy to them. And when I left them, what had seemed bitter to me was turned into sweetness of soul and body. And afterwards I delayed a little and left the world.[4]

We struggle to grasp the profundity of this experience. Michael Cusato, O.F.M., describes this elemental event in these words:

> On that fateful day, perhaps for the very first time in his life, Francis came into contact with the world of real, suffering human beings – people of flesh and blood like himself – men and women whom he had been taught by the value system reigning in Assisi not only to flee in horror but also to ignore, despise, account for nothing and render virtually invisible. But now, in that moment of transforming grace, Francis came to realize that God so loved the world that, through Christ's coming in human flesh, all men and women without exceptions, even the seemingly most repulsive among us, were revealed to be the bearers of the presence of God – tabernacles as it were of the incarnate Christ; that all possessed the same inestimable dignity and worth given by God to every creature; that all, in other words were *fratres et sorores*, brothers and sisters, of the same creator God.[5]

Jean François Godet-Calogeras in an essay entitled: "Clare of Assisi: A Woman's Life" speaks of mercy thus:

> The Father is the one who engenders life. But God, as fully revealed by Jesus Christ, is a merciful God, a God full of mercy. What is mercy, *misericordia*? It means having a heart sensitive to suffering and sorrow.

[4]Test 1-3; FA:ED I, 124.

[5]M. Cusato, "*Esse Ergo Mitem Et Humilem Corde, Hoc Est Esse Vere Fratrem Minorem*: Bonaventure of Bagnoregio and the Reformulation of the Franciscan Charism," in *Charisma und religiöse Gemeinschaften im Mittelalter*, G. Andenna, M. Breitenstein, G. Melville, eds. (Münster, LIT Verlag, 2004), 347-48.

This, therefore, means that God is not a revenging or hostile God. But there is more, far more. The Latin word for *misericordia*, corresponds in the Bible to a Hebrew notion of "being a womb for someone." To be merciful to someone means to be capable of taking that person into one's very entrails, having the entrails of a mother. The Father of mercies is a father-mother who, at one and the same time, engenders life and nourishes it, protects it, cares for it, helps it to grow.[6]

This is what Francis does. He takes the lepers into himself – a profound act of God. It is a transformative action. To be so engaged with another that you are transformed. Francis is transformed – he can never "not see" a leper or any person for that matter. To do so would be like a "mother who forgets the child of her womb." Just imagine the implications of this act!

In this encounter, Michael Cusato would go on to say:

> This is what can be called Francis's insight into the universal fraternity of all creatures.... Moreover, everything – all actions and attitudes – that ruptures the bonds of this fraternity of creatures is what Francis means in his *Testament* by being "in sin." To do penance is to distance himself from all those forms of power, wealth and violence that threaten to break the bonds of this human fraternity, setting human beings over each other and against each other.[7]

This conversion experience opened Francis to see and know the unfolding of God's love. "If you knew me, you would also know my Father...."[8] In particular, this love is expressed for Francis in Christ who embraces the human condition of frailty and vulnerability in the Incarnation.

> The most high Father made known from heaven through His holy angel Gabriel this Word of the Father – so worthy, so holy and glorious – in the womb of the holy and glorious Virgin Mary, from whose womb he received the flesh of our humanity and frailty. Though He was rich, He wished, together with the most Blessed Virgin, His mother, to choose poverty in the world beyond all else.[9]

From this perspective, Francis seeks to follow the "poverty and humility of Jesus Christ" especially in his beliefs concerning the Incarnation, Passion and Eucharist. As Francis looks to Jesus he sees that:

---

[6]J-F. Godet, *Clare of Assisi: A Woman's Life* (Chicago: Haversack, 1991), 67-68.

[7]Cusato, 348.

[8]Francis states in his writings that Jesus is the revelation of the Father as in Adm I; FA:ED I, 128.

[9]2LtF 4-5; FA:ED I, 46.

Jesus did not force or coerce anyone to follow him. Rather, Jesus simply and unreservedly loved. Letting go of personal power so that others might find their own power. Perhaps the most notable aspect of the life and ministry of Jesus is that he spent no time seeking prestige, but he constantly interacted with ordinary people, especially the powerless poor, widows and children of his day. In freedom, humans can choose to respond to love or reject it. Paradoxically, as Francis learned by following Jesus, when humans surrender to love, they are most powerful and most free.[10]

For Francis, the poverty, humility, and obedience of Jesus to the will of the Father are all wrapped up together – in Jesus, the glory of God the Father is revealed, namely, "God is love" (1 John 4:8).

As I have engaged the text, I have come to understand that if I am to "observe the holy Gospel of Our Lord Jesus Christ…"[11] following in His footsteps after the example of Francis, poverty ultimately means to imitate what is happening in the Trinity. The Divine Word experienced the love of God within the Trinity; Jesus came to reveal the hidden nature of God as One who loves.[12] In other words, within the Trinity, the Father gives himself totally, perfectly and completely to the Son and the Son receives that love totally, perfectly and completely. The love exchange produces the Holy Spirit. In turn, the Eternal Word gives himself totally, perfectly and completely to us in the Incarnation for our redemption and for the Father's glorification. It is from this perspective, to reveal the love and goodness of God the Father; the Word comes to live among us – to glorify the Father. Demetrius Dumm, O.S.B. writes: "Biblical glorification of a person means the external manifestation of the person's deeper hidden nature. The ultimate role of Jesus is to make evident in our world the true, hidden nature of God … the full revelation of God's love and goodness."[13] Jesus lived in loving service so we would know God's love; and therefore, it is the means in which I am called to live my life – in self-emptying. How did he do that? Chapter IV Article 21 says: "Though rich beyond measure (2 Cor 8:9), he emptied himself for our sake (Phil 2: 7) and with the holy virgin, His Mother, Mary, He chose poverty in this world." Ilia Delio in her article, "The Dangerous Memory of Francis," writes:

---

[10]D.M. Nothwehr, *The Franciscan View of the Human Person: Some Central Elements*, (St. Bonaventure: Franciscan Institute Publications, 2005), 11.

[11]*Rule and Life*, Art. 1, 5.

[12]D. Dumm, *A Mystical Portrait of Jesus: New Perspectives on John's Gospel* (Collegeville, The Liturgical Press, 2001), 161-62.

[13]Dumm, 161-62.

For Francis, however, radical dependency means relational dependency. It is striving to attain one's authentic human existence by being in relation to someone other than one's self; that is, by being in relationship to God and to one's neighbor. Although Francis was not a trained theologian and bequeathed few writings, it is striking that in his writings he rarely speaks of poverty. Indeed, in his "Salutation of the Virtues" he places wisdom not poverty at the principal virtue.[14] In those places where he does speak of poverty, he places poverty in relationship to Jesus Christ and to fraternal love.

The significance of poverty for Francis is integrally related to love and must be considered within the context of love."[15]

Thaddée Matura, O.F.M. wrote: "The strongest and most demanding love is that which is required of me with regard to those to whom I have committed my life."[16] In commenting on this, Clare Andrew D'Auria, O.S.F. states:

> Such love presupposes an essential poverty, that active self-emptying love that frees our hearts from self-interest: that on-going conversion by which we live without appropriating anything to ourselves. This kind of poverty facilitates the building up of the bonds of community/ fraternity (ER VI: 10).[17]

This is the invitation of our poverty – to embrace our creaturehood, our dependence on God so that the hidden nature of God is revealed. What an invitation!!! The implications of our creaturehood are then implied in our Rule:

—"…having something to eat and something to wear, with these we are content…"

—"Let them particularly beware of money."

—"Let them be happy to live among the outcast…"

—"…live in this world as pilgrims and strangers."

—"…neither appropriate nor defend anything as their own…"[18]

---

[14]SalV 1; FA:ED I, 164-65.

[15]I. Delio, "The Dangerous Memory of Francis," *The Cord* 48.5 (September/October 1998): 219.

[16]T. Matura, "Fraternity: Human Reality and the Gospel Sign," *The Cord* 30.4 (April 1980): 116.

[17]C.A. D'Auria, "Franciscan Evangelical Life and the Third Order Regular Charism," *The Cord* 44.11 (November 1994): 312.

[18]*Rule and Life*, 21-22, 11.

## AND FROM HERE...

Today, twenty-five years later, I realize that it is only now that the richness and profound wisdom regarding the fundamental value of poverty as contained in the Rule is dawning within me. I have been influenced and taught, not only by the Rule, but also by sisters who have grappled with living a Franciscan lifestyle under the guidance of the Rule. Francis, when "pondering within himself about the qualities and virtues which should abound in a good Lesser Brother," would say:

> "a good Lesser Brother is one who would possess the life and qualities of the following holy brothers: namely, the faith and love of poverty which Brother Bernard most perfectly had; the simplicity and purity of Brother Leo who was truly a man of most holy purity; the courtly bearing of Brother Angelo who...."[19]

I, too, could name sisters who possess some aspect of poverty like a "the light of God's love refracted through the prism of the virtue of love (poverty) to form a million colorful rays of light."[20] I could name sisters with attributes of poverty: the qualities of availability, presence, generosity in speech, simplicity of life, joy in the midst of physical diminishment, non-judgmental, gratitude for others gifts.... I will never be socio-economically poor. I am well educated; I have the support and love of my Franciscan congregation as well as my family and friends. My day-to-day living is not precarious. I have "discretionary funds" a.k.a. a budget, though limited. I have health insurance! I may live simply and at times work with people who are socio-economically poor, but I can "walk away" – I have a choice in the matter. Besides, I do not find value in degradation. The poverty of socio-economics often damages a person's sense of self and their dignity while destroying their lives. My poverty is one that must reveal the extravagant love that God has for us humans. It does have material implications that challenge me personally and as a community member. More demanding are all the ways in which I find myself not embracing my relationship to God as "daughter" (creature not creator). It challenges all the direct and subtle appropriations I make in my life regarding: *my* thoughts, *my* decisions, *my* ministry, *my* involvement with my religious congregation and the community at large, *my* expertise... The list can go on.

---

[19] 2MP 85; FA:ED III, 333.
[20] Dumm, 163.

UPON REFLECTION, I OFFER THE FOLLOWING THOUGHTS FOR CONSIDERATION:

1. While Francis trusted the Spirit of God at work within each person, he was also a man of discernment. Can we risk exposing ourselves (to be vulnerable) to members of our own congregations in an honest dialogue, without becoming defensive, as to how I am/we are being called to grow in our embrace of poverty?

2. Trace your own journey as you have experienced Gospel poverty. Where has the challenge been and what is it today?

3. Does my fraternity reflect the Trinity – as persons in relationship?

4. Name the attributes of poverty as seen in the life of Jesus, i.e.: availability, presence, self-emptying, ability to name the good in others, generosity. Then name people in your community who exemplify that attribute.

5. What contact do I have with the material poor?

6. Articulate one attribute of poverty you would like to grow into during the next period of time. Name concrete behaviors that will demonstrate this attribute in your life.

7. John Shea, in *The Relentless Widow,* says: "The cross is what the disciples have knowingly initiated by pursuing compassion and reconciliation in the midst of people who will not tolerate the efforts of unity. The suffering of the cross is the result of persisting in love in a loveless world. It is so difficult a task that if one moves away from it for a moment, one may move away from it forever. Therefore, the followers of Jesus must take up their cross daily."[21] How am I committed to efforts of unity, of love?

8. Remember your initial desire and passion to follow the poor Christ and recommit yourself to that ideal.

I trust that God will continue to unfold in us the mystery of His love discovered by living our Rule.

---

[21]J. Shea, *The Relentless Widow: The Spiritual Wisdom of the Gospels for Christian Teachers and Preachers* (Collegeville: Liturgical Press, 2006), 168.

# Thomas Barton, O.S.F.

## MINORITY, SUBVERTING THE DOMINANT PARADIGM[1]

His Holiness, Blessed John XXIII in convoking the Second Vatican Council instructed us to throw open the windows to let in the vibrant fresh air of the Holy Spirit. Another beloved Pontiff, John Paul II, invited us to open the doors to Christ. During this time of renewal we have witnessed the church describe itself as the People of God on pilgrimage. We are a pilgrim people; we are becoming a pilgrim Church.

The literature of the Franciscan Pilgrimage Program, Milwaukee, Wisconsin, USA states that for Christians "a pilgrimage is a going out of one's known environment into the unknown in order to know the mind of Christ."[2] Pilgrimage, as described by the late Joseph Doino, O.F.M. is "extroverted mysticism" and "prayer of the feet."[3] Pilgrimage is not unique to Christianity. Indeed, we know that Jesus himself went on pilgrimage at the age of 12, with Mary and Joseph to Jerusalem. Pilgrimage is an essential feature and a liminal experience of many of the world's major religious expressions. Whether the destination of a pilgrimage is Jerusalem or Mecca, Canterbury or Rome, Varanasi or Bodhgaya, the purpose of pilgrimage is to deepen one's God experience or to enter the mystery of God. As a pilgrim guide myself, I know how much the act of pilgrimage requires of us to leave behind. This liminal experience, indeed, often offers us the challenge to reflect deeply on our lives and our God relationship, and in the light of the pilgrimage experience, to leave behind whatever is not for life.

We are a people whose time has come. We, the Third Order of Penance of St. Francis of Assisi, have come into our own, finally, after all these centuries. In the interim 50 years since the Second Vatican Council the entire Third Order, Secular and Regular, has undergone a profound period of reflection and renewal that has culminated in the writing of a new rule of life for each part of the Third Order. What a true blessing it is to be alive today, and, for the first time in Franciscan history, for

---

[1]Dan Edwards is a college student who is also employed at Mt. Alvernia, Centerport, NY. He has a bumper sticker emblazoned on his car that reads, "subvert the dominant paradigm." I am indebted to Dan for this idea. By the "dominant paradigm" I understand the phrase "it's all about me" as a way of living for a significant number of people today. Franciscan life is all about the following of Jesus, especially by living the four dominant values of our rule: minority, conversion, contemplation and poverty.

[2]The Order of Friars Minor, Assumption of the Blessed Virgin Mary Province, Milwaukee, Wisconsin, sponsors the Franciscan Pilgrimage Programs. The literature that is sent to newly registered pilgrims has this line in it.

[3]Joseph Doino, O.F.M., class notes in his course "Franciscan Spirituality," at the Franciscan Institute, St. Bonaventure University, St. Bonaventure, NY, Spring 1989.

all to have equal access to the words and writings of Francis of Assisi in our own vernacular language. We have written for ourselves, with the excellent encouragement and direction of other Franciscans and scholars, our own rules. In this time we have heeded the pontiffs' calls to open the windows and throw open the doors. In this last half-century the entire Third Order has undergone a pilgrimage in faith.

The invitation to write this essay in celebration of the Silver Anniversary of the signing of the Rule of 1982, the John Paul II Rule, is an honor and a distinct privilege. I undertake this writing as an act of praise to God, deep love for the brothers of my own congregation, the Franciscan Brothers of Brooklyn, and in gratitude to my Franciscan sisters and brothers whose good example, beyond all else, has continually pointed me to Jesus Christ. We are companions on this pilgrimage, following in Jesus' footprints. As I wrote this essay, I have kept in mind the motifs of pilgrimage and minority through the experiences described below.

I wish to state that there are three excerpts that have emerged on my personal pilgrimage which have become as essential to me as oxygen is to the human body. Since I have taken liberty with two of these, I will provide the paraphrase, and give the reference for the exact wording. The first comes from the holy Scripture: whatsoever you do to the least, or allow the least to do to you, that you do to me (Mt 25: 40).[4] Francis wrote that those who live among Saracens and other believers, or who remain among them, could do so in two ways. They are not to engage in arguments or disputes. When they see that it pleases the Lord then they may announce the Word of God.[5] The Rule of the Secular Franciscan Order, 1978 calls those Franciscans to go "from Gospel to life, and life to Gospel."[6] Finally, Thomas of Celano declared, "Many people ... began to come to Saint Francis for they desired to serve under his constant training and leadership ... to all he gave a norm of life and to those of every rank he sincerely pointed out the way of salvation."[7]

Raffaele Pazzelli, T.O.R., in his seminal work *St. Francis and the Third Order* indicates that in the First Version of the *Letter to the Faithful* that he referred to as the *recensio prior* – and which Early Documents calls the "Earlier Exhortation" – contains "core ideas by which Francis tried to shape the life of the Brothers and Sisters of Penance associated with

---

[4]*The New Jerusalem Bible*, H. Wansbrough, ed. (New York: Darton, Longman & Todd, 1985).

[5]ER XVI:7; FA:ED I, 74.

[6]R. Stewart, *De Illis Qui Faciunt Penitentiam: The Rule of the Secular Franciscan Order: Origins, Development, Interpretation* (Rome: Istituto Storico dei Cappuccini, 1991), 438.

[7]1C XV:37; FA:ED I, 216-17.

him."[8] I believe the key then to understanding the vocation of the Third Order Franciscan, as minors, is to be found in these words:

> We are spouses when the faithful soul is joined by the Holy Spirit to Our Lord Jesus Christ. We are brothers to Him when we do the will of the Father who is in heaven. We are mothers when we carry Him in our heart and body through a divine love and a pure and sincere conscience and give birth to Him through a holy activity which must shine as an example before others.[9]

In the course of my travels, I had many opportunities to visit carpet-weaving factories of Northern India. For hours I would watch the intricate weaving of woolen strands of bright and vivid colors into what we might call "Persian carpets." How distinct and individual the spools of wool were. Yet, their individuality disappeared when they became a piece of the carpet that was being woven. And so it is with the values that uphold the Rule, when they are lived in the context of our *fraternitas*: minority, contemplation, poverty and penance. They form a pattern that we call Franciscan. To be clear, there are very few who can embody the entire value structure. Yet Francis himself appreciated that fact when he was asked who was the ideal/model lesser brother. "And he used to say that a good Lesser Brother is one who would possess the life and qualities of the following holy brothers: namely, the faith and love of poverty which Brother Bernard most perfectly had; the simplicity and purity of Brother Leo … the courtly bearing of Brother Angelo…."[10]

I was asked to reflect specifically on minority through the prism of experience. I will write about my own experience, from my own congregation and from the greater Third Order Regular family. As a very young child I understood that we were not all the same and we were not all alike. In my family there was an uncle who had lost a leg in battle during World War II, and from my family and him I understood that people could be differently abled and very capable, too. In my life as a Franciscan, too, I have been called to be with differently abled individuals, far outside the formal educational structure in which most of my Franciscan brothers minister.

---

[8]R. Pazzelli, *St. Francis and the Third Order* (Chicago: Franciscan Herald Press, 1989): 113.

[9]1LtF 1:8-10 ; FA:ED I, 42.

[10]2MP 85; FA:ED III, 333.

## Special Education/GRID

My educational ministry was not in the mainstream of academic education as it has been for many of my brothers. I was allowed and encouraged to study Special Education of the Mentally Retarded at Teachers College, Columbia University. Then for fourteen years I served as a classroom teacher or independence trainer.[11]

As the population of persons with developmental disabilities aged, and group homes began to come into existence, I had a desire to learn more about the aging population, and was encouraged to pursue a position on the pastoral staff of a parish in Brooklyn, New York. Many of the parishioners were elderly, frail Caucasian women who had been live-in domestics in the Brownstone homes. Now pensioned off, many were living in single rooms in hotels and apartment buildings. Often they needed assistance with coordinating appointments, medication, home health aides, transferring into assisted living, or finally, to heaven. I was happy to assist, and eager to learn, with one eye on the aging developmentally delayed population. I confess that I was not really emotionally prepared to undertake this position then. End of life issues are difficult; being alone at the end of life is tragic. I learned to be in awe at how aged people embraced Sister Death.

There is a saying in Brooklyn: "You make plans and God laughs." Such was the case with my plan for the elderly. The parish under consideration is in a now very upscale, Brownstone section of Brooklyn Heights. One day one year into this ministry, Msgr. Frank Murphy, our pastor, asked me to go to the local hospital to visit a parishioner. "This one is different, he is male." That would be unique; all the other clients were aged women. Notepad and pen in hand, off I went to the hospital to meet the man and see what could be done for him. I did not know that what I was about to encounter would change my life.

The sight that greeted me was of a twenty-ish, emaciated, almost blind man covered with bruises known as Kaposi Sarcoma, who was on the verge of death. Cancer, I thought to myself. All I could do then was give him a drink of water, and put some ice cubes in his mouth. I asked the nurse, who knew me from the parish, the nature of his illness, and she whispered "GRID." I didn't know what that was, and she would not say.

Returning to the office I looked in the medical encyclopedia, and there was no such term. Asking around, no one knew the meaning. The next day when I returned to visit, the same nurse told me that he had died, and that the family had him cremated immediately. The family was from "out of town" and the undertaker was not at liberty to provide any

---

[11]In those days it was very common to refer to educators by their subject. So, for most of those days I was commonly referred to as "the retarded teacher".

information to me. That was my introduction to the deep, dark world of AIDS, and the social implications of that condition. In those days the condition was described as GRID, Gay Related Infectious Disease.

When I asked the pastor about GRID, he said that I should be ready, because there were a number of men in the parish suffering from the same condition. Fortunately, many of them were taking their treatments and hospitalizations at the three Catholic hospitals in Manhattan who were open to their care. These were St. Vincent's, St. Clare's and the Cabrini Medical Center, a witness of love overcoming fear. Also, very fortunately we learned very early that this disease was not contagious and is in fact, very difficult to transmit. Then, too, I was not really prepared for the case load of clients primarily young men, all beginning their lives, facing end of life issues, and who were not at all eager to rush into the waiting embrace of Sister Death. You can imagine the depth of despair, alienation, outrage, emotional exhaustion and severe pain that accompanied their final days. And I did not yet know that God was preparing me to meet this condition closer to home.

At the same time that I joined the pastoral staff, I was elected by the brothers to our congregational formation team, and appointed as the post-novitiate director for brothers in temporary vows. In the course of those years, I became acquainted with the dozen brothers in temporary profession in remarkably intimate detail. More, surely, than had been the case when I was in that level of profession with my directors.

One of these young brothers was often ill, and required frequent hospitalization; he was forced to drop out of college. My pastor and the superior general gave me the freedom to spend whatever time was needed with this brother. Gradually, very sparingly, and quite tentatively, his life story was opened up to me in a way that required me to be the most minor I have ever been, voluntarily or involuntarily. At the particular medical center where this brother was being treated, one of the Catholic ones, I was very much known as "the Brother from the Church in Brooklyn."[12]

One day, an unknown male nurse whispered to me "Boy is this a lucky one," meaning my Franciscan brother. "How so?" I asked. His reply all but knocked me off my feet. "When they get in here their lovers almost always run away. How nice you are to him and you stayed around." Those words are etched in my memory and on my heart. Being so stunned, and shocked, I could not at all respond except to say "He's very important to me." All I could think is that we were Franciscan Brothers. The paradigm was asserting itself.

---

[12]At this time there were a number of parishioners in treatment.

I walked home across the Brooklyn Bridge that day, and over the space of a few hours had to deeply commit myself to this brother, irrespective of whatever the thoughts of others were – the dominant paradigm, and to myself. Francis's words in *Admonition XIX* came into my memory then, in a way it had never been before, "What a person is before God that he is and no more."[13] I did speak with some friends about this, and about my shock, and my feelings. I had to be a mother to this brother regarding his personal care and medical attention, a father in terms of what we would call reality checks and boundary issues, and especially brotherly as I represented him to the congregation and others. If others perceived this as a different type of relationship, what to do? The brother did not renew his vows and left the congregation. He was not bitter or angry. Later there was a beautiful reconciliation, and finally, he was buried with the brothers in Holy Cross Cemetery, Brooklyn, New York. Much later in India, I spoke to whichever group would listen, as well as in the Philippines, Bangladesh and Korea. I consider HIV prevention education as my main educational apostolate, and I will do that forever.

## India

Having completed a degree in Franciscan Studies at St. Bonaventure University, an invitation was extended to me to join the fledgling faculty of Shanthi Sadhana, the Franciscan Institute of Spirituality in India. There, it was my privilege to serve as lecturer for five years, 1992-93 and 1996-2000. Over those years, the opportunity was given to me to teach the *Rule and Life of the Third Order Regular* many times.

I heard some few simple things in India that have helped me enormously. "Franciscans have upside down values" and "Franciscans practice downward mobility." Minority took on a particular meaning for me especially then as a resident alien who needed local governmental permission to leave the city of Bangalore for more than three consecutive days and a special permit to leave the country.

One of the privileges that I had then was to enroll in Manassa Gangothri, The University of Mysore, Karnataka State, South India in the School of Christian Studies. As a doctoral student I pursued research on a very part-time basis, while teaching for Shanthi Sadhana.

Once each academic term, each of the doctoral students is required to present thirty minutes of their current research and to answer any questions. Generally, the presentations were dull and plodding. We students were not much interested in the work of the others. The topics, which were either theological or spiritual in nature, were often erudite and not easily accessible. Sisters, three diocesan priests and I were the students.

---

[13]Adm XIX; FA:ED I, 135.

Also, there were two young Hindu men studying Christianity as an academic subject at the Masters level.

When it was my turn to present, I did what we all did and began to read from the prepared text. A brief while into the reading I noted that one of the Sisters was writing furiously, and glancing briefly in her direction I observed a look of absolute anger. I knew that had nothing to do with myself, and I plodded on. During the exchange, I learned that a flash point in Indians' consciousness is the subject of minority, for indeed all Christians in India are members of a very miniscule, yet extremely influential, socially powerful subgroup.[14] Try as I did, I was unable to win over anyone to my viewpoint of the value of minority. I did quote Scripture, Philippians 2:6-11, "though he was in the form of God, Jesus did not deem equality with God something to be grasped at. Rather he emptied himself …"[15] as a way of embracing the subject. Despite the mention of the exemplary life of Francis and Clare of Assisi, with a collection of examples, no one was convinced. The exchange went well beyond the allotted time, and sparked a significant number of remarks in the subsequent presentations during the course of that year. I might mention that the departmental chairperson was profuse in his compliments as to how I managed to spark some "interesting discussion"! I was really startled, and still am today, reflecting on that. That was the first time I was ever called upon to defend this Franciscan value.

## FROM MATRON TO MOTHER

During this same time I was invited to lead a study on the new Rule for the silver jubilee preparation for some Franciscan Sisters. They were all very competent in their fields of study and they expected to be lectured to. They were thrilled to be invited to share their own life experiences as a part of our study. Truly, their experiences and insights were remarkably profound.

When we approached the subject of minority, I was a bit more aware than previously, and I was prepared for some tension or disagreement. One jubilarian, the matron of a hospital in Kerala, South India, very prominent in this geographic region, offered one of her experiences. She was both the superior of the convent and the head of this hospital. Every day going from the convent to the hospital she would inevitably pass a group of beggars who gathered at the compound gate. Having her few favorites, she would toss a rupee coin to each of them and carry on. One day, however, she had no coins. She turned to one particular man to state that. He replied, "Mother, today you looked at me." Sister told us that

---

[14]In America that flash point would have been poverty.
[15]Philippians 2:6-11.

she went immediately back into the convent, to her room, where, she said, she wept for the entire day at the understanding of what she had let her life become. The cares and worries of the house and office had been such, she felt, that she disregarded those around her, i.e. the beggars, which the dominant paradigm suggests. She has transformed the paradigm remarkably in her years since that coin-less encounter.

Our rule has something to say. "In the charity which God is (1 Jn 4:16) all the brothers and sisters, whether they are praying or serving or working should strive to be humble (i.e. minor) in everything."[16]

### FROM BROTHER TO BROTHER

The Franciscan Brothers of Brooklyn received a high school from the bishop of Brooklyn unexpectedly in the early 1960s. As we usually do, we staffed the school to the hilt with forty Brothers, the best of the high school teachers. As was the case then, all the positions of authority and the responsible decision makers were Brothers. The 1960s in America were times of change in all aspects of life, compounded towards the end by the very unpopular Vietnam War. One of the slogans of the age was "question authority" and another "don't trust anyone over thirty."

In this particular school there was a growing movement towards unionization, which finally led to a strike. Of course, the Brothers could not support the strike, they believed, and as they crossed the picket line daily, relationships changed with lay colleagues that may even today be estranged.[17] I was living in a friary with some of the Brothers from that school, and so I witnessed the cost to them of doing "what was expected," even if they personally believed the strikers were correct. What does the *dominant paradigm* say about that? During the course of the next few years, when "self placement" came into practice, Brothers sought out positions in other schools and very few transferred in. Rather rapidly the Brother number dwindled down to a handful from the initial forty. Gradually, this worked to the betterment of the relationship between those who remained, or came at other times, and the faculty. I think the profound transition was evident when the position of campus minister was created and a Brother was asked to provide that ministry to students, faculty and staff. To date, and for the last fifteen years, a Brother has served in that capacity. The Franciscan Brothers who have remained in that educational setting have worked diligently to transform their own relationship with those with whom they minister. None any longer serve

---

[16]*Rule and Life of the Brothers and Sisters of the Third Order Regular of St. Francis: 25th Anniversary Edition*, J.F. Godet-Calogeras, trans. (Washington: Franciscan Federation, 2007), Art. 31, 15.

[17]One Brother did respect the picket line. Several years later, he returned to the school as principal.

in administration, or as a department chair. Indeed they have moved from being Brother to brother.

### FAITH

After returning from India in 1993, I joined the staff of the Franciscan Aids Initiative, FAITH Services, sponsored by the Franciscan Sisters of the Poor Health System in New Jersey and administered by the Brothers of the Poor of St. Francis. In those days the staff of fifteen was comprised of nine Franciscans: eight Third Order Regular and one Capuchin priest. During the eleven years ministering at FAITH Services, I buried at least 200 people. More that two-thirds died in the period between 1993-1996.

I wish to remember one very sad individual in this essay. Born in the Bronx, New York and baptized in Union City, New Jersey, Eligio was born a biological male but, according to him, always believed himself to be female. In his adolescent years he was sexually very active, and in addition to many other common sexually transmitted diseases he acquired the HIV virus. When Eligia was assigned to my case management she was in the process of being sexually reassigned, although, as time would tell, she was unable to complete this transgendering process.

We worked in triads in FAITH then. My colleagues were Nancy, a New-Jersey born Puerto Rican woman, and Sr. Joy, a Japanese-born, Peruvian-raised, Felician Sister. Nancy accompanied me to Eligia's wake. Eligia's partner Kevin had been banned from the wake by the parents, which was the first issue that greeted me. After I knelt down at the casket to pray, Nancy anticipated what I would do. She all but grabbed me in a bear hug and turned me away. Eligia had been dressed as a man, with an artificial mustache, crew cut hair and heavy bunting to disguise the enhanced breast development. I was so shocked, furious, and upset by this disregard of her rights, I would have been blunt and very forceful about the violation. But Nancy wisely pointed out the parents. The sight broke my heart. Two very frail, sorrowful, perplexed immigrants doing the very best they could to deal with life, death and grief. "Hermano, hermano" the mother wailed as I went to greet them. All in Spanish they told the pitiful story of the brief, and flamboyant life of their dear, dear child. How beautiful the funeral was, and how beautiful the Catholic Church was on that day for these unfortunate, perplexed immigrants from the Dominican Republic. The one concession I was able to get that day was that Kevin could attend the funeral.

## A Cloud of Witnesses

As Francis entered his time of conversion, he embraced a dual question: "Who are you my dearest God? And what am I?"[18] At the end of his life Francis made a bold declaration: "I have done *what is mine*; may *Christ teach* you what is yours."[19]

How does one get to that point? By practice. By practicing acts of minority. By consciously deciding at every possible moment to be the lesser, the minor, in any situation, and most importantly, when the lesser role is put upon us, to accept that willingly as did Francis. In *The Earlier Rule* for the Lesser Brothers, Francis wrote a directive about how they were to be among the Saracens and other believers. I have paraphrased that at the beginning of this essay. The following is the exact quotation: "As for the brothers who go, they can live spiritually among the Saracens and nonbelievers in two ways. One way is not to engage in arguments or disputes but to be *subject to every human creature for God's sake* and to acknowledge that they are Christians. The other way is to announce the Word of God, when they see it pleases the Lord, in order that [unbelievers] may believe in almighty God, the Father, the Son and the Holy Spirit...."[20] By "others" we can take it to mean those whose practice is different from ours. We are not to engage in disputes. When we see that it pleases the Lord then, and only then, are we free to proclaim the Word of God. What follows are the stories of some who gave their lives in service to Christ.

## Sister Rani Maria, F.C.C.

Sister Rani Maria, F.C.C. was a Franciscan Clarist who was born in the state of Kerala, India.[21] After entering the community she opted to go to a province in the North, to work for "the uplift" of the under-privileged. Until the arrival of Rani the pastoral work of the sisters and priests from the Indore Diocese was principally to care for the spiritual needs of fifteen Catholic tribal families, plus some regular visits to the area villages to provide "unorganized humanitarian aid" for which she was murdered.

Rani Maria was a trained social worker who had earned a masters degree in sociology. After being a missionary for sixteen years in other parts of Northern India she arrived on May 18, 1992 in Udalnagar, and

---

[18]*St. Francis of Assisi: Writings and Early Biographies*, Marion Habig, ed. (Chicago: Franciscan Herald Press, 1973): 1444.

[19]2C CLXII214; FA:ED II, 386.

[20]ER XVI:5-7; FA:ED I, 74.

[21]Material was provided by the Roman Catholic Diocese of Indore, Northern India through a fax sent by Sister Celine, FCC of the IFC-TOR Office, Rome Italy. All quotations are from this one source.

"she began to put things in order, and things in Udalnagar took a turn for the better." Initially accompanied by her Franciscan Sisters, she began to visit the local villages primarily to assess the situation and to meet the people. In a very short while she "was convinced that the poor villagers had unconsciously fallen prey to the 'debt-trap' laid by the tradesmen of Udalnagar. She also found the villagers over-dependent on the moneylenders." Being illiterate they were generally unaware of the programs and opportunities that the central government has to offer for loans, projects and training. Rani spent her days educating and organizing small groups into savings associations, credit unions and educational projects. She brought awareness to the villagers of the various "self help" projects offered, which would allow them to buy seeds, fertilizers and to create irrigation projects. "These projects went against the interest of the local oppressive money lenders and other vested interests." "Injustice done to the people pained her to the heart. Sr. Lissa, another Franciscan Clarist commented, "Many a time I have seen her sitting in the chapel crying because the government officials were non-cooperative."

Rani Maria is remembered as a woman of prayer. Before she would leave the convent for a village visit she would spend some time with the Scriptures. Psalm 119 was a favorite of hers. *Your word is a lamp to my feet and a light to my path.* The superior of the community remembers "she would boldly speak about the Word of God to anyone who cared to listen. The village meetings always began with a reading from the holy Scriptures and a small prayer service."

The immediate cause of the murder of Rani Maria was that she helped a group of "poor, illiterate, Catholic villagers to be bailed out of police custody after a fight with a local mafia leader...." On February 25, 1995, when she was on her way to a home visit in Kochi, Kerala she was assaulted in a passenger bus. The bus was stopped, Sr. Rani was dragged off the bus and brutally stabbed more than forty times, and no passenger would come to her assistance. "There is no doubt that ... this was a preplanned and well executed murder." The Diocese of Indore reflected that "the murder has apparently succeeded in doing away with Sr. Rani Maria ... but the life of Sr. Rani Maria cannot be over with her death." More than 12,000 people from every aspect of Indian life and society attended her funeral.

In her personal prayer book, there was a listing of eight intentions she prayed for daily. Among those are these: *My apostolate—to do for the glory of God and the salvation of souls, and to have two priests and three sisters from my own brothers' and sisters' families in the future.* Meanwhile the Franciscan Clarist Sisters "continued to receive anonymous phone calls and threats." Sr. Deena, who came as a replacement for Rani Maria said, "… The sisters are undeterred and all the more determined now."

## BROTHER LARRY TIMMONS, O.S.F.

Brother Larry Timmons, O.S.F. was a Franciscan Brother from Mt. Bellew, Ireland, the mother congregation of my own.[22] As a young brother he went to Kenya to the new mission. For a number of years he was involved in the brothers' schools in Baraka, Molo and then Lare, Nakuru.

Community development, particularly in the area of agriculture and food production, was made urgent by the semi-famine situations caused by drought and crop failures in the Lare area. He became involved in a water project, plus the acquisition and distribution of food and seed to the local community. His interest developed in the areas of subsistence farming methods and the development of basic skills such as sewing, knitting, carpentry work and mechanics. In late 1996 he built Mtakatifu Clara Mwangaza, St. Clare's Polytechnic Institute. He had a keen interest in the improvement of the people's diet, which included projects such as rabbit breeding, poultry production, the improvement of the milk cows and cattle in the area. All these projects are a part of the wider service offered by the Franciscan Brothers, and all initiatives were undertaken with full consultation and the total involvement and support of the people of Lare. "Larry was very much on the side of the local people and wherever he saw an injustice he spoke out about it." In the 1990s Nakuru District was badly affected by ethnic conflict. The Lare District was not spared in this conflict. Many people were killed, homes were burned and the population displaced. Larry worked tirelessly to promote peace and justice and challenged the government to fulfill its responsibilities and to address the root causes of violence.

In the very early hours of Wednesday, January 22, 1997 Larry was killed during a robbery of his home. Approximately twenty robbers entered the Brothers' compound and stole 1300 euros. A policeman, Francis Kamanzi Mbaiya, entered the compound during this time and began to fire his gun. Nineteen rounds were fired, and one killed Larry instantly; all the robbers escaped. The robbers had bludgeoned the faithful night watchman, James Kamani, as they entered. He died also. In early 2004 the police officer was found guilty of manslaughter and sentenced to ten years in prison. No one has been arrested in the murder of Mr. Kamani. The Franciscan Brothers and the local community are carrying on the work created by Brother Larry Timmons.

---

[22]Brother Peter Roddy, O.S.F., Superior General provided materials electronically that includes the obituary and necrology of Brother Larry Timmons, O.S.F. All quotations are from this source.

## BROTHER GEORGE KUZHIDANDAM, C.M.S.F.

George was baptized Varghese in the parish church of St. Lawrence, Canarra, Karnataka state, India, in August 1957.[23] He joined the Franciscan Missionary Brothers in 1985 and made first profession October 4, 1989. His ministerial assignments were in both Northern and Southern India.

In addition to his teaching assignment he was given the responsibility to direct the Boys' Home at Navada, Mathura, which he did until his death, June 7, 2000. "His innocence and childlike simplicity, his love and care for the boys were visible in all his dealings and activities." As a musician and accomplished singer he contributed much to the lively nature of the mission.

During the three months leading up to his death there were "a chain of attacks that took place in the Archdiocese of Agra." On the night of his death, Brother George was sleeping alone outside in the courtyard of the boys' home. While the other brothers had accompanied the children on an outing to New Delhi, during this vacation time he remained at the orphanage with one boy who was ill. "A group of men surrounded him, armed with *lathis*[poles] and iron rods; they beat him and tortured him cruelly to death.... The gruesome murder evoked restlessness and anxiety among the Christians all over the country and protest marches, rallies and Inter-religious prayer meetings were organized everywhere." Pope John Paul II wrote a letter of condolence, stating "the sad news of the death of Brother George Kuzhikandam, C.M.S.F., at the hands of the extremists was communicated to us in Rome. Brother George thus continues to lengthen the list of martyrs who have washed their robes white in the 'blood of the Lamb' (Rev 7:14) in your country." None of those extremists has yet been brought to justice. The work of the Franciscan Missionary Brothers in Navada, Mathura continues.

As I began to write this essay, I used the image of pilgrimage, "a going out of one's known experience in order to know the mind of Christ Jesus." Most of the time the mind of Christ Jesus, as we are given to know his mind, leads us to unusual, and very interesting situations and people. For most of us, these are not very dramatic or even noticeable, yet for those who embrace them, they can be life-changing moments.

In one of the reflections written for *All Praise Be Yours*, the twenty-fifth anniversary booklet of the Franciscan Federation of the Sisters and Brothers of the U.S.A., one of our sisters commented: "Our gift to the

---

[23]Brother Thaddeus, Regional Superior of North America, the Franciscan Missionary Brothers, St. Francis Friary, Rockaway Park, New York provided materials electronically that contained the obituary for Brother George, C.M.S.F. All quotations are from this material.

Church is not all about what we do for the sake of the Reign of God, it is all about who we are."[24]

As we celebrate the silver anniversary of the Rule of 1982, the John Paul II Rule, and as we embrace the future together as Franciscan sisters and brothers let us encourage each other to continue through the value of minority to "subvert the dominant paradigm."

---

[24]N. Celaschi, *All Praise Be To You* (Washington: Franciscan Federation, 2007), 6.

# TESTIMONIES

# OF THE RULE "COMPANIONS"

# 7

## Testimonies of the Rule "Companions"

### Jean François Godet-Calogeras

#### We who lived and worked together...

**W**e end this Source Book with the words of the artisans of the *Rule and Life of the Brothers and Sisters of the Third Order Regular of Saint Francis*, the members of the International Work Group.

*Ad perpetuam rei memoriam,*[1] let us recall the sisters and brother who composed the final draft of the new Rule. Margaret Carney, of the Sisters of St. Francis of the Providence of God, came from Pittsburgh, Pennsylvania; Ignatia Gomez, of the Mission Sisters of Ajmer, from India; Thaddeus Horgan, of the Society of Atonement, from Garrison, New York; Marianne Jungbluth, of the Franziskanerinnen von der Heiligen Familie (Mayen, Germany), from Eupen, Belgium; Marie Benoît Lucbernet, of the Soeurs de Saint François d'Assise, from Montpelier, France; Maria Honoria Montalvo, of the Hermanas Franciscanas de María Inmaculada, from Columbia;  and Maria Luiza Piva, of the Irmãs Catequistas Franciscanas, from Brazil.

In the spring of 1980, I was asked to serve as facilitator of the Work Group. I did not belong to the Third Order Regular, but I had been working with several congregations in Belgium and France. I was chosen because of my expertise in the writings of Francis and Clare and the early Franciscan documents, and because of my facility with languages. But, even if the gift of tongues is traditionally recognized as a gift of the Spirit since the first Pentecost after Jesus' Resurrection, it did not take long to realize that other gifts of the Spirit were needed!

The first meeting of the Work Group, in Reute, Germany at the beginning of September 1980, was a failure. We had begun to work immedi-

---

[1]A well-known traditional formula opening papal documents: For a perpetual memorial.

ately trying to blend various documents that only had in common their Franciscan origin. The text we produced was definitely not satisfactory, but it also reflected the lack of concord and harmony within the Work Group. The linguistic skills and the help of translators had not been enough to bring the Work Group together.

The second meeting took place in Brussels, Belgium during May, 1981. This time the members of the Work Group took another approach. They began by looking together at the origins of Franciscan life, at the emergence of the Franciscan movement as described in the early Franciscan documents, in particular the *Testament* of Francis. In doing so, we became more obedient to one another, that is, we listened carefully and respectfully to one another, and we began to recognize and appreciate each other. We prayed together, we enjoyed eating and drinking together. We entered into a relationship of sisters and brothers. We became a *fraternitas* and understood anew what Franciscan life meant, and which are its essential elements. We then became truly inspired and joyfully drafted the text of the new Rule. We knew then what we had to write, and together we found and selected words of Francis and Clare to compose our text.

At the end of the Brussels session, we were understandably tired from the work we had accomplished. But the predominant feeling was one of peace, joy and happiness: the document the Work Group delivered to the BFI and the CFI was not only written with words of Francis and Clare, it also expressed what we had experienced together, living and working as sisters and brothers. Anything could happen to the text. That experience could never be erased and had marked our lives forever.

The Work Group met a third time to prepare for the General Assembly scheduled for March, 1982 in Rome. The *fraternitas* born in Brussels got back together in New York in time to celebrate Christmas 1981. We were welcomed by a host who would rapidly become our brother and our friend, Thomas Grady, of the Franciscan Brothers of Brooklyn. That third meeting had its share of tensions and difficulties. Although our *fraternitas* was put to the test, our relationship as sisters and brothers was strengthened. During this difficult time our brother Tom supported and encouraged us as a mother, after Francis's heart. We were most grateful to him.

And here we are, after all those years. All of us have continued our Franciscan journey with its ups and downs, with moments of happiness but also of tribulations. Our brother Thaddeus ended his life's journey and passed away eighteen years ago. We remember. We remember all of that. Our hearts are filled with gratitude. And every day is a new beginning.

# Margaret Carney, O.S.F. and †Thaddeus Horgan, S.A.

## MEMORY AND MOTIVE

In 1979 Thaddeus Horgan and I were appointed to serve on the International Work Group which would eventually author the text of the 1982 Rule. I was selected to represent the Federation of U.S.A. sisters. Thaddeus would represent the institutes of men who followed the TOR Rule. From our first encounter at St. Onofrio, Generalate of the Atonement Friars in Rome, we developed a partnership that included hard work, shared prayer, ever-extending circles of new friends, moments of hilarity and days of super-saturated stress.We were given a mandate by our respective superiors. We were rewarded with a rare friendship and unfathomable experience of the workings of the Holy Spirit in contemporary Franciscan life.

For the next two years we faithfully executed our duties as members of the Work Group and even managed to host our colleagues in the United States for one of our sessions. After the Rome Assembly, we set to work helping to devise an educational program that would prepare other Franciscan sisters and brothers to teach the new *Rule and Life* text in depth and in earnest. The program – to be presented five times over the next two years – was called *Roots and Wings.* However, we no sooner had the design approved when Thaddeus announced his intention to leave the States and take up a mission in a very poor area of Jamaica.

The dramatic debates we experienced about Franciscan poverty and solidarity had impacted him deeply. Accustomed to service as a respected ecumenical theologian traveling in official capacities, he now longed to give his energies to the deep Franciscan soul-call: to find joy and meaning at the margins of the world. I was heartsick that he would leave me and others with the task of education at home, but I knew better than to argue. This was the Spirit at work and obedience was the only response allowed.

After three years of intense service, he was called back to the States to accept a position in the National Conference of Catholic Bishops. Thus he moved from pastoring a parish that was jointly conducted by Episcopal and Roman Catholic clergy, to being associate director of the Secretariat for Ecumenical and Inter-religious Affairs. This appointment would benefit from his years at the *Centro Pro Unione* which he founded in Rome at the close of Vatican II. During the Council sessions Thaddeus served as adviser and host to delegations of Council fathers and Protestant observers and the Center, still a hub of ecumenical work today, was the outcome of that work.

Soon after his return, his own Graymoor congregation asked him to dedicate a day of education on the Rule to them. Would I come and join him for the presentations, they asked? Of course! After a three year hiatus, Thaddeus and I stepped right into our partnership patterns and pulled off a workshop that ended on a high note in the late afternoon. In the short time we had that day, we had managed to catch up on each other's family, work, health, ecclesiastical gossip and news of Franciscan friends. We parted. He was on his way to dinner with a friend in Connecticut. I was returning to meetings at my Pittsburgh convent. That night he died of a heart attack.

The Gospel we heard proclaimed on that last morning of his life was the Emmaus story. He and I had walked a long road together. Unlike the confused disciples in Galilee, we had always had the assurance of the One journeying beside us. We had the consolation of playing a small but life-changing part in an historic event in our Franciscan family. We had struggled to be understood and to understand on some very difficult days. We contended with questions of ethical responsibility and historical accountability. And on that April Easter-week day – the last, though we did not know it – we spent the flying hours well. We were sharing our love for our penitential vocation and the Rule that would define it. The blow of his death was numbing, but the realization of how he was gifted in those last hours in his religious community, in his world, placed a halo of gratitude around the days of mourning that followed.

May the parable of the last day, a day dedicated to teaching and cherishing that which Francis and Clare pioneered for us, remain with me and with all of us. May it be, for all who share this on-going task, a memory and a motive to persevere to the end in true faith and penance.

# Ignatia Gomez, M.S.A.

I am glad to share with you my experience of living out the TOR Rule over these 25 years.

In the first place I must say that being with the "Work Group" studying, reading, listening to the experts and sharing with one another was a great learning experience for me. I got to know our dear Father Francis better and I began to ask myself – "what would Francis do in my place?" I do this even now. This has helped me over the years to imbibe his attitudes and act as he would have.

After the Rule was approved and sent out to the various congregations, I went round to many congregations to explain the Rule. This sharing was always a reminder to me to live it as well as possible. It also helped me to foster a greater unity and fellowship with all the members of the Franciscan family.

As I have always been a delegate to our General and Provincial Chapters, I have exerted a fairly good influence on the younger members of our fraternity. Besides this I have been a General Councilor for 12 years and this is my sixth year as Provincial Councilor. Having been Secretary General for 12 years and Provincial Secretary for 4 years has helped me to convey a lot of my Franciscan attitudes to the members of my fraternity, both by my words and deeds. The simplicity of my life is expressed through the dress I wear, the hard work I put in, my attitude towards food, place of work, detachment from things, sharing of personal money allotted to us for sundries etc., care of my health and not making importunate demands whether in health or illness.

A spirit of obedience to God's will and obedience to my superiors gives me a lot of peace and helps me to pray. I accept whatever is unpleasant or irksome to me with resignation to God's will as did our Father Francis. This is part of my penance and spirit of self-denial.

Even though life for me is quite hectic, I am generally peaceful. I try to disseminate this peace to the patients, their companions, our staff and all those whom I encounter from day to day. My peace comes through my faith and trust in Jesus. The Eucharist, the source and summit of our Christian living, nourishes and fortifies me daily. Many today try to dissuade us from praying the Prayer of the Church daily. They say that it can be replaced by other forms of prayer, but remembering the words of Our Father Francis, we, in all our communities, celebrate the Liturgy of the Hours daily (RNB XXIII:8).

My spirit of poverty urges me to associate myself with the poor and the middle class. We reach out to the people living in the slums and in the villages. Through our hospitals and educational institutions we look after those who have no one to care for them and we help school drop-outs to be educated through non-formal education. We help the unemployed to find employment and also have detoxification programs for drug addicts and alcoholics. A lot of medical services are provided gratis and concessions are given in the hospitals to needy patients since there is no health insurance in our country.

Even in our schools where the children are expected to pay fees we give a lot of financial assistance to deserving children. Scholarships for higher education are given to the poor students who cannot afford to pursue their studies at the universities.

Many of our sisters work directly for the liberation of battered women and preventing the killing of female infants. We save children from being aborted. We work against sex determination, customs of dowry, child marriage and other forms of exploitation. Water harvesting, employment, Natural Family Planning and AIDS Awareness Programs are regular features in our ministries. A few of our Sisters who have studied law are engaged in educating women in legal matters so that they can be saved from being exploited.

We realize that the harvest indeed is great but the laborers are few. We therefore constantly pray to the Lord of the harvest and ask for genuine vocations to the priestly and religious life. We pray and make determined efforts to recruit candidates to our way of life. We spend a lot of time, energy and money educating these young candidates and forming them to our Gospel life.

On-going formation for all of us is given much importance so that we all strive towards a constant conversion of heart.

And the text of the TOR Rule is read frequently as a reminder to the senior members and explained to the novices and junior members so that it truly becomes our way of life.

# Marianne Jungbluth, F.H.F.

## RULE AND LIFE – A JOURNEY FROM 1980 UNTIL 2008

I nearly missed it, the Kairos, in Spring 1980. I had been asked to serve as representative of the sisters and brothers in the German-speaking areas for the newly created "Work Group" for the drafting of the TOR Rule. After long reflection, I decided to decline this offer. But I didn't count on the heartfelt resistance of those people who had asked me: the founders and leaders of the Franciscan Committee for the Third Order Regular in Germany, Sr. Ethelburga Häcker, O.S.F. and Fr. Lothar Hardick, O.F.M. They believed in me and I said, "Yes." Later, it turned out that this decision changed my life. To make a long story short, at the International Franciscan General Assembly in Rome in March, 1982, I was selected for the Inter-Franciscan Committee for the German-speaking areas. This organization was formally born on April 15, 1982 in Reute, the exact location where the International Work Group had met in September, 1980.

For the second time, God's Spirit had clearly called me to a special service within the Franciscan family. And today this service reaches far beyond the three-nation triangle (Belgium, Germany, the Netherlands), where I was initially located. The "Spirit of the Rule," often mentioned during our meetings, has embraced my whole life. After the Rule was accepted, I experienced first-hand how – with the enthusiastic work of the previously mentioned leaders of German Franciscan communities– brothers and sisters were exposed to the new Rule in conferences, spiritual exercises, retreats and commentaries. Some communities, who had delayed to submit their new constitutions to Rome, began to create them in correlation to the chapters of the new Rule. It was a time of new creation and of feeding from a (nearly) unknown spring.

I was grateful to feel the joy over a new-found identity, a new "us" as sisters and brothers of the Third Order Regular in communion with the Franciscan family worldwide. The foundation of the "International Franciscan Conference – TOR" added to this joy. Now "we" could speak with one voice in the Church and in the world.

Of course, there have been moments of exhaustion during the last 25 years. And, unfortunately, numerous sisters and brothers were not able to make our new Rule fruitful for their own Franciscan spirituality. But last year with its important anniversaries – Eighth centenary of Elizabeth of Thuringia's birth, the twenty-fifth anniversary of Inter-Franciscan Committee for German-speaking areas, the twenty-fifth anniversary of the renewed Rule of the Third Order Regular – led to new beginnings. This feeling of renewal will be strengthened in 2009 with the joyful celebration of the eighth centenary of the Franciscan Movement. The German-speaking Committee mentioned above, and I personally, have declared this to be of utmost importance.

The seed, planted many years ago, has borne fruit: St. Francis and his way of living the Gospel have become closer than ever to us, the sisters and brothers of the Third Order Regular. And in this very moment I feel deeply moved and much gratitude for all those who joined me at the beginning of my journey in spring 1980, the day of that first telephone call, and who are still traveling along to this day.

# Marie-Benoît Lucbernet, S.S.F.A.

## The "Rule and Life" of 1982: A Turning Point in our History

This Rule, prepared by all the Franciscan Institutes was approved December 8, 1982, and given to us by Pope John Paul II. The Church promulgated this Rule to all Franciscan religious institutions so that they would share a single vision. This point of connection forms one entity, a single family, from the institutes. From 1955 to 1982, the progression of spiritual development, the return to the sources and the desire to live the life portrayed in them has caused us to become aware of our common heritage.

This Rule roots us in our origins and identity. It is a founding text that states our membership, and reflects meaning and direction for our life in the world.

### Unity in diversity

In fact, if the Rule is common to the Franciscan family, every institute can emphasize a particular aspect of the charism. Thus our one Rule can reflect our diversity. It is a step towards reconciling national and international interests.

International understanding was not the original intent of the work, but it came as a gift. The spiritual issues that resulted are many and varied, and whether we will make use of these treasures remains to be seen.

### Enrichment and diversification on a global level

As the different projects on the origin of the Rule have shown, we – that is each of our institutions – have helped to refine the spirituality of the TOR. They have contributed to the charism through developing a particular aspect of the spirituality, or emphasizing a particular value of Franciscan life.

Working through circumstances, the Spirit inspired an awareness of four major tendencies to arise in the history of the TOR. When combined, they became universal treasures: conversion, contemplation, poverty, and minority. These same gifts were woven into the tapestry of *fraternitas*.

We are at a point where our work has opened new horizons on the value of the "other" to us. Though familiar, the ways in which they are lived and practiced throughout the world – in other languages, contexts and cultures – could only be enriching. Both dialogue and new beginnings grow from this mutual enrichment.

Thus the value of conversion seen in the spirit of reconciliation (that is, the mission of peace, of non-violence) appears necessary in a world plagued by continual violence and ethnic war.

This type of conversion opens the way to interreligious dialogue, without which neither familial understanding nor acceptance of other cultures is possible.

"Our cloister, it is the world," the *Sacrum Commercium* calls us to the contemplation of God through everyday work, in His creation, in the life of those around us, and also through new technologies, developments in human science.

At the same time, one of our objectives is to discern communally ways in which we can live the spirit of the Rule in a world that presents new ethical questions, puts forth new vocations, and reveals new challenges.

Another way of living minority is needed, one that flows from mercy, one that is lived in service, in clemency, and in compassion to the ultimate extent of the Cross.

The spiritual issue is not so much to find something new as it is to live the spirit of the Rule in today's world, within a common discernment of brothers and sisters of all cultures.

Today, the *Rule and Life* of TOR is:

—a spiritual text that inspires personal, brotherly, and sisterly conversion;

—a reference text that both grows from and facilitates continued unity;

— and also a prophetic text.

The prophetic aspects of the Rule challenge our understanding and draw us into the future. We live the same Rule and the same Franciscan spirituality so that we might accomplish our common mission.

This bond creates and sustains itself around three themes:

### 1. A common history

The very history of the TOR binds us together. We know it is always difficult to return to the source, but we must understand our historical foundations so that we might then move beyond the particularities.

### 2. A common spirituality

Our shared way of life fosters a common sensitivity, a heart that beats to the same rhythm. The Rule of 1982 articulates this unity, based on a fraternal life, with the four fundamental values cited above: conversion, contemplation, poverty, and minority.

### 3. A COMMON MISSION

Although it must comprise different overtones according to our history, our origins, our precepts, we have a common mission if we are convinced that the message we must spread together is a message of peace, charity and service.

The Rule originates in a desire to live and deepen Franciscan spirituality, which then nourishes the tenacity to follow its path, to put in place the structures that serve it, which are themselves open to the Spirit: to dialogue, to understanding and to acceptance of diversity. In all this we contemplate God at work in our lives.

In combining time and space, the tapestry of intuition and institution revealed the fruits of unity, solidarity, fraternity, vitality, communion, openness to new mission in other places, and many other possibilities.

We must continue on this journey, persevering in our efforts of unity, solidarity, and mutual reliance. More than ever, this prophetic text invites us to go further in internationality, in globalization.

Indeed, we have history to demonstrate that there are many ways of following St. Francis. There are close to four hundred institutes of Franciscan women in the modern world, yet it seems improbable that the Spirit would wish four hundred radically different ways of following St. Francis. Such diversity can only be the result of human design; however, would it have to be that way if a spiritual point of view were adopted? (Michel Dortel-Claudot, S.J.).

I leave us with this question: "Can we dream of a federation on a global scale?"

## María Honoria Montalvo Lenin, F.M.I.

As a participant in the Work Group to prepare the *Rule and Life of the Brothers and Sisters of the Third Order Regular of Saint Francis*, on the twenty-fifth anniversary of its historical elaboration, I recall the eighth of March when the General Ministers took a historical vote to approve the Rule. It is of utmost importance to exalt and bless the work of Divine Providence and the action of the Holy Spirit that made it possible to write the Rule and Life of the Third Order Regular. For the first time in history, the Rule was written with the words of Francis, even though his words were born in the Church of the thirteenth century.

It is not easy to define the supernatural impact that the approval of this *Rule and Life* has initiated in me. As a Franciscan, I give the first place to God in every occasion, with a profound conviction of faith in the one God who gives primacy to His loving intimate relationship with His brothers and sisters, a relationship which originated in Jesus Christ and is realized through the Spirit running through Him, in permanent adoration and praise in union with all of creation.

Enlightened by the Gospel and the sources of Franciscan history, we have received our Franciscan inheritance woven together by many foundresses and founders. Given our admirable spirituality, the *Rule and Life* actually defines and consolidates the work of our religious consecration as an invitation to "persevere" in penitence, that is to say, to be involved in a constant process of conversion, contemplation, poverty, and minority. These lasting dispositions are indispensable and mark the identification of my life in search of God. These considerations help interpret the signs of the times for *today*, and confirm that the magisterial Church needs the Franciscan life.

In assuming the consequences of following Jesus Christ during these past twenty-five years and in living a permanent and committed state of life, I have followed the *Rule and Life* at the side of the Virgin Mary, taking into consideration her humility as a servant. I continue the project of my life in the spirit of prayer and poverty, with a permanent commitment of service to promote the reign of God.

In thirty-two paragraphs, our *Rule and Life of the Third Order Regular of Saint Francis*, in its extraordinary journey in the light of the Gospel, encapsulates a model for evangelical life. This document is divided into nine chapters with seventy biblical references, the majority being from the New Testament. Our *Rule and Life* is now and will continue to be in the future, a source of spirituality for current Franciscan congregations, and those that the Spirit of God will in the years to come offer to our world as a gift of Franciscan grace.

# Maria Luiza Piva, C.F.

*What it meant for me to be part of the work group that elaborated the text for the Rule and Life of the Brothers and Sisters of the Third Order Regular of Saint Francis*

Calling to mind the process of elaborating the text of the *Rule and Life of the Brothers and Sisters of the Third Order Regular of Saint Francis* twenty-five years ago brings me much joy. Participating in the work commission that elaborated it was a real school that permitted me to know more and to live better the project of Franciscan and Clarian evangelical life.

Sharing life with the brothers and sisters from various continents, researching the sources, valuing the contributions of the Franciscan congregations from the whole world, seeking together the way to write the text – that is how the participative work happened, in the Assemblies, the celebrations. All this made the opportunity an experience that was unique and marked the lives of everyone in the group.

The process of living and experiencing this for various years was also a great incentive and an invitation to deepen the content about the life of Francis and Clare and about the spirituality they proposed.

Paying attention to this inspiration, I dedicated a time to study and to deepen the Franciscan and Clarian themes. In these twenty-five years then, I was able to contribute in a more effective form to the Franciscan family of Brazil, giving courses and retreats about the Franciscan and Clarian Sources, about the *Rule and Life of the Third Order of Saint Francis* and about other themes that helped to make the Francisclarian evangelical life project more concrete. For six years, I also participated in the coordination of the Franciscan spirituality course that lasted for a period of four months each semester.

When the *Rule and Life* … celebrated 20 years, there was a whole movement to return to the content. Here in Brazil this happened with the support of the International Franciscan Conference of the Third Order Regular, along with the Franciscan family of Brazil, and the Itinerant School project. We formed a coordination team of three sisters and one brother and organized three gatherings in different regions lasting from ten to fifteen days for men and women who were animators of formation in their congregations. In all the gatherings, the participation of the groups was very alive and real.

In these last two years, some congregations or provinces continued requesting assistance to study and reflect on the *Rule and Life,* showing that its content continues to be inspirational today.

I feel that the willingness and joy with which I dedicated myself to this work resulted, in great part, from the fact that I had participated actively in the process of elaborating this *Form of Life*, with all the richness of its content and life.

For all of life that has happened, I raise to God a hymn of praise with Clare of Assisi: Blessed be You, my Lord, who created me! (LegCl 46).

# Thomas Grady, O.S.F.

As we arrive at the end of this *Historical Source Book* commemorating the 25th Anniversary of the promulgation of the *Rule and Life of the Third Order Regular* (TOR), the question, as posed to me by the editors for a concluding reflection, is this: "What is the significance, for today and tomorrow, of the events recorded in these pages from twenty-five years ago?"

Contributors to this book have spent more than a quarter century working on the clarification of our charism. Indeed, many worked for decades uncovering the treasures of our penitential/evangelical charism before the monumental work of creating a collaborative, cohesive, international text in the 1970s and 80s. And so, it seems that this ongoing project of discovery and implementation has no clear beginning or end. Rather, it is a major historical moment in the eternal working of the Holy Spirit moving us closer to an incarnation of the Gospel of Christ in our times and circumstances, just as the same timeless Spirit moved previous generations and will continue the outpouring of grace and insight into a Franciscan future. Our task is to make the charism visible so that it will attract others who will enflesh it in times yet to come.

As the ocean waves that come and go carry the water, which represents divinity according to Thich Nhat Hanh[1] and intuited as such by Francis in his *Canticle of Creation*, we, too, come and go as drops of water in waves comprised of the divine essence. This twenty-five-year period we celebrate is but a moment in the longer "Now" in which "the Alpha and Omega" is, like an ocean, ever alive.

This longer "Now" contains centuries of Franciscan life, from the 1209 verbal approval of Francis's Gospel way of life and his *Letter to the Faithful* to the "Now" of 1982-2007 during which we have worked to *be* those "faithful." The moment flows on into the future wherein sisters and brothers will take the work recorded in this volume and live it in circumstances and structures, both global and local, which are not at all clear from our particular vantage points.

The one desire of our way of life is to have "the Spirit of God at work within them."[2] That intergenerational desire constitutes one extended moment in salvation history, though its manifestations are many.

Consider, for example, the circumstances in which brothers and sisters have taken this one *Rule and Life* into their own historical contexts since the 1982 approval. More than a few have had their lives taken in the effort,

---

[1]Brian Pierce, *We Walk the Path Together* (New York: Orbis, 2005), 53-56.

[2]TOR Rule 32, Jean François Godet-Calogeras, trans. *The Rule and Life of the Brothers and Sisters of the Third Order Regular of St. Francis: 1982-2007 25th Anniversary Edition* (Washington: Franciscan Federation, 2007), 16.

as recorded elsewhere in this volume. Entire congregations have struggled to live our common commitment in times of war and places of misery. I think of our sisters in Lebanon, who have begun and ended this twenty-five year period amid violent conflicts at heavy personal costs. And yet, one of the greatest joys to those who translated and published the texts was to see the first edition of the *Rule and Life* in Arabic. Our Rule is the companion the sisters in Lebanon sought in their struggles. How unchained the charism is by time, place, language or circumstance!

In 2007 Franciscans across the United States and in other countries reflected prayerfully on different articles of our Rule each day throughout Lent. Such reflection is very unifying. Hopefully, it will lead to coordinated efforts of witness by Gospel-living – literal Franciscan actions as followers of the Incarnate Christ. There are so very many situations in need of loving hands and hearts; we hear daily of genocides, wars and violations of human rights, isolationism, shows of power, greed, terror and destruction of earth and atmosphere. One could get discouraged; but collectively we cannot. The Spirit is within us.

The groundbreaking work done by scholars and leaders of TOR congregations in the 1970s was complicated and fraught with challenges. Inter-Franciscan collaboration was new to most TOR institutes. Eventually cooperation replaced competition. The process led not only to a universally-accepted and treasured text for our *Rule and Life*, but also led to the establishment, in 1985, of a permanent forum, the International Franciscan Conference, through which such collaboration could continue. By the 1990s informal as well as formal networks among the various institutes had formed. Brothers from Brooklyn, for example were able to assist brothers from India in establishing their presence in the United States. In the globalized world of the twenty-first century we must continue unifying our witness to conversion, contemplation, poverty and minority – our particular patrimonial gifts for the world.

We have another gift to cultivate as well, *la vita fraternal*, to create familial relations in place of the polarization so endemic to our increasingly pluralistic societies. That wasn't so easy, even for us, in the 1970s, but after 30 years of experience, this generation of TOR Franciscans could witness another way to live as sisters/brothers for all.

The earlier chapters of this source book chronicle the stages of the development of our *Rule and Life*. It is a remarkable story of sisterhood/brotherhood blossoming from ancient seeds among Franciscan penitents and watered by the breath of the Holy Spirit. It is a story of dedication to scholarship on our penitential charism as well as determination to have one unified text for our one family. Margaret Carney and Jean François Godet-Calogeras have presented the contents and processes of the various stages of our Rule's development. They were witnesses and workers at each stage, in struggles as well as celebrations.

Other than responding to surveys about the various drafts of the texts and submitting papers to the *Madrid Statement* group, as all tertiaries in the United States were invited to do, I was not a personal witness to this historic project except for one moment. The "moment" extended from December 26, 1981 through January 3, 1982. After Brussels, the Work Group needed one more as yet unscheduled meeting before presenting the final draft of the proposed Rule for approval of the Major Superiors in Rome in March of 1982. The only time available for everyone in the group was the holiday-holyday week. They came to the United States and worked at a retreat house of the Franciscan Brothers at Oyster Bay on Long Island, New York. As host of the Work Group, I became a witness to their work.

This "moment" has held special significance for me ever since. I'm really not sure why. It has something to do with expanding my experience of brotherhood. First of all, members of the Work Group were women (the usual TOR majority) and men from various institutes, continents and language groups – a novelty for me at the time. I had nothing to do with the task at hand: preparing a final draft and process for presentation to the Rome Assembly. Rather, I was in a supportive role, organizing my brothers to serve the group's needs.

Looking back twenty-five years, I think the significance of those days for me was not so much witnessing the *Rule and Life* being created, but experiencing it being shared in concrete, fraternal actions. A humorous example is the group's need for homemade bread for supper European-style. During the Federation Assembly in 1981 Ann Carville, O.S.F. and Margaret Carney, O.S.F. took me aside to explain the necessary preparations from us, the hosts. Top of the list was the bread. "No problem," I said. They didn't believe these brothers from Brooklyn "got it." Upon returning home I put out an alert for bread, and had sufficient volunteers to have varieties of homemade breads throughout the meeting. On the first day of the meeting Margaret arrived with a station wagon filled with bread from the Sisters in Whitehall – just to "make sure." We had a deep freezer crammed with the new bread that probably served the retreat center for several months. So, our sisters discovered their brothers could cook. The Europeans decided we must be "lay Brothers." We are. They couldn't connect the facts that the kitchen cooks were also college professors. On the other hand, folks from the southern hemisphere seemed to be delighted! So, roles were upturned, people served one another and were willing to be served, and community was created more completely by tending to the dinner table, as well as the Eucharistic table and the work table. We celebrated Christmas week at the Cathedral in Brooklyn and New Year's Eve with a party for many TOR communities from the New York metropolitan area and lightened, yet enlivened, the prevailing work mood. As the days progressed we seemed able to communicate socially with decreasing need for translators – we were connecting and communicating more personally, albeit by hand gestures and faulted words, simply by living together and enjoying *la vita fraternal.*

The Work Group really worked hard those days and nights. We supported them with simple acts, heretofore untold tales: Margaret, in her customary style, needed an iron; Jean François needed a liquid nightcap with conversation by the fire in the cozy library; Thaddeus needed a clearer translation of *Sicut;*[3] Sister Ignatia from India needed a serious shopping spree, American-style;[4] Sister Louise, coordinator, needed a phone to consult with the Friar Minor "expert" in Europe! (I did not understand a word spoken on the one phone in a public hallway, but knew there was "trouble.") The next day I prayed in the chapel during the hours the Work Group was in session. Considered together, these events were an experience of conversion and minority on a small but intimate scale. It was a special time, a "moment" that continues "now," and always reminds me that our *Rule and Life* is very human indeed, a fit dwelling place for the Holy Spirit.

The future holds known and unknown opportunities to incarnate the Gospel "by word and work,"[5] celebrating our common desire: "the Spirit of God at work within us."[6] As drops of Sister Water, "humble and precious" in the divine wave,[7] let us continue plumbing the depths of our evangelical way of life in the ongoing "Now" of conversion, exploring the opportunities that lie deep within our diverse yet united family of penitents.

> And the end of all our exploring
> Will be to arrive where we started
> And to know the place for the first time.
> Through the unknown, remembered gate
> When the last of earth to discover
> Is that which was the beginning.[8]

---

[3]*Sicut* is the opening word of Article 18 of the *Rule and Life* meaning "to be" rather than "seem to be" poor.

[4]This was made possible by a trip to the "city" – Manhattan – thanks to the Franciscan Handmaids of Mary who loaned us a van from their Harlem motherhouse, which also allowed some cultural events: a play about St. Francis, a visit to the observation deck of the now iconic World Trade Center.

[5]TOR Rule 29; *Rule and Life*, 14.

[6]TOR Rule 32; *Rule and Life*, 16.

[7]Brian Pierce, 53-56.

[8]T.S. Eliot, *Four Quarterts* (New York: Hartcourt, 1943), 39.